THE BELT AND ROAD
COOPERATION AND PARTNERSHIP
MODEL AGREEMENT

「一帶一路」
合作與夥伴關係協議範本

EDITED BY GUIGUO WANG AND RAJESH SHARMA

王貴國　RAJESH SHARMA 編

發起人 Initiators

Prof. Wang, Guiguo
王貴國教授

Title 職稱	浙江大學 文科資深教授	Nationality 國家	China 中國	Gender 性別	Male 男

Prof. Wang Guiguo is the President of Zhejiang University Academy of International Strategy and Law, and University Professor of Law, Zhejiang University; President of International Academy of the Belt and Road (Hong Kong); Eason-Weinmann Chair of International and Comparative Law Emeritus, School of Law, Tulane University, USA; Chairman of the Hong Kong WTO Research Institute; Chairman of the National Committee (HK) and Titular Member of the International Academy of Comparative Law; Vice President of the Chinese Society of International Economic Law. Prof.Wang, holder of the JSD degree from Yale and LL.M. degree from Columbia, has published more than 20 books and more than 100 academic articles in both Chinese and English.

王貴國教授係浙江大學國際戰略與法律研究院院長、浙江大學文科資深教授;「一帶一路」國際研究院（香港）院長;美國杜蘭大學法學院 Eason-Weinmann 國際法與比較法榮休教授;香港世界貿易組織研究中心主席、比較法國際（海牙）科學院名譽院士、比較法國際（海牙）科學院香港委員會主席;中國國際經濟法學會副會長。王貴國教授為美國耶魯大學法哲學博士和美國哥倫比亞大學法學碩士,曾出版中英文著作 20 餘部以及學術論文百餘篇。

Prof. Addis, Adeno

Title 職稱	美國杜蘭大學 法學教授	Nationality 國家	United States 美國	Gender 性別	Male 男

Prof. Adeno Addis holds the W. R. Irby Chair and is the W. Ray Forrester Professor of Public and Constitutional Law at Tulane University School of Law (U.S.). He is an internationally recognized scholar whose expertise spans a range of areas, but primarily focusing on constitutional law, international law, human rights, and political and legal theory. He has taught at other law schools as a visiting professor both in the United States and in other countries.

Adeno Addis 教授擔任 W. R. Irby 主席,是杜蘭法學院（美國）的公共和憲法法學教授,國際著名法學家。他的專業領域廣泛,主要集中在憲法、國際法、人權以及政治和法律理論。他曾在美國和澳大利亞、德國、中國香港、日本等國家和地區的法學院擔任客座教授。

Prof. Adhikari, Bipin

Title 職稱	加德滿都大學 法學教授	Nationality 國家	Nepal 尼泊爾	Gender 性別	Male 男

Prof. Bipin Adhikari is a law professor at Kathmandu University and a senior lawyer in Nepal. He specializes in various fields, including constitutional law, federalism, infrastructure law, regulatory theory, political economy, and public policy. Additionally, he shows keen interest in the Belt and Road Initiative in his region.

Bipin Adhikari 教授是加德滿都大學的法學教授，也是尼泊爾的資深律師。他的專業領域包括憲法、聯邦制、基礎設施法、監管理論、政治經濟學和公共政策。此外，對他所在地區的「一帶一路」倡議表現出濃厚的興趣。

Mrs. Alayan, Jocelyne

Title 職稱	法律專家	Nationality 國家	Turkey 土耳其	Gender 性別	Female 女

Mrs. Jocelyne Alayan is a cross-border legal consultant with extensive experience in multiple jurisdiction practice and conflicts, MENA laws, international contracts drafting and legal translation. Mrs. Alayan received her Bachelor of Law (LL.B) from Beirut Arab University, Alexandria University and Lebanese University. She holds a Diploma in Private Law and a Master of Law (LL. M) in Private International Law with a thesis entitled "Legislative Competence in Consumption Contracts Concluded through Internet" from Beirut Arab University, after graduation Mrs. Alayan enrolled in Beirut Bar Association.

Jocelyne Alayan 女士是一名跨境法律顧問，在多個司法管轄區的實踐和衝突、中東和北非法律、國際合同起草和法律翻譯方面擁有豐富的經驗。Alayan 夫人在貝魯特阿拉伯大學、亞歷山大大學和黎巴嫩大學獲得法學學士學位。她擁有貝魯特阿拉伯大學私法文憑和國際私法碩士學位，畢業論文題為「通過互聯網簽訂的消費合同的立法權能」。畢業後，Alayan 女士進入貝魯特律師協會。

Prof. Amasike, Chukwudi Joseph

Title 職稱	尼日利亞 前首席大法官	Nationality 國家	Nigeria 尼日利亞	Gender 性別	Male 男

Prof. Amasike, Chukwudi Joseph was the former Chairman/Chief Judge, Federal Government of

Nigeria, Tax Appeal Court/Tribunal. He had worked as Special Adviser to the Honourable Attorney General of the Federation and Minister of Justice of Nigeria and at different times was Chairman/ Member of the Federal Government of Nigeria National Committees. Professor C. J. Amasike is the Chairman of the Governing Council, International Dispute Resolution Institute [IDRI].

Amasike, Chukwudi Joseph 教授曾任尼日利亞聯邦政府稅務上訴法院 / 審裁處主席 / 首席法官。他曾擔任尼日利亞聯邦總檢察長和司法部長的特別顧問，並在不同時期擔任尼日利亞聯邦政府各國家委員會的主席 / 成員。Amasike, Chukwudi Joseph 教授是國際爭端解決研究所理事會主席。

Mr. Changaroth, Anil

Title 職稱	爭端解決專家	Nationality 國家	Singapore 新加坡	Gender 性別	Male 男

Mr. Anil Changaroth, an international accredited Arbitrator and Mediator, and an Advocate & Solicitor of Singapore, a Solicitor of England and Wales, and a Barrister at Law. Anil currently is the Country Representative (Singapore) for Dispute Resolution Board Foundation and the Chair of Law Society of Singapore newly formed ESG working group.

Anil Changaroth 是一名國際認可的仲裁員和調解員以及新加坡、英格蘭和威爾士律師。2012-2014 年任新加坡建築法學會主席。Anil 目前是爭議解決委員會基金會的國家代表（新加坡）和新加坡律師協會新成立的 ESG 工作組主席。

Prof. Cooray, Anthony

Title 職稱	斯里蘭卡科倫坡大學前法學院院長倫敦大學教授	Nationality 國家	United Kingdom 英國	Gender 性別	Male 男

Professor Anton Cooray is a Professor of Law at City University of London and Senior Associate Research Fellow of the Institute of Advanced Legal Studies, University of London. He was Dean of the Law School of University of Colombo, Sri Lanka, and Associate Dean of Law at City University of Hong Kong. He was the Chairman of the Hong Kong Town Planning Appeal Board and Deputy Chairman of the Hong Kong Town Planning Board panel of members and was a World Bank consultant on legal and judicial reform in Sri Lanka and has conducted a series of training programmes for judges, State Counsel and academics from Sri Lanka.

安東‧庫雷教授是倫敦城市大學法學教授、倫敦大學高級法律研究所高級副研究員。他曾任斯里蘭卡科倫坡大學法學院院長和香港城市大學法學院副院長。他曾擔任香港城市規劃上訴委員會主席和香港城市規劃委員會委員團副主席，並曾擔任世界銀行斯里蘭卡法律和司法改革顧問，為斯里蘭卡的法官、國家律師和學者舉辦了一系列培訓課程。

Prof. Franceschi, De Alberto

Title 職稱	歐洲科學院院士	Nationality 國家	**Italy** **意大利**	Gender 性別	**Male** **男**

Prof. Alberto De Franceschi is Full Professor of Private Law, Digital Law and Sustainability, and International Trade Law at the at the University of Ferrara, elected member of the Academia Europaea, Co-chairman of the European Law Institute's Digital Law Special Interest Group, and of the European Law Institute's Sustainability and Environmental Law Special Interest Group. Delegate of the Italian Ministry of Justice at the G7, at the United Nations Commission for International Trade Law (UNCITRAL) – Working Group IV on E-Commerce, at the Hague Conference on Private International Law (HCCH) and at the International Institute for the Unification of Private Law (UNIDROIT).

Alberto, De Franceschi 教授是帕爾馬大學的私法、數字法和可持續性發展、國際貿易法教授，歐洲科學院院士，歐洲法律研究所數字法特別小組和歐洲法律研究所可持續性和環境法特別小組的聯合主席。意大利司法部代表，出席七國集團會議、聯合國國際貿易法委員會電子商務第四工作組、海牙國際私法會議和國際統一私法協會。

Mr. Galih Permadi Siwi

Title 職稱	企業家	Nationality 國家	**Indonesia** **印度尼西亞**	Gender 性別	**Male** **男**

Mr. Galih Permadi Siwi S.T., M.B.A. is a member of management team of PT Wijaya Karya (Persero) Tbk which is the largest and most prominent state-owned enterprises (SOEs) in Indonesia. With an educational background in Mechanical Engineering and Business Administration, he has 15 years of experience in project management and engineering management. He has participated the Indonesia-China High-Speed Railway Project (KCIC). His company, as the largest consortium shareholder, is responsible for developing the Jakarta-Bandung high-speed rail project, which is one of the Indonesian government's National Strategic Projects (PSN) as outlined in Presidential Regulation No. 3/2016.

Galih Permadi Siwi 先生是印度尼西亞最大的國有建築公司 PT Wijaya Karya（Persero）Tbk 的管理團隊成員。他擁有機械工程和工商管理的教育背景，在項目管理和工程管理方面擁有 15 年的經驗，曾參與印尼—中國高鐵項目（KCIC）工程。其所在的公司作為最大股東負責中國—印尼合作開發建設雅加達—萬隆高鐵項目，該項目是印度尼西亞總統第 3/2016 號條例所述的國家戰略項目之一。

Prof. Gu, Minkang
顧敏康教授

Title 職稱	香港城市大學 原副院長	Nationality 國家	China (Hong Kong) 中國香港	Gender 性別	Male 男

Professor Gu, Minkang is Associate Co-Director of Academy for Applied Policy Studies and Education Futures, and Project Director of Office of the President. He was the Dean of Faculty of Law and Head of Credit Risk Management School, Xiangtan University, China. He was also Associated Dean of School of Law, City University of Hong Kong. He worked for the same university as a Lecturer in Law for 5 years. During that time, he visited the Rule University of Bochum (Germany) as a Visiting Scholar for a year. Subsequently in 1993, he went to the United States and successfully completed his legal study in the Willamette University College of Law and earned Doctor of Jurisprudence in 1996. He also went to France and earned a degree in Master of European Business Law.

顧敏康教授是香港教育大學應用政策研究及教育未來學院聯席副院長和校長室項目總監。他曾經是湘潭大學法學部部長、信用風險管理學院院長、教授、博士生導師，也曾經是香港城市大學法律學院副院長，教授。他在華東政法大學工作五年，期間去德國魯爾大學做訪問學者。他於 1993 年去美國留學並於 1996 年獲得威拉姆特大學法學院法律博士；他還曾去法國進修並獲得歐洲商法碩士學位。

Ms. Habeeb, Suha

Title 職稱	馬爾代夫律師	Nationality 國家	Maldives 馬爾代夫	Gender 性別	Female 女

Ms. Habeeb, Suha has been engaged as an attorney in the Maldives, since 2020. She graduated with a Bachelor of Laws (LL.B) Honors degree from the University of West of England in 2019, and was called to the Bar of the Maldives, the following year. She is currently working as an 'Attorney-at-Law' at SHC Law & Tax, a leading commercial law firm in the Maldives.

Suha Habeeb 女士自 2020 年以來一直在馬爾代夫擔任律師。她於 2019 年畢業於西英格蘭大學，獲得法學榮譽學士學位，並於次年獲得馬爾代夫律師資格。她目前在馬爾代夫領先的商業律師事務所 SHC Law & Tax 擔任律師。

Prof. Helal Mehtab, Farhana

Title 職稱	孟加拉國綠色大學 法學院院長	Nationality 國家	Bangladesh 孟加拉	Gender 性別	Female 女

Prof. Helal Mehtab, Farhana is the Dean of the Faculty of Law at Green University of Bangladesh (GUB). She is the first female Dean of the Faculty of Law among the private universities in Bangladesh.

Mehtab, Farhana Helal 教授是孟加拉國綠色大學的法學院院長，她是孟加拉私立大學中第一位女性法學院院長。

Ms. Huang, Jianwen
黃建雯女士

| Title 職稱 | 中國律師 | Nationality 國家 | China 中國 | Gender 性別 | Female 女 |

Ms. Huang Jianwen is the Director-in-chief of King & Wood Mallesons Belt & Road Center for International Cooperation and Facilitation, the head of KWM's life science team and the legal consultant of National Medical Products Administration. She specializes in domestic and cross-border investments and M&A, licensing, compliance and corporate matters.

黃建雯律師是金杜律師事務所「一帶一路」國際合作與促進中心主任、醫藥醫療板塊負責人、國家藥品監督管理局法律顧問。黃建雯律師的主要執業領域為境內外投資和兼併收購、技術許可、商業合規與公司業務。

Ms. Hyang Ismalya Mihardja

| Title 職稱 | 國際爭端解決專家 | Nationality 國家 | Indonesia 印度尼西亞 | Gender 性別 | Female 女 |

Hyang I. Mihardja, S.H., MBA., has 20 years of professional experience and is executive director of EYR Centre for Legal Studies, a recognised expert in conflict resolution. She is a representative of the Pusat Mediasi Nasional - Indonesian Mediation Centre (PMN) which is a Board Member of the Asia Pacific Centre for Arbitration and Mediation (APCAM). Her competency has been recognized by the national standard BNSP and is accredited by the Supreme Court of the Republic of Indonesia. She graduated from University of Indonesia Law School, and got MBA degree from School of Business and Management, Institute Technology Bandung. She is certified on Mediator's Skills from Vrije Universiteit cooperate with Van Vollenhoven Institute, Netherland.

Hyang I. Mihardja，MBA。她擁有 20 年的專業經驗，是 EYR 法律研究中心的執行主任，也是公認的衝突解決專家。她是印尼國家調解中心（PMN）的代表，該中心是亞太仲裁與調解中心（APCAM）的董事會成員。其能力資格獲國家標準 BNSP 及印度尼西亞共和國最高法院的認可。她畢業於印度尼西亞大學法學院，並獲得萬隆理工學院工商管理學院 MBA 學位。她持有荷蘭自由大學與 Van Vollenhoven 研究所合作的調解員資格證書。

Ms. Ilyas, Suma

Title 職稱	馬爾代夫法律專家	Nationality 國家	Maldives 馬爾代夫	Gender 性別	Female 女

Ms. Ilyas Suma is currently working as an Associate at Law & Tax firm. She carries out corporate and commercial law assignments including foreign investment regulatory approvals, business registrations, due diligence enquires, security registrations, intellectual property, litigation matters, and etc. She is the founder and president of Maldives Moot Court Society (MMCS), a training platform for young budding lawyers and students to enhance practical legal skills. She holds a Bachelor's of Shari'ah and Law with honours from the Maldives National University.

Ilyas Suma 女士目前在法律與稅務事務所擔任律師。她負責公司和商業法律事務，包括外國投資監管審批、商業登記、盡職調查查詢、證券登記、知識產權、訴訟事宜等。Ms. Ilyas Suma 還是馬爾代夫模擬法庭協會（MMCS）的創始人和主席，該協會是一個培訓年輕律師和學生提高實際法律技能的培訓平台。她擁有馬爾代夫國立大學的伊斯蘭教法和法律學士學位。

Prof. Ishikawa, Tomoko

Title 職稱	日本名古屋大學 法學院副院長、教授	Nationality 國家	Japan 日本	Gender 性別	Female 女

Prof. Ishikawa, Tomoko is vice dean and professor at Nagoya University in Japan. She has served as an ICSID Conciliator, appointed by the Chairman of the Administrative Council (2017-2023), a member of the Legal Advisory Committee of the Energy Charter Treaty, an arbitrator at Shenzhen Court of International Arbitration, and a mediator at the Kyoto International Mediation Centre. Her professional experiences include serving as an Associate Judge at Tokyo District Court and holding the position of Deputy Director at the International Legal Affairs Bureau of the Ministry of Foreign Affairs of Japan, where she worked on bilateral/trilateral investment treaties, Free Trade Agreements, and WTO dispute settlement.

石川朝子教授是日本名古屋大學副院長兼教授。她曾擔任 ICSID 調解員，由行政理事會主席任命（2017-2023），能源憲章條約法律諮詢委員會成員，深圳國際仲裁院仲裁員，京都國際調解中心調解員。她的專業經歷包括在東京地方法院擔任助理法官，並擔任日本外務省國際法律事務局副局長，負責雙邊 / 三邊投資條約、自由貿易協定和世貿組織爭端解決。

Prof. Junngam, Nartnirun

| Title 職稱 | 泰國國立法政大學
法學教授 | Nationality 國家 | Thailand
泰國 | Gender 性別 | Male
男 |

Prof. Nartnirun Junngam teaches at the Faculty of Law, Thammasat University. His areas of interest include public international law, international economic law, and international dispute settlement. He was a Visiting Fellow at the Lauterpacht Centre for International Law at the University of Cambridge and guest speaker at Yale Law School.

Nartnirun Junngam 教授在泰國國立法政大學法律系任教。他的研究領域包括國際公法、國際經濟法和國際爭端解決。他是劍橋大學勞特派特國際法中心的訪問學者，也是耶魯大學法學院的客座演講嘉賓。

Prof. Kamardeen, Naazima

| Title 職稱 | 科倫坡大學
法學院商法系主任、教授 | Nationality 國家 | Sri Lanka
斯里蘭卡 | Gender 性別 | Female
女 |

Prof. Naazima Kamardeen is Professor and Chair of Commercial Law, Department of Commercial Law, Faculty of Law, University of Colombo. Naazima Kamardeen, holding a Doctor of Philosophy degree from the University of Colombo, Sri Lanka, a Master of Laws degree in International Legal Studies from Georgetown University USA, is also an Attorney-at-Law of the Supreme Court of Sri Lanka. She is a member of the Law Commission of Sri Lanka. She has authored two books.

Naazima Kamardeen 教授是科倫坡大學法學院商法系教授兼商法系主任。Naazima Kamardeen 在斯里蘭卡科倫坡大學獲得哲學博士學位，在美國喬治敦大學獲得國際法律研究碩士學位，也是斯里蘭卡最高法院的律師。她是斯里蘭卡法律委員會的成員，出版了兩本專著。

Prof. Kawashima, Fujio

| Title 職稱 | 神戶大學
法學教授 | Nationality 國家 | Japan
日本 | Gender 性別 | Male
男 |

Prof. Kawashima, Fujio is a professor of the Graduate School of Law at Kobe University. He holds B.A. in Law (University of Tokyo 1990). He specializes in international economic law and competition law. His research interests include WTO dispute settlement, trade and competition policy and development of competition law in Asian countries.

川島富士雄教授是神戶大學法學院的教授。他擁有法學學士學位（1990 年東京大學）。專攻國際經濟法和競爭法。主要研究方向為 WTO 爭端解決、貿易與競爭政策、亞洲國家競爭法發展等。

Dr. Lee, Yuk Lun Alan
李鋈麟先生

Title 職稱	「一帶一路」國際 研究院副院長	Nationality 國家	China (Hong Kong) 中國香港	Gender 性別	Male 男

Dr. Lee, Yuk Lun Alan is Justice of the Peace; Vice president, International Academy of the Belt and Road, China; He was awarded Bronze Bauhinia Star (SBS) in 2018 by HKSAR Government.

李鋈麟博士是太平紳士；「一帶一路」國際研究院副院長；於 2018 年獲香港特別行政區政府授勳銅紫荊星章。

Mr. Letten, James

Title 職稱	美國前聯邦檢察官	Nationality 國家	United States 美國	Gender 性別	Male 男

Mr. James Letten, a partner at the US law firm of Butler Snow LLP, previously served as Tulane University Law School's first Assistant Dean for Experiential Learning. Prior to that, he served 30 years with the United States Department of Justice– the last 12 as the presidentially-appointed United States Attorney in New Orleans—and upon his retirement was the longest serving U.S. Attorney in the US.

James Letten 先生，美國 Butler Snow 律師事務所合夥人，曾擔任杜蘭大學法學院（Tulane University law School）首任體驗式學習助理院長。在此之前，他在美國司法部工作了 30 年。其中有 12 年是由總統任命的聯邦檢察官，是美國任職時間最長的聯邦檢察官。

Prof. Leung, Mei-fun
梁美芬教授

Title 職稱	全國人大代表 香港城市大學 法學院教授	Nationality 國家	China (Hong Kong) 中國香港	Gender 性別	Female 女

Prof. Leung Mei-fun, NPC deputy, Professor of School of Law in City University of Hong Kong; She is a Barrister-at Law, Hong Kong; She is an arbitrator (CIETAC). Besides, she is a member of the Hong Kong Basic Law Committee; Member of the Hong Kong Legislative Council. She is Hong Kong Special Administrative Region deputy to the National People's Congress.

梁美芬教授為全國人大代表，香港城市大學法學院教授，香港執業大律師，中國國際經濟貿易仲裁委員會仲裁員，全國人大常委會香港基本法委員會委員，香港立法會議員，香港特別行政區第十四屆全國人民代表大會代表。

Ms. Lykova Natalia Andreevna

Title 職稱	俄羅斯律師	Nationality 國家	**Russia** **俄羅斯**	Gender 性別	**Female** **女**

Ms. Lykova Natalia Andreevna is a lawyer, arbitrator and mediator specializing in international law and foreign economic activities. She is the President of the Association of Mediators and Intermediaries of the Asia-Pacific region, CEO of the law firm Vintsere Co., Ltd., arbitrator of the Russian Arbitration Center of the Russian Institute of Modern Arbitration and a number of other arbitration bodies. She teaches mediation at the Far Eastern Federal University, Vladivostok State University, the Russian Customs Academy (Vladivostok branch) and other institutions.

Lykova Natalia Andreevna 女士是一名律師、仲裁員和調解員，專注國際法和外國經濟活動方面的工作。她是亞太地區調解員和調解員協會主席，Vinsere 律師事務所首席執行官。俄羅斯現代仲裁學會俄羅斯仲裁中心及其他數家仲裁機構的仲裁員。她在遠東聯邦大學、符拉迪沃斯托克國立大學、俄羅斯海關學院（符拉迪沃斯托克分校）等機構講授調解課程。

Prof. Ma, Guang
馬光教授

Title 職稱	浙江大學 光華法學院副教授	Nationality 國家	**China** **中國**	Gender 性別	**Male** **男**

Prof. MA Guang is an Associate Professor of international law at Guanghua Law School of Zhejiang University of China. He also serves as Executive Director of the Institute of International Law at Zhejiang University. He was awarded LL.B Degree from China University of Political Science and Law and LL.M. and Ph.D. from Korea University. Professor Ma is an arbitrator and also a licensed lawyer in China. His interest fields include international trade law, law of the sea, humanitarian law, international law of cyberspace, personal information protection law.

馬光教授，浙江大學光華法學院國際法副教授，浙江大學國際法研究所執行主任。中國政法大學學士，高麗大學法學碩士、博士。馬教授同時是中國的仲裁員和執業律師。主要研究領域為國際貿易法、海洋法、人道法、網絡空間國際法、個人資訊保護法。

Ambassador Datuk Manickham, Supperamaniam

| Title 職稱 | 馬來西亞前駐 WTO 大使 | Nationality 國家 | Malaysia 馬來西亞 | Gender 性別 | Male 男 |

Ambassador Datuk Manickham, Supperamaniam joined the Malaysian Administrative and Diplomatic Service in 1970 and served the Ministry of International Trade and Industry for a period of 34 years in various capacities including Senior Trade Commissioner of Malaysia to Hong Kong and China, Director, Department of International Trade, Deputy Secretary-General (Trade) and Ambassador/Permanent Representative of Malaysia to the World Trade Organization.

Datuk Manickham, Superamaniam 大使先生於 1970 年加入馬來西亞行政和外交事務處，並在國際貿易和工業部服務了 34 年，擔任過馬來西亞駐香港和中國高級貿易專員，國際貿易司司長，副秘書長（貿易）和馬來西亞駐世界貿易組織大使 / 常駐代表。

Mr. Merle, Alexis

| Title 職稱 | 毛里裘斯律師 | Nationality 國家 | Mauritius 毛里裘斯 | Gender 性別 | Male 男 |

Mr. Alexis Merle is a practicing Barrister-at-Law known for his pragmatic approach to legal matters. He took on the role of Registrar at the Mediation and Arbitration Center (Mauritius) Ltd ('MARC'), where he oversees arbitration and mediation matters in line with the MARC Rules.

Alexis Merle 先生是一名執業大律師，以其對法律事務的務實態度而聞名。他在調解與仲裁中心（毛里裘斯）有限公司擔任書記官長，根據 MARC 規則監督仲裁和調解事宜。

Prof. Munyantwali, Swithin J.

| Title 職稱 | 烏干達法律專家 法學教授 | Nationality 國家 | Uganda 烏干達 | Gender 性別 | Male 男 |

Prof. Swithin J. Munyantwali is Vice Chairman and co-founder of the International Law Institute African Centre for Legal Excellence, and the ILI-South African Centre for Excellence, affiliates of the International Law Institute (ILI), in Washington, DC. Munyantwali is Senior Advisor to Appleton Luff, an international law firm. Munyantwali has served as a party-appointed arbitrator under the auspices of the International Chamber of Commerce (power and telecoms), and the World Bank International Centre for the Settlement of Investment Disputes (energy).

Swithin J. Munyantwali 教授是位於華盛頓特區的國際法研究所（ILI）附屬機構——國際法

研究所非洲卓越法律中心和 IL—南非卓越法律中心的副主席和聯合創始人。Munyantwali 是國際精品律師事務所 Appleton Luff 的高級顧問。曾在國際商會（電力和電信）和世界銀行國際投資爭端解決中心（能源）的主持下擔任當事方指定的仲裁員。

Mr. Nguyen Trung Nam

Title 職稱	爭端解決專家	Nationality 國家	Vietnam 越南	Gender 性別	Male 男

Mr. Nguyen Trung Nam is one of the few top-tiered project & energy lawyers in Vietnam who are highly regarded by many international publications. He is dual-qualified and practices in both Vietnam and England and Wales as a senior partner of EPLegal. He is Deputy Director of Vietnam Mediation Center ("VMC"). He is also the Managing Director and co-founder of Vietnam Institute for International Arbitration ("VIArb").

Nguyen 先生是越南為數不多的頂級項目和能源律師之一，受到國際出版界的高度評價。他擁在越南和英格蘭和威爾士的律師執業資格。Nguyen 先生現為越南調解中心（VMC）副主任，越南國際仲裁協會（「VIArb」）的董事總經理及聯合創始人。

Chief Justice Nisar, Mian Saqib

Title 職稱	巴基斯坦 前首席大法官	Nationality 國家	Pakistan 巴基斯坦	Gender 性別	Male 男

Nisar, Mian Saqib, is a Pakistani jurist who served as the 25th Chief Justice of Pakistan from 31 December 2016 till 17 January 2019. He has previously served as the Law Secretary. He also served as a visiting professor of law at the University of Punjab where he provided instructions on constitutional law.

首席大法官 Mian Saqib Nisar 是巴基斯坦法學家，2016 年 12 月 31 日至 2019 年 1 月 17 日擔任巴基斯坦第 25 任首席大法官。他曾擔任律政司司長。他還擔任旁遮普邦大學的客座法學教授，提供關於憲法的指導。

Prof. Nurgozhay-eva, Roza

Title 職稱	納扎爾巴耶夫大學 法學教授	Nationality 國家	Kazakhstan 哈薩克斯坦	Gender 性別	Female 女

Prof. Roza Nurgozhayeva joined the Nazarbayev University in September 2021 as Assistant Professor of Law. Prior to joining the school, Dr. Nurgozhayeva served as Vice President-General Counsel at Nazarbayev University and practiced law for more than seven years in the banking industry. Her research interests include comparative law, corporate governance, corporate law, state-owned enterprises, emerging markets and law, law and sustainable development.

Roza Nurgozhayeva 教授於 2021 年 9 月加入納扎爾巴耶夫大學，擔任法學助理教授。在加入學校之前，Nurgozhayeva 博士曾擔任納扎爾巴耶夫大學的副總裁兼總法律顧問，並在銀行業從事法律工作超過七年，主要研究方向為比較法、公司治理、公司法、國有企業、新興市場與法律、法律與可持續發展。

Prof. Park, Nohyoung
朴魯馨教授

Title 職稱	高麗大學法學院 前院長、法學教授	Nationality 國家	Korea 韓國	Gender 性別	Male 男

Prof. Park, Nonyoung is Professor and currently the Dean of School of Law, and the Director of the Cyber Law Centre of Korea University. He graduated from the College of Law of the Korea University (LL.B., 1981) and from the Graduate School of the Korea University (LL.M., 1983). He also graduated from Harvard Law School (LL.M., 1985) and from the University of Cambridge (Ph.D. in international law, 1990). His main research interests cover international economic law, negotiation and mediation, cybersecurity and privacy. Member of the Research Committee on FTAs of R.O. Korea, R.O. Korea

朴魯馨教授是韓國高麗大學法學院院長，法學教授，網絡法律中心主任；他畢業於高麗大學法學院（法學學士，1981 年）和高麗大學研究生院（法學碩士，1983 年）。他還畢業於哈佛大學法學院（法學碩士，1985 年）和劍橋大學（國際法博士，1990 年）。主要研究方向為國際經濟法、談判與調解、網絡安全和隱私。韓國自由貿易協定研究小組成員。

Mr. Pereira, Cesar C. Arb FCiarb

Title 職稱	巴西法律專家	Nationality 國家	Brazil 巴西	Gender 性別	Male 男

Mr. Cesar Pereira C.Arb FCiarb is a partner at Justen, Pereira, Oliveira & Talamini (Brazil), co-head of the firm's infrastructure and arbitration departments. He has a Doctorate and Masters in Public Law from PUC/SP (Brazil) and has been a visiting scholar at various universities. He is also a on the roster of arbitrators of numerous international arbitral institutions and often serves as arbitrator or legal expert in domestic and international disputes. He is a Chartered Arbitrator and Fellow of the Chartered Institute of Arbitrators (Ciarb) and was the first chairperson of the Ciarb Brazil Branch.

Cesar Pereira 先生是 Justen, Pereira, Oliveira & Talamini（巴西）律師事務所的合夥人，也是

該事務所基礎設施和仲裁部門的聯席主管。他擁有 PUC/SP（巴西）公法博士和碩士學位，曾在多所大學任訪問學者。他是多個國際仲裁機構的仲裁員，經常在國內和國際爭議中擔任仲裁員或法律專家。他是英國特許仲裁員協會的特許仲裁員和會員，也是特許仲裁人學會巴西分會的首任主席。

Prof. Porcelli, Stephano

| Title 職稱 | 布雷西亞大學 法學教授 | Nationality 國家 | Italy 意大利 | Gender 性別 | Male 男 |

Prof. Dr. Stefano Porcelli is currently a faculty member at the School of Law at the University of Brescia, after being teaching for several years at the School of Juris Master at the China University of Political Science and Law (CUPL). He obtained a Ph.D. at the University of Rome Tor Vergata and a Ph.D. at the School of Civil and Commercial Law at the CUPL (thesis written and defended in Chinese Mandarin language). He is also member of several research centers and think tanks and is responsible of the Research Observatory on the Law of Persons of the Latin-American Legal Studies Center at the University of Rome Tor Vergata.

Stefano Porcelli（司德法）教授現任意大利布雷西亞大學的法學院教授，曾在中國政法大學法學碩士學院任教多年。他在羅馬第二大學和中國政法大學民商法學院獲得博士學位，是幾個研究中心和智庫的成員，並負責羅馬第二大學拉丁美洲法律研究中心的人格法研究觀察站。

Prof. Prisekina, Natalia G.

| Title 職稱 | 遠東聯邦大學 法學院系主任 | Nationality 國家 | Russia 俄羅斯 | Gender 性別 | Female 女 |

Prof. Natalia G. Prisekina, Professor of International Public and Private Law and Head for International Relations, School of Law, Far Eastern Federal University; Partner and Head of the Far Eastern Office of "Pepeliaev Group" law firm; Head of the Vladivostok Branch of the International Commercial Arbitration Court at the Chamber of Commerce and Industry of the Russian Federation (ICAC); Honorary Consul of the Republic of Chile; Deputy Chairman of the Council of the Primorsky Regional Branch of the All-Russian Public Organization "Association of Lawyers of Russia" for International Relations.

Natalia G. Prisekina 教授是遠東聯邦大學法學院國際公法和私法教授、國際關係系主任；「Pepeliaev Group」律師事務所遠東辦事處合夥人兼負責人；俄羅斯聯邦工商會（ICAC）國際商事仲裁法庭海參崴分院院長；智利共和國名譽領事；全俄公共組織「俄羅斯律師協會」國際關係濱海邊疆區分會理事會副主席。

Mr. Rameez, Sulaiman

Title 職稱	國際爭端解決專家	Nationality 國家	The United Arab Emirates 阿聯酋	Gender 性別	Male 男

Mr. Rameez is a corporate and transactional lawyer with a focus on commercial, real estate, employment law, technology transactions, intellectual property (IP), non-profit and charitable organizations, and privacy and data protection. He routinely handles a variety of transactional matters and has also appeared in all levels of Court and before several tribunals in a wide range of commercial litigation and arbitration. Sulaiman has also delivered lectures and training on commercial law and arbitration.

Rameez 先生是一名公司和商事律師，專注於商業、房地產、勞動法、技術交易、知識產權、非營利和慈善組織以及隱私和數據保護。他經常處理各種各樣的交易事務，並在各級法院和多個仲裁庭出庭，處理商業訴訟和仲裁。Rameez 先生也曾舉辦商法和仲裁培訓項目講座。

Ms. Senin, Ruby Valles

Title 職稱	菲律賓律師	Nationality 國家	Phillipines 菲律賓	Gender 性別	Female 女

Ms. Senin, Ruby Valles is a member of the Philippine Bar whose work focuses on supporting businesses in navigating the legal landscape in commercial transactions and disputes. She merges her legal background with her multifaceted experience in international humanitarian operations. Her interests include leveraging the transformative process of alternative dispute resolutions to various contexts of conflicts in bridging gaps between diverse stakeholders.

塞寧律師是菲律賓律師協會的成員，她的工作重點是企業的商業交易和糾紛，包括國際人道主義方面的法律問題。她的興趣含不同環境下的替代性爭議解決變革，以彌合不同利益相關者間的差距。

Mr. Sentíes, Hector Flores

Title 職稱	墨西哥律師	Nationality 國家	Mexico 墨西哥	Gender 性別	Male 男

Mr. Sentíes, Hector Flores is Abascal, Flores y Segovia's Partner. In International commercial arbitration, with almost 15 years of experience in the field of alternative dispute resolution, he has acted as arbitrator, secretary and counsel in national and international arbitrations, ad hoc and institutional, ordinary or expedited, with seats in Mexico City, New York, Miami and Houston, under several rules including the rules of arbitration of the International Chamber of Commerce (ICC), International Centre for Dispute Resolution (ICDR), the Commercial Rules of the American Arbitration Association (AAA), Cámara Nacional de Comercio de la Ciudad de México (CANACO) and Centro de Arbitraje de México (CAM).

Sentíes, Hector Flores 先生是 Abascal, Flores y Segovia 的合夥人。在國際商事仲裁方面，他在替代性爭議解決領域擁有近 15 年的經驗，並基於包括國際商會（ICC）、國際爭議解決中心（ICDR）、《美國仲裁協會商業規則》（AAA）、CANACO 和 CAM 的規則，在國內和國際仲裁中擔任仲裁員、秘書和法律顧問，包括臨時仲裁和機構仲裁、普通仲裁或快速仲裁，在墨西哥城、紐約、邁阿密和休斯頓設有席位。

Prof. Sharma, Rajesh

Title 職稱	澳大利亞墨爾本皇家理工大學國際爭端解決專家	Nationality 國家	**Australia** **澳大利亞**	Gender 性別	**Male** **男**

Prof. Rajesh Sharma is Senior Lecturer, Legal and Dispute Studies, Criminology and Justice, RMIT University, Melbourne, Australia, Adjunct Professor at Academy of International Dispute Resolution and Professional Negotiation (AIDRN). Prof. Sharma also worked in Hong Kong and Macao for many years.

Sharma Rajesh 是澳大利亞墨爾本皇家理工大學法律與爭議研究、犯罪學與司法高級講師，國際爭議解決與專業談判學會（AIDRN）兼職教授。Sharma 教授也曾在香港和澳門工作多年。

Prof. Shetreet, Shimon

Title 職稱	希伯來大學法學教授	Nationality 國家	**Israel** **以色列**	Gender 性別	**Male** **男**

Prof. Shimon Shetreet is a Professor of Law at the Hebrew University of Jerusalem, Israel. He is a leading academic figure for public law and the judiciary, writer and editor of many published articles and books in the field. He served as Ministers in several mini-stries, Israel.

Shimon Shetreet 教授是以色列耶路撒冷希伯來大學的法學教授。他是公法和私法領域的主要學術人物，也是該領域許多已發表文章和書籍的作者和編輯。他曾在以色列政府擔任多個部長級職位。

Prof. Singh, Swaran

| Title 職稱 | 尼赫魯大學政治學教授
亞洲學者協會主席 | Nationality 國家 | India
印度 | Gender 性別 | Male
男 |

Prof. Swaran Singh teaches at Jawaharlal Nehru University (New Delhi) and is president of Association of Asia Scholars, director of India for Washington-based the Millennium Project's South Asia Foresight Network, Fellow of Canadian Global Affairs Institute (Calgary), Member of Governing Body of Society of Indian Ocean Studies (New Delhi) and formerly visiting professor at various universities. He has published 15 book and numerous articles.

Swaran Singh 教授任教於尼赫魯大學（新德里），現任亞洲學者協會主席，華盛頓千年專案南亞遠見網絡印度部主任，加拿大全球事務研究所（卡爾加里）研究員，印度洋研究學會理事機構（新德里）成員，曾在多所大學任訪問教授。他出版了 15 本著作和多篇文章。

Prof. Stychin, Carl

| Title 職稱 | 倫敦大學高級研究學院
高級法律研究所所長 | Nationality 國家 | United Kingdom
英國 | Gender 性別 | Male
男 |

Prof. Stychin , Carl is Director of Instutite of Advanced Legal Studies, School of Advanced Study, University of London. In 2014, Professor Stychin was made a Fellow of the Academy of Social Sciences in recognition of his contribution to the socio-legal study of gender and sexuality. He is a former Chair of the Committee of Heads of UK Law Schools (CHULS).

Stychin, Carl 教授是倫敦大學高級研究學院高級法律研究所所長。2014 年，他被任命為社會科學院院士，以表彰他在性別和性行為的社會法律研究方面的貢獻。他是英國法學院校長委員會（CHULS）的前任主席。

Prof. Verschraegen, Bea

| Title 職稱 | 維也納大學
比較法和國際私法教授 | Nationality 國家 | Austria
奧地利 | Gender 性別 | Female
女 |

Prof. Verschraegen, Bea is a professor of comparative law and private international law at the University of Vienna from 1998-2018. At the same time, she taught at the Pan European University Bratislava from 2004-2014, where she initiated several cooperation agreements as Vice-Rector for International Affairs. She is also Présidente honoraire de la Commission Internationale de l'État Civil (CIEC, France), adjunct professor at various domestic and foreign universities, and a registered mediator and arbitrator.

Verschraegen, Bea 教授於 1998-2018 年在維也納大學擔任比較法和國際私法教授。2004-2014 年，她在泛歐大學任教，擔任國際事務副校長。她是 État 國際民事委員會榮譽會長（CIEC，法國）、在多所國內外大學任兼職教授，係註冊調解員和仲裁員。

Prof. Willems, Jane

Title 職稱	國際仲裁專家	Nationality 國家	France 法國	Gender 性別	Female 女

Prof. Willems, Jane, with over 20 years' experience, has appeared as counsel in international arbitration and regularly sits as arbitrator in international arbitrations. Ms. Willems has been appointed as chairman, party-appointed arbitrator and sole arbitrator. Ms. Willems is an Associate Professor of Law and the Associate Director of the International Arbitration and Dispute Settlement (IADS) Program at Tsinghua University School of Law in Beijing.

Jane Willems 教授，在國際仲裁中擔任法律顧問，並經常擔任國際仲裁仲裁員，擁有超過 20 年的經驗，Willems 女士被任命為主席、當事人指定仲裁員和獨任仲裁員。她是北京清華大學法學院法學副教授、國際仲裁與爭端解決（IADS）項目副主任。

Mr. Xi, Yushan
席與善先生

Title 職稱	企業家	Nationality 國家	China (Hong Kong) 中國香港	Gender 性別	Male 男

Mr. Xi, Yushan is a well-known Hong Kong current affairs commentator and social activist. He was the chief guest commentator of the Phoenix TV Current Affairs Debate. He founded and served as the managing director of ANCENT.

席與善先生，香港著名時事評論員、社會活動家，曾任鳳凰衛視《時事辯論會》主嘉賓評論員，創辦並任安迅國際董事總經理。

Prof. Yi, Lori

Title 職稱	啓明大學 法學教授	Nationality 國家	Korea 韓國	Gender 性別	Female 女

Prof. Lori Yi has worked as a law professor in Keimyung University, Daegu in Korea since 2005. She is vice -president of Korean Association of Arbitration Studies in 2023. She is a mediator of Personal Information Dispute Mediation Committee, Open Data Mediation Committee (ODMC), the Korea Agency of Medical Mediation and Arbitration, and Conflict Management Committee of Daegu

Metropolitan City. She published a number of articles on the mediation system and mediation training and has conducted various mediations projects.

Lori Yi 教授從 2005 年開始在大丘啓明大學擔任法學教授。她將於 2023 年擔任韓國仲裁學會副會長。她是個人資訊糾紛調解委員會、開放數據調解委員會（ODMC）、韓國醫療調解和仲裁機構、大丘市衝突管理委員會的調解員。她發表了許多關於調解制度和調解培訓的文章，並進行了多項調解研究項目。

Prof. Zadi, Kashif Imran

| Title 職稱 | 巴基斯坦管理科技大學 法律與政策學院 代理院長、主任 | Nationality 國家 | Pakistan 巴基斯坦 | Gender 性別 | Male 男 |

Prof. Zadi, Kashif Imran is an associate Professor, Acting Dean/Director, School of Law and Policy, University of Management and Technology, Lahore, Pakistan. He obtained his JSD degree from Zhejiang University, China.

Zadi, Kashif Imran 教授是巴基斯坦管理科技大學法律與政策學院副教授，代理院長 / 主任。他自浙江大學獲得法學博士學位。

Mr. Zhang, Jun
張軍先生

| Title 職稱 | 「一帶一路」商貿法律 服務研究院 院長、律師 | Nationality 國家 | China 中國 | Gender 性別 | Male 男 |

Zhang, Jun, currently serves as the Founding Partner, and Director of Beijing Gongheng Law Firm. He is the president of the Belt and Road Trade and Legal Services Research Institute;External Supervisor at the Law School of China University of Political Science and Law;Special Contributor to the People's Daily Lawyer's Mailbox Column; He is an arbitrator at Hainan International Arbitration Court, Hainan Arbitration Commission, and Beihai International Arbitration Court; He is Deputy Director of the Commercial and Economic Committee of Beijing Chaoyang District Lawyers Association

張軍，現任北京市公衡律師事務所律所主任，任中國政法大學、中國品牌協會與公衡律所合辦的「一帶一路」商貿法律服務研究院院長、中國政法大學法學院校外導師、《人民日報》律師信箱特約撰稿律師、海南國際仲裁院、海南仲裁委員會、北海國際仲裁院仲裁員、北京朝陽區律協商事與經濟委員會副主任。

Prof. Zhao, Jun
趙駿教授

Title 職稱	浙江大學光華法學院 副院長、教授	Nationality 國家	China 中國	Gender 性別	Male 男

Zhao, Jun, Professor, supervisor of Ph.D. students, Vice Dean of Guanghua Law School, Zhejiang University. Professor Zhao's expertise is in the area of international economic law and he has published widely in top journals like Social Sciences in China.

趙駿教授，博士生導師，浙江大學光華法學院副院長。主要研究國際經濟法領域，並在《中國社會科學》等頂級期刊上發表了大量文章。

Prof. Zhao, Yun
趙雲教授

Title 職稱	香港大學 法學教授	Nationality 國家	China (Hong Kong) 中國香港	Gender 性別	Male 男

Prof. Zhao, Yun is Henry Cheng Professor in International Law and Associate Dean of Faculty of Law at the University of Hong Kong (HKU). Prof. Zhao is currently Representative of Regional Office for Asia and the Pacific (ROAP) of the Hague Conference on Private International Law (HCCH); Standing Council Member of Chinese Society of International Law and Council Member of Chinese Law Society; Chair Professor at Xiamen University (2020-2023). He is listed as arbitrator in several international arbitration commissions. He has published widely on various topics including particularly Space Law, Dispute Resolution, and E-commerce Law.

趙雲教授，香港大學法律學院鄭家純基金國際法教授兼副院長；海牙國際私法會議亞太區域辦事處代表；中國法學會理事；中國國際法學會常務理事；廈門大學講座教授。國內國際多家仲裁機構仲裁員。主要研究領域包括爭議解決、外空法和電子商務法。

專家起草組 Expert Drafting Group

Prof. Wang, Guiguo
王貴國教授

Title 職稱	浙江大學 文科資深教授	Nationality 國家	China 中國	Gender 性別	Male 男

Prof. Wang Guiguo is the President of Zhejiang University Academy of International Strategy and Law, and University Professor of Law, Zhejiang University; President of International Academy of the Belt and Road (Hong Kong); Eason-Weinmann Chair of International and Comparative Law Emeritus, School of Law, Tulane University, USA; Chairman of the Hong Kong WTO Research Institute; Chairman of the National Committee (HK) and Titular Member of the International Academy of Comparative Law; Vice President of the Chinese Society of International Economic Law. Prof.Wang, holder of the JSD degree from Yale and LL.M. degree from Columbia, has published more than 20 books and more than 100 academic articles in both Chinese and English.

王貴國教授係浙江大學國際戰略與法律研究院院長、浙江大學文科資深教授;「一帶一路」國際研究院(香港)院長;美國杜蘭大學法學院 Eason-Weinmann 國際法與比較法榮休教授;香港世界貿易組織研究中心主席、比較法國際(海牙)科學院名譽院士、比較法國際(海牙)科學院香港委員會主席;中國國際經濟法學會副會長。王貴國教授為美國耶魯大學法哲學博士和美國哥倫比亞大學法學碩士,曾出版中英文著作 20 餘部以及學術論文百餘篇。

Prof. Addis, Adeno

Title 職稱	美國杜蘭大學 法學教授	Nationality 國家	United States 美國	Gender 性別	Male 男

Prof. Adeno Addis holds the W. R. Irby Chair and is the W. Ray Forrester Professor of Public and Constitutional Law at Tulane University School of Law (U.S.). He is an internationally recognized scholar whose expertise spans a range of areas, but primarily focusing on constitutional law, international law, human rights, and political and legal theory. He has taught at other law schools as a visiting professor both in the United States and in other countries.

Adeno Addis 教授擔任 W. R. Irby 主席,是杜蘭法學院(美國)的公共和憲法法學教授,國際著名法學家。他的專業領域廣泛,主要集中在憲法、國際法、人權以及政治和法律理論。他曾在美國和澳大利亞、德國、香港、日本等國家和地區的法學院擔任客座教授。

Prof. Gu, Minkang
顧敏康教授

| Title 職稱 | 香港城市大學 原副院長 | Nationality 國家 | China (Hong Kong) 中國香港 | Gender 性別 | Male 男 |

Professor Gu, Minkang is Associate Co-Director of Academy for Applied Policy Studies and Education Futures, and Project Director of Office of the President. He was the Dean of Faculty of Law and Head of Credit Risk Management School, Xiangtan University, China. He was also Associated Dean of School of Law, City University of Hong Kong. He worked for the same university as a Lecturer in Law for 5 years. During that time, he visited the Rule University of Bochum (Germany) as a Visiting Scholar for a year. Subsequently in 1993, he went to the United States and successfully completed his legal study in the Willamette University College of Law and earned Doctor of Jurisprudence in 1996. He also went to France and earned a degree in Master of European Business Law.

顧敏康教授是香港教育大學應用政策研究及教育未來學院聯席副院長和校長室項目總監。他曾經是湘潭大學法學部部長、信用風險管理學院院長、教授、博士生導師，也曾經是香港城市大學法律學院副院長，教授。他在華東政法大學工作五年，期間去德國魯爾大學做訪問學者。他於 1993 年去美國留學並於 1996 年獲得威拉姆特大學法學院法律博士；他還曾去法國進修並獲得歐洲商法碩士學位。

Ms. Huang, Jianwen
黃建雯女士

| Title 職稱 | 中國律師 | Nationality 國家 | China 中國 | Gender 性別 | Female 女 |

Ms. Huang Jianwen is the Director-in-chief of King & Wood Mallesons Belt & Road Center for International Cooperation and Facilitation, the head of KWM's life science team and the legal consultant of National Medical Products Administration. She specializes in domestic and cross-border investments and M&A, licensing, compliance and corporate matters.

黃建雯律師是金杜律師事務所「一帶一路」國際合作與促進中心主任、醫藥醫療板塊負責人、國家藥品監督管理局法律顧問。黃建雯律師的主要執業領域為境內外投資和兼併收購、技術許可、商業合規與公司業務。

Prof. Ishikawa, Tomoko

| Title 職稱 | 日本名古屋大學
法學院副院長、教授 | Nationality 國家 | Japan
日本 | Gender 性別 | Female
女 |

Prof. Ishikawa, Tomoko is vice dean and professor at Nagoya University in Japan. She has served as an ICSID Conciliator, appointed by the Chairman of the Administrative Council (2017-2023), a member of the Legal Advisory Committee of the Energy Charter Treaty, an arbitrator at Shenzhen Court of International Arbitration, and a mediator at the Kyoto International Mediation Centre. Her professional experiences include serving as an Associate Judge at Tokyo District Court and holding the position of Deputy Director at the International Legal Affairs Bureau of the Ministry of Foreign Affairs of Japan, where she worked on bilateral/trilateral investment treaties, Free Trade Agreements, and WTO dispute settlement.

石川朝子教授是日本名古屋大學副院長兼教授。她曾擔任 ICSID 調解員,由行政理事會主席任命(2017-2023),能源憲章條約法律諮詢委員會成員,深圳國際仲裁院仲裁員,京都國際調解中心調解員。她的專業經歷包括在東京地方法院擔任助理法官,並擔任日本外務省國際法律事務局副局長,負責雙邊 / 三邊投資條約、自由貿易協定和世貿組織爭端解決。

Prof. Junngam, Nartnirun

| Title 職稱 | 泰國國立法政大學
法學教授 | Nationality 國家 | Thailand
泰國 | Gender 性別 | Male
男 |

Prof. Nartnirun Junngam teaches at the Faculty of Law, Thammasat University. His areas of interest include public international law, international economic law, and international dispute settlement. He was a Visiting Fellow at the Lauterpacht Centre for International Law at the University of Cambridge and guest speaker at Yale Law School.

Nartnirun Junngam 教授在泰國國立法政大學法律系任教。他的研究領域包括國際公法、國際經濟法和國際爭端解決。他是劍橋大學勞特派特國際法中心的訪問學者,也是耶魯大學法學院的客座演講嘉賓。

Prof. Kawashima, Fujio

| Title 職稱 | 神戶大學
法學教授 | Nationality 國家 | Japan
日本 | Gender 性別 | Male
男 |

Prof. Kawashima, Fujio is a professor of the Graduate School of Law at Kobe University. He holds B.A. in Law (University of Tokyo 1990). He specializes in international economic law and competition law. His research interests include WTO dispute settlement, trade and competition policy and development of competition law in Asian countries.

川島富士雄教授是神戶大學法學院的教授。他擁有法學學士學位（1990 年東京大學）。專攻國際經濟法和競爭法。主要研究方向為 WTO 爭端解決、貿易與競爭政策、亞洲國家競爭法發展等。

Mr. Letten, James

Title 職稱	美國前聯邦檢察官	Nationality 國家	United States 美國	Gender 性別	Male 男

Mr. James Letten, a partner at the US law firm of Butler Snow LLP, previously served as Tulane University Law School's first Assistant Dean for Experiential Learning. Prior to that, he served 30 years with the United States Department of Justice– the last 12 as the presidentially-appointed United States Attorney in New Orleans—and upon his retirement was the longest serving U.S. Attorney in the US.

James Letten 先生，美國 Butler Snow 律師事務所合夥人，曾擔任杜蘭大學法學院（Tulane University law School）首任體驗式學習助理院長。在此之前，他在美國司法部工作了 30 年。其中有 12 年是由總統任命的聯邦檢察官，是美國任職時間最長的聯邦檢察官。

Prof. Leung, Mei-fun
梁美芬教授

Title 職稱	全國人大代表 香港城市大學 法學院教授	Nationality 國家	China (Hong Kong) 中國香港	Gender 性別	Female 女

Prof. Leung Mei-fun, NPC deputy, Professor of School of Law in City University of Hong Kong; She is a Barrister-at Law, Hong Kong; She is an arbitrator (CIETAC). Besides, she is a member of the Hong Kong Basic Law Committee; Member of the Hong Kong Legislative Council. She is Hong Kong Special Administrative Region deputy to the National People's Congress.

梁美芬教授為全國人大代表，香港城市大學法學院教授，香港執業大律師，中國國際經濟貿易仲裁委員會仲裁員，全國人大常委會香港基本法委員會委員，香港立法會議員，香港特別行政區第十四屆全國人民代表大會代表。

Prof. Ma, Guang
馬光教授

Title 職稱	浙江大學 光華法學院副教授	Nationality 國家	China 中國	Gender 性別	Male 男

Prof. MA Guang is an Associate Professor of international law at Guanghua Law School of Zhejiang University of China. He also serves as Executive Director of the Institute of International Law at Zhejiang University. He was awarded LL.B Degree from China University of Political Science and Law and LL.M. and Ph.D. from Korea University. Professor Ma is an arbitrator and also a licensed lawyer in China. His interest fields include international trade law, law of the sea, humanitarian law, international law of cyberspace, personal information protection law.

馬光教授，浙江大學光華法學院國際法副教授，浙江大學國際法研究所執行主任。中國政法大學學士，高麗大學法學碩士、博士。馬教授同時是中國的仲裁員和執業律師。主要研究領域為國際貿易法、海洋法、人道法、網絡空間國際法、個人資訊保護法。

Ambassador Datuk Manickham, Supperamaniam

Title 職稱	馬來西亞 前駐 WTO 大使	Nationality 國家	Malaysia 馬來西亞	Gender 性別	Male 男

Ambassador Datuk Manickham, Supperamaniam joined the Malaysian Administrative and Diplomatic Service in 1970 and served the Ministry of International Trade and Industry for a period of 34 years in various capacities including Senior Trade Commissioner of Malaysia to Hong Kong and China, Director, Department of International Trade, Deputy Secretary-General (Trade) and Ambassador/Permanent Representative of Malaysia to the World Trade Organization.

Datuk Manickham, Superamaniam 大使先生於 1970 年加入馬來西亞行政和外交事務處，並在國際貿易和工業部服務了 34 年，擔任過馬來西亞駐香港和中國高級貿易專員，國際貿易司司長，副秘書長（貿易）和馬來西亞駐世界貿易組織大使 / 常駐代表。

Chief Justice Nisar, Mian Saqib

Title 職稱	巴基斯坦 前首席大法官	Nationality 國家	Pakistan 巴基斯坦	Gender 性別	Male 男

Nisar, Mian Saqib, is a Pakistani jurist who served as the 25th Chief Justice of Pakistan from 31 December 2016 till 17 January 2019. He has previously served as the Law Secretary. He also served as a visiting professor of law at the University of Punjab where he provided instructions on constitutional law.

首席大法官 Mian Saqib Nisar 是巴基斯坦法學家，2016 年 12 月 31 日至 2019 年 1 月 17 日擔任巴基斯坦第 25 任首席大法官。他曾擔任律政司司長。他還擔任旁遮普邦大學的客座法學教授，提供關於憲法的指導。

Prof. Park, Nohyoung
朴魯馨教授

Title 職稱	高麗大學法學院 前院長、法學教授	Nationality 國家	Korea 韓國	Gender 性別	Male 男

Prof. Park, Nonyoung is Professor and currently the Dean of School of Law, and the Director of the Cyber Law Centre of Korea University. He graduated from the College of Law of the Korea University (LL.B., 1981) and from the Graduate School of the Korea University (LL.M., 1983). He also graduated from Harvard Law School (LL.M., 1985) and from the University of Cambridge (Ph.D. in international law, 1990). His main research interests cover international economic law, negotiation and mediation, cybersecurity and privacy. Member of the Research Committee on FTAs of R.O. Korea, R.O. Korea

朴魯馨教授是韓國高麗大學法學院院長，法學教授，網絡法律中心主任；他畢業於高麗大學法學院（法學學士，1981 年）和高麗大學研究生院（法學碩士，1983 年）。他還畢業於哈佛大學法學院（法學碩士，1985 年）和劍橋大學（國際法博士，1990 年）。主要研究方向為國際經濟法、談判與調解、網絡安全和隱私。韓國自由貿易協定研究小組成員。

Prof. Porcelli, Stephano

Title 職稱	布雷西亞大學 法學教授	Nationality 國家	Italy 意大利	Gender 性別	Male 男

Prof. Dr. Stefano Porcelli is currently a faculty member at the School of Law at the University of Brescia, after being teaching for several years at the School of Juris Master at the China University of Political Science and Law (CUPL). He obtained a Ph.D. at the University of Rome Tor Vergata and a Ph.D. at the School of Civil and Commercial Law at the CUPL (thesis written and defended in Chinese Mandarin language). He is also member of several research centers and think tanks and is responsible of the Research Observatory on the Law of Persons of the Latin-American Legal Studies Center at the University of Rome Tor Vergata.

Stefano Porcelli（司德法）教授現任意大利布雷西亞大學的法學院教授，曾在中國政法大學法學碩士學院任教多年。他在羅馬第二大學和中國政法大學民商法學院獲得博士學位，是幾個研究中心和智庫的成員，並負責羅馬第二大學拉丁美洲法律研究中心的人格法研究觀察站。

Prof. Sharma, Rajesh

| Title 職稱 | 澳大利亞墨爾本 皇家理工大學 國際爭端解決專家 | Nationality 國家 | **Australia** 澳大利亞 | Gender 性別 | **Male** 男 |

Prof. Rajesh Sharma is Senior Lecturer, Legal and Dispute Studies, Criminology and Justice, RMIT University, Melbourne, Australia, Adjunct Professor at Academy of International Dispute Resolution and Professional Negotiation (AIDRN). Prof. Sharma also worked in Hong Kong and Macao for many years.

Sharma Rajesh 是澳大利亞墨爾本皇家理工大學法律與爭議研究、犯罪學與司法高級講師，國際爭議解決與專業談判學會（AIDRN）兼職教授。Sharma 教授也曾在香港和澳門工作多年。

Prof. Singh, Swaran

| Title 職稱 | 尼赫魯大學政治學教授 亞洲學者協會主席 | Nationality 國家 | **India** 印度 | Gender 性別 | **Male** 男 |

Prof. Swaran Singh teaches at Jawaharlal Nehru University (New Delhi) and is president of Association of Asia Scholars, director of India for Washington-based the Millennium Project's South Asia Foresight Network, Fellow of Canadian Global Affairs Institute (Calgary), Member of Governing Body of Society of Indian Ocean Studies (New Delhi) and formerly visiting professor at various universities. He has published 15 book and numerous articles.

Swaran Singh 教授任教於尼赫魯大學（新德里），現任亞洲學者協會主席，華盛頓千年專案南亞遠見網絡印度部主任，加拿大全球事務研究所（卡爾加里）研究員，印度洋研究學會理事機構（新德里）成員，曾在多所大學任訪問教授。他出版了 15 本著作和多篇文章。

Prof. Yi, Lori

| Title 職稱 | 啓明大學 法學教授 | Nationality 國家 | **Korea** 韓國 | Gender 性別 | **Female** 女 |

Prof. Lori Yi has worked as a law professor in Keimyung University, Daegu in Korea since 2005. She is vice -president of Korean Association of Arbitration Studies in 2023. She is a mediator of Personal Information Dispute Mediation Committee, Open Data Mediation Committee (ODMC), the Korea Agency of Medical Mediation and Arbitration, and Conflict Management Committee of Daegu Metropolitan City. She published a number of articles on the mediation system and mediation training and has conducted various mediations projects.

Lori Yi 教授從 2005 年開始在大丘啓明大學擔任法學教授。她將於 2023 年擔任韓國仲裁學會副會長。她是個人資訊糾紛調解委員會、開放數據調解委員會（ODMC）、韓國醫療調解和仲裁機構、大丘市衝突管理委員會的調解員。她發表了許多關於調解制度和調解培訓的文章，並進行了多項調解研究項目。

Prof. Zadi, Kashif Imran

Title 職稱	巴基斯坦管理科技大學 法律與政策學院 代理院長、主任	Nationality 國家	Pakistan 巴基斯坦	Gender 性別	Male 男

Prof. Zadi, Kashif Imran is an associate Professor, Acting Dean/Director, School of Law and Policy, University of Management and Technology, Lahore, Pakistan. He obtained his JSD degree from Zhejiang University, China.

Zadi, Kashif Imran 教授是巴基斯坦管理科技大學法律與政策學院副教授，代理院長 / 主任。他自浙江大學獲得法學博士學位。

Prof. Zhao, Jun
趙駿教授

Title 職稱	浙江大學光華法學院 副院長、教授	Nationality 國家	China 中國	Gender 性別	Male 男

Zhao, Jun, Professor, supervisor of Ph.D. students, Vice Dean of Guanghua Law School, Zhejiang University. Professor Zhao's expertise is in the area of international economic law and he has published widely in top journals like Social Sciences in China.

趙駿教授，博士生導師，浙江大學光華法學院副院長。主要研究國際經濟法領域，並在《中國社會科學》等頂級期刊上發表了大量文章。

翻譯與編輯組
Editors and Translators Group

Dong, Yao
董堯

Nationality 國家	**China** **中國**	Gender 性別	**Female** **女**

PhD student, major in international law, at Guanghua Law School, Zhejiang University; research assistant of the Academy of International Strategy and Law, specializing in dispute resolution, international investment, and climate change. She holds an LLM degree from Tulane University, USA and an LLM in international law from the City University of Hong Kong. She participated in the translation of UNIDROIT Principles of International Commercial Contracts—An Article by Article Commentary (China Law Press, 2021). She has published an article entitled "Investors' Legal Expectations in International Investment Arbitration" (Legal Daily, July 20, 2022).

浙江大學光華法學院 2019 級國際法博士生。國際戰略與法律研究院研究助理，研究方向為爭端解決、國際投資、氣候變化。美國杜蘭大學法律碩士，香港城市大學國際經濟法碩士。曾參與翻譯《國際統一私法協會國際商事合同通則：逐條評述》（法律出版社，2021年），曾發表文章〈國際投資仲裁中的投資者合法期待〉（《法治日報》，2022 年 7 月 20 日）。

Wang, Xin
王欣

Nationality 國家	**China** **中國**	Gender 性別	**Female** **女**

Wang Xin, PhD, Lecturer of the School of Law, Guangdong University of Foreign Studies, Member of the Association for Legal Education, Guangdong Law Society. Ms. Wang obtained her Doctor of Philosophy from Zhejiang University. Ms. Wang's research interests include international trade law, cybersecurity as well as interdisciplinary studies between international relations and international law. She has published research articles with the *Journal of World Trade*, *Asian Journal of WTO & International Health Law and Policy*, etc. and has chaired several projects commissioned by provincial authorities.

王欣，博士，廣東外語外貿大學法學院講師，廣東省法學會法學教育研究會理事。畢業於浙江大學，獲哲學博士學位。主要研究領域包括國際貿易法、網絡安全以及國際關係與國際法交叉研究。曾在 *Journal of World Trade*、*Asian Journal of WTO & International Health Law and Policy* 等刊物上發表論文數篇，主持省級橫向課題數項。

Weng, Yi
翁怡

Nationality 國家	China 中國	Gender 性別	Female 女

Dr. Weng, Yi, holding a Ph.D. in Law from the University of Manchester, is currently a postdoctoral researcher at the Guanghua Law School of Zhejiang University. Dr. Weng specializes in international private law, international investment law, and cross-border arbitration. She has authored several articles in both English and Chinese in journals including the *International Journal of Law, Policy, and The Family*, and the *Journal of Anhui University (Philosophy and Social Sciences Edition)*. She has also participated in multiple research projects.

翁怡，英國曼徹斯特大學法學博士，浙江大學光華法學院博士後，主要研究方向為國際私法、國際投資法和涉外仲裁。在 *International Journal of Law, Policy, and The Family*，《安徽大學學報（哲學社會科學版）》等期刊發表中英文論文數篇，參與多項省部級課題。

Wu, Haowen
吳灝文

Nationality 國家	China 中國	Gender 性別	Male 男

WU, Haowen, J.S.D., City University of Hong Kong; Postdoctor, Zhejiang University. Associate Researcher of the School of Government, Shenzhen University. He has published multiple articles and few books mainly focusing on issues concerning international trade law and social governance, and conducted more than 20 policy reports.

吳灝文，香港城市大學法學博士，浙江大學法學博士後。深圳大學政府管理學院副研究員。主要就國際貿易法、社會治理等主題，發表中英文文章十餘篇，出版專著數部，近 20 篇諮政報告。

Yang, Zhaojun
楊朝軍

Nationality 國家	China 中國	Gender 性別	Male 男

Yang Zhaojun holds a master degree in international law from the Law School of Hunan Normal University. During his study at Hunan Normal University, he published a number of articles, some of which were commended by the Ministry of Commerce and the National Copyright Administration. After graduation, he worked as a lawyer and since 2015, he has been a member of the Foreign Affairs, Anti-dumping and Countervailing Committee by the Lawyers' Association of Hunan Province, appointed as the professional legal practical tutor by the Law School of Science and Technology

University and the Law School of Hunan Normal University respectively. Since 2019, he has been a PhD candidate in international law at the Guanghua Law School of Zhejiang University, China.

楊朝軍，畢業於湖南師範大學法學院，獲國際法碩士學位。在校期間發表論文多篇，其中部分論文獲中國商務部、國家版權局表彰。畢業後一直從事律師工作，2015 年起被湖南省律師協會選為涉外及雙反專委會委員、長沙理工大學法學院實踐教學指導老師、湖南師範大學法學院法律實務技能授課老師。2019 年入學中國浙江大學光華法學院，修讀國際法學博士學位。

Zhang, Jun
張軍

| Nationality 國家 | China 中國 | Gender 性別 | Male 男 |

Zhang Jun, Founding Partner and Director of Beijing Gongheng Law Firm. President of the Belt and Road Trade and Legal Services Research Institute; External Supervisor at the Law School of China University of Political Science and Law; Special Contributor to the People's Daily Lawyer's Mailbox Column; Arbitrator at Hainan International Arbitration Court, Hainan Arbitration Commission, and Beihai International Arbitration Court; Deputy Director of the Commercial and Economic Committee of Beijing Chaoyang District Lawyers Association

張軍，現任北京市公衡律師事務所律所主任，任中國政法大學、中國品牌協會與公衡律所合辦的「一帶一路」商貿法律服務研究院院長、中國政法大學法學院校外導師、《人民日報》律師信箱特約撰稿律師、海南國際仲裁院、海南仲裁委員會、北海國際仲裁院仲裁員、北京朝陽區律協商事與經濟委員會副主任。

Zhu, Yongqian
朱永倩

| Nationality 國家 | China 中國 | Gender 性別 | Female 女 |

Zhu Yongqian, a candidate of Ph.D. in international law, Guanghua Law School and research assistant of Academy of International Strategy and Law, majoring in international economic law and cyberspace law. She obtained her master degree of International Law from Anhui University of Finance and Economics and participated in the exchange programme at Solbridge International School of Business in South Korea. She has participated in the National Social Science Program and the Program of Ministry of Natural Resources, etc. She has published 7 articles in journals such as *Pacific Journal* and *Journal of International and Comparative Law*.

朱永倩，浙江大學國際法學博士生，浙江大學國際戰略與法律研究院研究助理，研究方向為國際經濟法與網絡空間法。安徽財經大學國際法學碩士，韓國 Solbridge 國際商學院交換生。曾參與國家社科項目與自然資源部項目等，在《太平洋學報》、*Journal of International and Comparative Law* 等期刊上發表文章 7 篇。

編者序

在迎來「一帶一路」倡議提出十周年之際，「一帶一路」國際研究院（香港）和浙江大學國家戰略與法律研究院聯合國際專家完成了《「一帶一路」合作與夥伴關係協議範本》（以下簡稱《協議範本》）的起草，並獲來自於世界五大洲 31 個國家近 50 位專家的支持，共同向世界推薦，深感榮幸！

世界正處於百年未有之大變局，變化與交替無處不在，無時不在，「逝者如斯夫，不舍晝夜」，「俯仰之間已陳跡」。然「萬物負陰而抱陽」，有變則有不變，變囿於不變之中，變與不變相互作用。這也就是古人所說的，「天生烝民，有物有則」，則即規律、即「道」。

在此變化的世界，全球化的大勢並沒有改變，但當下全球化的形態和內容發生了變化，代表了多極世界的特點。「一帶一路」倡議以實現人格尊嚴和世界和平為己任，搭建了一個國際合作的平台。古人云：「事督乎法，法出乎權，權出乎道」，而「道法自然」；自然即本然，即本來如此，無任何外力的干預。

「一帶一路」的有效實施需要與之相適應的秩序（包括程序和實體規則），以便為當事方提供具透明度及拘束力的行為規範和標準，正所謂「不以規矩，不能成方圓」。「一帶一路」係國際社會的公共產品，與之相關的規則和規範不僅應基於並反映各參加國的文化、傳統和價值，亦應反映人類社會的整體價值。「一帶一路」倡議自提出時起，歷經十年，得到國際社會的廣泛支持，反映了世界發展的趨勢。

「一帶一路」國際研究院（香港）和浙江大學國際戰略與法律研究院有機會參與其中，深感榮幸。我們先後舉辦了「一帶一路」國際法律系列論壇，出版了《「一帶一路」的國際法律視野》，並於 2015 年組織國際專家起草了《「一帶一路」爭端解決機制》（藍皮書），由近 30 個國家的專家學者作為發起人共同推出。《「一帶一路」爭端解決機制》（藍皮書）先後被譯成數種外國文字，並在國外出版發行。

《「一帶一路」爭端解決機制》（藍皮書）獲中國政府認可；中國貿促會作為發起人，參照《「一帶一路」爭端解決機制》《藍皮書》的具體建議籌組了國際商事爭端預防與解決組織；該組織於 2020 年在北京正式開業，處理商事爭端。「一帶一路」國際研究院和浙江大學國際戰略與法律研究院直接參與了國際商事爭端預防與解決組織的調解、仲裁和上訴程序等規則的起草與制定。

「大車無輗，小車無軏，其何以行之哉？」輗和軏都是車的關鍵，缺之車則不可以為用，或不成為車。其他事情亦然；每項事業的成功均需相應的秩序。「一帶一路」倡議的目的是造福人類，實現《聯合國憲章》下的人格尊嚴與世界和平，需要與之相適應的規則，即秩序。「凡事豫則立，不豫則廢。言前定則不跆，事前定則不困，行前定則不疚，道前定則不窮」。為「一帶一路」倡議之有效實施量身定製一套秩序不僅需要，而且必要。

所有秩序都包括程序和實體兩個方面，缺一不可。《「一帶一路」爭端解決機制》（藍皮書）針對的是爭議解決的程序方面。故「一帶一路」國際研究院和浙江大學國際戰略與法律研究院於 2018 年組織了十餘個國家的二十餘位專家共同起草了《協議範本》，並獲來自於世界五大洲 31 個國家近 50 位專家的支持，共同向世界推薦，希望並鼓勵「一帶一路」參與國及其他國家在簽訂自由貿易等協定時作為範本參考。這也是「一帶一路」倡議得到國際社會廣泛歡迎與支持的有力證據。

《協議範本》共 15 章，以發展中國家的需要為依歸，反映了「一帶一路」參與國的文化、歷史和傳統，強調主權原則、發展權、可持續發展、數字經濟、公共衛生、基礎設施、環境和爭端解決等方面，同時注重與人類社會整體發展間的平衡。基於此理念，《協議範本》既有對現行國際秩序的繼承，又有基於「一帶一路」倡議宗旨和內涵的對當代國際秩序的發展興革。

我們認為，改進國際法律秩序「如四時之錯行，如日月之代明」，必要性不可否認，不能回避。然任何興革和改進均應「隨時而變，因俗而動」，而不是為了標新立異。古人云：「人法地，地法天，天法道，道法自然」，說的是任何事物的發生、發展都不可脫離其「道」，即事物的本然。與「一帶一路」倡議相關的秩序亦需師法自然，反映「一帶一路」的本然狀態，符合其發展的規律。

　　我們的建議只是一些國際學者和專家的意見，意在為列國參加「一帶一路」倡議盡微薄之力。我們遵循的價值理念是師法自然，盡力使我們的建議符合世界發展的「道」，並希望依「道」起草的《協議範本》得到同樣「尊道而貴德」的列國政府和國際專家的認可、批評與鞭策。

王貴國

2023 年 9 月 3 日

CONTENTS

CHAPTER - 3   SUSTAINABLE DEVELOPMENT   10

CHAPTER - 4   TRANSPARENCY AND ANTI-CORRUPTION   14

CHAPTER - 5 FACILITATION OF GOODS, SERVICES AND SERVICE PROVIDERS

CHAPTER - 7   INVESTMENT   65

CHAPTER - 9   PUBLIC HEALTH   120

CHAPTER - 10   FINANCE   123

CHAPTER - 11   INFRASTRUCTURE

CHAPTER - 12   COMPETITION   150

CHAPTER - 13   ENVIRONMENT   158

CHAPTER - 14   LABOUR STANDARDS   162

CHAPTER - 15   DISPUTE SETTLEMENT   175

目錄

第七章　投資　　　　　　　　　　　　　　　　239

第九章　公共衛生　291

第十章　金融　294

第十一章　基礎設施　303

第十二章　競爭 319

THE BELT AND ROAD

COOPERATION AND PARTNERSHIP
MODEL AGREEMENT

CHAPTER - 1
GENERAL PRINCIPLES AND DEFINITIONS

Section A. General Principles

Article 1: General Scope and Framework

The Contracting Parties acknowledge that the Belt and Road Initiative ("BRI") provides a good framework for strengthening economic cooperation and development with clearly defined goals, guiding principles and areas of priorities. It is a major step forward for building a sense of community among the participating countries in the BRI.

According to the "Vision and Actions on Jointly Building Silk Road Economic Belt and 21st-Century Maritime Silk Road", as published in 2015, the general key characteristics of the BRI includes the promotion of shared development and prosperity, peace and friendship through enhancing mutual understanding, trust and exchange.

Article 2: Sovereignty

The BRI is based on the principle of the sovereign equality of all Contracting Parties.

Article 3: Good Faith and Pacta Sunt Servanda

This Agreement is binding upon the Contracting Parties. All Contracting Parties shall act and discharge their obligations of this Agreement in good faith to enjoy the benefits of the BRI.

Article 4: Sustainable Development

The Contracting Parties commit to incorporate principle of sustainable development including the UN Sustainable Development Goals in all BRI.

The Contracting Parties ensure BRI projects as defined herein are comprehensive enough to result in increased efficiency and effectiveness and promote sustainable development with poverty reduction and social inclusivity.

Article 5: Rule of Law

The Contracting Parties are committed to implement BRI projects including infrastructure development, finance, investment, intellectual property rights and other related aspects of the BRI projects following rule of law.

Article 6: Non-Discrimination

The Contracting Parties shall apply the rules and procedures relating to BRI projects in a non-discriminatory or non-arbitrary manner and based on market principles.

Article 7: Treatment

The Contracting Parties shall treat each other including their investments, businesses and people on the basis of fairness, objectivity, and accord Most-Favoured Nation Treatment, National Treatment and fair and equitable treatment.

The Contracting Parties shall protect rights of labour and provide safety and security to labour involved in carrying out of BRI projects in their respective territories.

Article 8: Transparency and Anti-Corruption

The Contracting Parties agree to commit to Transparency principle in general.

All information on policies, laws, regulations, administrative rulings, licensing, certification, qualification and registration requirements, technical regulations, standards, guidelines, procedures and practices and other relevant matters relating to BRI projects shall be made available by the Contracting Parties to all interested parties, consistently and in a timely manner, at no cost or at a reasonable cost.

The Contracting Parties affirm to resolve to eliminate bribery and corruption in BRI projects.

The Contracting Parties recognise the need to build integrity within both public and private sectors and each sector has complementary responsibilities in this regard.

Article 9: Due Process

The Contracting Parties shall respect all legal rights that are owed to a person and shall accord due process including access to adequate appeal procedure in accordance with the applicable laws of the respective Contracting Parties.

Article 10: Mutual Respect and Trust

The Contracting Parties agree that the BRI should be pursued in the spirit of mutual respect and trust premised on the understanding that the participating countries in the BRI are at different stages of development, have different perspectives, different capabilities and different priorities.

Article 11: Mutual Benefits

The Contracting Parties agree that the BRI must promote a balanced program that is responsive to the interests and needs of its participating countries; all must benefit to a similar and substantial degree.

The Contracting Parties agree that BRI projects must focus on result rather than form, and achievement rather than policy.

Article 12: Regional Solidarity

The Contracting Parties recognise that the maintenance of close and growing relationships among the participating countries in the BRI in the BRI is crucial to all and therefore friendship and regional solidarity must link and bind the participating countries in the BRI in the BRI together.

Article 13: Cooperation between Government and Stakeholders

The Contracting Parties agree that the progressive initiation, design and implementation of projects must be pursued by close cooperation among government authorities and businesses and stakeholders.

Article 14: Standardisation of Business Practices and Ethics

The Contracting Parties ensure that all BRI projects must be implemented on the basis of international best practices. Any disparity in terms of business practices and ethics should be addressed through standardised approaches.

Article 15: Communications, Cooperation and Consultations

The Contracting Parties shall endeavour to facilitate and promote effective mechanisms for exchanges with the business and trading community and investors including opportunities for consultation when formulating, implementing and reviewing rules and procedures relating to BRI projects.

The Contracting Parties shall endeavour to engage the business sector and community-based organisations even more effectively, both in terms of providing easier access to official information on implementation and by obtaining timely feedback on policies or measures being proposed, particularly when they have a project facilitation goal.

The Contracting Parties must involve participation of all actors including Civil societies, non-government organizations, Business Sector, Public Sector and Academia when formulating, implementing and reviewing rules and procedures relating to BRI projects.

Article 16: Simplification and Efficiency of Rules

The Contracting Parties shall strive to simplify the rules and procedures relating to BRI projects by fostering responsive regulatory practices, in order to reduce burdensome, restrictive or unnecessary measures.

Article 17: Consistency and Predictability of Rules

The Contracting Parties shall endeavour to apply rules and procedures relating to BRI projects in a consistent, predictable and uniform manner, so as to minimise uncertainty. Rules and procedures shall be applied in a non-discretionary manner and shall provide clear and precise procedural guidance to the appropriate authorities with standard policies and operating procedures.

Article 18: Harmonisation and Mutual Recognition of Rules

While maintaining the right to regulate or set rules to pursue legitimate objectives such as the protection of health, safety or public morals and the conservation of exhaustible natural resources, the Contracting Parties agree that the regulations, rules and procedures relating to BRI projects shall be harmonised subject to domestic regulation on the basis of international standards and facilitated through mutual recognition, where appropriate.

Article 19: Modernisation and Use of New Technology

The Contracting Parties shall, review and update, if necessary, the rules and procedures relating to BRI projects, including new information and new business practices, and based on the adoption, where appropriate, of modern techniques and new technology.

The Contracting Parties are committed to promote Digital Trade, Cyber Security and respect Intellectual Property Rights.

Article 20: Amicable and Peaceful Resolution of Dispute

The Contracting Parties shall resolve all disputes related to BRI projects in an amicable and peaceful manner so that peace, security and justice in the Belt and Road countries or region are not endangered.

Section B. Definitions

Article 21: General Definitions

For the purposes of this Agreement, unless otherwise provided:

"BRI projects" mean the projects that are initiated and developed in connection with or as measures for the implementation of the BRI.

"GATS" means the General Agreement on Trade in Services, contained in Annex 1B to the WTO Agreement;

"IMF" means the International Monetary Fund;

"IMF Articles of Agreement" means the Articles of Agreement of the International Monetary Fund adopted at Bretton Woods on 22 July 1944;

"Personal information" means any information relating to an identified or identifiable natural person;

"WCO" shall mean the World Customs Organization established in 1952.

"TRIPS Agreement" means the Agreement on Trade-Related Aspects of Intellectual Property Rights, contained in Annex 1C to the WTO Agreement.

"UNCITRAL" means the United Nations Commission on International Trade Law.

"WTO Agreement" means the Marrakesh Agreement Establishing the World Trade Organization, done on April 15, 1994.

CHAPTER - 2
RIGHT TO DEVELOPMENT

Article 1: Definition

1. The **"right to development"** with reference to this Agreement means right by virtue of which every Contracting Party and individuals of the Contracting Parties are entitled to participate in, contribute to, and enjoy economic, social and cultural development, in which all economic rights and free trade can be fully realized.

2. The **"right to development"** herein also means that the full realization of the rights under this Agreement and other international agreements and declarations which are ratified by the Contracting Parties.

Article 2: States as a Duty Bearers of Right to Development for Own People

1. The Contracting Parties and individuals of the Contracting Parties are the central subjects of development and should be the active participants and beneficiaries of the right to development.

2. The Contracting Parties and individuals of the Contracting Parties have a responsibility for development, individually and collectively, taking into account the need for full respect for their rights as well as their duties to the community, which alone can ensure the free and complete fulfilment of the object of this Agreement, and they should therefore promote and protect an appropriate political, social and economic order for development.

3. The Contracting Parties shall formulate appropriate national development policies for promoting and implementing the right to development and in the fair distribution of the benefits resulting therefrom.

Article 3: States Acting as Collective Duty Bearers of Right to Development at Global and Regional Level

1. The Contracting Parties shall formulate provisions which are favourable to the realization of the right to development.

2. The provisions relating to the right to development requires full respect for the principles of international law concerning friendly relations and co-operation among States in accordance with the Charter of the United Nations.

3. The Contracting Parties have the duty to co-operate with each other in ensuring development and eliminating obstacles to development. The Contracting Parties shall realize their rights and fulfill their duties in such a manner as to promote the right to development as a new international economic order based on sovereign equality, interdependence, mutual interest and co-operation among all the Contracting Parties.

Article 4: States as a Duty Bearers of Right to Development for Others

Necessary measures shall be taken for the development of developing Contracting Parties. The mutual cooperation of the Contracting Parties is compulsory to provide the developing and least-developed Contracting Parties with appropriate means and facilities to foster their comprehensive development.

Article 5: Observing Trade Rules

The Contracting Parties shall take resolute steps to eliminate the massive and flagrant violations of trade rules.

Article 6: Right to Development without Discrimination

1. The Contracting Parties shall co-operate with a view to promote, encourage and strengthen the respect for and observance of the right to development for all without any discrimination.

2. The right to development is indivisible and interdependent; equal attention and urgent consideration shall be given for its implementation, promotion and protection to achieve the goals of this Agreement.

3. The Contracting Parties shall take steps to eliminate obstacles to development resulting from failure to observe civil and political rights, as well as economic, social and cultural rights.

Article 7: Eradication of Social Injustice

The Contracting Parties shall ensure to take effective measures for appropriate economic and social reforms with a view to eradicating all social injustices.

Article 8: Public and Stakeholders Participation

The Contracting Parties shall encourage popular participation in all spheres as an important factor in development and in the full realization of the right to development.

Article 9: Progressive Enhancement of Right to Development

The Contracting Parties shall take necessary steps to ensure the full exercise and progressive enhancement of the right to development, including formulation, adoption and implementation of policy, legislative and other measures at the national and international levels.

Article 10: People-to-People Connectivity

The Contracting Parties shall encourage the people-to-people connectivity to promote dialogue, research and policies for the protection of the right to development.

Article 11: Relationship with Other Provisions

All the aspects of the right to development set forth here are indivisible and interdependent and each of them should be considered in the context of the whole.

CHAPTER - 3

SUSTAINABLE DEVELOPMENT

Article 1: Objectives and Goals

1. According to the General Principles of this Agreement, the Contracting Parties commit to incorporate principle of sustainable development including the UN Sustainable Development Goals in the BRI projects.

2. The Contracting Parties ensure BRI projects are comprehensive enough to result in increased efficiency and effectiveness and promote sustainable development with poverty reduction and social inclusivity.

Article 2: Sustainable Infrastructure Development

1. The Contracting Parties agree to develop quality, reliable, sustainable and resilient infrastructure, including regional and transborder infrastructure, by implementing BRI projects, to support economic development and human well-being, with a focus on affordable and equitable access for all in the Belt and Road countries by providing enhanced financial, technological and technical support.

2. The Contracting Parties agree to assist in upgrading existing infrastructure and retrofit industries in form of BRI projects, to make them sustainable, with increased resource-use efficiency and greater adoption of clean and environmentally sound technologies and industrial processes, with all Belt and Road countries and regions taking action in accordance with their respective capabilities.

3. The Contracting Parties agree to promote inclusive and sustainable industrialization and, significantly raise industry's share of employment and gross domestic product, in line with national circumstances of the Belt and Road countries and regions.

Article 3: Debt Sustainability

The Contracting Parties commit to mobilize additional financial resources for Belt and Road countries from multiple sources for BRI projects and assist Belt and Road countries in attaining long-term debt sustainability through coordinated policies aimed at fostering debt financing, debt relief and debt restructuring, as appropriate.

Article 4: Sustainable Investment

1. Investment policies of the Contracting Parties should establish open, non-discriminatory, transparent and predictable conditions for investment. Investment policies of the Contracting Parties should provide legal certainty and strong protection to investors and investments, tangible and intangible, including access to effective mechanisms for the prevention and settlement of disputes, as well as to enforcement procedures. Dispute settlement procedures of a Contracting Party should be fair, open and transparent, with appropriate safeguards to prevent abuse.

2. Regulation relating to investment of a Contracting Party should be developed in a transparent manner with the opportunity for all stakeholders to participate, and embedded in an institutional framework based on the rule of law.

3. Investment policies and other policies of a Contracting Party that impact on investment should be coherent at both the national, regional and international levels and aimed at fostering investment, consistent with the objectives of sustainable development and inclusive growth of a Belt and Road country and region.

3. Policies for investment promotion of a Contracting Party should maximize economic benefit, be effective and efficient, aimed at attracting and retaining investment, and matched by facilitation efforts that promote transparency and are conducive for investors to establish, conduct and expand their businesses.

4. Investment policies of a Contracting Party should promote and facilitate the observance by investors of regional and international best practices and applicable instruments of responsible business conduct and corporate governance.

Article 5: Sustainable Production and Consumption

The Contracting Parties agree to implement the principle of sustainable consumption and production aiming at "doing more and better with less," for the BRI projects so that net welfare gains from the BRI projects and economic activities can increase by reducing resource use, degradation and pollution along the whole life cycle, while increasing quality of life in the Belt and Road countries and regions.

Article 6: Clean Energy

1. The Contracting Parties agree, wherever possible, in form of the BRI projects, to build, expand infrastructure and upgrade technology for supplying modern and sustainable energy services for all the Belt and Road countries and regions.

2. The Contracting Parties agree to enhance cooperation to facilitate access to clean energy research and technology, including renewable energy, energy efficiency and advanced and cleaner fossil-fuel technology, and promote investment in energy infrastructure and clean energy technology through the BRI projects wherever possible.

Article 7: Sustainable Work and Economic Growth

1. The Contracting Parties agree to create the conditions in BRI projects that allow people to have quality job opportunities and decent working conditions for whole working population in Belt and Road countries and region.

2. The Contracting Parties agree to take immediate and effective measures to eradicate forced labour, end modern slavery and human trafficking and secure the prohibition of child labour in all its forms in the BRI projects.

3. The Contracting Parties agree to protect labour rights and promote safe and secure working environments for all workers, including migrant workers, in particular women migrants, and those in precarious employment in the BRI projects.

Article 8: Sustainable Cities and Communities

1.The Contracting Parties agree to enhance inclusive and sustainable urbanization and capacity for participatory, integrated and sustainable human settlement planning and management in the Belt and Road countries while implementing the BRI projects.

2. With regards to the BRI projects relating to connectivity, the Contracting Parties agree to provide access to safe, affordable, accessible and sustainable transport systems for all, improving road safety, notably by expanding public transport, with special attention to the needs of those in vulnerable situations, women, children, persons with disabilities and older persons.

Article 9: Climate Change

The Contracting Parties agree to integrate climate change measures into national policies, strategies and planning to strengthen resilience and adaptive capacity for all the BRI projects to climate-related hazards and natural disasters in the Belt and Road countries and regions.

Article 10: Protection of Life Below Water

1. With regards to the BRI projects relating to ocean, river and water sources, the Contracting Parties agree to sustainably manage and protect marine and coastal ecosystems to avoid significant adverse impacts, including by strengthening their resilience, and take action for their restoration in order to achieve healthy and productive oceans.

2. With regards to BRI projects on land, the Contracting Parties agree to prevent and significantly reduce marine pollution of all kinds, in particular from land-based activities, including marine debris and nutrient pollution.

Article 11: Protection of Life on Land

1. The Contracting Parties agree to ensure the conservation, restoration and

sustainable use of terrestrial and inland freshwater ecosystems and their services, in particular forests, wetlands, mountains and dry lands, in line with obligations under international agreements while executing the BRI projects.

2. The Contracting Parties agree to promote the implementation of sustainable management of all types of forests, halt deforestation, restore degraded forests and substantially increase afforestation and reforestation in the Belt and Road countries and region while executing the BRI projects.

3. The Contracting Parties agree to combat desertification, restore degraded land and soil, including land affected by desertification, drought and floods, if that comes within the are of the BRI projects and strive to achieve a land degradation-neutral in the Belt and Road countries and region while executing the BRI projects.

4. The Contracting Parties agree to ensure the conservation of mountain ecosystems, including their biodiversity, in order to enhance their capacity to provide benefits that are essential for sustainable development during implementation of the BRI projects.

5. The Contracting Parties agree to integrate ecosystem and biodiversity values into the BRI projects planning, and development processes.

6. The Contracting Parties agree to mobilize and significantly increase financial resources from all sources to conserve and sustainably use of biodiversity and ecosystems together with implementation of the BRI projects.

Article 12: Peace, Justice and Strong Institution

1. The Contracting Parties subscribe and agree to resolve all disputes related to the BRI projects in an amicable and peaceful manner under the auspices of the International Centre for Dispute Prevention and Settlement Organization (ICDPASO) so that peace, security and justice in the Belt and Road countries or region are not endangered.

2. The Contracting Parties also agree, through implementing the BRI projects and related activities, to:

    (a) Promote the rule of law at the national and international levels and ensure equal access to justice for all while implementing the BRI projects;

    (b) Eliminate corruption and bribery in all their forms in relations to the implementation of the BRI projects;

    (c) Ensure responsive, inclusive, participatory and representative decision-making at all levels in execution of the BRI projects;

    (d) Strengthen relevant national institutions, including through international cooperation, for building capacity at all levels, in particular in developing and least developed countries and regions of the BRI, to prevent violence and combat terrorism and crime;

    (e) Promote and enforce non-discriminatory laws and policies for sustainable development.

CHAPTER - 4
TRANSPARENCY AND ANTI-CORRUPTION

Article 1: Definitions

For the purpose of this Chapter:

"Foreign public official" shall mean any person holding a legislative, executive, administrative or judicial office of a foreign country, whether appointed or elected; and any person exercising a public function for a foreign country, including for a public agency or public enterprise.

"Official of a public international organization" shall mean an international civil servant or any person who is authorized by such an organization to act on behalf of that organization.

"Public official" means:

(i) any person holding a legislative, executive, administrative or judicial office of a Contracting Party, whether appointed or elected, whether permanent or temporary, whether paid or unpaid, irrespective of that person's seniority;

(ii) any other person who performs a public function for a Contracting Party, including for a public agency or public enterprise, or provides a public service, as defined under the Contracting Party's law and as applied in the pertinent area of that Contracting Party's law; or

(iii) any other person defined as a public official under a Contracting Party's domestic law.

"Small and medium enterprise" means any small and medium enterprise, including any micro enterprise, and may be further defined, where applicable, in accordance with the respective laws, regulations, or national policies of each Contracting Party.

Article 2: Scope of Application

The scope of this Chapter is limited to measures to promote transparency and to eliminate bribery and corruption with respect to any matter covered by this Agreement.

Article 3 Transparency

1. Each Contracting Party shall ensure that its policies, laws, regulations, administrative rulings, licensing, certification, qualification and registration requirements, technical regulations, standards, guidelines, procedures and practices and any changing or amendment to its policies, laws, regulations, administrative rulings, licensing, certification, qualification and registration requirements, technical regulations, standards, guidelines, procedures and practices, related to any matter covered by this Agreement are made available to all Parties and interested persons by means of publication preferably in an official journal of national circulation and/or an official website. Each Contracting Party shall inform the other Parties about such an official journal of national circulation and/or official website consistently and in a timely manner.

2. Each Contracting Party shall, consistent with its legal system, publish a policy proposal, discussion document, summary of the regulation or other document that contains sufficient detail to inform other Parties about whether and how their trade or investment interests may be affected.

Article 4: Notification of Proposed or Actual Measures

Each Contracting Party shall, consistent with its legal system, adopt such measures as may be necessary, to notify the other Contracting Party, any proposed or actual measure that may materially affect the operation of this Agreement or otherwise substantially affect another Contracting Party's interests under this Agreement.

Article 5: Strengthening Systems to Promote Transparency

Each Contracting Party shall, in accordance with the fundamental principles of its domestic law, endeavour to adopt, maintain and strengthen systems that promote transparency, including the transparency of technical trade measures, and prevent conflicts of interest.

Article 6: Maintaining Anti-Corruption Policies and Evaluation

1. Each Contracting Party shall, consistent with its principles of domestic law, develop and implement or maintain effective and coordinated anti-corruption policies that reflect the principles of the rule of law, transparency and accountability; and, promote integrity among its public officials.

2. Each Contracting Party shall endeavour to periodically evaluate relevant legal instruments and administrative measures with a view to determining their adequacy to prevent and fight corruption.

Article 7: Criminalization

1. Each Contracting Party shall, in accordance with its fundamental legal principles, adopt or maintain such legislation and other measures as may be necessary to establish as criminal offences, when committed intentionally:

   (a) the promise, offering or giving to a public official, directly or indirectly, of an undue advantage, for the official or another person or entity, in order that the official act or refrain from acting in the exercise of his or her official duties;

   (b) the solicitation or acceptance by a public official, directly or indirectly, of an undue advantage, for the official or another person or entity, in order that the official act or refrain from acting in the exercise of his or her official duties;

   (c) the promise, offering or giving to a foreign public official or an official of a public international organisation, directly or indirectly, of an undue advantage, for the official or another person or entity, in order that the official act or refrain from acting in relation to the performance of or the exercise of his or her official duties, in order to obtain or retain business or other undue advantage in relation to the conduct of international business; and

   (d) the aiding or abetting, or conspiracy in the commission of any of the offences described in subparagraphs (a) through (c).

2. Each Contracting Party shall make the commission of an offence described in subparagraphs (a) through (d) liable to sanctions that take into account the gravity of that offence.

Article 8: Liability of Legal Persons

Each Contracting Party shall adopt such measures as may be necessary, in accordance with its principles of domestic law, to establish the liability of legal persons for offences established in accordance with Article 7.

Article 9: Compensation

Each Contracting Party shall take such measures as may be necessary, consistent with principles of its domestic law, to ensure that entities or persons who have suffered damage as a result of an act of corruption have the right to initiate legal proceedings against those responsible for that damage in order to obtain compensation.

Article 10: Illicit Enrichment

Consistent with its domestic laws and the fundamental principles of its legal system, each Contracting Party that has not yet done so shall take the necessary measures to adopt such legislation and other measures as may be necessary to establish as a criminal offence, when committed intentionally, illicit enrichment, that is, a significant increase in the assets of a public official that he or she cannot reasonably explain in relation to his or her lawful income during the performance of his or her functions.

Article 11: Enforcement of Anti-Corruption Laws

Each Contracting Party shall, in accordance with the fundamental principles of its legal system, effectively enforce its laws or other measures adopted or maintained to comply with provisions of this Chapter.

Article 12: Effective Prevention of Money Laundering

Each Contracting Party shall ensure the existence and effective enforcement of anti-money laundering legislation that provide for substantial criminal penalties for the laundering of the proceeds of corruption and crime consistent with its domestic legal system.

Article 13: Mutual Legal Assistance

1. Each Contracting Party shall, to the fullest extent possible under its laws and relevant treaties and arrangements, provide prompt and effective legal assistance to another Contracting Party for the purpose of criminal investigations and proceedings brought by a Contracting Party concerning offences within the scope of this Agreement and for non-criminal proceedings within the scope of this Agreement brought by a Contracting Party against a legal person. The requested Contracting Party shall inform the requesting Contracting Party, without delay, of any additional information or documents needed to support the request for assistance and, where requested, of the status and outcome of the request for assistance.

2. Where a Contracting Party makes mutual legal assistance conditional upon the existence of dual criminality, dual criminality shall be deemed to exist if the offence for which the assistance is sought is within the scope of this Agreement.

3. A Contracting Party shall not decline to render mutual legal assistance for criminal matters within the scope of this Agreement on the ground of bank secrecy.

Article 14: Capacity Building and Training Program

1. The Contracting Parties shall intensify cooperation on capacity building for effective prevention and detection of corruption including corruption-related money laundering, developing a specific training program on anti-corruption for officials in various areas, such as on providing technical assistance on operational activities and surveillance of the movement of corruption.

2. The Contracting Parties shall endeavour to develop training program on anti-corruption for directors and managers of businesses and raise awareness among private

sector stakeholders.

Article 15: Integrity in Public Service

Each Contracting Party shall establish systems of government hiring of public officials that assure openness, equity and efficiency and promote hiring of individuals of the highest levels of competence and integrity and develop systems for transparent hiring and promotion to help avoid abuses of patronage, nepotism and favouritism.

Article 16: Independence and Autonomy

Each Contracting Party shall ensure that those in charge of the prevention, investigation, prosecution and adjudication of corruption offences enjoy the independence and autonomy appropriate to their functions, are free from improper influence and have effective means for gathering evidence, protecting the persons who help the investigative authorities in combating corruption and preserving the confidentiality of investigations.

Article 17: Effective Disciplinary Measures

Each Contracting Party shall ensure that the rules relating to the rights and duties of public officials take into account the requirements of the fight against corruption and provide for appropriate and effective disciplinary measures in order to promote further specification of the behaviour expected from public officials by appropriate means, such as codes of conduct.

Article 18: Public Information

Each Contracting Party shall ensure that the general public and the media have freedom to receive and impart public information and in particular information on corruption matters in accordance with its domestic law and in a manner that would not compromise the operational effectiveness of the administration or, in any other way, be detrimental to the interest of governmental agencies and individuals.

Article 19: Participation of Private Sector and Civil Society

1. Each Contracting Party shall take appropriate measures, within its means and in accordance with fundamental principles of its legal system, to promote the active participation of individuals and groups outside the public sector, such as enterprises, civil society, non-governmental organisations and community-based organisations, in the prevention of and the fight against corruption in matters affecting international trade or investment, and to raise public awareness regarding the existence, causes and gravity of, and the threat posed by, corruption. To this end, a Contracting Party may:

(a) undertake public information activities and public education programmes that contribute to non-tolerance of corruption;

(b) adopt or maintain measures to encourage professional associations and other non-governmental organisations, if appropriate, in their efforts to encourage and assist enterprises, in particular SMEs, in developing internal controls, ethics and compliance programmes or measures for preventing and detecting bribery and corruption in international trade and investment;

(c) adopt or maintain measures to encourage company management to make statements in their annual reports or otherwise publicly disclose their internal controls, ethics and compliance programmes or measures, including those that contribute to preventing and detecting bribery and corruption in international trade and investment; and

(d) adopt or maintain measures that respect, promote and protect the freedom to seek, receive, publish and disseminate information concerning corruption.

2. Each Contracting Party shall endeavour to encourage private enterprises, taking into account their structure and size, to:

(a) develop and adopt sufficient internal auditing controls to assist in preventing and detecting acts of corruption in matters affecting international trade or investment; and

(b) ensure that their accounts and required financial statements are subject to appropriate auditing and certification procedures.

3. Each Contracting Party shall take appropriate measures to ensure that its relevant anti- corruption bodies are known to the public and shall provide access to those bodies, if appropriate, for the reporting, including anonymously, of any incident that may be considered to constitute an offence described in Article 7 (Criminalization).

Article 20: Relationship with other Agreements

Unless defeating the objectives and purposes of the present Chapter, nothing contained in this Chapter shall affect the rights and obligations of the Contracting Parties under such other treaties as United Nations Convention Against Corruption, done at New York on October 31, 2003, United Nations Convention against Transnational Organized Crime, done at New York on November 15, 2000, the Convention on Combating Bribery of Foreign Public Officials in International Business Transactions, with its Annex, done at Paris on November 21, 1997, the Inter-American Convention Against Corruption, done at Caracas on March 29, 1996, or the African Union Convention on Preventing and Combating Corruption, done at Maputo on July 11, 2003.

CHAPTER - 5

FACILITATION OF GOODS, SERVICES AND SERVICE PROVIDERS

SECTION A

The Contracting Parties agree to reduce or eliminate existing administrative red tape to facilitate free and seamless cross border movement, including movement in transit, of goods, services and service suppliers necessary for carrying out the BRI projects. In this regard, the Contracting Parties agree to simplify their paper work, modernise procedure and harmonising customs requirements for expediting the movement, release, and clearance of goods, services and service providers, including in transit.

Article 1: Sharing and Availability of Information

1. Sharing of Information

1.1 Each Contracting Party shall promptly publish and share the following information in a non-discriminatory and easily accessible manner in order to enable governments, traders, and other stakeholders to become acquainted with them:

(a) procedures for importation, exportation, and transit (including port, airport, and other entry-point procedures), and required forms and documents;

(b) applied rates of duties and taxes of any kind imposed on or in connection with importation or exportation;

(c) fees and charges imposed by or for administrative authorities on or in connection with importation, exportation or transit;

(d) rules for the classification or valuation of products for customs purposes;

(e) laws, regulations, and administrative rulings of general application relating to rules of origin;

(f) import, export or transit restrictions or prohibitions;

(g) penalty provisions for breaches of import, export, or transit formalities;

(h) procedures for appeal or review;

(i) agreements or parts thereof with any country or countries relating to importation, exportation, or transit; and

(j) procedures relating to the administration of tariff quotas.

1.2 Nothing in these provisions shall be construed as requiring the publication or provision of information other than in the English language.

2. Information Available Through Internet

2.1 Each Contracting Party shall make available, and update to the extent possible and as appropriate, the following through the internet:

(a) a description of its procedures for importation, exportation, and transit, including procedures for appeal or review, that informs governments, traders, and other interested parties of the practical steps needed for importation, exportation, and transit;

(b) the forms and documents required for importation into, exportation from, or transit through the territory of that Contracting Party;

(c) contact information on its enquiry point(s).

2.2 Whenever practicable, the description referred to in subparagraph 2.1(a) shall also be made available in English.

3. Enquiry Points

3.1 Each Contracting Party shall, within its available resources, establish or maintain one or more enquiry points to answer reasonable enquiries of governments, traders, and other interested parties on matters covered by paragraph 1.1 and to provide the required forms and documents referred to in subparagraph 1.1(a).

3.2 The Contracting Parties of a customs union or involved in regional integration other than Belt and Road jurisdictions may establish or maintain common enquiry points at the regional level to satisfy the requirement of paragraph 3.1 for common procedures.

3.3 The Contracting Parties are encouraged not to require the payment of a fee for answering enquiries and providing required forms and documents. If any, Contracting Parties shall limit the amount of their fees and charges to the approximate cost of services rendered.

3.4 The enquiry points shall answer enquiries and provide the forms and documents within a reasonable time period set by each Contracting Party, which may vary depending on the nature or complexity of the request.

3.5 The Contracting Parties are encouraged to make available further trade-related information through the internet, including relevant trade-related legislation and other items referred to in paragraph 1.

4. Notification

Each Contracting Party shall notify the Committee on Trade Facilitation of Belt and Road established under paragraph 1.1 of Article 23 (referred to in this Agreement as the "Committee") of:

    (a) the official place(s) where the items in subparagraphs 1.1(a)to (j) have been published;

    (b) the Uniform Resource Locators of website(s) referred to in paragraph 2.1; and

    (c) the contact information of the enquiry points referred to in paragraph 3.1.

Article 2: Opportunity to Comment, Information before Entry into Force, and Consultations

1. Opportunity to Comment and Information before Entry into Force

1.1 Each Contracting Party shall, to the extent practicable and in a manner consistent with its domestic law and legal system, provide opportunities and an appropriate time period to traders and other interested parties to comment on the proposed introduction or amendment of laws and regulations of general application related to the movement, release, and clearance of goods, including goods in transit.

1.2 Each Contracting Party shall, to the extent practicable and in a manner consistent with its domestic law and legal system, ensure that new or amended laws and regulations of general application related to the movement, release, and clearance of goods, including goods in transit, are published or information on them made otherwise publicly available, as early as possible before their entry into force, in order to enable traders and other interested parties to become acquainted with them.

1.3 Changes to duty rates or tariff rates, measures that have a relieving effect, measures the effectiveness of which would be undermined as a result of compliance with paragraphs 1.1 or 1.2, measures applied in urgent circumstances, or minor changes to domestic law and legal system are each excluded from paragraphs 1.1 and 1.2.

2. Consultations

Each Contracting Party shall, as appropriate, provide for regular consultations between its border agencies and traders or other stakeholders located within its territory.

Article 3: Advance Rulings

1. Each Contracting Party shall issue an advance ruling in a reasonable, time-bound manner to the applicant that has submitted a written request containing all necessary information. If a Contracting Party declines to issue an advance ruling, it shall promptly notify the applicant in writing, setting out the relevant facts and the basis for its decision.

2. A Contracting Party may decline to issue an advance ruling to the applicant where the question raised in the application:

(a) is already pending in the applicant's case before any governmental agency, appellate tribunal, or court; or

(b) has already been decided by any appellate tribunal or court.

3. The advance ruling shall be valid for a reasonable period of time after its issuance unless the law, facts, or circumstances supporting that ruling have changed.

4. Where the Contracting Party revokes, modifies, or invalidates the advance ruling, it shall provide written notice to the applicant setting out the relevant facts and the basis for its decision. Where a Contracting Party revokes, modifies, or invalidates advance rulings with retroactive effect, it may only do so where the ruling was based on incomplete, incorrect, false, or misleading information.

5. An advance ruling issued by a Contracting Party shall be binding on that Contracting Party in respect of the applicant that sought it. The Contracting Party may provide that the advance ruling is binding on the applicant.

6. Each Contracting Party shall publish, at a minimum:

(a) the requirements for the application for an advance ruling, including the information to be provided and the format;

(b) the time period by which it will issue an advance ruling; and

(c) the length of time for which the advance ruling is valid.

7. Each Contracting Party shall provide, upon written request of an applicant, a review of the advance ruling or the decision to revoke, modify, or invalidate the advance ruling.

8. Each Contracting Party shall endeavour to make publicly available any information on advance rulings which it considers to be of significant interest to other interested parties, taking into account the need to protect commercially confidential information.

9. Definitions and scope:

(a) An advance ruling is a written decision provided by a Contracting Party to the applicant prior to the importation of a good covered by the application that sets forth the treatment that the Contracting Party shall provide to the good at the time of importation with regard to:

(i) the good's tariff classification; and

(ii) the origin of the good.

(b) In addition to the advance rulings defined in subparagraph (a), Contracting Parties are encouraged to provide advance rulings on:

    (i) the appropriate method or criteria, and the application thereof, to be used for determining the customs value under a particular set of facts;

    (ii) the applicability of the Contracting Party's requirements for relief or exemption from customs duties;

    (iii) the application of the Contracting Party's requirements for quotas, including tariff quotas; and

    (iv) any additional matters for which a Contracting Party considers it appropriate to issue an advance ruling.

(c) An applicant is an exporter, importer or any person with a justifiable cause or a representative thereof.

(d) A Contracting Party may require that the applicant have legal representation or registration in its territory. To the extent possible, such requirements shall not restrict the categories of persons eligible to apply for advance rulings, with particular consideration for the specific needs of small and medium-sized enterprises. These requirements shall be clear and transparent and not constitute a means of arbitrary or unjustifiable discrimination.

Article 4: Procedures for Appeal or Review

1. Each Contracting Party shall provide that any person to whom customs issues an administrative decision has the right, within its territory, to:

(a) an administrative appeal to or review by an administrative authority higher than or independent of the official or office that issued the decision; and/or

(b) a judicial appeal or review of the decision.

2. The legislation of a Contracting Party may require that an administrative appeal or review be initiated prior to a judicial appeal or review.

3. Each Contracting Party shall ensure that its procedures for appeal or review are carried out in a non-discriminatory manner.

4. Each Contracting Party shall ensure that, in a case where the decision on appeal or review under subparagraph 1(a) is not given either:

(a) within set periods as specified in its laws or regulations; or

(b) without undue delay the petitioner has the right to either further appeal to or further review by the administrative authority or the judicial authority or any other recourse to the judicial authority. The Contracting Parties may also enter into negotiations in good faith or have recourse to the Dispute Resolution Mechanism as specified in Chapter 14 (Dispute Settlement) of this Agreement.

5. Each Contracting Party shall ensure that the person referred to in paragraph 1 is provided with the reasons for the administrative decision so as to enable such a person to have recourse to procedures for appeal or review where necessary.

6. Each Contracting Party is encouraged to make the provisions of this Article applicable to an administrative decision issued by a relevant border agency other than customs.

Article 5: Other Measures to Enhance Impartiality, Non-Discrimination and Transparency

1. Notifications for enhanced controls or inspections

Where a Contracting Party adopts or maintains a system of issuing notifications or guidance to its concerned authorities for enhancing the level of controls or inspections at the border in respect of foods, beverages, or feedstuffs covered under the notification or guidance for protecting human, animal, or plant life or health within its territory, the following disciplines shall apply to the issuance, termination, or suspension of such notification or guidance:

    (a) the Contracting Party may, as appropriate, issue the notification or guidance based on risk;

    (b) the Contracting Party may issue the notification or guidance so that it applies uniformly only to those points of entry where the sanitary and phytosanitary conditions on which the notification or guidance are based apply;

    (c) the Contracting Party shall promptly terminate or suspend the notification or guidance when circumstances giving rise to it no longer exist, or if changed circumstances can be addressed in a less trade-restrictive manner; and

    (d) when the Contracting Party decides to terminate or suspend the notification or guidance, it shall, as appropriate, promptly publish the announcement of its termination or suspension in a non-discriminatory and easily accessible manner, or inform the exporting Contracting Party or the importer.

2. Detention

A Contracting Party shall promptly inform the carrier or importer(s) in case of detention of goods declared for importation, for inspection by customs or any other competent authority.

3. Test Procedures

3.1 A Contracting Party may, upon request, grant an opportunity for a second test in case the first test result of a sample taken upon arrival of goods declared for importation shows an adverse finding.

3.2 A Contracting Party shall either publish, in a non-discriminatory and easily accessible manner, the name and address of any laboratory where the test can be carried out or provide this information to the importer(s) when it is granted the opportunity provided under paragraph 3.1.

3.3 A Contracting Party shall consider the result of the second test, if any, conducted under paragraph 3.1, for the release and clearance of goods and, if appropriate, may accept the results of such test.

Article 6: Disciplines on Fees and Charges Imposed on or in Connection with Importation, Exportation and Penalties

1. General Disciplines on Fees and Charges Imposed on or in Connection with Importation and Exportation

1.1 The provisions of paragraph 1 shall apply to all fees and charges other than import and export duties and other than taxes within the purview of Article III of GATT 1994 imposed by Contracting Parties on or in connection with the importation or exportation of goods.

1.2 Information on fees and charges shall be published in accordance with Article 1. This information shall include the fees and charges that will be applied, the reason for such fees and charges, the responsible authority and when and how payment is to be made.

1.3 An adequate time period shall be accorded between the publication of new or amended fees and charges and their entry into force, except in urgent circumstances. Such fees and charges shall not be applied until information on them has been published.

Each Contracting Party shall periodically review its fees and charges with a view to reducing their number and diversity, where practicable.

2. Specific disciplines on Fees and Charges for Customs Processing Imposed on or in Connection with Importation and Exportation

Fees and charges for customs processing:
    (i) shall be limited in amount to the approximate cost of the services rendered on or in connection with the specific import or export operation in question; and
    (ii) are not required to be linked to a specific import or export operation provided they are levied for services that are closely connected to the customs processing of goods.

3.Penalty Disciplines

3.1 For the purpose of paragraph 3, the term "penalties" means those imposed by a Contracting Party's customs administration for a breach of the Contracting Party's customs laws, regulations, or procedural requirements.

3.2 Each Contracting Party shall ensure that penalties for a breach of a customs law, regulation, or procedural requirement are imposed only on the person(s) responsible for the breach under its laws.

3.3 The penalty imposed shall depend on the facts and circumstances of the case and shall be commensurate with the degree and severity of the breach.

3.4 Each Contracting Party shall ensure that it maintains measures to avoid:

(a) conflicts of interest in the assessment and collection of monetary penalties and duties; and

(b) creating an incentive for the assessment or collection of a monetary penalty that is inconsistent with paragraph 3.3.

3.5 Each Contracting Party shall ensure that when a penalty is imposed for a breach of customs laws, regulations, or procedural requirements, an explanation in writing is provided to the person(s) upon whom the penalty is imposed specifying the nature of the breach and the applicable law, regulation or procedure under which the amount or range of penalty for the breach has been prescribed.

3.6 When a person voluntarily discloses to a Contracting Party's customs administration the circumstances of a breach of a customs law, regulation, or procedural requirement prior to the discovery of the breach by the customs administration, the Contracting Party is encouraged to, where appropriate, consider this fact as a potential mitigating factor when establishing a penalty for that person.

3.7 The provisions of this paragraph shall apply to the penalties on traffic in transit referred to in Article 11.

Article 7: Release and Clearance of Goods

1. Pre-arrival Processing

1.1 Each Contracting Party shall adopt or maintain procedures allowing for the submission of import documentation and other required information, including manifests, in order to begin processing prior to the arrival of goods with a view to expediting the release of goods upon arrival.

1.2 Each Contracting Party shall, as appropriate, provide for advance lodging of documents in electronic format for pre-arrival processing of such documents.

2. Electronic Payment

Each Contracting Party shall, to the extent practicable, adopt or maintain procedures allowing the option of electronic payment for duties, taxes, fees, and charges collected by customs incurred upon importation and exportation.

3. Separation of Release from Final Determination of Customs Duties, Taxes, Fees and Charges

3.1 Each Contracting Party shall adopt or maintain procedures allowing the release of goods prior to the final determination of customs duties, taxes, fees, and charges, if such a determination is not done prior to, or upon arrival, or as rapidly as possible after arrival and provided that all other regulatory requirements have been met.

3.2 As a condition for such release, a Contracting Party may require:

(a) payment of customs duties, taxes, fees, and charges determined prior to or upon arrival of goods and a guarantee for any amount not yet determined in the form of a surety, a deposit, or another appropriate instrument provided for in its laws and regulations; or

(b) a guarantee in the form of a surety, a deposit, or another appropriate instrument provided for in its laws and regulations.

3.3 Such guarantee shall not be greater than the amount the Contracting Party requires to ensure payment of customs duties, taxes, fees, and charges ultimately due for the goods covered by the guarantee.

3.4 In cases where an offence requiring imposition of monetary penalties or fines has been detected, a guarantee may be required for the monetary penalties and fines that may be imposed.

3.5 The guarantee as set out in paragraphs 3.2 and 3.4 shall be discharged when it is no longer required.

3.6 Nothing in these provisions shall affect the right of a Contracting Party to examine, detain, seize or confiscate or deal with the goods in any manner not otherwise inconsistent with the Contracting Party's rights and obligations in WTO and other international agreements including binding instruments in the BRI projects.

4. Risk Management

4.1 Each Contracting Party shall, to the extent possible, adopt or maintain a risk management system for customs control.

4.2 Each Contracting Party shall design and apply risk management in a manner as to avoid arbitrary or unjustifiable discrimination, or a disguised restriction on international trade.

4.3 Each Contracting Party shall concentrate customs control and, to the extent possible other relevant border controls, on high-risk consignments and expedite the release of low-risk consignments. A Contracting Party also may select, on a random basis, consignments for such controls as part of its risk management.

4.4 Each Contracting Party shall base risk management on an assessment of risk through appropriate selectivity criteria. Such selectivity criteria may include, inter alia, the Harmonized System code of WCO, nature and description of the goods, country of origin, country from which the goods were shipped, value of the goods, compliance record of traders, and type of means of transport.

5. Post-clearance Audit

5.1 With a view to expediting the release of goods, each Contracting Party shall adopt or maintain post-clearance audit to ensure compliance with customs and other related laws and regulations.

5.2 Each Contracting Party shall select a person or a consignment for post-clearance audit in a risk-based manner, which may include appropriate selectivity criteria. Each Contracting Party shall conduct post-clearance audits in a transparent manner. Where a person is involved in the audit process and conclusive results have been achieved the Contracting Party shall, without delay, notify the person whose record is audited of the results, the person's rights and obligations, and the reasons for the results.

5.3 The information obtained in post-clearance audit may be used in further administrative or judicial proceedings.

5.4 The Contracting Parties shall, wherever practicable, use the result of post-clearance audit in applying risk management.

6. Establishment and Publication of Average Release Times

6.1 The Contracting Parties are encouraged to measure and publish their average release time of goods periodically and in a consistent manner, according to its needs and capacity, using tools such as, inter alia, the Time Release Study of the WCO.

6.2 The Contracting Parties are encouraged to share with the Committee their experiences in measuring average release times, including methodologies used, bottlenecks identified, and any resulting effects on efficiency.

7. Trade Facilitation Measures for Authorized Operators

7.1 Each Contracting Party shall provide additional trade facilitation measures related to import, export, or transit formalities and procedures, pursuant to paragraph 7.3, to operators who meet specified criteria, hereinafter called authorized operators. Alternatively, a Contracting Party may offer such trade facilitation measures through customs procedures generally available to all operators and is not required to establish a separate scheme.

7.2 The specified criteria to qualify as an authorized operator shall be related to compliance, or the risk of non-compliance, with requirements specified in a Contracting Party's laws, regulations or procedures.

(a) Such criteria, which shall be published, may include:

(i) an appropriate record of compliance with customs and other related laws and regulations;

(ii) a system of managing records to allow for necessary internal controls;

(iii) financial solvency, including, where appropriate, provision of a sufficient security or guarantee; and

(iv) supply chain security.

(b) Such criteria shall not:

(i) be designed or applied so as to afford or create arbitrary or unjustifiable discrimination between operators where the same conditions prevail; and

(ii) to the extent possible, restrict the participation of small and medium-sized enterprises.

7.3 The trade facilitation measures provided pursuant to paragraph 7.1 shall include at least three of the following measures:

(a) low documentary and data requirements, as appropriate;

(b) low rate of physical inspections and examinations, as appropriate;

(c) rapid release time, as appropriate;

(d) deferred payment of duties, taxes, fees, and charges;

(e) use of comprehensive guarantees or reduced guarantees;

(f) a single customs declaration for all imports or exports in a given period; and

(g) clearance of goods at the premises of the authorized operator or another place authorized by customs.

7.4 The Contracting Parties are encouraged to develop authorized operator schemes on the basis of international standards, where such standards exist, except when such standards would be an inappropriate or ineffective means for the fulfilment of the legitimate objectives pursued.

7.5 In order to enhance the trade facilitation measures provided to operators, the Contracting Parties shall afford to other Contracting Parties the possibility of negotiating mutual recognition of authorized operator schemes.

7.6 The Contracting Parties shall exchange relevant information within the Committee about authorized operator schemes in force.

8. Expedited Shipments

8.1 Each Contracting Party shall adopt or maintain procedures allowing for the expedited release of at least those goods entered through air cargo facilities to persons who apply for such treatment, while maintaining customs control. If a Contracting Party employs criteria limiting who may apply, the Contracting Party may, in published criteria, require that the applicant shall, as conditions for qualifying for the application of the treatment described in paragraph 8.2 to its expedited shipments:

(a) provide adequate infrastructure and payment of customs expenses related to processing of expedited shipments in cases where the applicant fulfils the Contracting Party's requirements for such processing to be performed at a dedicated facility;

(b) submit in advance of the arrival of an expedited shipment the information necessary for the release;

(c) be assessed fees limited in amount to the approximate cost of services rendered in providing the treatment described in paragraph 8.2;

(d) maintain a high degree of control over expedited shipments through the use of internal security, logistics, and tracking technology from pick-up to delivery;

(e) provide expedited shipment from pick-up to delivery;

(f) assume liability for payment of all customs duties, taxes, fees, and charges to the customs authority for the goods;

(g) have a good record of compliance with customs and other related laws and regulations;

(h) comply with other conditions directly related to the effective enforcement of the Contracting Party's laws, regulations, and procedural requirements, that specifically relate to providing the treatment described in paragraph 8.2.

8.2 Subject to paragraphs 8.1 and 8.3, the Contracting Parties shall:

(a) minimize the documentation required for the release of expedited shipments in accordance with paragraph 1 of Article 10 and, to the extent possible, provide for release based on a single submission of information on certain shipments;

(b) provide for expedited shipments to be released under normal circumstances as rapidly as possible after arrival, provided the information required for release has been submitted;

(c) endeavour to apply the treatment in subparagraphs (a) and (b) to shipments of any weight or value;

(d) recognize that a Contracting Party is permitted to require additional entry procedures, including declarations and supporting documentation and payment of duties and taxes, and to limit such treatment based on the type of good, provided the treatment is not limited to low value goods such as documents; and

(e) provide, to the extent possible, for a *de minimis* shipment value or dutiable amount for which customs duties and taxes will not be collected, aside from certain prescribed goods. Internal taxes, such as value added taxes and excise taxes, applied to imports consistently with Article III of the GATT

1994 are not subject to this provision.

8.3 Nothing in paragraphs 8.1 and 8.2 shall affect the right of a Contracting Party to examine, detain, seize, confiscate or refuse entry of goods, or to carry out post-clearance audits, including in connection with the use of risk management systems. Further, nothing in paragraphs 8.1 and 8.2 shall prevent a Contracting Party from requiring, as a condition for release, the submission of additional information and the fulfilment of non-automatic licensing requirements.

9. Perishable Goods[1]

9.1 With a view to preventing avoidable loss or deterioration of perishable goods, and provided that all regulatory requirements have been met, each Contracting Party shall provide for the release of perishable goods:

    (a) under normal circumstances within the shortest possible time; and

    (b) in exceptional circumstances where it would be appropriate to do so, outside the business hours of customs and other relevant authorities.

9.2 Each Contracting Party shall give appropriate priority to perishable goods when scheduling any examinations that may be required.

9.3 Each Contracting Party shall either arrange or allow an importer to arrange for the proper storage of perishable goods pending their release. The Contracting Party may require that any storage facilities arranged by the importer have been approved or designated by its relevant authorities. The movement of the goods to those storage facilities, including authorizations for the operator moving the goods, may be subject to the approval, where required, of the relevant authorities. The Contracting Party shall, where practicable and consistent with domestic legislation, upon the request of the importer, provide for any procedures necessary for release to take place at those storage facilities.

9.4 In cases of significant delay in the release of perishable goods, and upon written request, the importing Contracting Party shall, to the extent practicable, provide a communication on the reasons for the delay.

Article 8: Border Agency Cooperation

1. Each Contracting Party shall ensure that its authorities and agencies responsible for border controls and procedures dealing with the importation, exportation, and transit of goods cooperate with one another and coordinate their activities in order to facilitate trade.

2. Each Contracting Party shall, to the extent possible and practicable, cooperate on

---

1   For the purposes of this provision, perishable goods are goods that rapidly decay due to their natural characteristics, in particular in the absence of appropriate storage conditions.

mutually agreed terms with other Contracting Parties with whom it shares a common border with a view to coordinating procedures at border crossings to facilitate cross-border trade. Such cooperation and coordination may include:

    (a) alignment of working days and hours;

    (b) alignment of procedures and formalities;

    (c) development and sharing of common facilities;

    (d) joint controls;

    (e) establishment of one stop border post control.

Article 9: Formalities Connected with Importation, Exportation and Transit

1. Formalities and Documentation Requirements

1.1 With a view to minimizing the incidence and complexity of import, export, and transit formalities and to decreasing and simplifying import, export, and transit documentation requirements and taking into account the legitimate policy objectives and other factors such as changed circumstances, relevant new information, business practices, availability of techniques and technology, international best practices, and inputs from interested parties, each Contracting Party shall review such formalities and documentation requirements and, based on the results of the review, ensure, as appropriate, that such formalities and documentation requirements are:

    (a) adopted and/or applied with a view to a rapid release and clearance of goods, particularly perishable goods;

    (b) adopted and/or applied in a manner that aims at reducing the time and cost of compliance for traders and operators;

    (c) the least trade restrictive measure chosen where two or more alternative measures are reasonably available for fulfilling the policy objective or objectives in question; and

    (d) not maintained, including parts thereof, if no longer required.

1.2 The Committee of Belt and Road shall develop procedures for the sharing by Contracting Parties of relevant information and best practices, as appropriate.

2. Acceptance of Copies

2.1 Each Contracting Party shall, where appropriate, endeavour to accept paper or electronic copies of supporting documents required for import, export, or transit formalities.

2.2 Where a government agency of a Contracting Party already holds the original of such a document, any other agency of that Contracting Party shall accept a paper or electronic copy, where applicable, from the agency holding the original in lieu of the original document.

2.3 A Contracting Party shall not require an original or copy of export declarations submitted to the customs authorities of the exporting Contracting Party as a requirement for importation.

3. Use of International Standards

3.1 The Contracting Parties are encouraged to use relevant international standards or parts thereof as a basis for their import, export, or transit formalities and procedures, except as otherwise provided for in this Agreement.

3.2 The Contracting Parties are encouraged to take part, within the limits of their resources, in the preparation and periodic review of relevant international standards by appropriate international organizations.

3.3 The Committee shall develop procedures for the sharing by the Contracting Parties of relevant information, and best practices, on the implementation of international standards, as appropriate.

3.4 The Committee may also invite relevant international organizations to discuss their work on international standards. As appropriate, the Committee may identify specific standards that are of particular value to the Contracting Parties.

4. Single Window

4.1 The Contracting Parties shall endeavour to establish or maintain a single window, enabling traders to submit documentation and/or data requirements for importation, exportation, or transit of goods through a single entry point to the participating authorities or agencies. After the examination by the participating authorities or agencies of the documentation and/or data, the results shall be notified to the applicants through the single window in a timely manner.

4.2 In cases where documentation and/or data requirements have already been received through the single window, the same documentation and/or data requirements shall not be requested by participating authorities or agencies except in urgent circumstances and other limited exceptions which are made public.

4.3 The Contracting Parties shall notify the Committee of the details of operation of the single window.

4.4 The Contracting Parties shall, to the extent possible and practicable, use information technology to support the single window.

5. Preshipment Inspection

5.1 The Contracting Parties shall not require the use of preshipment inspections in relation to tariff classification and customs valuation.

5.2 Without prejudice to the rights of the Contracting Parties to use other types of preshipment inspection not covered by paragraph 5.1, the Contracting Parties are encouraged not to introduce or apply new requirements regarding their use.

6. Use of Customs Brokers

6.1 Without prejudice to the important policy concerns of some Contracting Parties that currently maintain a special role for customs brokers, from the entry into force of this Agreement Contracting Parties shall not introduce the mandatory use of customs brokers.

6.2 Each Contracting Party shall notify the Committee and publish its measures on the use of customs brokers. Any subsequent modifications thereof shall be notified and published promptly.

6.3 With regard to the licensing of customs brokers, the Contracting Parties shall apply rules that are transparent and objective.

7. Common Border Procedures and Uniform Documentation Requirements

7.1 Each Contracting Party shall, subject to paragraph 7.2, apply common customs procedures and uniform documentation requirements for release and clearance of goods throughout its territory.

7.2 Nothing in this Article shall prevent a Contracting Party from:
   (a) differentiating its procedures and documentation requirements based on the nature and type of goods, or their means of transport;
   (b) differentiating its procedures and documentation requirements for goods based on risk management;
   (c) differentiating its procedures and documentation requirements to provide total or partial exemption from import duties or taxes;
   (d) applying electronic filing or processing; or
   (e) differentiating its procedures and documentation requirements in a manner consistent with the Agreement on the Application of Sanitary and Phytosanitary Measures of WTO.

8. Rejected Goods

8.1 Where goods presented for import are rejected by the competent authority of a Contracting Party on account of their failure to meet prescribed sanitary or phytosanitary regulations or technical regulations, the Contracting Party shall, subject to and consistent with its laws and regulations, allow the importer to re-consign or to return the rejected goods to the exporter or another person designated by the exporter.

8.2 When such an option under paragraph 8.1 is given and the importer fails to exercise it within a reasonable period of time, the competent authority may take a different course of action to deal with such noncompliant goods.

9. Temporary Admission of Goods and Inward and Outward Processing

9.1 Temporary Admission of Goods

Each Contracting Party shall allow, as provided for in its laws and regulations, goods to be brought into its customs territory conditionally relieved, totally or partially, from payment of import duties and taxes if such goods are brought into its customs territory for a specific purpose, are intended for re-exportation within a specific period, and have not undergone any change except normal depreciation and wastage due to the use made of them.

9.2 Inward and Outward Processing

(a) Each Contracting Party shall allow, as provided for in its laws and regulations, inward and outward processing of goods. Goods allowed for outward processing may be re-imported with total or partial exemption from import duties and taxes in accordance with the Contracting Party's laws and regulations.

(b) For the purposes of this Article, the term "inward processing" means the customs procedure under which certain goods can be brought into a Contracting Party's customs territory conditionally relieved, totally or partially, from payment of import duties and taxes, or eligible for duty drawback, on the basis that such goods are intended for manufacturing, processing, or repair and subsequent exportation.

(c) For the purposes of this Article, the term "outward processing" means the customs procedure under which goods which are in free circulation in a Contracting Party's customs territory may be temporarily exported for manufacturing, processing, or repair abroad and then re-imported.

Article 10: Freedom of Transit

1. Any regulations or formalities in connection with traffic in transit imposed by a Contracting Party shall not be:

(a) maintained if the circumstances or objectives giving rise to their adoption no longer exist or if the changed circumstances or objectives can be addressed in a   reasonably available less trade-restrictive manner;

(b) applied in a manner that would constitute a disguised restriction on traffic in transit.

2. Traffic in transit shall not be conditioned upon collection of any fees or charges imposed in respect of transit, except the charges for transportation or those

commensurate with administrative expenses entailed by transit or with the cost of services rendered.

3. The Contracting Parties shall not seek, take, or maintain any voluntary restraints or any other similar measures on traffic in transit. This is without prejudice to existing and future national regulations, bilateral or multilateral arrangements related to regulating transport, consistent with WTO rules.

4. Each Contracting Party shall accord to products which will be in transit through the territory of any other Contracting Party treatment no less favourable than that which would be accorded to such products if they were being transported from their place of origin to their destination without going through the territory of such other Contracting Party.

5. The Contracting Parties are encouraged to make available, where practicable, physically separate infrastructure (such as lanes, berths and similar) for traffic in transit.

6. Formalities, documentation requirements, and customs controls in connection with traffic in transit shall not be more burdensome than necessary to:

    (a) identify the goods; and

    (b) ensure fulfilment of transit requirements.

7. Once goods have been put under a transit procedure and have been authorized to proceed from the point of origination in a Contracting Party's territory, they will not be subject to any customs charges nor unnecessary delays or restrictions until they conclude their transit at the point of destination within the Contracting Party's territory.

8. The Contracting Parties shall not apply technical regulations and conformity assessment procedures within the meaning of the Agreement on Technical Barriers to Trade of WTO to goods in transit.

9. The Contracting Parties shall allow and provide for advance filing and processing of transit documentation and data prior to the arrival of goods.

10. Once traffic in transit has reached the customs office where it exits the territory of a Contracting Party, that office shall promptly terminate the transit operation if transit requirements have been met.

11. Where a Contracting Party requires a guarantee in the form of a surety, deposit or other appropriate monetary or non-monetary instrument for traffic in transit, such guarantee shall be limited to ensuring that requirements arising from such traffic in transit are fulfilled.

12. Once the Contracting Party has determined that its transit requirements have been satisfied, the guarantee shall be discharged without delay.

13. Each Contracting Party shall, in a manner consistent with its laws and regulations, allow comprehensive guarantees which include multiple transactions for same operators or renewal of guarantees without discharge for subsequent consignments.

14. Each Contracting Party shall make publicly available the relevant information it uses to set the guarantee, including single transaction and, where applicable, multiple transaction guarantee.

15. Each Contracting Party may require the use of customs convoys or customs escorts for traffic in transit only in circumstances presenting high risks or when compliance with customs laws and regulations cannot be ensured through the use of guarantees. General rules applicable to customs convoys or customs escorts shall be published in accordance with Article 1.

16. The Contracting Parties shall endeavour to cooperate and coordinate with one another with a view to enhancing freedom of transit. Such cooperation and coordination may include, but is not limited to, an understanding on:

    (a) charges;

    (b) formalities and legal requirements; and

    (c) the practical operation of transit regimes.

17. Each Contracting Party shall endeavour to appoint a national transit coordinator to which all enquiries and proposals by other Contracting Parties relating to the good functioning of transit operations can be addressed.

Article 11: Customs Cooperation

1. Measures Promoting Compliance and Cooperation

1.1 The Contracting Parties agree on the importance of ensuring that traders are aware of their compliance obligations, encouraging voluntary compliance to allow importers to self-correct without penalty in appropriate circumstances, and applying compliance measures to initiate stronger measures for non-compliant traders.

1.2 The Contracting Parties are encouraged to share information on best practices in managing customs compliance, including through the Committee. The Contracting Parties are encouraged to cooperate in technical guidance or assistance and support for capacity building for the purposes of administering compliance measures and enhancing their effectiveness.

2. Exchange of Information

2.1 Upon request and subject to the provisions of this Article, the Contracting Parties shall exchange the information set out in subparagraphs 6.1(b) and/or (c) for the purpose of verifying an import or export declaration in identified cases where there are reasonable grounds to doubt the truth or accuracy of the declaration.

2.2 Each Contracting Party shall notify the Committee of the details of its contact point for the exchange of this information.

3. Verification

A Contracting Party shall make a request for information only after it has conducted appropriate verification procedures of an import or export declaration and after it has inspected the available relevant documentation.

4. Request

4.1 The requesting Contracting Party shall provide the requested Contracting Party with a written request, through paper or electronic means in English, including:

    (a) the matter at issue including, where appropriate and available, the number identifying the export declaration corresponding to the import declaration in question;

    (b) the purpose for which the requesting Contracting Party is seeking the information or documents, along with the names and contact details of the persons to whom the request relates, if known;

    (c) where required by the requested Contracting Party, confirmation of the verification where appropriate;

    (d) the specific information or documents requested;

    (e) the identity of the originating office making the request;

    (f) reference to provisions of the requesting Contracting Party's domestic law and legal system that govern the collection, protection, use, disclosure, retention, and disposal of confidential information and personal information.

4.2 If the requesting Contracting Party is not in a position to comply with any of the subparagraphs of paragraph 4.1, it shall specify this in the request.

5. Protection and Confidentiality

5.1 The requesting Contracting Party shall, subject to paragraph 5.2:

    (a) hold all information or documents provided by the requested Contracting Party strictly in confidence and grant at least the same level of such protection and confidentiality as that provided under the domestic law and legal system of the requested Contracting Party as described by it under subparagraphs 6.1(b)　or (c);

    (b) provide information or documents only to the customs authorities dealing with the matter at issue and use the information or documents solely for the purpose stated in the request unless the requested Contracting Party agrees otherwise in writing;

    (c) not disclose the information or documents without the specific written permission of the requested Contracting Party;

(d) not use any unverified information or documents from the requested Contracting Party as the deciding factor towards alleviating the doubt in any given circumstance;

(e) respect any case-specific conditions set out by the requested Contracting Party regarding retention and disposal of confidential information or documents and personal data; and

(f) upon request, inform the requested Contracting Party of any decisions and actions taken on the matter as a result of the information or documents provided.

5.2 A requesting Contracting Party may be unable under its domestic law and legal system to comply with any of the subparagraphs of paragraph 5.1. If so, the requesting Contracting Party shall specify this in the request.

5.3 The requested Contracting Party shall treat any request and verification information received under paragraph 4 with at least the same level of protection and confidentiality accorded by the requested Contracting Party to its own similar information.

6. Provision of Information

6.1 Subject to the provisions of this Article, the requested Contracting Party shall promptly:

(a) respond in writing, through paper or electronic means;

(b) provide the specific information as set out in the import or export declaration, or the declaration, to the extent it is available, along with a description of the level of protection and confidentiality required of the requesting Contracting Party;

(c) if requested, provide the specific information as set out in the following documents, or the documents, submitted in support of the import or export declaration, to the extent it is available: commercial invoice, packing list, certificate of origin and bill of lading, in the form in which these were filed, whether paper or electronic, along with a description of the level of protection and confidentiality required of the requesting Contracting Party;

(d) confirm that the documents provided are true copies;

(e) provide the information or otherwise respond to the request, to the extent possible, within 90 days from the date of the request.

6.2 The requested Contracting Party may require, under its domestic law and legal system, an assurance prior to the provision of information that the specific information will not be used as evidence in criminal investigations, judicial proceedings, or in non-customs proceedings without the specific written permission of the requested

Contracting Party. If the requesting Contracting Party is not in a position to comply with this requirement, it should specify this to the requested Contracting Party.

7. Postponement or Refusal of a Request

7.1 A requested Contracting Party may postpone or refuse part or all of a request to provide information, and shall inform the requesting Contracting Party of the reasons for doing so, where:

(a) it would be contrary to the public interest as reflected in the domestic law and legal system of the requested Contracting Party;

(b) its domestic law and legal system prevents the release of the information. In such a case it shall provide the requesting Contracting Party with a copy of the relevant, specific reference;

(c) the provision of the information would impede law enforcement or otherwise interfere with an on-going administrative or judicial investigation, prosecution or proceeding;

(d) the consent of the importer or exporter is required by its domestic law and legal system that govern the collection, protection, use, disclosure, retention, and disposal of confidential information or personal data and that consent is not given; or

(e) the request for information is received after the expiration of the legal requirement of the requested Contracting Party for the retention of documents.

7.2 In the circumstances of paragraphs 4.2, 5.2, or 6.2, execution of such a request shall be at the discretion of the requested Contracting Party.

8. Reciprocity

If the requesting Contracting Party is of the opinion that it would be unable to comply with a similar request if it was made by the requested Contracting Party, or if it has not yet implemented this Article, it shall state that fact in its request. Execution of such a request shall be at the discretion of the requested Contracting Party.

9. Administrative Burden

9.1 The requesting Contracting Party shall take into account the associated resource and cost implications for the requested Contracting Party in responding to requests for information. The requesting Contracting Party shall consider the proportionality between its fiscal interest in pursuing its request and the efforts to be made by the requested Contracting Party in providing the information.

9.2 If a requested Contracting Party receives an unmanageable number of requests for information or a request for information of unmanageable scope from one or more requesting Contracting Party(s) and is unable to meet such requests within a reasonable time, it may request one or more of the requesting Contracting Party(s) to prioritize with a view to agreeing on a practical limit within its resource constraints. In the absence of a mutually-agreed approach, the execution of such requests shall be at the discretion of the requested Contracting Party based on the results of its own prioritization.

10. Limitations

A requested Contracting Party shall not be required to:
    (a) modify the format of its import or export declarations or procedures;
    (b) call for documents other than those submitted with the import or export declaration as specified in subparagraph 6.1(c);
    (c) initiate enquiries to obtain the information;
    (d) modify the period of retention of such information;
    (e) introduce paper documentation where electronic format has already been introduced;
    (f) translate the information;
    (g) verify the accuracy of the information; or
    (h) provide information that would prejudice the legitimate commercial interests of particular enterprises, public or private.

11. Unauthorized Use or Disclosure

11.1 In the event of any breach of the conditions of use or disclosure of information exchanged under this Article, the requesting Contracting Party that received the information shall promptly communicate the details of such unauthorized use or disclosure to the requested Contracting Party that provided the information and:
    (a) take necessary measures to remedy the breach;
    (b) take necessary measures to prevent any future breach; and
    (c) notify the requested Contracting Party of the measures taken under subparagraphs (a)   and (b).

11.2 The requested Contracting Party may suspend its obligations to the requesting Contracting Party under this Article until the measures set out in paragraph 11.1 have been taken.

12. Bilateral and Regional Agreements

12.1 Nothing in this Article shall prevent a Contracting Party from entering into or maintaining a bilateral, plurilateral, or regional agreement for sharing or exchange of customs information and data, including on a secure and rapid basis such as on an automatic basis or in advance of the arrival of the consignment.

12.2 Nothing in this Article shall be construed as altering or affecting a Contracting Party's rights or obligations under such bilateral, plurilateral, or regional agreements, or as governing the exchange of customs information and data under such other agreements.

SECTION B. Institutional Arrangements and Final Provisions

Article 12: Institutional Arrangements

1. The Committee on Facilitation of the Belt and Road

1.1 A Committee on Facilitation is hereby established.

1.2 The Committee shall be open for participation by all Contracting Parties and shall elect its own Chairperson. The Committee shall meet as needed and envisaged by the relevant provisions of this Agreement, but no less than once a year, for the purpose of affording Contracting Parties the opportunity to consult on any matters related to the operation of this Agreement or the furtherance of its objectives. The Committee shall carry out such responsibilities as assigned to it under this Agreement or by the Contracting Parties. The Committee shall establish its own rules of procedure.

1.3 The Committee may establish such subsidiary bodies as may be required. All such bodies shall report to the Committee.

1.4 The Committee shall develop procedures for the sharing by Contracting Parties of relevant information and best practices as appropriate.

1.5 The Committee shall maintain close contact with other international organizations in the field of trade facilitation, such as the WCO, with the objective of securing the best available advice for the implementation and administration of this Agreement and in order to ensure that unnecessary duplication of effort is avoided. To this end, the Committee may invite representatives of such organizations or their subsidiary bodies to:

    (a) attend meetings of the Committee; and

    (b) discuss specific matters related to the implementation of this Agreement.

1.6 The Committee shall review the operation and implementation of this Agreement four years from its entry into force, and periodically thereafter.

1.7 Contracting Parties are encouraged to raise before the Committee questions relating to issues on the implementation and application of this Agreement.

1.8 The Committee shall encourage and facilitate ad hoc discussions among Contracting Parties on specific issues under this Agreement with a view to reaching a mutually satisfactory solution promptly.

2. National Committee on Facilitation

Each Contracting Party shall establish and/or maintain a national committee on trade facilitation or designate an existing mechanism to facilitate both domestic coordination and implementation of the provisions of this Agreement.

Article 13: Final Provisions

1. For the purpose of this Agreement, the term "Contracting Party" is deemed to include the competent authority of that Contracting Party.

2. All provisions of this Agreement are binding on all Contracting Parties.

CHAPTER - 6

DIGITAL ECONOMY

Section A. Definitions

Article 1: Definitions

For the purposes of this Chapter:

"Computing facilities" means computer servers and storage devices for processing or storing information for commercial use;

"Covered investment" means a covered investment as defined in (Investment Chapter, Definitions);

"Covered person" means:

    (a) an investor of a Contracting Party as defined in (Investment Chapter, Definitions), or

    (b) a service supplier of a Contracting Party as defined in (Cross-border Services Chapter, Definitions), but does not include a covered person as defined in (Financial Services Chapter, Definitions);

"Digital product" means a computer programme, text, video, image, sound recording or other product that is digitally encoded, produced for commercial sale or distribution, and that can be transmitted electronically;[2,3]

"Electronic authentication" means the process or act of verifying the identity of a Contracting Party to an electronic communication or transaction and ensuring the integrity of an electronic communication;

---

2 For greater certainty, digital product does not include a digitised representation of a financial instrument, including money.

3 The definition of digital product should not be understood to reflect a Contracting Party's view on whether trade in digital products through electronic transmission should be categorised as trade in services or trade in goods.

"**Electronic invoicing**" means the automated creation, exchange and processing of a request for payment between a supplier and a buyer using a structured digital format;

"**Electronic payments**" means a payer's transfer of a monetary claim acceptable to a payee made through electronic means;

"**Electronic signature**" means data in electronic form that is in, affixed to, or logically associated with, an electronic document or message, and that may be used to identify the signatory in relation to the electronic document or message and indicate the signatory's approval of the information contained in the electronic document or message;

"**Electronic transmission or transmitted electronically**" means a transmission made using any electromagnetic means, including by photonic means;

"**Government information**" means non-proprietary information, including data, held by the central level of government;

"**Personal information**" means any information, including data, about an identified or identifiable natural person;

"**Trade administration documents**" means forms issued or controlled by a Contracting Party that must be completed by or for an importer or exporter in connection with the import or export of goods;

"**Unsolicited commercial electronic message**" means an electronic message which is sent for commercial or marketing purposes to an electronic address, without the consent of the recipient or despite the explicit rejection of the recipient, through an Internet access service supplier or, to the extent provided for under the laws and regulations of each Contracting Party, other telecommunications service.

Section B. Scope and General Provisions

Article 2: Scope and General Provisions[4]

1. The Contracting Parties recognize the economic growth and opportunities provided by digital trade and the importance of frameworks that promote consumer confidence in digital trade and of avoiding unnecessary barriers to its use and

---

4   In the event of any inconsistency between this Chapter and other Chapters, the other Chapters shall prevail to the extent of the inconsistency.

development.

2. The objectives of this Chapter are also to:

    (a) promote electronic commerce among the Contracting Parties and the wider use of digital trade globally;

    (b) contribute to creating an environment of trust and confidence in the use of digital trade; and

    (c) enhance cooperation among the Contracting Parties regarding development of digital trade.

3. This Chapter shall apply to measures adopted or maintained by a Contracting Party that affect trade by electronic means.

4. This Chapter shall not apply to:

    (a) government procurement; or

    (b) information held or processed by or on behalf of a Contracting Party, or measures related to such information, including measures related to its collection.

Section C. Digital Products

Article 3: Customs Duties

1. No Contracting Party shall impose customs duties on electronic transmissions, including content transmitted electronically, between a person of one Contracting Party and a person of another Contracting Party.

2. For greater certainty, paragraph 1 shall not preclude a Contracting Party from imposing internal taxes, fees or other charges on content transmitted electronically, provided that such taxes, fees or charges are imposed in a manner consistent with this Agreement.

Article 4: Non-Discriminatory Treatment of Digital Products

1. No Contracting Party shall accord less favourable treatment to digital products created, produced, published, contracted for, commissioned or first made available on commercial terms in the territory of another Contracting Party, or to digital products of which the author, performer, producer, developer or owner is a person of another

Contracting Party, than it accords to other like digital products.[5]

2. Paragraph 1 shall not apply to the extent of any inconsistency with the rights and obligations in Chapter-8 (Intellectual Property Rights).

3. The Contracting Parties understand that this Article does not apply to subsidies or grants provided by a Contracting Party, including government-supported loans, guarantees and insurance.

4. This Article shall not apply to broadcasting.

Section D. Electronic Commerce

Article 5: Domestic Electronic Transactions Framework

1. Each Contracting Party shall maintain a legal framework governing electronic transactions consistent with the principles of the UNCITRAL Model Law on Electronic Commerce 1996 or the United Nations Convention on the Use of Electronic Communications in International Contracts, done at New York, November 23, 2005.

2. Each Contracting Party shall endeavour to:

(a) avoid any unnecessary regulatory burden on electronic transactions; and

(b) facilitate input by interested persons in the development of its legal framework for electronic transactions.

(c) adopt the UNCITRAL Model Law on Electronic Transferable Records (2017).

Article 6: Electronic Authentication and Electronic Signatures

1. Except in circumstances otherwise provided for under its law, a Contracting Party shall not deny the legal validity of a signature solely on the basis that the signature is in electronic form.

2. No Contracting Party shall adopt or maintain measures for electronic authentication that would:

(a) prohibit parties to an electronic transaction from mutually determining the appropriate authentication methods for that transaction; or

---

5   For greater certainty, to the extent that a digital product of a non-Contracting Party is a "like digital product", it will qualify as an "other like digital product" for the purposes of this paragraph.

(b) prevent parties to an electronic transaction from having the opportunity to establish before judicial or administrative authorities that their transaction complies with any legal requirements with respect to authentication.

3. Notwithstanding paragraph 2, a Contracting Party may require that, for a particular category of transactions, the method of authentication meets certain performance standards or is certified by an authority accredited in accordance with its law.

4. The Parties shall encourage the use of interoperable electronic authentication.

Article 7: Electronic Invoicing

1. The Contracting Parties recognise the importance of electronic invoicing to increase the efficiency, accuracy and reliability of commercial transactions. Each Contracting Party also recognises the benefits of ensuring that the systems used for electronic invoicing within its territory are interoperable with the systems used for electronic invoicing in the other Contracting Party's territory.

2. Each Contracting Party shall endeavour to ensure that the implementation of measures related to electronic invoicing in its territory supports cross-border interoperability between the Contracting Parties' electronic invoicing frameworks. To this end, each Contracting Party shall base its measures relating to electronic invoicing on international frameworks.

3. The Contracting Parties recognise the economic importance of promoting the global adoption of interoperable electronic invoicing systems. To this end, the Contracting Parties shall share best practices and collaborate on promoting the adoption of interoperable systems for electronic invoicing.

4. The Contracting Parties shall collaborate on initiatives which promote, encourage, support or facilitate the adoption of electronic invoicing by enterprises. To this end, the Contracting Parties shall endeavour to:
    (a) promote the existence of policies, infrastructure and processes that support electronic invoicing; and
    (b) generate awareness of, and build capacity for, electronic invoicing.

Article 8: Electronic Payments

1. To facilitate the rapid growth of electronic payments, in particular those provided by non-bank, non-financial institution and FinTech enterprises, the Contracting Parties recognise the importance of developing an efficient, safe and secure environment for cross-border electronic payments, including by:
    (a) fostering the adoption and use of internationally accepted standards for electronic payments;
    (b) promoting interoperability and the interlinking of electronic payment

infrastructures; and

    (c) encouraging innovation and competition in electronic payments services.

2. To this end, each Contracting Party shall:

    (a) make regulations on electronic payments, including in relation to regulatory approval, licensing requirements, procedures and technical standards, publicly available;

    (b) endeavour to finalise decisions on regulatory or licensing approvals in a timely manner;

    (c) not arbitrarily or unjustifiably discriminate between financial institutions and non-financial institutions in relation to access to services and infrastructure necessary for the operation of electronic payment systems;

    (d) adopt, for relevant electronic payment systems, international standards for electronic payment messaging, for electronic data exchange between financial institutions and services suppliers to enable greater interoperability between electronic payment systems;

    (e) facilitate the use of open platforms and architectures such as tools and protocols provided for through Application Programming Interfaces ("APIs") and encourage payment service providers to safely and securely make APIs for their products and services available to third parties, where possible, to facilitate greater interoperability, innovation and competition in electronic payments; and

    (f) facilitate innovation and competition and the introduction of new financial and electronic payment products and services in a timely manner, such as through adopting regulatory and industry sandboxes.

3. In view of paragraph 1, the Contracting Parties recognise the importance of upholding safety, efficiency, trust and security in electronic payment systems through regulations, and that the adoption and enforcement of regulations and policies should be proportionate to the risks undertaken by the payment service providers.

Article 9: Paperless Trading

1. Each Contracting Party shall endeavour to:

    (a) make trade administration documents available to the public in electronic form; and

    (b) accept trade administration documents submitted electronically as the legal equivalent of the paper version of those documents.

    (c) Whenever practicable, each Contracting Party shall provide trade administration documents referred to in sub-paragraph (a)   in English.

2. Noting the obligations in the WTO Trade Facilitation Agreement, each Contracting Party shall establish or maintain a single window that enables persons

to submit trade administration documents and data requirements for importation, exportation, or transit of goods through a single entry point to the participating authorities or agencies.

3. Each Contracting Party shall establish or maintain a seamless, trusted and secure interface with the other Contracting Party's single window to facilitate the exchange of data relating to trade administration documents, which may include:

(a) certificates of origin;

(b) certificates of non-manipulation; and

(c) any other documents, as jointly determined by the Contracting Parties.

4. The Contracting Parties shall endeavour to develop data exchange systems to support the exchange of data relating to the trade administration documents referred to in paragraph 3 between the competent authorities of each Contracting Party.

5. Each Contracting Party shall:

(a) hold all exchanged data referred to in paragraphs 3 and 4 strictly in confidence and grant at least the same level of such protection and confidentiality as that provided under the domestic law and legal system of the disclosing Contracting Party;

(b) provide exchanged data referred to in paragraphs 3 and 4 only to the customs authorities responsible and use the data solely for the purpose jointly determined by the Contracting Parties; and

(c) not disclose the exchanged data referred to in paragraphs 3 and 4 without the specific written permission of the disclosing Contracting Party.

6. Each Contracting Party recognises the importance of the exchange of electronic records used in commercial trading activities between enterprises within its territory. To this end, the Contracting Parties shall, where appropriate, facilitate the use and exchange of electronic records used in commercial cross-border trading activities of enterprises between their respective territories, including supporting the development of data exchange systems.

7. The Contracting Parties recognise that the data exchange systems referred to in paragraphs 4 and 6 should, as far as possible, be compatible and interoperable with each other. To this end, the Contracting Parties shall endeavour to work towards the development and adoption of internationally-recognised standards in the development and governance of the data exchange systems.

8. The Contracting Parties shall cooperate and collaborate on initiatives which promote, encourage, support and/or facilitate the use and adoption of the data exchange systems referred to in this Article, including, but not limited to, through:

(a) sharing of information and experiences, including the exchange of best practices, in the area of development and governance of the data exchange systems; and

(b) collaboration on pilot projects in the development and governance of data exchange systems.

9. The Contracting Parties shall cooperate bilaterally and in international fora to promote acceptance of electronic versions of trade administration documents and electronic records used in commercial trading activities between enterprises.

10. In developing initiatives that provide for the use of paperless trading, each Contracting Party shall endeavour to take into account the methods agreed by international organisations.

Article 10 Express Shipments

1. The Contracting Parties recognise that electronic commerce plays an important role in increasing trade. To facilitate air express shipments, each Contracting Party shall ensure its customs procedures are applied in a manner that is predictable, consistent and transparent.

2. Each Contracting Party shall adopt or maintain expedited customs procedures for air express shipments while maintaining appropriate customs control and selection. These procedures shall:

(a) provide for information necessary to release an express shipment to be submitted and processed before the shipment arrives;

(b) allow a single submission of information covering all goods contained in an express shipment, such as a manifest, through, if possible, electronic means;[6]

(c) to the extent possible, provide for the release of certain goods with a minimum of documentation;

(d) under normal circumstances, provide for express shipments to be released within four hours of submission of the necessary customs documents, provided the shipment has arrived; and

(e) apply to express shipments of any weight or value, recognising that a Contracting Party may require formal entry procedures as a condition for release, including a declaration and supporting documentation and payment of customs duties, based on the good's weight or value.

3. If a Contracting Party does not provide the treatment in paragraphs 2(a) through (e) to all shipments, that Contracting Party shall provide a separate and expedited customs procedure that provides such treatment for air express shipments.

4. To the extent possible, each Contracting Party shall:

(a) set a de minimis value in its law below which it will not collect customs duties or taxes on shipments;

(b) not collect customs duties or taxes on shipments below its set value; and

---

6 For greater certainty, additional documents may be required as a condition for release.

(c) review, as appropriate, its set value, taking into account relevant factors such as rates of inflation, effect on trade facilitation, impact on risk management, administrative cost of collecting duties compared to the amount of duties, cost of cross-border trade transactions, impact on SMEs or other factors related to the collection of customs duties.

5. Paragraph 4 shall not apply to shipments of restricted or controlled goods, such as goods subject to import licensing or similar requirements.

Article 11: Principles on Access to and Use of the Internet for Digital Trade

Subject to applicable policies, laws and regulations, the Contracting Parties recognise the benefits of consumers in their territories having the ability to:

(a) access and use services and applications of a consumer's choice available on the Internet, subject to reasonable network management;[7]

(b) connect the end-user devices of a consumer's choice to the Internet, provided that such devices do not harm the network; and

(c) access information on the network management practices of a consumer's Internet access service supplier.

Article 12: Internet Interconnection Charge Sharing

The Contracting Parties recognise that a supplier seeking international Internet connection should be able to negotiate with suppliers of another Contracting Party on a commercial basis. These negotiations may include negotiations regarding compensation for the establishment, operation and maintenance of facilities of the respective suppliers.

Article 13: Unsolicited Commercial Electronic Messages[8]

1. Each Contracting Party shall adopt or maintain measures regarding unsolicited commercial electronic messages that:

(a) require suppliers of unsolicited commercial electronic messages to facilitate the ability of recipients to prevent ongoing reception of those messages;

(b) require the consent, as specified according to the laws and regulations of each Contracting Party, of recipients to receive commercial electronic messages; or

(c) otherwise provide for the minimisation of unsolicited commercial electronic

---

7   The Contracting Parties recognise that an Internet access service supplier that offers its subscribers certain content on an exclusive basis would not be acting contrary to this principle.

8   A Contracting Party is not required to apply this Article before the date on which it implements its legal framework regarding unsolicited commercial electronic messages.

messages.

2. Each Contracting Party shall provide recourse against suppliers of unsolicited commercial electronic messages that do not comply with the measures adopted or maintained pursuant to paragraph 1.

3. The Parties shall endeavour to cooperate in appropriate cases of mutual concern regarding the regulation of unsolicited commercial electronic messages.

Article 14: Source Code

1. No Contracting Party shall require the transfer of, or access to, source code of software owned by a person of another Party, as a condition for the import, distribution, sale or use of such software, or of products containing such software, in its territory.

2. For the purposes of this Article, software subject to paragraph 1 is limited to mass-market software or products containing such software and does not include software used for critical infrastructure.

3. Nothing in this Article shall preclude:

    (a) the inclusion or implementation of terms and conditions related to the provision of source code in commercially negotiated contracts; or

    (b) a Contracting Party from requiring the modification of source code of software necessary for that software to comply with laws or regulations which are not inconsistent with this Agreement.

4. This Article does not preclude a government agency, law enforcement agency, regulatory body or judicial authority ("Relevant Body") of a Contracting Party from requiring a person of the other Contracting Party to preserve or make available the source code of software, or an algorithm expressed in that source code, to the Relevant Body for an investigation, inspection, examination, enforcement action, or judicial or administrative proceeding,[9] subject to safeguards against unauthorised disclosure under the laws and regulations of the Contracting Party.

5. This Article shall not be construed to affect requirements that relate to patent applications or granted patents, including any orders made by a judicial authority in relation to patent disputes, subject to safeguards against unauthorised disclosure under the law or practice of a Contracting Party.

Article 15: Online Consumer Protection

1. The Contracting Parties recognise the importance of adopting and maintaining transparent and effective measures to protect consumers from fraudulent and deceptive commercial activities when they engage in digital trade. Accordingly, the Contracting

---

9 Such disclosure shall not be construed to negatively affect the software source code's status as a trade secret, if such status is claimed by the trade secret owner.

Parties shall promote, as appropriate, cooperation and coordination on matters of mutual interest related to fraudulent and deceptive commercial activities, including in the enforcement of their consumer protection laws.[10]

2. For the purposes of this Article, fraudulent and deceptive commercial activities refer to those commercial practices that are fraudulent or deceptive and cause actual harm to consumers, or that pose a potential threat of such harm if not prevented. For example:

(a) making a misrepresentation of material fact, including an implied factual misrepresentation, that may cause significant detriment to the economic interests of a misled consumer;

(b) failing to deliver products or provide services to a consumer after the consumer is charged; or

(c) charging or debiting a consumer's financial, digital or other accounts without authorisation.

3. Each Contracting Party shall adopt or maintain consumer protection laws to proscribe fraudulent and deceptive commercial activities that cause harm or potential harm to consumers engaged in online commercial activities.

4. The Contracting Parties recognise the importance of cooperation between their respective national consumer protection agencies or other relevant bodies on activities related to cross-border digital trade in order to enhance consumer welfare. To this end, the Contracting Parties affirm to cooperation with respect to online commercial activities.

5. To this end, the Contracting Parties shall promote, as appropriate and subject to the laws and regulations of each Contracting Party, cooperation on matters of mutual interest related to fraudulent and deceptive commercial activities that cause actual harm to consumers, or that pose an imminent threat of such harm if not prevented, including in the enforcement of their consumer protection laws, with respect to online commercial activities.

6. The Contracting Parties recognise the benefits of mechanisms, including alternative dispute resolution, to facilitate the resolution of claims over electronic commerce transactions.

---

10 The Contracting Parties shall endeavour to cooperate and coordinate on the matters set out in this Article through the relevant national public bodies or officials responsible for consumer protection policy, laws or enforcement, as determined by each Party and compatible with their respective laws, regulations and important interests and within their reasonably available resource.

Section E. Protection of Personal Information and Data

Article 16: Personal Information Protection[11]

1. The Contracting Parties recognise the economic and social benefits of protecting the personal information of users of digital trade and the contribution that this makes to enhancing consumer confidence in digital trade.

2. To this end, each Contracting Party shall adopt or maintain a legal framework that provides for the protection of the personal information of the users of digital trade. In the development of its legal framework for the protection of personal information, each Contracting Party should take into account principles and guidelines of relevant international bodies.[12]

3. Each Contracting Party shall endeavour to adopt non-discriminatory practices in protecting users of digital trade from personal information protection violations occurring within its jurisdiction.

4. Each Contracting Party shall publish information on the personal information protections it provides to users of digital trade, including how:

    (a) individuals can pursue remedies; and

    (b) businesses can comply with any legal requirements pertaining to personal information protection.

5. Recognising that the Contracting Parties may take different legal approaches to protecting personal information, each Contracting Party shall encourage the development of mechanisms to promote compatibility and interoperability between these different regimes. These mechanisms may include the recognition of regulatory outcomes, whether accorded autonomously or by mutual arrangement, or broader international frameworks. To this end, the Contracting Parties shall endeavour to exchange information on any such mechanisms applied in their jurisdictions and explore ways to extend these or other suitable arrangements to promote compatibility and interoperability between them.

---

11 A Contracting Party is not required to apply this Article before the date on which that Party implements its legal framework that provides for the protection of personal data of the users of digital trade.

12 For greater certainty, a Party may comply with the obligation in this paragraph by adopting or maintaining measures such as a comprehensive privacy, personal information or personal data protection laws, sector-specific laws covering privacy, or laws that provide for the enforcement of voluntary undertakings by enterprises relating to privacy.

6. The Contracting Parties shall endeavour to jointly promote the adoption of common cross-border information transfer mechanisms.

Article 17: Access to and Use of Public Telecommunications Services

1. Each Contracting Party shall ensure that an enterprise of any Contracting Party may use public telecommunications services for the movement of information in its territory or across its borders, including for intra-corporate communications, and for access to information contained in databases or otherwise stored in machine-readable form in the territory of any Contracting Party.

2. A Contracting Party may take measures that are necessary to ensure the security and confidentiality of messages and to protect the privacy of personal information of end-users of public telecommunications networks or services, provided that those measures are not applied in a manner that would constitute a means of arbitrary or unjustifiable discrimination or a disguised restriction on trade in services.

3. Each Contracting Party shall ensure that suppliers of public telecommunications services in its territory take reasonable steps to protect the confidentiality of commercially sensitive information of, or relating to, suppliers and end-users of public telecommunications services obtained as a result of interconnection arrangements and that those suppliers only use that information for the purpose of providing these services.

Article 18: Open Government Data

1. The Contracting Parties recognise that facilitating public access to and use of government information may foster economic and social development and innovation;

2. The Contracting Parties shall endeavour to cooperate to identify ways in which the Contracting Parties can expand access to and use of open government data, with a view to enhancing and generating business opportunities;

3. Cooperation under this Article may include activities such as:
   (a) encouraging the development of new products and services based on open government data sets; and
   (b) fostering the use and develop open government data licensing models in the form of standardised public licences available online, which will allow open government data to be freely accessed, used and shared by anyone for any purpose permitted by the Contracting Parties' respective laws and regulations, and which rely on open government data formats.

Section F. Cross-border Data Flow

Article 19: Cross-Border Transfer of Information by Electronic Means

1. The Parties recognise that each Contracting Party may have its own regulatory requirements concerning the transfer of information by electronic means.

2. Each Contracting Party shall allow the cross-border transfer of information by electronic means, including personal information, when this activity is for the conduct of the business of a covered person subject to paragraph 3.

3. Nothing in this Article shall prevent a Contracting Party from adopting or maintaining measures inconsistent with paragraph 2 to achieve a legitimate public policy objective, provided that the measure:

   (a) is not applied in a manner which would constitute a means of arbitrary or unjustifiable discrimination or a disguised restriction on trade; and

   (b) does not impose restrictions on transfers of information greater than are required to achieve the objective.

Article 20: Location of Computing Facilities

1. The Contracting Parties recognise that each Contracting Party may have its own regulatory requirements regarding the use of computing facilities, including requirements that seek to ensure the security and confidentiality of communications.

2. No Contracting Party shall require a covered person to use or locate computing facilities in that Contracting Party's territory as a condition for conducting business in that territory subject to paragraph 3.

3. Nothing in this Article shall prevent a Contracting Party from adopting or maintaining measures inconsistent with paragraph 2 to achieve a legitimate public policy objective, provided that the measure:

   (a) is not applied in a manner which would constitute a means of arbitrary or unjustifiable discrimination or a disguised restriction on trade; and

   (b) does not impose restrictions on the use or location of computing facilities greater than are required to achieve the objective.

Section G. Cooperation

Article 21: Cooperation

1. Recognizing the global nature of digital trade, the Contracting Parties shall endeavour to:

    (a) exchange information and share experiences on regulations, policies, enforcement and compliance regarding digital trade, including:

        (i) personal information protection, particularly with the view to strengthening existing international mechanisms for cooperation in the enforcement of laws protecting privacy;

        (ii) security in electronic communications;

        (iii) electronic authentication;

        (iv) government use of digital tools and technologies to achieve better government performance; and

        (v) Information and Communication Technology Products that Use Cryptography;

    (b) cooperate and maintain a dialogue on the promotion and development of mechanisms that further global interoperability of privacy regimes;

    (c) participate actively in regional and multilateral fora to promote the development of digital trade;

    (d) encourage development by the private sector of methods of self-regulation that foster digital trade, including codes of conduct, model contracts, guidelines and enforcement mechanisms;

    (e) promote access for persons with disabilities to information and communications technologies; and

    (f) promote, through international cross-border cooperation initiatives, the development of mechanisms to assist users to submit cross-border complaints regarding protection of personal information.

2. The Parties shall consider establishing a forum to address any of the issues listed above, or any other matter pertaining to the operation of this chapter.

Article 22: SMEs and Startups

1. The Contracting Parties recognise the significant role of small and medium-sized enterprises (SMEs) and startups in maintaining dynamism and enhancing competitiveness in the digital economy;

2. The Contracting Parties recognise the integral role of the private sector in

the cooperation of the SMEs and startups cooperation to be implemented under this Chapter;

3. With a view to more robust cooperation between the Contracting Parties to enhance trade and investment opportunities for SMEs and startups in the digital economy, the Contracting Parties shall

    (a) continue cooperation with the other Contracting Parties to exchange information and best practices in leveraging on digital tools and technology to improve the access of SMEs and startups access to capital and credit, the participation of SMEs and startups participation in government procurement opportunities and other areas that could help SMEs and startups adapt to the digital economy; and

    (b) encourage participation by the Contracting Parties' SMEs and startups in platforms that could help them link with international suppliers, buyers and other potential business partners; and

4. The Contracting Parties shall endeavour to enhance digital dialogues of SMEs and startups dialogues. Such dialogues may include private sector, non-government organisations, academia and other stakeholders from each Contracting Party.

Article 23: Data Innovation

1. The Contracting Parties recognise that digitalisation and the use of data in the digital economy promote economic growth. To support the cross-border transfer of information by electronic means and promote data-driven innovation in the digital economy, the Contracting Parties further recognise the need to create an environment that enables and supports, and is conducive to, experimentation and innovation, including through the use of regulatory sandboxes where applicable.

2. The Contracting Parties shall endeavour to support data innovation through:

    (a) collaborating on data-sharing projects, including projects involving researchers, academics and industry, using regulatory sandboxes as required to demonstrate the benefits of the cross-border transfer of information by electronic means;

    (b) cooperating on the development of policies and standards for data portability; and

    (c) sharing research and industry practices related to data innovation.

Article 24: Competition in the Digital Economy

1. Recognising that the Contracting Parties can benefit by sharing their experiences in enforcing competition law and in developing and implementing competition policies to address the additional challenges that arise from the digital economy, the Contracting Parties shall endeavour to:

(a) exchange information and share best practices on the competition policies and effective competition law enforcement activities to promote and protect a competitive environment in digital markets;

(b) ensure that the Contracting Parties' digital markets are open, contestable and efficient; and

(c) strengthen cooperation between the Contracting Parties by providing advice or training, including through the exchange of officials, in order to identify and mitigate anticompetitive practices in digital markets.

2. The Parties shall cooperate, as appropriate, on issues of competition law enforcement in digital markets, including through consultation and exchange of information.

Article 25: Standards, Technical Regulations and Conformity Assessment Procedures for Digital Economy

1. The Contracting Parties recognise the importance and contribution of standards, technical regulations and conformity assessment procedures in fostering a well-functioning digital economy and reducing barriers to trade by increasing compatibility, interoperability, and reliability.

2. The Contracting Parties shall endeavour to participate and cooperate in areas of mutual interest at regional, multilateral or international fora that both Parties are party to, to promote development of standards relating to the digital economy and adoption thereof, in accordance with the principles and procedures as below:

(a) Information and procedure regarding standards development shall be easily accessible, notified and communicated through established mechanisms to the members of standardising bodies;

(b) Standards development process should allow open and non-discriminatory participation to the extent practicable;

(c) The standards development process should ensure that adopted standards are impartial and coherent, and promote their application and dissemination; and

(d) The standardising bodies should continue their efforts and cooperate to maintain standards to be effective and relevant to the objectives and circumstances.

3. The Contracting Parties recognise that mechanisms which facilitate the cross-border recognition of conformity assessment results can support the digital economy. Such mechanisms include:

(a) voluntary arrangements between relevant conformity assessment bodies; and

(b) the use of regional or international recognition agreements or arrangements that both Contracting Parties are party to.

4. To this end, the Contracting Parties shall endeavour to:

(a) exchange information, share experiences and views, including cooperation on technical assistance/capacity building and dialogues relating to the development and application of standards, technical regulations and conformity assessment procedures that are related to the digital economy, on mutually determined terms and conditions;

(b) participate actively in regional, multilateral and international fora that both Contracting Parties are party to, to develop standards that are related to the digital economy and to promote adoption thereof in the areas of mutual interest;

(c) identify, develop, and promote joint initiatives in the field of standards that are related to the digital economy;

(d) upon request of the other Contracting Party, give positive consideration to proposals for cooperation on matters of mutual interest on standards, technical regulations and conformity assessment procedures relating to the digital economy; and

(e) foster cooperation between governmental and non-governmental bodies of the Parties, on matters of mutual interest, including cross border research or test-bedding projects, to develop a greater understanding, between the Contracting Parties and industry, of standards, technical regulations and conformity assessment procedures.

5. The Contracting Parties acknowledge the importance of information exchange and transparency with regard to the preparation, adoption and application of standards, technical regulations and conformity assessment procedures on the digital economy. Each Contracting Party shall endeavour to:

(a) upon request, provide information on standards, technical regulations and conformity assessment procedures relating to its digital economy, in print or electronically, within a reasonable period of time agreed by the Contracting Parties and, if possible, within 60 days; and

(b) upon request, provide, if already available, the full text or summary in English.

Section H. Cybersecurity

Article 26: Cybersecurity Cooperation

1. The Contracting Parties recognise that threats to cybersecurity undermine confidence in digital trade. Accordingly, the Parties shall endeavour to:

(a) build the capabilities of their national entities responsible for cybersecurity incident response; and

(b) strengthen existing collaboration mechanisms for cooperating to identify and mitigate malicious intrusions or dissemination of malicious code that affect electronic networks and use those mechanisms to swiftly address cybersecurity incidents, as well as the sharing of information for awareness and best practices.

2. Given the evolving nature of cybersecurity threats, the Contracting Parties recognise that risk-based approaches may be more effective than prescriptive regulation in addressing those threats. Accordingly, each Contracting Party shall endeavour to employ, and encourage enterprises within its jurisdiction to use, risk-based approaches that rely on consensus-based standards and risk management best practices to identify and protect against cybersecurity risks and to detect, respond to, and recover from cybersecurity events.

3. Where in their mutual interest, the Contracting Parties shall cooperate in the field of cyber issues by sharing best practices and through cooperative practical actions aimed at promoting and protecting an open, free, stable, peaceful and secure cyberspace based on the application of existing international law and norms for responsible State behaviour and cyber confidence-building measures.

Article 27: Online Safety and Security

1. The Contracting Parties recognise that a safe and secure online environment supports the digital economy.

2. The Contracting Parties recognise the importance of taking a multi-stakeholder approach to addressing online safety and security issues.

3. The Contracting Parties shall endeavour to cooperate to advance collaborative solutions to global issues affecting online safety and security.

Section I. Transparency

Article 28: Transparency

1. Each Contracting Party shall publish as promptly as possible or, where that is not practicable, otherwise make publicly available, including on the internet where feasible, all relevant measures of general application pertaining to or affecting the operation of this Chapter.

2. Each Contracting Party shall respond as promptly as possible to a relevant request from another Party for specific information on any of its measures of general application pertaining to or affecting the operation of this Chapter.

CHAPTER - 7

INVESTMENT

SECTION A

Article 1: Definitions

For purposes of this Chapter:

"Central level of government" means:

    (a) for [Country], [   ]; and

    (b) for [Country], [   ];

"Centre" means the International Centre for Settlement of Investment Disputes ("ICSID") established by the ICSID Convention.

"Claimant" means an investor of a Contracting Party that is a party to an investment dispute with the other Contracting Party.

"Covered investment" means, with respect to a Contracting Party, an investment in its territory of an investor of the other Contracting Party in existence as of the date of entry into force of this Chapter or established, acquired, or expanded thereafter.

"Disputing parties" means the claimant and the respondent.

"Disputing party" means either the claimant or the respondent.

"Enterprise" means any entity constituted or organized under applicable law, whether or not for profit, and whether privately or governmentally owned or controlled, including a corporation, trust, partnership, sole proprietorship, joint venture, association, or similar organization; and a branch of an enterprise.

"Enterprise of a Contracting Party" means an enterprise constituted or organized under the law of a Contracting Party, and a branch located in the territory of a Contracting

Party and carrying out business activities there.

"Existing" means in effect on the date of entry into force of this Chapter.

"Freely usable currency" means "freely usable currency" as determined by the International Monetary Fund under its *Articles of Agreement.*

"Government procurement" means the process by which a government obtains the use of or acquires goods or services, or any combination thereof, for governmental purposes and not with a view to commercial sale or resale, or use in the production or supply of goods or services for commercial sale or resale.

"ICSID Additional Facility Rules" means the *Rules Governing the Additional Facility for the Administration of Proceedings by the Secretariat of the International Centre for Settlement of Investment Disputes.*

"ICSID Convention" means the *Convention on the Settlement of Investment Disputes between States and Nationals of Other States,* done at Washington, March 18, 1965.

"Investment" means every asset that an investor owns or controls, directly or indirectly, that has the characteristics of an investment, including such characteristics as the commitment of capital or other resources, the expectation of gain or profit, or the assumption of risk. Forms that an investment may take include:

(a) an enterprise;

(b) shares, stock, and other forms of equity participation in an enterprise;

(c) bonds, debentures, other debt instruments, and loans;

(d) futures, options, and other derivatives;

(e) turnkey, construction, management, production, concession, revenue-sharing, and other similar contracts;

(f) intellectual property rights;

(g) licenses, authorizations, permits, and similar rights conferred pursuant to domestic law;[13] and

(h) other tangible or intangible, movable or immovable property, and related property rights, such as leases, mortgages, liens, and pledges.

"Investment agreement" means a written agreement[14] between a national

---

13 For greater certainty, the term "investment" does not include an order or judgment entered in a judicial or administrative action.

14 "Written agreement" refers to an agreement in writing, executed by both parties, whether in a single instrument or in multiple instruments, that creates an exchange of rights and obligations, binding on both parties under the law applicable under Paragraph 2 of Article 33. For greater certainty, (a) a unilateral act of an administrative or judicial authority, such as a permit, license, or authorization issued by a Party solely in its regulatory capacity, or a decree, order, or judgment, standing alone; and (b) an administrative or judicial consent decree or order, shall not be considered a written agreement.

authority[15] of a Contracting Party and a covered investment or an investor of the other Contracting Party, on which the covered investment or the investor relies in establishing or acquiring a covered investment other than the written agreement itself, that grants rights to the covered investment or investor:

    (a) with respect to natural resources that a national authority controls, such as for their exploration, extraction, refining, transportation, distribution, or sale;

    (b) to supply services to the public on behalf of the Contracting Party, such as power generation or distribution, water treatment or distribution, or telecommunications; or

    (c) to undertake infrastructure projects, such as the construction of roads, bridges, canals, dams, or pipelines, that are not for the exclusive or predominant use and benefit of the government.

"Investment authorization"[16] means an authorization that the foreign investment authority of a Contracting Party grants to a covered investment or an investor of the other Contracting Party.

"Investor of a non-Contracting Party" means, with respect to a Contracting Party, an investor that attempts to make, is making, or has made an investment in the territory of that Contracting Party, that is not an investor of either Contracting Party.

"Investor of a Contracting Party" means a Contracting Party or state enterprise thereof, or a national or an enterprise of a Contracting Party, that attempts to make, is making, or has made an investment in the territory of the other Contracting Party; provided, however, that a natural person who is a dual national shall be deemed to be exclusively a national of the State of his or her dominant and effective nationality.

"Measure" includes any law, regulation, procedure, requirement, or practice.

"National" means:

    (a) for [Country], [   ]; and

    (b) for [Country], [   ].

"New York Convention" means the United Nations Convention on the Recognition and Enforcement of Foreign Arbitral Awards, done at New York, June 10, 1958.

"Non-disputing Contracting Party" means the Contracting Party that is not a party to an investment dispute.

"Person" means a natural person or an enterprise.

"Person of a Contracting Party" means a national or an enterprise of a

---

15 For purposes of this definition, "national authority" means (a) for [Country], [ ].; and (b) for [Country], [ ].

16 For greater certainty, actions taken by a Party to enforce laws of general application, such as competition laws, are not encompassed within this definition.

Contracting Party.

"Protected information" means confidential business information or information that is privileged or otherwise protected from disclosure under a Contracting Party's law.

"Regional level of government" means:

    (a) for [Country], [   ]; and

    (b) for [Country], [   ].

"Respondent" means the Contracting Party that is a Contracting Party to an investment dispute.

"Secretary-General" means the Secretary-General of ICSID.

"State enterprise" means an enterprise owned, or controlled through ownership interests, by a Contracting Party.

"Territory" means:

    (a) with respect to [Country], [ ];

    (b) with respect to [Country], [ ].

    (c) with respect to each Contracting Party, the territorial sea and any area beyond the territorial sea of the Contracting Party within which, in accordance with customary international law as reflected in the United Nations Convention on the Law of the Sea, the Contracting Party may exercise sovereign rights or jurisdiction.

"TRIPS Agreement" means the Agreement on Trade-Related Aspects of Intellectual Property Rights, contained in Annex 1C to the WTO Agreement.[17]

"UNCITRAL Arbitration Rules" means the arbitration rules of the United Nations Commission on International Trade Law.

"WTO Agreement" means the Marrakesh Agreement Establishing the World Trade Organization, done on April 15, 1994.

Article 2: Scope and Coverage

1. This Chapter applies to measures adopted or maintained by a Contracting Party relating to:

    (a) investors of the other Contracting Party;

    (b) covered investments; and

    (c) with respect to Articles 8 [Performance Requirements], 12 [Investment and Environment], and 13 [Investment and Labour], all investments in the territory of the Contracting Party.

2. A Contracting Party's obligations under Section A shall apply:

---

17 For greater certainty, "TRIPS Agreement" includes any waiver in force between the Contracting Parties of any provision of the TRIPS Agreement granted by WTO Members in accordance with the WTO Agreement.

(a) to a state enterprise or other person when it exercises any regulatory, administrative, or other governmental authority delegated to it by that Contracting Party;[18] and

(b) to the adminstrative subdivisions of that Contracting Party.

3. For greater certainty, this Chapter does not bind either Contracting Party in relation to any act or fact that took place or any situation that ceased to exist before the date of entry into force of this Chapter.

Article 3: Relationship to Other Agreements

1. Recognising the Contracting Parties' intention for this Agreement to coexist with their existing international agreements, each Contracting Party affirms: (a) in relation to existing international agreements to which all Contracting Parties are party, including the WTO Agreement, its existing rights and obligations with respect to the other Contracting Parties; and (b) in relation to existing international agreements to which that Contracting Party and at least one other Contracting Party are party, its existing rights and obligations with respect to that other Contracting Party or Contracting Parties, as the case may be.

2. If a Contracting Party considers that a provision of this Agreement is inconsistent with a provision of another agreement to which it and at least one other Contracting Party are party, on request, the relevant Contracting Parties to the other agreement shall consult with a view to reaching a mutually satisfactory solution. This paragraph is without prejudice to a Contracting Party's rights and obligations under Section B.[19]

Article 4: National Treatment

1. Each Contracting Party shall accord to investors of the other Contracting Party treatment no less favourable than that it accords, in like circumstances, to its own investors with respect to the establishment, acquisition, expansion, management, conduct, operation, and sale or other disposition of investments in its territory.

2. Each Contracting Party shall accord to covered investments treatment no less favourable than that it accords, in like circumstances, to investments in its territory of its own investors with respect to the establishment, acquisition, expansion, management, conduct, operation, and sale or other disposition of investments.

3. The treatment to be accorded by a Contracting Party under paragraphs 1 and 2

---

18 For greater certainty, government authority that has been delegated includes a legislative grant, and a government order, directive or other action transferring to the state enterprise or other person, or authorizing the exercise by the state enterprise or other person of, governmental authority.

19 For the purposes of application of this Agreement, the Contracting Parties agree that the fact that an agreement provides more favorable treatment of goods, services, investments or persons than that provided for under this Agreement does not mean that there is an inconsistency within the meaning of paragraph 2.

means, with respect to a regional level of government, treatment no less favourable than the treatment accorded, in like circumstances, by that regional level of government to natural persons resident in and enterprises constituted under the laws of other regional levels of government of the Contracting Party of which it forms a part, and to their respective investments.

Article 5: Most-Favored-Nation Treatment

1. Each Contracting Party shall accord to investors of the other Contracting Party treatment no less favourable than that it accords, in like circumstances, to investors of any non-Contracting Party with respect to the establishment, acquisition, expansion, management, conduct, operation, and sale or other disposition of investments in its territory.

2. Each Contracting Party shall accord to covered investments treatment no less favourable than that it accords, in like circumstances, to investments in its territory of investors of any non-Contracting Party with respect to the establishment, acquisition, expansion, management, conduct, operation, and sale or other disposition of investments.

3. For greater certainty, the treatment referred to in this Article does not encompass international dispute resolution procedures or mechanisms, such as those included in Section B (Investor-State Dispute Settlement).

Article 6: Minimum Standard of Treatment[20]

1. Each Contracting Party shall accord to covered investments treatment in accordance with customary international law, including fair and equitable treatment and full protection and security.

2. For greater certainty, Paragraph 1 prescribes the customary international law minimum standard of treatment of aliens as the minimum standard of treatment to be afforded to covered investments. The concepts of "fair and equitable treatment" and "full protection and security" do not require treatment in addition to or beyond that which is required by that standard, and do not create additional substantive rights. The obligation in Paragraph 1 to provide:

    (a) "fair and equitable treatment" includes the obligation not to deny justice in criminal, civil, or administrative adjudicatory proceedings in accordance with the principle of due process embodied in the principal legal systems of the world; and

    (b) "full protection and security" requires each Contracting Party to provide the level of police protection required under customary international law.

---

20 Article 6 [Minimum Standard of Treatment] shall be interpreted in accordance with Annex A.

3. A determination that there has been a breach of another provision of this Chapter, or of a separate international agreement, does not establish that there has been a breach of this Article.

4. Notwithstanding Paragraph 5(b) [subsidies and grants] of Article 16, each Contracting Party shall accord to investors of the other Contracting Party, and to covered investments, non-discriminatory treatment with respect to measures it adopts or maintains relating to losses suffered by investments in its territory owing to armed conflict or civil strife.

5. Notwithstanding Paragraph 4, if an investor of a Contracting Party, in the situations referred to in Paragraph 4, suffers a loss in the territory of the other Contracting Party resulting from:

    (a) requisitioning of its covered investment or part thereof by the latter's forces or authorities; or

    (b) destruction of its covered investment or part thereof by the latter's forces or authorities, which was not required by the necessity of the situation, the latter Contracting Party shall provide the investor restitution, compensation, or both, as appropriate, for such loss. Any compensation shall be prompt, adequate, and effective in accordance with Article 8 [Expropriation and Compensation] (2) through (4), *mutatis mutandis*.

6. Paragraph 4 does not apply to existing measures relating to subsidies or grants that would be inconsistent with Article 3 [National Treatment] but for Paragraph 5(b) [subsidies and grants] of Article 16 (Non-Conforming Measures).

Article 7: Treatment in Case of Armed Conflict or Civil Strife

1. Notwithstanding Article 16 (Non-Conforming Measures), each Contracting Party shall accord to investors of another Contracting Party and to covered investments non-discriminatory treatment with respect to measures it adopts or maintains relating to losses suffered by investments in its territory owing to armed conflict or civil strife.

2. Notwithstanding Paragraph 1, if an investor of a Contracting Party, in a situation referred to in Paragraph 1, suffers a loss in the territory of another Contracting Party resulting from:

    (a) requisitioning of its covered investment or part thereof by the latter's forces or authorities; or

    (b) destruction of its covered investment or part thereof by the latter's forces or authorities, which was not required by the necessity of the situation,

the latter Contracting Party shall provide the investor restitution, compensation or both, as appropriate, for that loss.

3. Paragraph 1 shall not apply to existing measures relating to subsidies or grants that would be inconsistent with Article 4 (National Treatment) but for Article 16 (Non-

Conforming Measures).

Article 8: Expropriation and Compensation[21]

1. Neither Contracting Party may expropriate or nationalize a covered investment either directly or indirectly through measures equivalent to expropriation or nationalization ("expropriation"), except:

    (a) for a public purpose;

    (b) in a non-discriminatory manner;

    (c) on payment of prompt, adequate, and effective compensation; and

    (d) in accordance with due process of law and Paragraphs 1-3 of Article 6 (Minimum Standard of Treatment).

2. The compensation referred to in paragraph 1(c) shall:

    (a) be paid without delay;

    (b) be equivalent to the fair market value of the expropriated investment immediately before the expropriation took place ("the date of expropriation");

    (c) not reflect any change in value occurring because the intended expropriation had become known earlier; and

    (d) be fully realizable and freely transferable.

3. If the fair market value is denominated in a freely usable currency, the compensation referred to in Paragraph 1(c) shall be no less than the fair market value on the date of expropriation, plus interest at a commercially reasonable rate for that currency, accrued from the date of expropriation until the date of payment.

4. If the fair market value is denominated in a currency that is not freely usable, the compensation referred to in Paragraph 1(c) – converted into the currency of payment at the market rate of exchange prevailing on the date of payment – shall be no less than:

    (a) the fair market value on the date of expropriation, converted into a freely usable currency at the market rate of exchange prevailing on that date, plus

    (b) interest, at a commercially reasonable rate for that freely usable currency, accrued from the date of expropriation until the date of payment.

5. This Article does not apply to the issuance of compulsory licenses granted in relation to intellectual property rights in accordance with the TRIPS Agreement, or to the revocation, limitation, or creation of intellectual property rights, to the extent that such issuance, revocation, limitation, or creation is consistent with the TRIPS Agreement.

6. For greater certainty, a Contracting Party's decision not to issue, renew or maintain a subsidy or grant, or decision to modify or reduce a subsidy or grant,

---

21 Article 8 [Expropriation] shall be interpreted in accordance with Annexes A and B.

(a) in the absence of any specific commitment under law or contract to issue, renew or maintain that subsidy or grant; or

(b) in accordance with any terms or conditions attached to the issuance, renewal, modification, reduction and maintenance of that subsidy or grant, standing alone, does not constitute an expropriation.

Article 9: Transfers

1. Each Contracting Party shall permit all transfers relating to a covered investment to be made freely and without delay into and out of its territory. Such transfers include:

(a) contributions to capital;

(b) profits, dividends, capital gains, and proceeds from the sale of all or any part of the covered investment or from the partial or complete liquidation of the covered investment;

(c) interest, royalty payments, management fees, and technical assistance and other fees;

(d) payments made under a contract, including a loan agreement;

(e) payments made pursuant to Paragraphs 4-5 of Article 6 (Minimum Standard of Treatment); and

(f) payments arising out of a dispute.

2. Each Contracting Party shall permit transfers relating to a covered investment to be made in a freely usable currency at the market rate of exchange prevailing at the time of transfer.

3. Each Contracting Party shall permit returns in kind relating to a covered investment to be made as authorized or specified in a written agreement between the Contracting Party and a covered investment or an investor of the other Contracting Party.

4. Notwithstanding Paragraphs 1 through 3, a Contracting Party may prevent a transfer through the equitable, non-discriminatory, and good faith application of its laws relating to:

(a) bankruptcy, insolvency, or the protection of the rights of creditors;

(b) issuing, trading, or dealing in securities, futures, options, or derivatives;

(c) criminal or penal offenses;

(d) financial reporting or record keeping of transfers when necessary to assist law enforcement or financial regulatory authorities; or

(e) ensuring compliance with orders or judgments in judicial or administrative proceedings.

Article 10: Performance Requirements

1. Neither Contracting Party may, in connection with the establishment,

acquisition, expansion, management, conduct, operation, or sale or other disposition of an investment of an investor of a Contracting Party or of a non-Contracting Party in its territory, impose or enforce any requirement or enforce any commitment or undertaking:[22]

> (a) to export a given level or percentage of goods or services;
>
> (b) to achieve a given level or percentage of domestic content;
>
> (c) to purchase, use, or accord a preference to goods produced in its territory, or to purchase goods from persons in its territory;
>
> (d) to relate in any way the volume or value of imports to the volume or value of exports or to the amount of foreign exchange inflows associated with such investment;
>
> (e) to restrict sales of goods or services in its territory that such investment produces or supplies by relating such sales in any way to the volume or value of its exports or foreign exchange earnings;
>
> (f) to transfer a particular technology, a production process, or other proprietary knowledge to a person in its territory;
>
> (g) to supply exclusively from the territory of the Contracting Party the goods that such investment produces or the services that it supplies to a specific regional market or to the world market; or
>
> (h) (i) to purchase, use, or accord a preference to, in its territory, technology of the Contracting Party or of persons of the Contracting Party[23]; or
>
> (ii) that prevents the purchase or use of, or the according of a preference to, in its territory, particular technology,

so as to afford protection on the basis of nationality to its own investors or investments or to technology of the Contracting Party or of persons of the Contracting Party.

2. Neither Contracting Party may condition the receipt or continued receipt of an advantage, in connection with the establishment, acquisition, expansion, management, conduct, operation, or sale or other disposition of an investment in its territory of an investor of a Contracting Party or of a non-Contracting Party, on compliance with any requirement:

> (a) to achieve a given level or percentage of domestic content;
>
> (b) to purchase, use, or accord a preference to goods produced in its territory, or

---

22 For greater certainty, a condition for the receipt or continued receipt of an advantage referred to in paragraph 2 does not constitute a "commitment or undertaking" for the purposes of paragraph 1.

23 For purposes of this Article, the term "technology of the Contracting Party or of persons of the Contracting Party" includes technology that is owned by the Contracting Party or persons of the Contracting Party, and technology for which the Contracting Party holds, or persons of the Contracting Party hold, an exclusive license.

to purchase goods from persons in its territory;

 (c) to relate in any way the volume or value of imports to the volume or value of exports or to the amount of foreign exchange inflows associated with such investment; or

 (d) to restrict sales of goods or services in its territory that such investment produces or supplies by relating such sales in any way to the volume or value of its exports or foreign exchange earnings.

3. (a) Nothing in Paragraph 2 shall be construed to prevent a Contracting Party from conditioning the receipt or continued receipt of an advantage, in connection with an investment in its territory of an investor of a Contracting Party or of a non-Contracting Party, on compliance with a requirement to locate production, supply a service, train or employ workers, construct or expand particular facilities, or carry out research and development, in its territory.

 (b) Paragraphs 1(f) and (h) do not apply:

  (i) when a Contracting Party authorizes use of an intellectual property right in accordance with Article 31 of the TRIPS Agreement, or to measures requiring the disclosure of proprietary information that fall within the scope of, and are consistent with, Article 39 of the TRIPS Agreement; or

  (ii) when the requirement is imposed or the commitment or undertaking is enforced by a court, administrative tribunal, or competition authority to remedy a practice determined after judicial or administrative process to be anticompetitive under the Contracting Party's competition laws.[24]

 (c) Provided that such measures are not applied in an arbitrary or unjustifiable manner, and provided that such measures do not constitute a disguised restriction on international trade or investment, Paragraphs 1(b), (c), (f), and (h), and 2(a) and (b), shall not be construed to prevent a Contracting Party from adopting or maintaining measures, including environmental measures:

  (i) necessary to secure compliance with laws and regulations that are not inconsistent with this Chapter;

  (ii) necessary to protect human, animal, or plant life or health; or

  (iii) related to the conservation of living or non-living exhaustible natural resources.

 (d) Paragraphs 1(a), (b), and (c), and 2(a) and (b), do not apply to qualification requirements for goods or services with respect to export promotion and foreign aid programs.

 (e) Paragraphs 1(b), (c), (f), (g), and (h), and 2(a) and (b), do not apply to

---

24 The Contracting Parties recognise that a patent does not necessarily confer market power.

government procurement.

(f) Paragraphs 2(a) and (b) do not apply to requirements imposed by an importing Contracting Party relating to the content of goods necessary to qualify for preferential tariffs or preferential quotas.

(g) Paragraphs (1)(h) and (1)(i) shall not be construed to prevent a Contracting Party from adopting or maintaining measures to protect legitimate public welfare objectives, provided that such measures are not applied in an arbitrary or unjustifiable manner, or in a manner that constitutes a disguised restriction on international trade or investment.

4. For greater certainty, Paragraphs 1 and 2 do not apply to any commitment, undertaking, or requirement other than those set out in those Paragraphs.

5. This Article does not preclude enforcement of any commitment, undertaking, or requirement between private parties, where a Contracting Party did not impose or require the commitment, undertaking, or requirement.

6. Investors and their enterprises operating within its territory of each Contracting Party shall endeavour to voluntarily incorporate internationally recognised standards of corporate social responsibility in their practices and internal policies, such as statements of principle that have been endorsed or are supported by the Contracting Parties. These principles may address issues such as labour, the environment, human rights, community relations and anti-corruption.

Article 11: Senior Management and Boards of Directors

1. Neither Contracting Party may require that an enterprise of that Contracting Party that is a covered investment appoint to senior management positions natural persons of any particular nationality.

2. A Contracting Party may require that a majority of the board of directors, or any committee thereof, of an enterprise of that Contracting Party that is a covered investment, be of a particular nationality, or resident in the territory of the Contracting Party, provided that the requirement does not materially impair the ability of the investor to exercise control over its investment.

Article 12: Publication of Laws and Decisions Related to Investment

1. Each Contracting Party shall ensure that its:

(a) laws, regulations, procedures, and administrative rulings of general application; and

(b) adjudicatory decisions

respect to any matter covered by this Chapter is promptly published or otherwise made publicly available.

2. For purposes of this Article, "administrative ruling of general application" means

an administrative ruling or interpretation that applies to all persons and fact situations that fall generally within its ambit and that establishes a norm of conduct but does not include:

    (a) a determination or ruling made in an administrative or quasi-judicial proceeding that applies to a particular covered investment or investor of the other Contracting Party in a specific case; or

    (b) a ruling that adjudicates with respect to a particular act or practice.

Article 13: Transparency and Anti-corruption

1. Subject to Chapter-4 (Transparency and Anti-Corruption) of this Agreement, the Contracting Parties agree to consult periodically on ways to improve the transparency practices set out in this Article, Article 12 and Article 32.

2. Publication

To the extent possible, each Contracting Party shall:

    (a) publish in advance any measure referred to in Paragraph 1(a) of Article 12 that it proposes to adopt; and

    (b) provide interested persons and the other Contracting Party a reasonable opportunity to comment on such proposed measures.

3. With respect to proposed regulations of general application of its central level of government respecting any matter covered by this Chapter that are published in accordance with paragraph 2(a), each Contracting Party:

    (a) shall publish the proposed regulations in a single official journal of national circulation and shall encourage their distribution through additional outlets;

    (b) should in most cases publish the proposed regulations not less than 60 days before the date public comments are due;

    (c) shall include in the publication an explanation of the purpose of and rationale for the proposed regulations; and

    (d) shall, at the time it adopts final regulations, address significant, substantive comments received during the comment period and explain substantive revisions that it made to the proposed regulations in its official journal or in a prominent location on a government Internet site.

4. With respect to regulations of general application that are adopted by its central level of government respecting any matter covered by this Chapter, each Contracting Party:

    (a) shall publish the regulations in a single official journal of national circulation and shall encourage their distribution through additional outlets; and

    (b) shall include in the publication an explanation of the purpose of and rationale for the regulations.

5. Provision of Information

(a) On request of the other Contracting Party, a Contracting Party shall promptly provide information and respond to questions pertaining to any actual or proposed measure that the requesting Contracting Party considers might materially affect the operation of this Chapter or otherwise substantially affect its interests under this Chapter.

(b) Any request or information under this paragraph shall be provided to the other Contracting Party through the relevant contact points.

(c) Any information provided under this paragraph shall be without prejudice as to whether the measure is consistent with this Chapter.

6. Administrative Proceedings

With a view to administering in a consistent, impartial, and reasonable manner all measures referred to in Paragraph 1(a) of Article 12, each Contracting Party shall ensure that in its administrative proceedings applying such measures to particular covered investments or investors of the other Contracting Party in specific cases:

(a) wherever possible, covered investments or investors of the other Contracting Party that are directly affected by a proceeding are provided reasonable notice, in accordance with domestic procedures, when a proceeding is initiated, including a description of the nature of the proceeding, a statement of the authority under which the proceeding is initiated, and a general description of any issues in controversy;

(b) such persons are afforded a reasonable opportunity to present facts and arguments in support of their positions prior to any final administrative action, when time, the nature of the proceeding, and the public interest permit; and

(c) its procedures are in accordance with domestic law.

7. Review and Appeal

(a) Each Contracting Party shall establish or maintain judicial, quasi-judicial, or administrative tribunals or procedures for the purpose of the prompt review and, where warranted, correction of final administrative actions regarding matters covered by this Chapter. Such tribunals shall be impartial and independent of the office or authority entrusted with administrative enforcement and shall not have any substantial interest in the outcome of the matter.

(b) Each Contracting Party shall ensure that, in any such tribunals or procedures, the parties to the proceeding are provided with the right to:

(i) a reasonable opportunity to support or defend their respective positions; and

(ii) a decision based on the evidence and submissions of record or, where required by domestic law, the record compiled by the administrative authority.

(c) Each Contracting Party shall ensure, subject to appeal or further review as provided in its domestic law, that such decisions shall be implemented by, and shall govern the practice of, the offices or authorities with respect to the administrative action at issue.

8. Standards-Setting

(a) Each Contracting Party shall allow persons of the other Contracting Party to participate in the development of standards and technical regulations by its central government bodies.[25] Each Contracting Party shall allow persons of the other Contracting Party to participate in the development of these measures, and the development of conformity assessment procedures by its central government bodies, on terms no less favourable than those it accords to its own persons.

(b) Each Contracting Party shall recommend that non-governmental standardizing bodies in its territory allow persons of the other Contracting Party to participate in the development of standards by those bodies. Each Contracting Party shall recommend that non-governmental standardizing bodies in its territory allow persons of the other Contracting Party to participate in the development of these standards, and the development of conformity assessment procedures by those bodies, on terms no less favourable than those they accord to persons of the Contracting Party.

(c) Subparagraphs 8(a) and 8(b) do not apply to:

(i) sanitary and phytosanitary measures as defined in Annex A of the WTO Agreement on the Application of Sanitary and Phytosanitary Measures; or

(ii) purchasing specifications prepared by a governmental body for its production or consumption requirements.

(d) For purposes of Subparagraphs 8(a) and 8(b), "central government body", "standards", "technical regulations" and "conformity assessment procedures" have the meanings assigned to those terms in Annex 1 of the WTO Agreement on Technical Barriers to Trade. Consistent with Annex 1, the three latter terms do not include standards, technical regulations or conformity assessment procedures for the supply of a service.

9. Measures to combat corruption

Subject to Chapter-4 (Transparency and Anti-Corruption) of this Agreement:

---

25 A Contracting Party may satisfy this obligation by, for example, providing interested persons a reasonable opportunity to provide comments on the measure it proposes to develop and taking those comments into account in the development of the measure.

(a) Each Contracting Party shall adopt or maintain legislative and other measures as may be necessary to establish as criminal offences under its law, in matters that affect international trade or investment, when committed intentionally, by any person subject to its jurisdiction:

  (i) the promise, offering or giving to a public official, directly or indirectly, of an undue advantage, for the official or another person or entity, in order that the official act or refrain from acting in relation to the performance of or the exercise of his or her official duties;

  (ii) the solicitation or acceptance by a public official, directly or indirectly, of an undue advantage, for the official or another person or entity, in order that the official act or refrain from acting in relation to the performance of or the exercise of his or her official duties;

  (iii) the promise, offering or giving to a foreign public official or an official of a public international organisation, directly or indirectly, of an undue advantage, for the official or another person or entity, in order that the official act or refrain from acting in relation to the performance of or the exercise of his or her official duties, in order to obtain or retain business or other undue advantage in relation to the conduct of international business; and

  (iv) the aiding or abetting, or conspiracy in the commission of any of the offences described in Subparagraphs (i) through (iii).

(b) Each Contracting Party shall make the commission of an offence described in Paragraph 1 or 5 liable to sanctions that take into account the gravity of that offence.

(c) Each Contracting Party shall adopt or maintain measures as may be necessary, consistent with its legal principles, to establish the liability of legal persons for offences described in paragraph 1 or 5. In particular, each Contracting Party shall ensure that legal persons held liable for offences described in paragraph 1 or 5 are subject to effective, proportionate and dissuasive criminal or non-criminal sanctions, which include monetary sanctions.

(d) No Contracting Party shall allow a person subject to its jurisdiction to deduct from taxes expenses incurred in connection with the commission of an offence described in paragraph 1.

(e) In order to prevent corruption, each Contracting Party shall adopt or maintain measures as may be necessary, in accordance with its laws and regulations, regarding the maintenance of books and records, financial statement disclosures, and accounting and auditing standards, to prohibit the following acts carried out for the purpose of committing any of the offences described in Paragraph 1.

(i) the establishment of off-the-books accounts;

(ii) the making of off-the-books or inadequately identified transactions;

(iii) the recording of non-existent expenditure;

(iv) the entry of liabilities with incorrect identification of their objects;

(v) the use of false documents; and

(vi) the intentional destruction of bookkeeping documents earlier than foreseen by the law.

(f) Each Contracting Party shall consider adopting or maintaining measures to protect, against any unjustified treatment, any person who, in good faith and on reasonable grounds, reports to the competent authorities any facts concerning offences described in Paragraph 1 or 5.

Article 14: Investment and Environment

Subject to Chapter-3 (Sustainable Development) and Chapter-13 (Environment) of this Agreement:

1. The Contracting Parties recognise that their respective environmental laws and policies, and multilateral environmental agreements to which they are both party, play an important role in protecting the environment.

2. The Contracting Parties recognise that it is inappropriate to encourage investment by weakening or reducing the protections afforded in domestic environmental laws. Accordingly, each Contracting Party shall ensure that it does not waive or otherwise derogate from or offer to waive or otherwise derogate from its environmental laws[26] in a manner that weakens or reduces the protections afforded in those laws, or fail to effectively enforce those laws through a sustained or recurring course of action or inaction, as an encouragement for the establishment, acquisition, expansion, or retention of an investment in its territory.

3. The Contracting Parties recognise that each Contracting Party retains the right to exercise discretion with respect to regulatory, compliance, investigatory, and prosecutorial matters, and to make decisions regarding the allocation of resources to enforcement with respect to other environmental matters determined to have higher priorities. Accordingly, the Contracting Parties understand that a Contracting Party is in compliance with Paragraph 2 where a course of action or inaction reflects a reasonable exercise of such discretion, or results from a *bona fide* decision regarding the allocation of resources.

4. For purposes of this Article, "environmental law" means each Contracting

---

26 Paragraph 2 shall not apply where a Contracting Party waives or derogates from an environmental law pursuant to a provision in law providing for waivers or derogations.

Party's statutes or regulations, or provisions thereof, the primary purpose of which is the protection of the environment, or the prevention of a danger to human, animal, or plant life or health, through the:

(a) prevention, abatement, or control of the release, discharge, or emission of pollutants or environmental contaminants;

(b) control of environmentally hazardous or toxic chemicals, substances, materials, and wastes, and the dissemination of information related thereto; or

(c) protection or conservation of wild flora or fauna, including endangered species, their habitat, and specially protected natural areas,

in the Contracting Party's territory, but does not include any statute or regulation, or provision thereof, directly related to worker safety or health.

5. Nothing in this Chapter shall be construed to prevent a Contracting Party from adopting, maintaining, or enforcing any measure otherwise consistent with this Chapter that it considers appropriate to ensure that investment activity in its territory is undertaken in a manner sensitive to environmental concerns.

6. A Contracting Party may make a written request for consultations with the other Contracting Party regarding any matter arising under this Article. The other Contracting Party shall respond to a request for consultations within thirty days of receipt of such request. Thereafter, the Contracting Parties shall consult and endeavour to reach a mutually satisfactory resolution.

7. The Contracting Parties confirm that each Contracting Party may, as appropriate, provide opportunities for public participation regarding any matter arising under this Article.

Article 15: Investment and Labour

Subject to Chapter-14 (**Labour Standards**) of this Agreement:

1. The Contracting Parties reaffirm their respective obligations as members of the International Labour Organization("ILO") and their commitments under the *ILO Declaration on Fundamental Principles and Rights at Work and its Follow-Up.*

2. The Contracting Parties recognise that it is inappropriate to encourage investment by weakening or reducing the protections afforded in domestic labour laws. Accordingly, each Contracting Party shall ensure that it does not waive or otherwise derogate from or offer to waive or otherwise derogate from its labour laws where the waiver or derogation would be inconsistent with the labour rights referred to in Subparagraphs (a) through (e) of Paragraph 3, or fail to effectively enforce its labour laws through a sustained or recurring course of action or inaction, as an encouragement for the establishment, acquisition, expansion, or retention of an investment in its territory.

3. For purposes of this Article, "labour laws" means each Contracting Party's statutes or regulations, or provisions thereof, that are directly related to the following:

(a) freedom of association;

(b) the effective recognition of the right to collective bargaining;

(c) the elimination of all forms of forced or compulsory labour;

(d) the effective abolition of child labour and a prohibition on the worst forms of child labour;

(e) the elimination of discrimination in respect of employment and occupation; and

(f) acceptable conditions of work with respect to minimum wages, hours of work, and occupational safety and health.

4. A Contracting Party may make a written request for consultations with the other Contracting Party regarding any matter arising under this Article. The other Contracting Party shall respond to a request for consultations within thirty days of receipt of such request. Thereafter, the Contracting Parties shall consult and endeavour to reach a mutually satisfactory resolution.

5. The Contracting Parties confirm that each Contracting Party may, as appropriate, provide opportunities for public participation regarding any matter arising under this Article.

6. Entry and temporary stay of natural persons for business purposes

(a) This Paragraph applies to measures of the Contracting Parties concerning the entry and temporary stay in their territories of business visitors for establishment purposes and intra-corporate- transferees in accordance with Paragraph(d).

(b) This Paragraph shall not apply to measures affecting natural persons seeking access to the employment market of a Party, nor shall it apply to measures regarding citizenship, residence or employment on a permanent basis.

(c) Nothing in this Chapter shall prevent a Contracting Party from applying measures to regulate the entry of natural persons into, or their temporary stay in, its territory, including those measures necessary to protect the integrity of, and to ensure the orderly movement of natural persons across its borders, provided that such measures are not applied in such a manner as to nullify or impair the benefits[27] accruing to any Party under the terms of a specific commitment in this paragraph.

(d) For the purpose of this Paragraph:

(i) **'Business visitors for establishment purposes'** mean natural persons

---

27 The sole fact of requiring a visa for natural persons of certain countries and not for those of others shall not be regarded as nullifying or impairing benefits under a specific commitment.

working in a senior position who are responsible for setting up an enterprise. They do not offer or provide services or engage in any other economic activity than required for establishment purposes. They do not receive remuneration from a source located within the host Contracting Party.

(ii) **'Intra-corporate transferees'** mean natural persons who have been employed by a juridical person, or its branch or have been partners in it for at least one year and who are temporarily transferred to an enterprise that may be a subsidiary, branch or head company of the juridical person in the territory of the other Contracting Party[28]. The natural person concerned must belong to one of the following categories:

(iii) **"Managers"** means persons working in a senior position within a juridical person, who primarily direct the management of the enterprise, receiving general supervision or direction principally from the board of directors or from stockholders of the business or their equivalent, including at least: directing the enterprise or a department or sub-division thereof; and supervising and controlling the work of other supervisory, professional or managerial employees; and having the personal authority to recruit and dismiss or to recommend recruitment, dismissal or other personnel-related actions.

(iv) **"Specialists"** means persons working within a juridical person who possess specialised knowledge essential to the enterprise's production, research equipment, techniques, processes, procedures or management. In assessing such knowledge, account shall be taken not only of knowledge specific to the enterprise, but also of whether the person has a high level of qualification referring to a type of work or trade requiring specific technical knowledge, including membership of an accredited profession.

(e) The permissible length of stay shall be for a period of up to ninety days in any twelve months period for business visitors for establishment purposes, and up to three years for managers and specialists.

(f) Subject to relevant local reservations of a Contracting Party, if any, for business visitors and intra-corporate transferees:

(i) A Contracting Party shall allow the entry and temporary stay of intra-corporate transferees and business visitors for establishment purposes.

---

28 For greater certainty, managers and specialists may be required to demonstrate they possess the professional qualifications and experience needed in the enterprise to which they are transferred.

(ii) A Contracting Party shall not maintain or adopt, either on the basis of a territorial subdivision or on the basis of its entire territory, limitations in the form of numerical quotas or economic needs tests on the total number of natural persons that, in a specific sector, are allowed entry as business visitors for establishment purposes or that an investor may employ as intra-corporate transferees in a specific sector in the form of numerical quotas or economic needs tests either on the basis of a territorial subdivision or on the basis of its entire territory.

(iii) Each Contracting Party shall accord to Intra-corporate Transferees and Business Visitors for Establishment Purposes of the other Party national treatment with regard to their temporary stay in its Territory. For the purpose of this Paragraph, national treatment provided in Article 17 of GATS shall apply, mutatis mutandis.[29]

(g) For greater certainty, temporary entry granted in accordance with this Paragraph Article [Entry and temporary stay of natural persons for business purposes] does not replace the qualification requirements needed to carry out a profession or activity according to the applicable laws and regulations in force in the territory of the granting Contracting Party, provided such requirements are not inconsistent with its obligations under this Chapter.

Article 16: Non-Conforming Measures

1. Articles 4 (National Treatment), 5 (Most-Favored-Nation Treatment), 10 (Performance Requirements), and 11 (Senior Management and Boards of Directors) do not apply to:

(a) any existing non-conforming measure that is maintained by a Contracting Party at:

   (i) the central level of government, as set out by that Contracting Party in its Schedule to Annex I or Annex III,

   (ii) a regional level of government, as set out by that Contracting Party in its Schedule to Annex I or Annex III, or

   (iii) a local level of government;

(b) the continuation or prompt renewal of any non-conforming measure referred to in Subparagraph (a); or

(c) an amendment to any non-conforming measure referred to in subparagraph (a) to the extent that the amendment does not decrease the conformity of the

---

29 For greater certainty, the Contracting Parties agree that this commitment applies to all sectors of economic activity covered by the scope of commitments in this Chapter.

measure, as it existed immediately before the amendment, with Article 4 (National Treatment), 5 (Most-Favored-Nation Treatment), 10 (Performance Requirements), or 11 (Senior Management and Boards of Directors).

2. Articles 4 (National Treatment), 5 (Most-Favored-Nation Treatment), 10 (Performance Requirements), or 11 (Senior Management and Boards of Directors) do not apply to any measure that a Contracting Party adopts or maintains with respect to sectors, subsectors, or activities, as set out in its Schedule to Annex II.

3. Neither Contracting Party shall, under any measure adopted after the date of entry into force of this Chapter and covered by its Schedule to Annex II, require an investor of the other Contracting Party, by reason of its nationality, to sell or otherwise dispose of an investment existing at the time the measure becomes effective.

4. Neither Contracting Party shall, under any measure adopted after the date of entry into force of this Agreement for that Contracting Party and covered by its Schedule to Annex II, require an investor of another Contracting Party, by reason of its nationality, to sell or otherwise dispose of an investment existing at the time the measure becomes effective.

5. (a) Article 4 (National Treatment) shall not apply to any measure that falls within an exception to, or derogation from, the obligations which are imposed by:

(i) Article 4 (National Treatment); or

(ii) Article 3 of the TRIPS Agreement.

(b) Article 5 (Most-Favoured-Nation Treatment) shall not apply to any measure that falls within Article 5 of the TRIPS Agreement, or an exception to, or derogation from, the obligations which are imposed by:

(i) Article 4 (National Treatment); or

(ii) Article 4 of the TRIPS Agreement.

6. Articles 4 (National Treatment), 5 (Most-Favored-Nation Treatment), or 11 (Senior Management and Boards of Directors) do not apply to:

(a) government procurement; or

(b) subsidies or grants provided by a Contracting Party, including government-supported loans, guarantees, and insurance.

Article 17: Subrogation

If a Contracting Party, or any agency, institution, statutory body or corporation designated by the Contracting Party, makes a payment to an investor of the Contracting Party under a guarantee, a contract of insurance or other form of indemnity that it has entered into with respect to a covered investment, the other Contracting Party in whose territory the covered investment was made shall recognise the subrogation or transfer of any rights the investor would have possessed under this Chapter with respect to the covered investment but for the subrogation, and the investor shall be precluded from pursuing these rights to the extent of the subrogation.

Article 18: Special Formalities and Information Requirements

1. Nothing in Article 4 (National Treatment) shall be construed to prevent a Contracting Party from adopting or maintaining a measure that prescribes special formalities in connection with covered investments, such as a requirement that investors be residents of the Contracting Party or that covered investments be legally constituted under the laws or regulations of the Contracting Party, provided that such formalities do not materially impair the protections afforded by a Contracting Party to investors of the other Contracting Party and covered investments pursuant to this Chapter.

2. Notwithstanding Articles 4 (National Treatment), 5 (Most-Favored-Nation Treatment), a Contracting Party may require an investor of the other Contracting Party or its covered investment to provide information concerning that investment solely for informational or statistical purposes. The Contracting Party shall protect any confidential business information from any disclosure that would prejudice the competitive position of the investor or the covered investment. Nothing in this paragraph shall be construed to prevent a Contracting Party from otherwise obtaining or disclosing information in connection with the equitable and good faith application of its law.

Article 19: Non-Derogation

This Chapter shall not derogate from any of the following that entitle an investor of a Contracting Party or a covered investment to treatment more favourable than that accorded by this Chapter:

1. laws or regulations, administrative practices or procedures, or administrative or adjudicatory decisions of a Contracting Party;

2. international legal obligations of a Contracting Party; or

3. obligations assumed by a Contracting Party, including those contained in an investment authorization or an investment agreement.

Article 20: Denial of Benefits

1. A Contracting Party may deny the benefits of this Chapter to an investor of the other Contracting Party that is an enterprise of such other Contracting Party and to investments of that investor if persons of a non-Contracting Party own or control the enterprise and the denying Contracting Party:

    (a) does not maintain diplomatic relations with the non-Contracting Party; or

    (b) adopts or maintains measures with respect to the non-Contracting Party or a person of the non- Contracting Party that prohibit transactions with the enterprise or that would be violated or circumvented if the benefits of this Chapter were accorded to the enterprise or to its investments.

2. A Contracting Party may deny the benefits of this Chapter to an investor of the other Contracting Party that is an enterprise of such other Contracting Party and to investments of that investor if the enterprise has no substantial business activities in the territory of the other Contracting Party and persons of a non-Contracting Party, or of the denying Contracting Party, own or control the enterprise.

Article 21: Essential Security

The Contracting Parties agree to apply "Essential Security" measures in good faith and accept that any measures taken in the name of "Essential Security" shall be justiciable.

Nothing in this Chapter shall be construed:

1. to require a Contracting Party to furnish or allow access to any information the disclosure of which it determines to be contrary to its essential security interests; or

2. to preclude a Contracting Party from applying measures that it considers necessary for the fulfillment of its obligations with respect to the maintenance or restoration of international peace or security, or the protection of its own essential security interests.

Article 22: Disclosure of Information

Nothing in this Chapter shall be construed to require a Contracting Party to furnish or allow access to confidential information if the disclosure of which would impede law enforcement or otherwise be contrary to the public interest, or which would prejudice the legitimate commercial interests of particular enterprises, public or private.

Article 23: Financial Services

Subject to Chapter-10 (Finance) of this Agreement:

1. Notwithstanding any other provision of this Chapter, a Contracting Party shall not be prevented from adopting or maintaining measures relating to financial services for prudential reasons, including for the protection of investors, depositors, policy holders, or persons to whom a fiduciary duty is owed by a financial services supplier, or to ensure the integrity and stability of the financial system.[30] Where such measures do not conform with the provisions of this Chapter, they shall not be used as a means of avoiding the Contracting Party's commitments or obligations under this Chapter.

---

30 It is understood that the term "prudential reasons" includes the maintenance of the safety, soundness, integrity, or financial responsibility of individual financial institutions, as well as the maintenance of the safety and financial and operational integrity of payment and clearing systems.

2. (a) Nothing in this Chapter applies to non-discriminatory measures of general application taken by any public entity in pursuit of monetary and related credit policies or exchange rate policies. This paragraph shall not affect a Contracting Party's obligations under Article 9 (Transfers) or Article 10 (Performance Requirements).[31]

(b) For purposes of this paragraph, "public entity" means a central bank or monetary authority of a Contracting Party.

3. Where a claimant submits a claim to arbitration under Section B [Investor-State Dispute Settlement], and the respondent invokes paragraph 1 or 2 as a defense, the following provisions shall apply:

(a) The respondent shall, within 120 days of the date the claim is submitted to arbitration under Section B, submit in writing to the competent financial authorities[32] of both Contracting Parties a request for a joint determination on the issue of whether and to what extent Paragraph 1 or 2 is a valid defense to the claim. The respondent shall promptly provide the tribunal, if constituted, a copy of such request. The arbitration may proceed with respect to the claim only as provided in Subparagraph (d).

(b) The competent financial authorities of both Contracting Parties shall make themselves available for consultations with each other and shall attempt in good faith to make a determination as described in Subparagraph (a). Any such determination shall be transmitted promptly to the disputing parties and, if constituted, to the tribunal. The determination shall be binding on the tribunal.

(c) If the competent financial authorities of both Contracting Parties, within 120 days of the date by which they have both received the respondent's written request for a joint determination under subparagraph (a), have not made a determination as described in that Subparagraph, the tribunal shall decide the issue or issues left unresolved by the competent financial authorities. The provisions of Section B shall apply, except as modified by this Subparagraph.

(i) In the appointment of all arbitrators not yet appointed to the tribunal, each disputing Contracting Party shall take appropriate steps to ensure that the tribunal has expertise or experience in financial services law or practice. The expertise of particular candidates with respect to the

---

31 For greater certainty, measures of general application taken in pursuit of monetary and related credit policies or exchange rate policies do not include measures that expressly nullify or amend contractual provisions that specify the currency of denomination or the rate of exchange of currencies.

32 For purposes of this Article, "competent financial authorities" means, for [Country], [   ]; and for [Country], [   ].

particular sector of financial services in which the dispute arises shall be taken into account in the appointment of the presiding arbitrator.

(ii) If, before the respondent submits the request for a joint determination in conformance with subparagraph (a), the presiding arbitrator has been appointed pursuant to Paragraph 3 of Article 27, such arbitrator shall be replaced on the request of either disputing Contracting Party and the tribunal shall be reconstituted consistent with Subparagraph (c)(i). If, within 30 days of the date the arbitration proceedings are resumed under Subparagraph (d), the disputing parties have not agreed on the appointment of a new presiding arbitrator, the Secretary-General, on the request of a disputing party, shall appoint the presiding arbitrator consistent with Subparagraph (c)(i).

(iii) The tribunal shall draw no inference regarding the application of paragraph 1 or 2 from the fact that the competent financial authorities have not made a determination as described in Subparagraph (a).

(iv) The non-disputing Contracting Party may make oral and written submissions to the tribunal regarding the issue of whether and to what extent paragraph 1 or 2 is a valid defense to the claim. Unless it makes such a submission, the non-disputing Contracting Party shall be presumed, for purposes of the arbitration, to take a position on paragraph 1 or 2 not inconsistent with that of the respondent.

(d) The arbitration referred to in subparagraph (a)   may proceed with respect to the claim:

(i) 10 days after the date the competent financial authorities' joint determination has been received by both the disputing parties and, if constituted, the tribunal; or

(ii) 10 days after the expiration of the 120-day period provided to the competent financial authorities in subparagraph (c).

(e) On the request of the respondent made within 30 days after the expiration of the 120-day period for a joint determination referred to in Subparagraph (c), or, if the tribunal has not been constituted as of the expiration of the 120-day period, within 30 days after the tribunal is constituted, the tribunal shall address and decide the issue or issues left unresolved by the competent financial authorities as referred to in Subparagraph (c)   prior to deciding the merits of the claim for which paragraph 1 or 2 has been invoked by the respondent as a defense. Failure of the respondent to make such a request is without prejudice to the right of the respondent to invoke Paragraph 1 or 2 as a defense at any appropriate phase of the arbitration.

4. Where a dispute arises under Section C and the competent financial authorities

of one Contracting Party provide written notice to the competent financial authorities of the other Contracting Party that the dispute involves financial services, Section C shall apply except as modified by this paragraph and paragraph 5.

(a) The competent financial authorities of both Contracting Parties shall make themselves available for consultations with each other regarding the dispute, and shall have 180 days from the date such notice is received to transmit a report on their consultations to the Parties. A Contracting Party may submit the dispute to arbitration under Section C only after the expiration of that 180-day period.

(b) Either Contracting Party may make any such report available to a tribunal constituted under Section C to decide the dispute referred to in this Paragraph or a similar dispute, or to a tribunal constituted under Section B to decide a claim arising out of the same events or circumstances that gave rise to the dispute under Section C.

5. Where a Contracting Party submits a dispute involving financial services to arbitration under Section C in conformance with paragraph 4, and on the request of either Contracting Party within 30 days of the date the dispute is submitted to arbitration, each Contracting Party shall, in the appointment of all arbitrators not yet appointed, take appropriate steps to ensure that the tribunal has expertise or experience in financial services law or practice. The expertise of particular candidates with respect to financial services shall be taken into account in the appointment of the presiding arbitrator.

6. Notwithstanding Paragraphs 2-4 of Article 13 (Transparency and Anti-Corruption – Publication), each Contracting Party, to the extent practicable,

(a) shall publish in advance any regulations of general application relating to financial services that it proposes to adopt and the purpose of the regulation;

(b) shall provide interested persons and the other Contracting Party a reasonable opportunity to comment on such proposed regulations; and

(c) should at the time it adopts final regulations, address in writing significant substantive comments received from interested persons with respect to the proposed regulations.

7. The terms "financial service" or "financial services" shall have the same meaning as in Subparagraph 5(a) of the Annex on Financial Services of the GATS.

8. For greater certainty, nothing in this Chapter shall be construed to prevent the adoption or enforcement by a Contracting Party of measures relating to investors of the other Contracting Party, or covered investments, in financial institutions that are necessary to secure compliance with laws or regulations that are not inconsistent with this Chapter, including those related to the prevention of deceptive and fraudulent practices or that deal with the effects of a default on financial services contracts,

subject to the requirement that such measures are not applied in a manner which would constitute a means of arbitrary or unjustifiable discrimination between countries where like conditions prevail, or a disguised restriction on investment in financial institutions.

Article 24: Taxation

1. Except as provided in this Article, nothing in Section A shall impose obligations with respect to taxation measures.

2. Article 8 (Expropriation and Compensation) shall apply to all taxation measures, except that a claimant that asserts that a taxation measure involves an expropriation may submit a claim to arbitration under Section B only if:

    (a) the claimant has first referred to the competent tax authorities[33] of both Contracting Parties in writing the issue of whether that taxation measure involves an expropriation; and

    (b) within 180 days after the date of such referral, the competent tax authorities of both Contracting Parties fail to agree that the taxation measure is not an expropriation.

3. Subject to Paragraph 4, Paragraphs 2-4 of Article 10 (Performance Requirements) shall apply to all taxation measures.

4. Nothing in this Chapter shall affect the rights and obligations of either Contracting Party under any tax convention. In the event of any inconsistency between this Chapter and any such convention, that convention shall prevail to the extent of the inconsistency. In the case of a tax convention between the Contracting Parties, the competent authorities under that convention shall have sole responsibility for determining whether any inconsistency exists between this Chapter and that convention.

Article 25: Entry into Force, Duration, and Termination[34]

1. This Chapter shall enter into force thirty days after the date the Contracting Parties exchange instruments of ratification. It shall remain in force for a period of ten years and shall continue in force thereafter unless terminated in accordance with Paragraph 2.

2. A Contracting Party may terminate this Chapter at the end of the initial ten-year period or at any time thereafter by giving one year's written notice to the other Contracting Party.

3. For ten years from the date of termination, all other Articles shall continue to

---

33 For the purposes of this Article, the "competent tax authorities" means: (a) for [Country], [   ].; and (b) for [Country], [   ].

34 This provision will only apply a Contracting Party for its own unique reasons cannot commit to this Chapter as a single undertaking as part of the Agreement.

apply to covered investments established or acquired prior to the date of termination, except insofar as those Articles extend to the establishment or acquisition of covered investments.

SECTION B.
Dispute Settlement

Article 26: Consultation and Negotiation

1. In the event of an investment dispute, the claimant and the respondent should initially seek to resolve the dispute through consultation and negotiation, which may include the use of non-binding, third party procedures, such as good offices, conciliation or mediation.

2. The claimant shall deliver to the respondent a written request for consultations setting out a brief description of facts regarding the measure or measures at issue.

3. For greater certainty, the initiation of consultations and negotiations shall not be construed as recognition of the jurisdiction of the tribunal.

Article 27: Submission of a Claim to Arbitration

1. In the event that a disputing party considers that an investment dispute cannot be settled by consultation and negotiation:

    (a) the claimant, on its own behalf, may submit to arbitration under this Section a claim

        (i) that the respondent has breached

            (A) an obligation under Articles 3 through 10,

            (B) an investment authorization, or

            (C) an investment agreement;

        and

        (ii) that the claimant has incurred loss or damage by reason of, or arising out of, that breach; and

    (b) the claimant, on behalf of an enterprise of the respondent that is a juridical person that the claimant owns or controls directly or indirectly, may submit to arbitration under this Section a claim

   (i) that the respondent has breached

      (A) an obligation under Articles 3 through 10,

      (B) an investment authorization, or

      (C) an investment agreement;

  and

   (ii) that the enterprise has incurred loss or damage by reason of, or arising out of, that breach,

provided that a claimant may submit pursuant to Subparagraph (a)(i)(C) or (b)(i)(C) a claim for breach of an investment agreement only if the subject matter of the claim and the claimed damages directly relate to the covered investment that was established or acquired, or sought to be established or acquired, in reliance on the relevant investment agreement.

2. At least 90 days before submitting any claim to arbitration under this Section, a claimant shall deliver to the respondent a written notice of its intention to submit the claim to arbitration ("notice of intent"). The notice shall specify:

   (a) the name and address of the claimant and, where a claim is submitted on behalf of an enterprise, the name, address, and place of incorporation of the enterprise;

   (b) for each claim, the provision of this Chapter, investment authorization, or investment agreement alleged to have been breached and any other relevant provisions;

   (c) the legal and factual basis for each claim; and

   (d) the relief sought and the approximate amounts of damages claimed.

3. Provided that six months have elapsed since the events giving rise to the claim, a claimant may submit a claim referred to in Paragraph 1:

   (a) under the ICSID Convention and the ICSID Rules of Procedure for Arbitration Proceedings, provided that both the respondent and the non-disputing Contracting Party are parties to the ICSID Convention;

   (b) under the ICSID Additional Facility Rules, provided that either the respondent or the non-disputing Contracting Party is a party to the ICSID Convention;

   (c) under the UNCITRAL Arbitration Rules; or

   (d) under the Rules of Dispute Settlement Mechanism of the International Centre for Dispute Prevention and Settlement Organisation (ICDPASO);[35]

---

35 For greater certainty, if a party selects application of the Rules of the ICDPASO then the process of dispute settlement shall be subject that rules and not be subject to the dispute resolution rules of this Chapter. For greater certainty, Rules of the ICDPASO is deemed to be incorporated in this Chapter.

4. A claim shall be deemed submitted to arbitration under this Section when the claimant's notice of or request for arbitration ("notice of arbitration"):

   (a) referred to in Paragraph 1 of Article 36 of the ICSID Convention is received by the Secretary-General;

   (b) referred to in Article 2 of Schedule C of the ICSID Additional Facility Rules is received by the Secretary-General;

   (c) referred to in Article 3 of the UNCITRAL Arbitration Rules, together with the statement of claim referred to in Article 20 of the UNCITRAL Arbitration Rules, are received by the respondent; or

   (d) referred to under the Rules of the International Centre for Dispute Prevention and Settlment Organisation (ICDPASO) selected under Paragraph 3(d) is received by the respondent.

A claim asserted by the claimant for the first time after such notice of arbitration is submitted shall be deemed submitted to arbitration under this Section on the date of its receipt under the applicable arbitral rules.

5. The arbitration rules applicable under Paragraph 3, and in effect on the date the claim or claims were submitted to arbitration under this Section, shall govern the arbitration except to the extent modified by this Chapter.

6. The claimant shall provide with the notice of arbitration:

   (a) the name of the arbitrator that the claimant appoints; or

   (b) the claimant's written consent for the Secretary-General to appoint that arbitrator.

Article 28: Consent of Each Contracting Party to Arbitration

1. Each Contracting Party consents to the submission of a claim to arbitration under this Section in accordance with this Chapter.

2. The consent under Paragraph 1 and the submission of a claim to arbitration under this Section shall satisfy the requirements of:

   (a) Chapter II of the ICSID Convention (Jurisdiction of the Centre) and the ICSID Additional Facility Rules for written consent of the parties to the dispute; [and]

   (b) Article II of the New York Convention for an "agreement in writing."

Article 29: Conditions and Limitations on Consent of Each Contracting Party

1. No claim may be submitted to arbitration under this Section if more than three years have elapsed from the date on which the claimant first acquired, or should have first acquired, knowledge of the breach alleged under Paragraph 1 of Article 27 and

knowledge that the claimant [for claims brought under Paragraph 1(a) of Article 27] or the enterprise [for claims brought under Paragraph 1(b) of Article 27] has incurred loss or damage.

2. No claim may be submitted to arbitration under this Section unless:

    (a) the claimant consents in writing to arbitration in accordance with the procedures set out in this Chapter; and

    (b) the notice of arbitration is accompanied,

        (i) for claims submitted to arbitration under Paragraph 1(a) of Article 27, by the claimant's written waiver, and

        (ii) for claims submitted to arbitration under Paragraph 1(b) of Article 27, by the claimant's and the enterprise's written waivers

of any right to initiate or continue before any administrative tribunal or court under the law of either Contracting Party, or other dispute settlement procedures, any proceeding with respect to any measure alleged to constitute a breach referred to in Article 27.

3. Notwithstanding Paragraph 2(b), the claimant (for claims brought under Paragraph 1(a) of Article 27) and the claimant or the enterprise (for claims brought under Paragraph 1(b) of Article 27) may initiate or continue an action that seeks interim injunctive relief and does not involve the payment of monetary damages before a judicial or administrative tribunal of the respondent, provided that the action is brought for the sole purpose of preserving the claimant's or the enterprise's rights and interests during the pendency of the arbitration.

Article 30: Selection of Arbitrators

1. Unless the disputing parties otherwise agree, the tribunal shall comprise three arbitrators, one arbitrator appointed by each of the disputing parties and the third, who shall be the presiding arbitrator, appointed by agreement of the disputing parties.

2. The Secretary-General shall serve as appointing authority for an arbitration under this Section.

3. Subject to Paragraph 4 of Article 27, if a tribunal has not been constituted within 75 days from the date that a claim is submitted to arbitration under this Section, the Secretary-General, on the request of a disputing party, shall appoint, in his or her discretion, the arbitrator or arbitrators not yet appointed.

4. For purposes of Article 39 of the ICSID Convention and Article 7 of Schedule C to the ICSID Additional Facility Rules, and without prejudice to an objection to an arbitrator on a ground other than nationality:

    (a) the respondent agrees to the appointment of each individual member of a tribunal established under the ICSID Convention or the ICSID Additional Facility Rules;

(b) a claimant referred to in Paragraph 1(a)   of Article 27 may submit a claim to arbitration under this Section, or continue a claim, under the ICSID Convention or the ICSID Additional Facility Rules, only on condition that the claimant agrees in writing to the appointment of each individual member of the tribunal; and

(c) a claimant referred to in Paragraph 1(b)   of Article 27 may submit a claim to arbitration under this Section, or continue a claim, under the ICSID Convention or the ICSID Additional Facility Rules, only on condition that the claimant and the enterprise agree in writing to the appointment of each individual member of the tribunal.

Article 31: Conduct of the Arbitration

1. The disputing parties may agree on the legal place of any arbitration under the arbitral rules applicable under Paragraph 3 of Article 27. If the disputing parties fail to reach agreement, the tribunal shall determine the place in accordance with the applicable arbitral rules, provided that the place shall be in the territory of a State that is a party to the New York Convention.

2. The non-disputing Contracting Party may make oral and written submissions to the tribunal regarding the interpretation of this Chapter.

3. The tribunal shall have the authority to accept and consider amicus curiae submissions from a person or entity that is not a disputing party.

4. Without prejudice to a tribunal's authority to address other objections as a preliminary question, a tribunal shall address and decide as a preliminary question any objection by the respondent that, as a matter of law, a claim submitted is not a claim for which an award in favor of the claimant may be made under Article 37.

(a) Such objection shall be submitted to the tribunal as soon as possible after the tribunal is constituted, and in no event later than the date the tribunal fixes for the respondent to submit its counter-memorial (or, in the case of an amendment to the notice of arbitration, the date the tribunal fixes for the respondent to submit its response to the amendment).

(b) On receipt of an objection under this Paragraph, the tribunal shall suspend any proceedings on the merits, establish a schedule for considering the objection consistent with any schedule it has established for considering any other preliminary question, and issue a decision or award on the objection, stating the grounds therefor.

(c) In deciding an objection under this Paragraph, the tribunal shall assume to be true claimant's factual allegations in support of any claim in the notice of arbitration (or any amendment thereof) and, in disputes brought under the UNCITRAL Arbitration Rules, the statement of claim referred to in Article

20 of the UNCITRAL Arbitration Rules. The tribunal may also consider any relevant facts not in dispute.

(d) The respondent does not waive any objection as to competence or any argument on the merits merely because the respondent did or did not raise an objection under this Paragraph or make use of the expedited procedure set out in Paragraph 5.

5. In the event that the respondent so requests within 45 days after the tribunal is constituted, the tribunal shall decide on an expedited basis an objection under paragraph 4 and any objection that the dispute is not within the tribunal's competence. The tribunal shall suspend any proceedings on the merits and issue a decision or award on the objection(s), stating the grounds therefor, no later than 150 days after the date of the request. However, if a disputing party requests a hearing, the tribunal may take an additional 30 days to issue the decision or award. Regardless of whether a hearing is requested, a tribunal may, on a showing of extraordinary cause, delay issuing its decision or award by an additional brief period, which may not exceed 30 days.

6. When it decides a respondent's objection under paragraph 4 or 5, the tribunal may, if warranted, award to the prevailing disputing party reasonable costs and attorney's fees incurred in submitting or opposing the objection. In determining whether such an award is warranted, the tribunal shall consider whether either the claimant's claim or the respondent's objection was frivolous, and shall provide the disputing parties a reasonable opportunity to comment.

7. A respondent may not assert as a defense, counterclaim, right of set-off, or for any other reason that the claimant has received or will receive indemnification or other compensation for all or part of the alleged damages pursuant to an insurance or guarantee contract.

8. A tribunal may order an interim measure of protection to preserve the rights of a disputing party, or to ensure that the tribunal's jurisdiction is made fully effective, including an order to preserve evidence in the possession or control of a disputing party or to protect the tribunal's jurisdiction. A tribunal may not order attachment or enjoin the application of a measure alleged to constitute a breach referred to in Article 27. For purposes of this Paragraph, an order includes a recommendation.

9. (a) In any arbitration conducted under this Section, at the request of a disputing party, a tribunal shall, before issuing a decision or award on liability, transmit its proposed decision or award to the disputing parties and to the non-disputing Contracting Party. Within 60 days after the tribunal transmits its proposed decision or award, the disputing parties may submit written comments to the tribunal concerning any aspect of its proposed decision or award. The tribunal shall consider any such comments and issue its decision or award not later than 45 days after the expiration of the 60-day comment period.

(b) Subparagraph (a) shall not apply in any arbitration conducted pursuant to this Section for which an appeal has been made available pursuant to Paragraph 10.

10. In the event that an appellate mechanism for reviewing awards rendered by investor-State dispute settlement tribunals is developed in the future under other institutional arrangements, the Contracting Parties shall consider whether awards rendered under Article 37 should be subject to that appellate mechanism. The Contracting Parties shall strive to ensure that any such appellate mechanism they consider adopting provides for transparency of proceedings similar to the transparency provisions established in Article 32.

Article 32: Transparency of Arbitral Proceedings

1. Subject to Paragraphs 2 and 4, the respondent shall, after receiving the following documents, promptly transmit them to the non-disputing Contracting Party and make them available to the public:

    (a) the notice of intent;

    (b) the notice of arbitration;

    (c) pleadings, memorials, and briefs submitted to the tribunal by a disputing party and any written submissions submitted pursuant to Paragraphs 2 (Non-Disputing Contracting Party submissions) and 3 (Amicus Submissions) of Article 31 and Article 36 (Consolidation);

    (d) minutes or transcripts of hearings of the tribunal, where available; and

    (e) orders, awards, and decisions of the tribunal.

2. The tribunal shall conduct hearings open to the public and shall determine, in consultation with the disputing parties, the appropriate logistical arrangements. However, any disputing party that intends to use information designated as protected information in a hearing shall so advise the tribunal. The tribunal shall make appropriate arrangements to protect the information from disclosure.

3. Nothing in this Section requires a respondent to disclose protected information or to furnish or allow access to information that it may withhold in accordance with Article 21 (Essential Security) or Article 22 (Disclosure of Information).

4. Any protected information that is submitted to the tribunal shall be protected from disclosure in accordance with the following procedures:

    (a) Subject to Subparagraph (d), neither the disputing parties nor the tribunal shall disclose to the non-disputing Contracting Party or to the public any protected information where the disputing party that provided the information clearly designates it in accordance with Subparagraph (b);

    (b) Any disputing party claiming that certain information constitutes protected information shall clearly designate the information at the time it is submitted to the tribunal;

(c) A disputing party shall, at the time it submits a document containing information claimed to be protected information, submit a redacted version of the document that does not contain the information. Only the redacted version shall be provided to the non-disputing Contracting Party and made public in accordance with paragraph 1; and

(d) The tribunal shall decide any objection regarding the designation of information claimed to be protected information. If the tribunal determines that such information was not properly designated, the disputing party that submitted the information may (i)withdraw all or part of its submission containing such information, or (ii) agree to resubmit complete and redacted documents with corrected designations in accordance with the tribunal's determination and Sub-paragraph (c). In either case, the other disputing party shall, whenever necessary, resubmit complete and redacted documents which either remove the information withdrawn under (i) by the disputing party that first submitted the information or redesignate the information consistent with the designation under (ii) of the disputing party that first submitted the information.

5. Nothing in this Section requires a respondent to withhold from the public information required to be disclosed by its laws.

Article 33: Governing Law

1. Subject to paragraph 3, when a claim is submitted under Paragraph 1(a)(i)(A) or Paragraph 1(b)(i)(A) of Article 27, the tribunal shall decide the issues in dispute in accordance with this Chapter and applicable rules of international law.

2. Subject to Paragraph 3 and the other provisions of this Section, when a claim is submitted under Paragraph 1(a)(i)(B) or (C) of Article 27, or Paragraph 1(b)(i)(B) or (C) of Article 27, the tribunal shall apply:

(a) the rules of law specified in the pertinent investment authorization or investment agreement, or as the disputing parties may otherwise agree; or

(b) if the rules of law have not been specified or otherwise agreed:

(i) the law of the respondent, including its rules on the conflict of laws;[36] and

(ii) such rules of international law as may be applicable.

3. A joint decision of the Contracting Parties, each acting through its representative designated for purposes of this Article, declaring their interpretation of a provision of this Chapter shall be binding on a tribunal, and any decision or award issued by a

---

36 The "law of the respondent" means the law that a domestic court or tribunal of proper jurisdiction would apply in the same case.

tribunal must be consistent with that joint decision.

Article 34: Interpretation of Annexes

1. Where a respondent asserts as a defense that the measure alleged to be a breach is within the scope of an entry set out in Annex I, II, or III, the tribunal shall, on request of the respondent, request the interpretation of the Contracting Parties on the issue. The Contracting Parties shall submit in writing any joint decision declaring their interpretation to the tribunal within 90 days of delivery of the request.

2. A joint decision issued under Paragraph 1 by the Contracting Parties, each acting through its representative designated for purposes of this Article, shall be binding on the tribunal, and any decision or award issued by the tribunal must be consistent with that joint decision. If the Contracting Parties fail to issue such a decision within 90 days, the tribunal shall decide the issue.

Article 35: Expert Reports

Without prejudice to the appointment of other kinds of experts where authorized by the applicable arbitration rules, a tribunal, at the request of a disputing party or, unless the disputing parties disapprove, on its own initiative, may appoint one or more experts to report to it in writing on any factual issue concerning environmental, health, safety, or other scientific matters raised by a disputing party in a proceeding, subject to such terms and conditions as the disputing parties may agree.

Article 36: Consolidation

1. Where two or more claims have been submitted separately to arbitration under Paragraph 1 of Article 27 and the claims have a question of law or fact in common and arise out of the same events or circumstances, any disputing party may seek a consolidation order in accordance with the agreement of all the disputing parties sought to be covered by the order or the terms of Paragraphs 2 through 10.

2. A disputing party that seeks a consolidation order under this Article shall deliver, in writing, a request to the Secretary-General and to all the disputing parties sought to be covered by the order and shall specify in the request:

    (a) the names and addresses of all the disputing parties sought to be covered by the order;

    (b) the nature of the order sought; and

    (c) the grounds on which the order is sought.

3. Unless the Secretary-General finds within 30 days after receiving a request under Paragraph 2 that the request is manifestly unfounded, a tribunal shall be established under this Article.

4. Unless all the disputing parties sought to be covered by the order otherwise

agree, a tribunal established under this Article shall comprise three arbitrators:

(a) one arbitrator appointed by agreement of the claimants;

(b) one arbitrator appointed by the respondent; and

(c) the presiding arbitrator appointed by the Secretary-General, provided, however, that the presiding arbitrator shall not be a national of either Contracting Party.

5. If, within 60 days after the Secretary-General receives a request made under Paragraph 2, the respondent fails or the claimants fail to appoint an arbitrator in accordance with Paragraph 4, the Secretary-General, on the request of any disputing party sought to be covered by the order, shall appoint the arbitrator or arbitrators not yet appointed. If the respondent fails to appoint an arbitrator, the Secretary-General shall appoint a national of the disputing Contracting Party, and if the claimants fail to appoint an arbitrator, the Secretary-General shall appoint a national of the non- disputing Contracting Party.

6. Where a tribunal established under this Article is satisfied that two or more claims that have been submitted to arbitration under Paragraph 1 of Article 27 have a question of law or fact in common, and arise out of the same events or circumstances, the tribunal may, in the interest of fair and efficient resolution of the claims, and after hearing the disputing parties, by order:

(a) assume jurisdiction over, and hear and determine together, all or part of the claims;

(b) assume jurisdiction over, and hear and determine one or more of the claims, the determination of which it believes would assist in the resolution of the others; or

(c) instruct a tribunal previously established under Article 30 (Selection of Arbitrators) to assume jurisdiction over, and hear and determine together, all or part of the claims, provided that

(i) that tribunal, at the request of any claimant not previously a disputing party before that tribunal, shall be reconstituted with its original members, except that the arbitrator for the claimants shall be appointed pursuant to Paragraphs 4(a) and 5; and

(ii) that tribunal shall decide whether any prior hearing shall be repeated.

7. Where a tribunal has been established under this Article, a claimant that has submitted a claim to arbitration under Paragraph 1 of Article 27 and that has not been named in a request made under paragraph 2 may make a written request to the tribunal that it be included in any order made under paragraph 6, and shall specify in the request:

(a) the name and address of the claimant;

(b) the nature of the order sought; and

(c) the grounds on which the order is sought.

The claimant shall deliver a copy of its request to the Secretary-General.

8. A tribunal established under this Article shall conduct its proceedings in accordance with the UNCITRAL Arbitration Rules, except as modified by this Section.

9. A tribunal established under Article 30 [Selection of Arbitrators] shall not have jurisdiction to decide a claim, or a part of a claim, over which a tribunal established or instructed under this Article has assumed jurisdiction.

10. On application of a disputing party, a tribunal established under this Article, pending its decision under Paragraph 6, may order that the proceedings of a tribunal established under Article 30 (Selection of Arbitrators) be stayed, unless the latter tribunal has already adjourned its proceedings.

Article 37: Awards

1. Where a tribunal makes a final award against a respondent, the tribunal may award, separately or in combination, only:

(a) monetary damages and any applicable interest; and

(b) restitution of property, in which case the award shall provide that the respondent may pay monetary damages and any applicable interest in lieu of restitution.

A tribunal may also award costs and attorney's fees in accordance with this Chapter and the applicable arbitration rules.

2. Subject to paragraph 1, where a claim is submitted to arbitration under Paragraph 1(b) of Article 27:

(a) an award of restitution of property shall provide that restitution be made to the enterprise;

(b) an award of monetary damages and any applicable interest shall provide that the sum be paid to the enterprise; and

(c) the award shall provide that it is made without prejudice to any right that any person may have in the relief under applicable domestic law.

3. A tribunal may not award punitive damages.

4. An award made by a tribunal shall have no binding force except between the disputing parties and in respect of the particular case.

5. Subject to paragraph 6 and the applicable review procedure for an interim award, a disputing party shall abide by and comply with an award without delay.

6. A disputing party may not seek enforcement of a final award until:

(a) in the case of a final award made under the ICSID Convention,

(i) 120 days have elapsed from the date the award was rendered and no disputing party has requested revision or annulment of the award; or

(ii) revision or annulment proceedings have been completed; and

(b) in the case of a final award under the ICSID Additional Facility Rules, the UNCITRAL Arbitration Rules, or the rules selected pursuant to Paragraph 3(d) of Article 27.

  (i) 90 days have elapsed from the date the award was rendered and no disputing party has commenced a proceeding to revise, set aside, or annul the award; or

  (ii) a court has dismissed or allowed an application to revise, set aside, or annul the award and there is no further appeal.

7. Each Contracting Party shall provide for the enforcement of an award in its territory.

8. If the respondent fails to abide by or comply with a final award, on delivery of a request by the non-disputing Contracting Party, a tribunal shall be established under Article 41 (State-State Dispute Settlement). Without prejudice to other remedies available under applicable rules of international law, the requesting Contracting Party may seek in such proceedings:

  (a) a determination that the failure to abide by or comply with the final award is inconsistent with the obligations of this Chapter; and

  (b) a recommendation that the respondent abides by or complies with the final award.

9. A disputing party may seek enforcement of an arbitration award under the ICSID Convention or the New York Convention [or the Inter-American Convention] regardless of whether proceedings have been taken under Paragraph 8.

10. A claim that is submitted to arbitration under this Section shall be considered to arise out of a commercial relationship or transaction for purposes of Article I of the New York Convention (and Article I of the Inter-American Convention).

Article 38. General Exceptions

1. Article XX of GATT 1994 and its interpretative notes are incorporated into and made part of this Agreement, mutatis mutandis.

2. The Contracting Parties understand that the measures referred to in Article XX(b) of GATT 1994 include environmental measures necessary to protect human, animal or plant life or health, and that Article XX(g) of GATT 1994 applies to measures relating to the conservation of living and non-living exhaustible natural resources.

3. Paragraphs (a), (b) and (c) of Article XIV of GATS are incorporated into and made part of this Agreement, mutatis mutandis. The Contracting Parties understand that the measures referred to in Article XIV(b) of GATS include environmental measures necessary to protect human, animal or plant life or health.

4. Nothing in this Agreement shall be construed to prevent a Contracting Party from taking action, including maintaining or increasing a customs duty, that is authorized

by the Dispute Settlement Body of the WTO or is taken as a result of a decision by a dispute settlement panel under a free trade agreement to which the Contracting Party taking action and the Contracting Party against which the action is taken are party.

Article 39: Annexes and Footnotes

The Annexes and footnotes shall form an integral part of this Chapter.

Article 40: Service of Documents

Delivery of notice and other documents on a Contracting Party shall be made to the place named for that Contracting Party in Annex C.

SECTION C

Article 41: State-State Dispute Settlement

1. Subject to Paragraph 5, any dispute between the Contracting Parties concerning the interpretation or application of this Chapter, that is not resolved through consultations or other diplomatic channels, shall be submitted on the request of either Contracting Party to arbitration for a binding decision or award by a tribunal in accordance with applicable rules of international law. In the absence of an agreement by the Contracting Parties to the contrary, the UNCITRAL Arbitration Rules shall govern, except as modified by the Contracting Parties or this Chapter.

2. Unless the Contracting Parties otherwise agree, the tribunal shall comprise three arbitrators, one arbitrator appointed by each Contracting Party and the third, who shall be the presiding arbitrator, appointed by agreement of the Contracting Parties. If a tribunal has not been constituted within 75 days from the date that a claim is submitted to arbitration under this Section, the Secretary-General, on the request of either Contracting Party, shall appoint, in his or her discretion, the arbitrator or arbitrators not yet appointed.

3. Expenses incurred by the arbitrators, and other costs of the proceedings, shall be paid for equally by the Contracting Parties. However, the tribunal may, in its discretion, direct that a higher proportion of the costs be paid by one of the Contracting Parties.

4. Paragraph 3 of Article 31 (Amicus Curiae Submissions), Article 32 (Transparency

of Arbitral Proceedings), Paragraphs 1 and 3 of Article 33 (Governing Law), and Article 34 (Interpretation of Annexes) shall apply mutatis mutandis to arbitrations under this Article.

5. Paragraphs 1 through 4 shall not apply to a matter arising under Article 12 or Article 13.

Article 42: The Foreign Investment Commission

1. The Contracting Parties hereby establish the Foreign Investment Commission (hereinafter referred to as "the Commission"), comprising cabinet-level representatives of the Contracting Parties or their designees.

2. The Commission shall:
   (a) supervise the implementation of this Chapter;
   (b) oversee its further elaboration;
   (c) resolve disputes that may arise regarding its interpretation or application;
   (d) adopt binding interpretations of the provisions of this Chapter;
   (e) adopt mutually agreed solutions reached in a mediation procedure pursuant to the relevant rules of ICDPASO.
   (f) supervise the work of all committees and working groups established under this Chapter;
   (g) consider any other matter that may affect the operation of this Chapter.

3. The Commission may:
   (a) establish, and delegate responsibilities to, ad hoc or standing committees, working groups or expert groups;
   (b) seek the advice of non-governmental persons or groups; and
   (c) take such other action in the exercise of its functions as the Contracting Parties may agree.

4. The Commission shall establish its rules and procedures. All decisions of the Commission shall be taken by consensus, except as the Commission may otherwise agree.

5. The Commission shall convene at least once a year in regular session. Regular sessions of the Commission shall be chaired successively by each Contracting Party.

Annex A. Customary International Law

The Contracting Parties confirm their shared understanding that "customary international law" generally and as specifically referenced in Article 6 (Minimum Standard of Treatment) and Annex B (Expropriation) results from a general and consistent practice of States that they follow from a sense of legal obligation. With regard to Article 6 (Minimum Standard of Treatment), the customary international law minimum standard of treatment of aliens refers to all customary international law principles that protect the economic rights and interests of aliens.

Annex B. Expropriation

The Contracting Parties confirm their shared understanding that:

1. Paragraph 1 of Article 8 (Expropriation and Compensation) is intended to reflect customary international law concerning the obligation of States with respect to expropriation.

2. An action or a series of actions by a Contracting Party cannot constitute an expropriation unless it interferes with a tangible or intangible property right or property interest in an investment.

3. Paragraph 1 of Article 8 (Expropriation and Compensation) addresses two situations. The first is direct expropriation, where an investment is nationalized or otherwise directly expropriated through formal transfer of title or outright seizure.

4. The second situation addressed by Paragraph 1 of Article 8 (Expropriation and Compensation) is indirect expropriation, where an action or series of actions by a Contracting Party has an effect equivalent to direct expropriation without formal transfer of title or outright seizure.

  (a) The determination of whether an action or series of actions by a Contracting Party, in a specific fact situation, constitutes an indirect expropriation, requires a case-by- case, fact-based inquiry that considers, among other factors:

(i) the economic impact of the government action, although the fact that an action or series of actions by a Contracting Party has an adverse effect on the economic value of an investment, standing alone, does not establish that an indirect expropriation has occurred;

(ii) the extent to which the government action interferes with distinct, reasonable investment-backed expectations; and

(iii) the character of the government action.

(b) Except in rare circumstances, non-discriminatory regulatory actions by a Contracting Party that are designed and applied to protect legitimate public welfare objectives, such as public health, safety, and the environment, do not constitute indirect expropriations.

Annex C. Service of Documents on a Contracting Party

[Country]

Notices and other documents shall be served on [Country] by delivery to: [insert place of delivery of notices and other documents for [Country]]

[Country]

Notices and other documents shall be served on [Country] by delivery to: [insert place of delivery of notices and other documents for [Country]]

CHAPTER - 8
INTELLECTUAL PROPERTY RIGHTS

Article 1: Definitions

For the purposes of this Chapter, unless the contrary intention appears:

"Geographical indication" means an indication which identifies a good as originating in the territory of a Contracting Party, or a region or a locality in that territory, where a given quality, reputation or other characteristic of the good is essentially attributable to its geographical origin;

"Intellectual property rights" means to copyright and related rights, rights in trademarks, geographical indications, industrial designs, patents and layout-designs (topographies) of integrated circuits, rights in plant varieties, and rights in undisclosed information, as defined and described in the TRIPS Agreement;

"National of a Contracting Party" includes, in respect of the relevant right, an entity of that Contracting Party that would meet the criteria for eligibility for protection provided for in the agreements listed in Article 1.3 of the TRIPS Agreement;

"Paris Convention" means the Paris Convention for the Protection of Industrial Property, as revised at Stockholm, July 14, 1967;

"Performance" means a performance fixed in a phonogram unless otherwise specified;

"TRIPS Agreement" means the Agreement on Trade-Related Aspects of Intellectual Property Rights, contained in Annex 1C to the WTO Agreement; and

"WIPO" means the World Intellectual Property Organization.

Article 2: Objectives

1. The protection and enforcement of intellectual property rights should contribute to the promotion of technological innovation and to the transfer and dissemination of technology, to the mutual advantage of producers and users of technological knowledge and in a manner conducive to social and economic welfare, and to a balance between

the legitimate interest of rights holders, users and the public interest.

2. The objective of this Chapter is to reduce distortion and impediments to trade and investment by promoting deeper economic integration and cooperation for implementation of the BRI projects through the effective and adequate creation, utilisation, protection, and enforcement of intellectual property rights, while recognising:

(a) the Contracting Parties' different levels of economic development and capacity, and differences in national legal systems;

(b) the need to promote innovation and creativity;

(c) the need to maintain an appropriate balance between the rights of intellectual property right holders and the legitimate interests of users and the public interest including public health;

(d) the importance of facilitating the diffusion of information, knowledge, content, culture, and the arts; and

(e) that establishing and maintaining a transparent intellectual property system and promoting and maintaining adequate and effective protection and enforcement of intellectual property rights provide confidence to right holders and users and helps in execution of the BRI projects.

3. The protection and enforcement of intellectual property rights should contribute to the promotion of technological innovation and to the transfer and dissemination of technology, to the mutual advantage of producers and users of technological knowledge and in a manner conducive to social and economic welfare, and to a balance of rights and obligations.

Article 3: Principles

The Contracting Parties recognize that:

(a) intellectual property protection promotes economic and social development and can reduce distortion and obstruction to international trade;

(b) intellectual property systems should not themselves become barriers to legitimate trade;

(c) appropriate measures, provided they are consistent with the provisions of the TRIPS Agreement[37] and this Chapter, may be needed to prevent the abuse of intellectual property rights by right holders, or the resort to practices which unreasonably restrain trade, are anticompetitive or adversely affect the international transfer of technology.

---

37 For greater certainty, "TRIPS Agreement" includes any amending protocol in force and any waiver made between the Parties of any provision of the TRIPS Agreement granted by WTO Contracting Parties in accordance with the WTO Agreement.

Article 4: International Agreement

Each Contracting Party affirms its commitment to the TRIPS Agreement and any other multilateral agreement relating to intellectual property to which the Contracting Parties are party. The Contracting Parties are encouraged to observe their international obligations with regards to intellectual property. Any violation of TRIPS Agreement or other multilateral agreement relating to intellectual property which the Contracting Parties are party may not constitute violation of this Agreement and vice-versa any violation of this Agreement may not constitute violation of TRIPS Agreement and other multilateral agreement relating to intellectual property.

For greater certainty the Contracting Parties agree to incorporate provisions of TRIPS Agreement Part I (General Provisions and Basic Principles), Part II (Standards Concerning the availability, scope and use of Intellectual Property Rights), Part III (Enforcement of Intellectual Property Rights), Part IV (Acquisition, and maintenance of intellectual property rights and related *inte-partes* procedures) are part of this Agreement and Contracting Parties agree to abide it irrespective of whether a Contracting Party is member of WTO or not.

Article 5: National Treatment

1. In respect of all categories of intellectual property covered in this Chapter, each Contracting Party shall accord to nationals of another Contracting Party treatment no less favourable than it accords to its own nationals with regard to the protection of intellectual property rights, subject to the exceptions provided under the TRIPS Agreement and those multilateral agreements concluded under the auspices of WIPO to which the Contracting Parties are party.

2. For the purposes of this Article, "protection" includes matters affecting the availability, acquisition, scope, maintenance and enforcement of intellectual property rights, as well as those matters affecting the use of intellectual property rights covered by this Chapter.

3. A Contracting Party may derogate from paragraph 1 in relation to its judicial and administrative procedures, including requiring a national of another Contracting Party to designate an address for service of process in its territory, or to appoint an agent in its territory, provided that such derogation is:

    (a) necessary to secure compliance with laws or regulations that are not inconsistent with this Chapter; and

    (b) not applied in a manner that would constitute a disguised restriction on trade.

4. Paragraph 1 does not apply to procedures provided in multilateral agreements concluded under the auspices of WIPO relating to the acquisition or maintenance of intellectual property rights.

Article 6: Transparency

1. To assist with the transparency of the operation of its intellectual property system, each Contracting Party shall endeavour to make available on the Internet its laws, regulations, procedures and administrative rulings of general application concerning the protection and enforcement of intellectual property rights.

2. Each Contracting Party shall, subject to its law, endeavour to make available on the Internet information that it makes public concerning applications for trademarks, geographical indications, designs, patents and plant variety rights.

3. Each Contracting Party shall, subject to its law, make available on the Internet information that it makes public concerning registered or granted trademarks, geographical indications, designs, patents and plant variety rights, sufficient to enable the public to become acquainted with those registered or granted rights.

Article 7: Intellectual Property and Public Health

The Contracting Parties recognize the principles established in the Doha Declaration on the TRIPS Agreement and Public Health adopted on 14 November 2001 by the Ministerial Conference of the WTO and confirm that the provisions of this Chapter are without prejudice to this Declaration. In particular, the Contracting Parties have reached the following understandings regarding this Chapter:

(a) the Contracting Parties affirm the right to fully use the flexibilities as duly recognised in the Doha Declaration on the TRIPS Agreement and Public Health;

(b) the Contracting Parties agree that this Chapter does not and should not prevent a Contracting Party from taking measures to protect public health; and

(c) the Contracting Parties affirm that this Chapter can and should be interpreted and implemented in a manner supportive of each Contracting Party's right to protect public health and, in particular, to promote access to medicines for all.

In recognition of the Contracting Parties' commitment to access to medicines and public health, this Chapter does not and should not prevent the effective utilisation of Article 31bis of the TRIPS Agreement, and the Annex and Appendix to the Annex to the TRIPS Agreement.

The Contracting Parties recognise the importance of contributing to the international efforts to implement Article 31bis of the TRIPS Agreement, and the Annex and Appendix to the Annex to the TRIPS Agreement.

The Contracting Parties agree that in the situation of pandemic e.g. COVID-19 the operation of this Chapter may be temporarily suspended so that vaccine, medicine or related equipment could be made available to public at large in the Belt and Road jurisdictions or region. Once the situation of pandemic is controlled or sufficient vaccine or medicine or related equipment are made available then the operation of this Chapter will be restored. Any measures taken by the Contracting Parties during the suspension of this Chapter shall not be construed as violation of this Chapter.

Article 8: Exhaustion of Intellectual Property Rights

Nothing in this Chapter prevents the Contracting Parties from determining whether, and under what conditions, the exhaustion of intellectual property rights applies under their legal system.

Article 9: Procedures on Acquisition and Maintenance

The Contracting Parties shall:
- (a) continue to work to enhance its examination and registration systems, including through improving examination procedures and quality systems;
- (b) provide applicants with a communication in writing of the reasons for any refusal to grant or register an intellectual property right;
- (c) provide an opportunity for interested parties to oppose the grant or registration of an intellectual property right, or to seek either revocation, cancellation or invalidation of an existing intellectual property right;
- (d) require that opposition, revocation, cancellation or invalidation decisions be reasoned and in writing; and
- (e) for the purposes of this Article, "writing" and "communication in writing" includes writing and communications in an electronic form.

Article 10: Protection of Copyright and Related Rights

1. Without prejudice to the obligations set out in the international agreements to which both the Contracting Parties are party, each Contracting Party shall, in accordance with its laws and regulations and this Chapter grant and ensure adequate and effective protection to the authors of works and to performers, producers of phonograms and broadcasting organizations for their works, performances, phonograms and broadcasts, respectively.[38]

2. Each Contracting Party shall provide that authors, performers, producers of phonograms, and broadcasting organizations have the right to authorize or prohibit reproductions of their works, performances, phonograms and broadcasts, in any manner or form.

3. Each Contracting Party shall provide that the term of protection of broadcast shall not be less than 50 years after the taking place of a broadcasting, whether this

---

38 For greater certainty, work includes a cinematographic work, photographic work and computer program.

broadcasting is transmitted by wire or over the air, including by cable or satellite.

Article 11: Broadcasting and Communication to the Public

1. Performers and producers of phonograms shall enjoy the right to remuneration for the direct or indirect use of phonograms published for commercial purposes for broadcasting or for any communication to the public.

2. Each Contracting Party shall provide broadcasting organizations with the exclusive right to authorize or prohibit:

(a) the re-broadcasting of their broadcasts;

(b) the fixation of their broadcasts; and

(c) the reproduction of fixations, made without their consent, of their broadcasts.

Article 12: Limitations and Exceptions

Each Contracting Party shall confine limitations or exceptions to exclusive rights to certain special cases that do not conflict with a normal exploitation of the work, performance, phonogram or broadcasting, and do not unreasonably prejudice the legitimate interests of the right holder.

Article 13: Types of Signs as Trademarks

The Contracting Parties agree to cooperate on the means to protect types of signs as trademarks, including visual and sound signs. Additionally, each Contracting Party shall make best efforts to register scent marks. A Contracting Party may require a concise and accurate description, or graphical representation, or both, as applicable, of the trademark.

Article 14: Trademarks Protection

1. Each Contracting Party shall grant adequate and effective protection to trademark right holders of goods and services.

2. Neither Contracting Party may require, as a condition of registration, that signs be visually perceptible, nor may either Contracting Party deny registration of a trademark solely on the grounds that the sign of which it is composed is a sound.

3. Each Contracting Party shall provide that the owner of a registered trademark shall have the exclusive right to prevent all third parties not having the owner's consent from using in the course of trade identical or similar signs for goods or services that are identical or similar to those goods or services in respect of which the owner's trademark is registered, where such use would result in a likelihood of confusion. In the case of the use of an identical sign, for identical goods or services, a likelihood of confusion shall be presumed. The rights described above shall not prejudice any existing prior rights, nor shall they affect the possibility of Parties making rights available on the

basis of use.

4. Each Contracting Party shall provide that the signs having the nature of deception shall not be used as trademarks and shall not be registered as trademarks.

Article 15: Well-known Trademarks

The Contracting Parties shall provide protection for well-known trademarks at least in accordance with Article 16.2 and 16.3 of the TRIPS Agreement and Article 6 bis of the Paris Convention for the Protection of Industrial Property, done at Paris on 20 March 1883.

Article 16: Exceptions to Trademarks Rights

Each Contracting Party may provide limited exceptions to the rights conferred by a trademark, such as fair use of descriptive terms, provided that such exceptions take account of the legitimate interests of the owner of the trademark and of third parties.

Article 17: Geographical Indications

1. The Parties recognize that geographical indications may be protected through a trademark or sui generis system or other legal means.

2. Without prejudice to Articles 22 and 23 of the TRIPS Agreement, the Parties shall take all necessary measures, in accordance with this Chapter, to ensure mutual protection of the geographical indications that are used to refer to goods originating in the territory of the Parties.

Article 18: Patents Protection

1. Subject to the provisions of paragraphs 2 and 3, patents shall be available for any inventions, whether products or processes, in all fields of technology, provided that they are new, involve an inventive step, and are capable of industrial application.

2. Each Contracting Party may exclude from patentability inventions, the prevention within its territory of the commercial exploitation of which is necessary to protect ordre public or morality, including to protect human, animal or plant life or health or to avoid serious prejudice to the environment, provided that such exclusion is not made merely because the exploitation is prohibited by its law.

3. Each Contracting Party may also exclude from patentability:
    (a) diagnostic, therapeutic, and surgical methods for the treatment of humans or animals; and
    (b) plants and animals other than micro-organisms, and essentially biological processes for the production of plants or animals other than non-biological and microbiological processes.

4. Each Contracting Party may provide limited exceptions to the exclusive rights

conferred by a patent, provided that such exceptions do not unreasonably conflict with a normal exploitation of the patent and do not unreasonably prejudice the legitimate interests of the patent owner, taking into account of the legitimate interests of third parties.

5. Each Contracting Party may provide an applicant with accelerated examination for the patent application in accordance with domestic laws and regulations, on which topic the Contracting Parties agree to enhance cooperation.

Article 19: Plant Breeder's Rights

The Contracting Parties, through their competent agencies, shall cooperate to encourage and facilitate the protection and development of plant breeders' rights with a view to:

    (a) better harmonizing the plant breeders' rights administrative systems of Contracting Parties, including enhancing the protection of species of mutual interest and exchanging information;

    (b) reducing unnecessary duplicative procedures between their respective plant breeders' rights examination systems; and

    (c) contributing to the reform and further development of the international plant breeders' rights laws, standards and practices, including within the Belt and Road regions.

Article 20: Protection of Undisclosed Information

1. In the course of ensuring effective protection against unfair competition, each Contracting Party shall protect undisclosed information in accordance with paragraph 2.

2. Natural and legal persons shall have the possibility of preventing information lawfully within their control from being disclosed to, acquired by, or used by others without their consent in a manner contrary to honest commercial practices[39], so long as such information:

    (a) is secret, in that it is not, as a body or in the precise configuration and assembly of its components, generally known among or readily accessible to persons within the circles that normally deal with the kind of information in question;

    (b) has commercial value because it is secret; and

    (c) has been subject to reasonable steps under the circumstances, taken by the

---

39 For the purposes of this provision, "a manner contrary to honest commercial practices" shall mean, at least, practices such as breach of contract, breach of confidence and inducement to breach, and includes the acquisition of undisclosed information by third parties who knew, or were grossly negligent in failing to know, that such practices were involved in the acquisition.

person lawfully in control of the information, to keep it secret.

Article 21: Cooperation in the Area of Genetic Resources and Traditional Knowledge

1. The Contracting Parties recognize the relevance of intellectual property systems and traditional knowledge associated with genetic resources to each other, when that traditional knowledge is related to those intellectual property systems.

2. The Contracting Parties shall endeavour to cooperate through their respective agencies responsible for intellectual property, or other relevant institutions, to enhance the understanding of issues connected with traditional knowledge associated with genetic resources, and genetic resources.

3. The Contracting Parties shall endeavour to pursue quality patent examination, which may include:

   (a) that in determining prior art, relevant publicly available documented information related to traditional knowledge associated with genetic resources may be taken into account;

   (b) an opportunity for third parties to cite, in writing, to the competent examining authority prior art disclosures that may have a bearing on patentability, including prior art disclosures related to traditional knowledge associated with genetic resources;

   (c) if applicable and appropriate, the use of databases or digital libraries containing traditional knowledge associated with genetic resources; and

   (d) cooperation in the training of patent examiners in the examination of patent applications related to traditional knowledge associated with genetic resources.

Article 22: Enforcement

1. Each Contracting Party commits to implementing effective intellectual property enforcement systems with a view to eliminating trade in goods and services infringing intellectual property rights.

2. Each Contracting Party shall provide for criminal procedures and penalties in accordance with the TRIPS Agreement to be applied at least in cases of willful trademark counterfeiting or copyright piracy on a commercial scale. Remedies available shall include imprisonment and/or monetary fines sufficient to provide a deterrent, and consistent with the level of penalties applied for crimes of a corresponding gravity.

3. The Contracting Parties agree that for the purpose of dispute resolution through alternative means (ADR) particularly, arbitration and mediation, any dispute, whether directly or incidentally relating to intellectual property rights, including shall be considered as capable of being settled through arbitration and mediation and shall not

in violative of the Contracting Parties public policy. Intellectual property right disputes include:

(a) a dispute over the enforceability, infringement, subsistence, validity, ownership, scope, duration or any other aspect of an IPR;

(b) a dispute over a transaction in respect of an IPR; and

(c) a dispute over any compensation payable for an IPR.

Article 23: Border Measures

1. Each Contracting Party shall ensure that the requirements necessary for a right holder to initiate procedures to suspend the release of goods suspected of being counterfeit trademark or pirated copyright goods shall not unreasonably deter recourse to these procedures.

2. Where its competent authorities have made a determination that goods are counterfeit trademark or pirated copyright goods (or have detained such suspected goods), each Contracting Party shall provide that its competent authorities have the authority to inform the right holder of at least the names and addresses of the consignor and the consignee, and of the quantity of the goods in question.

3. Each Contracting Party shall provide that its customs authorities may initiate border measures ex officio with respect to imported or exported goods suspected of being counterfeit trademark or pirated copyright goods.

4. Each Contracting Party shall ensure that its laws, regulations or policies permit relevant competent authorities, on receipt of information or complaints, to take measures in accordance with its laws to prevent the export of counterfeit trademark or pirated copyright goods.

5. The Contracting Parties may exclude from the application of this Article the importation or exportation of small quantities of goods which are considered to be of a noncommercial nature.

Article 24: Cooperation

1. The Parties shall endeavour to cooperate on the subject matter covered by this Chapter, such as through appropriate coordination, training and exchange of information between the respective intellectual property offices of the Parties, or other institutions, as determined by each Contracting Party. Cooperation may cover areas such as:

(a) developments in domestic and international intellectual property policy;

(b) intellectual property administration and registration systems;

(c) education and awareness relating to intellectual property;

(d) intellectual property issues relevant to:

(i) small and medium-sized enterprises;

(ii) science, technology and innovation activities; and

(iii)the generation, transfer and dissemination of technology;

(e) policies involving the use of intellectual property for research, innovation and economic growth;

(f) implementation of multilateral intellectual property agreements, such as those concluded or administered under the auspices of WIPO; and

(g) technical assistance for developing countries.

2. The Contracting Parties will consider opportunities for continuing cooperation under established arrangements in areas of mutual interest that aim to improve the operation of the intellectual property rights system, including administrative processes, in each other's jurisdictions. This cooperation could include, but is not necessarily limited to:

(a) work sharing in patent examination;

(b) enforcement of intellectual property rights;

(c) strengthening partnership in areas such as:

(i) offering necessary collaboration upon request from the other Party on evidence collection, technical assistance and information sharing when fighting against cross-border intellectual property crimes;

(ii) exchanges and cooperation on online copyright enforcement;

(iii)technology transfer on energy-saving and green technologies;

(iv) other areas that the Parties have consensus on.

(d) raising public awareness on intellectual property issues;

(e) improvement of patent examination quality and efficiency; and

(f) reducing the complexity and cost of obtaining the grant of a patent.

3. Each Contracting Party will consider requests for assistance from the other Party in a public health crisis in accordance with Article 6 of this Chapter.

Article 25: Consultative Mechanism: Committee on Intellectual Property

1. For the purposes of the effective implementation and operation of this Chapter, the Parties hereby establish a Committee on Intellectual Property ("the Committee").

2. The functions of the Committee shall be to:

(a) review and monitor the implementation and operation of this Chapter;

(b) discuss any issues related to intellectual property covered by this Chapter; and

(c) report its findings to the BNR Joint Commission.

3. The Committee shall be composed of representatives of each Contracting Party.

4. The Committee shall meet at such venues and times and by such means as may be agreed by the Contracting Parties.

CHAPTER - 9
PUBLIC HEALTH

Article 1: Purpose and Scope of Application

1. The Contracting Parties uphold the preamble to the Constitution of the WHO, which states that the enjoyment of the highest attainable standard of health is one of the fundamental rights of every human being without distinction of race, religion, political belief, economic or social condition, and that unequal development in different countries in the promotion of health and control of disease, especially communicable disease, is a common danger.

2. The Contracting Parties reaffirm the principles established in the International Health Regulations (IHR) and commit to develop and maintain their pandemic preparedness and response capacities, including through Belt and Road projects, on the basis of equity, solidarity and in a good faith.

3. The Contracting Parties recognize the principles established in the Doha Declaration on the TRIPS Agreement and Public Health adopted on 14 November 2001 by the Ministerial Conference of the WTO and confirm that the provisions of this Chapter are without prejudice to this Declaration.

4. In particular, the Contracting Parties have reached the following understandings regarding this Chapter:

(a) the Contracting Parties affirm the right to fully use the flexibilities as duly recognised in the Doha Declaration on the TRIPS Agreement and Public Health;

(b) the Contracting Parties agree that this Chapter does not and should not prevent a Contracting Party from taking measures to protect public health; and

(c) the Contracting Parties affirm that this Chapter can and should be interpreted and implemented in a manner supportive of each Contracting Party's right to protect public health and, in particular, to promote access to medicines for all.

5. In recognition of the Contracting Parties' commitment to access to medicines and public health, this Chapter does not and should not prevent the effective utilisation of Article 31bis of the TRIPS Agreement, and the Annex and Appendix to the Annex to the TRIPS Agreement.

6. The Contracting Parties recognise the importance of contributing to the international efforts to implement Article 31bis of the TRIPS Agreement, and the Annex and Appendix to the Annex to the TRIPS Agreement.

7. The Contracting Parties agree that a pandemic situation is extraordinary in nature and agree that in the situation of Public Health Emergency of International Concern (PHEIC), e.g. COVID-19, the operation of Chapter-8 (Intellectual Property Rights) of this Agreement, Intellectual Property Rights (IPR) may be temporarily suspended so that vaccines, oxygen supplies, personal protective equipment, medicines or related equipment could be made available to public at large in the Belt and Road jurisdictions or region. Once the situation of pandemic is controlled or sufficient vaccine or medicine or related equipment are made available then the operation of Chapter-8 (Intellectual Property Rights) of this Agreement will be restored. Any measures taken by the Contracting Parties during the suspension of Chapter-8 (Intellectual Property Rights) of this Agreement shall not be construed as violation of this Chapter.

Article 2: Regional Solidarity in Prevention, Preparedness and Response

The Contracting Parties agree, wherever possible, in form of the Belt and Road projects, to support and strengthen regional planning, prevention, preparedness and response to the spread of diseases, including through health systems readiness and resilience, with particular regard to the needs of the Parties which are low or lower-middle income countries and in the spirit of friendship and regional solidarity with a shared commitment to leave no one behind.

Article 3: Information-sharing and Coordination

1. The Contracting Parties recognize and understand the importance of timely access to information, as well as efficient risk communication, and therefore, the Contracting Parties agree to strengthen regional capacity building to identify health threats including through research and development cooperation, technological and information sharing in Belt and Road countries and region.

2. Each Contracting Party shall, subject to its law, endeavour to counter the dissemination of false and misleading information about public health events, preventive and anti-epidemic measures and activities in the media, social networks and other ways of disseminating such information, thereby strengthening public trust.

3. Exchange of information between the Contracting Parties pursuant to the implementation of these Chapter shall be exclusively for peaceful purposes and to protect public in Belt and Road countries and region.

Article 4: Data Interoperability

1. The Contracting Party shall endeavour, to the extent possible, to provide each

other with technical assistance and disseminate information through socio-culturally appropriate messages and risk communication management and periodically updated early warning system for assessing and progressively updating the national, regional, or global risk, based on the best available knowledge.

2. In order to enhance data interoperability, the Contracting Parties shall, to the extent possible, endeavour to issue health documents and certificates in digital or paper form based on open standards and implemented as open source as well as safeguards to reduce the risk of abuse and falsification and to ensure the protection and security of personal data contained in such documents.

Article 5: Collaboration and Access to Health

The Contracting Parties recognize that pandemics have a disproportionately heavy impact on frontline workers, notably health workers, the poor and persons in vulnerable situations, in particular in developing countries, and agree to enhance regional cooperation to facilitate access to health products, healthcare technologies and know-how required for effective Public Health Response, through the Belt and Road projects, wherever possible.

Article 6: Predictable Supply Chain and Logistics Network

The Contracting Parties agree to make reasonable efforts to facilitate and coordinate, as appropriate, the movement of essential health care workers, ensuring protection of supply chains of essential medical products in PHEIC, and repatriating of travellers, avoiding, to the extent possible, unnecessary interference with regional traffic, trade, livelihoods, human rights, and equitable access to health products and health care technologies and know-how in Belt and Road countries and region.

Article 7: Strengthening Public Health Literacy

1. The Contracting Parties commit to increase public awareness, including through BRI projects, and promote science, public health and pandemic literacy in the population, based on science and evidence.

2. The Contracting Parties shall endeavour to contribute to research and inform policies on factors that hinder adherence to public health and social measures, confidence and uptake of vaccines, use of appropriate therapeutics and trust in science and government institutions in the Belt and Road countries.

CHAPTER - 10

FINANCE

Article 1: Definitions

"A Contracting Party" means a country which has ratified or acceded this Agreement;

"Financial service" means a service of a financial nature including insurance and insurance related services, banking and other financial services (excluding insurance), and services incidental or auxiliary to a service of a financial nature. Financial services include the following activities;

(a) insurance and insurance-related services

   (i) Direct insurance (including co-insurance) of life or non-life;

   (ii) Reinsurance and retrocession;

   (iii)Insurance intermediation, such as brokerage and agency; or

   (iv)Services auxiliary to insurance, such as consultancy, actuarial, risk assessment, and claim settlement services; and

(b) banking and other financial services (excluding insurance):

   (i)   Acceptance of deposits and other repayable funds from the public;

   (ii)   Lending of all types, including consumer credit, mortgage credit, factoring, and financing of commercial transactions;

   (iii) Financial leasing;

   (iv) All payment and money transmission services, including credit, charge and debit cards, travelers cheques, and bankers drafts;

   (v)   Guarantees and commitments;

   (vi) Trading for own account or for account of customers, whether on an exchange, in an over-the-counter market or otherwise, the following:

      (A) money market instruments (including cheques, bills or certificates of deposits);

      (B) foreign exchange;

      (C) derivative products including futures and options;

      (D) exchange rate and interest rate instruments, including products such as swaps and forward rate agreements;

     (E) transferable securities; or

     (F) other negotiable instruments and financial assets, including bullion;

(vii) Participation in issues of all kinds of securities, including underwriting and placement as agent (whether publicly or privately), and supply of services related to such issues;

(viii) Money broking;

(ix) Asset management, such as cash or portfolio management, all forms of collective investment management, pension fund management, custodial, depository, and trust services;

(x) Settlement and clearing services for financial assets, including securities, derivative products, and other negotiable instruments;

(xi) Provision and transfer of financial information, and financial data processing and related software; or

(xii) Advisory, intermediation and other auxiliary financial services on all the activities listed in sub-sub-paragraphs (i) through (xi), including credit reference and analysis, investment and portfolio research and advice, and advice on acquisitions and on corporate restructuring and strategy;

"Financial institution" means any financial intermediary or other enterprise that is authorized to do business and regulated or supervised as a financial institution under the law of a Contracting Party in whose territory it is located including a branch in the territory of the Contracting Party of that financial service supplier whose head offices are located in the territory of another Contracting Party;

"Financial service supplier" means an enterprise including public entity of a Contracting Party that is engaged in the business of supplying a financial service within the territory of that Contracting Party and that seeks to supply or supplies a financial service through the cross-border supply of that service;

"Public entity" means:

(a) a government, a central bank or a monetary authority of a Contracting Party or any entity owned or controlled by a Contracting Party, that is principally engaged in carrying out governmental functions or activities for governmental purposes, but does not include an entity principally engaged in supplying financial services on commercial terms; or

(b) a private entity that performs functions normally performed by a central bank or monetary authority when exercising those functions;

"Trade in financial services" means the supply of a financial service:

(a) from the territory of one Contracting Party into the territory of another Contracting Party;

(b) in the territory of a Contracting Party to a person of another Contracting Party; or

(c) by a national of a Contracting Party in the territory of another Contracting Party.

Article 2: Applicability

1. This Chapter applies to a measure adopted or maintained by a Contracting Party relating to:

   (a) Financial institutions of the Contracting Party;

   (b) An investor of the Contracting Party, and an investment of that investor, in a financial institution in the Contracting Party's territory; and

   (c) Cross-border trade in financial services.

2. This Chapter shall not apply to measures adopted or maintained by a Contracting Party relating to:

   (a) Activities or services forming part of a public retirement plan or statutory system of social security; or

   (b) Activities or services conducted for the account or with the guarantee or using the financial resources of the Contracting Party, including its public entities,

Except that this Chapter shall apply to the extent that a Contracting Party allows any of the activities or services referred to in subparagraph (a) or (b) to be conducted by its financial institutions in competition with a public entity or a financial institution.

3. This Chapter shall not apply to government procurement of financial services.

4. This Chapter shall not apply to subsidies or grants with respect to the cross-border supply of financial services, including government-supported loans, guarantees and insurance

Article 3: National Treatment

1. Each Contracting Party shall accord to investors of another Contracting Party treatment not less favourable than that it accords to its own investors, in like circumstances, with respect to the establishment, acquisition, expansion, management, conduct, operation, and sale or other disposition of financial institutions and investments in financial institutions in its territory.

2. Each Contracting Party shall accord to financial institutions of another Contracting Party, and to investments of investors of another Contracting Party in financial institutions, treatment no less favourable than that it accords to its own financial institutions, and to investments of its own investors in financial institutions, in like circumstances, with respect to the establishment, acquisition, expansion, management, conduct, operation, and sale or other disposition of financial institutions and investments.

3. For greater certainty, the treatment to be accorded by a Contracting Party under paragraphs 1 and 2 means, with respect to a regional level of government, treatment no less favourable than the most favourable treatment accorded, in like circumstances, by that regional level of government to investors, financial institutions and investments of investors in financial institutions, of the Contracting Party of which it forms a part.

4. For the purposes of the national treatment obligations a Contracting Party shall accord to cross-border financial service suppliers of another Contracting Party treatment no less favourable than that it accords to its own financial service suppliers, in like circumstances, with respect to the supply of the relevant service.

Article 4: Most-Favoured-Nation Treatment

Each Contracting Party shall accord to:
- (a) investors of another Contracting Party, treatment no less favourable than that it accords to investors of any other Contracting Party in like circumstances;
- (b) financial institutions of another Contracting Party, treatment no less favourable than that it accords to financial institutions of other Contracting Parties in like circumstances;
- (c) investments of investors of another Contracting Party in financial institutions, treatment no less favourable than that it accords to investments of investors of other Contracting Parties in like circumstances; and
- (d) cross-border financial service suppliers of another Contracting Party, treatment no less favourable than that it accords to cross-border financial service suppliers of other Contracting Parties in like circumstances.

Article 5: Market Access

Any Contracting Party shall not adopt or maintain a measure with respect to a financial institution of any other Contracting Party, or with respect to market access through establishment of a financial institution by an investor of another Contracting Party, on the basis of its entire territory or on the basis of the territory of a national, provincial, territorial, regional, or local level of government that:
- (a) imposes limitations on:
  - (i) the number of financial institutions, whether in the form of numerical quotas, monopolies, exclusive service suppliers or the requirement of an economic needs test;
  - (ii) the total value of financial service transactions or assets in the form of numerical quotas or the requirement of an economic needs test;
  - (iii) the total number of financial service operations or the total quantity of financial services output expressed in terms of designated numerical units in the form of quotas or the requirement of an economic needs test;

(iv) the participation of foreign capital in terms of maximum percentage limit on foreign shareholding in financial institutions or the total value of individual or aggregate foreign investment in financial institutions; or

(v) the total number of natural persons that may be employed in a particular financial service sector or that a financial institution may employ and who are necessary for, and directly related to, the performance of a specific financial service in the form of numerical quotas or the requirement of an economic needs test; or

(b) restricts or requires specific types of legal entity or joint venture through which a financial institution may perform an economic activity.

Article 6: Cross-Border Trade

1. Each Contracting Party shall permit, under terms and conditions that accord national treatment, cross-border financial service suppliers of another Contracting Party to supply the financial services.

2. Each Contracting Party shall permit persons located in its territory, and its nationals wherever located, to purchase financial services from cross-border financial service suppliers of another Contracting Party located in the territory of a Contracting Party other than the permitting Contracting Party. This obligation does not require a Contracting Party to permit those suppliers to do business or solicit in its territory. A Contracting Party may define "doing business" and "solicitation" for the purposes of this obligation provided that those definitions are not inconsistent with the provisions of this Chapter.

3. Without prejudice to other means of prudential regulation of cross-border trade in financial services, a Contracting Party may require the registration or authorisation of cross-border financial service suppliers of another Contracting Party and of financial instruments.

Article 7: Transfer and Processing of Information

1. Each Contracting Party shall permit a financial institution or a cross-border financial service supplier of another Contracting Party to transfer information in electronic or other form, into and out of its territory, for data processing if processing is required in the ordinary course of business of the financial institution or the cross-border financial service supplier.

2. Each Contracting Party shall maintain adequate safeguards to protect privacy, in particular with regard to the transfer of personal information. If the transfer of financial information involves personal information, such transfers should be in accordance with the legislation governing the protection of personal information of the territory of the Contracting Party where the transfer has originated.

Article 8: Prudential Measures

1. This Agreement does not prevent a Contracting Party from adopting or maintaining reasonable measures for prudential reasons, including:

(a) the protection of investors, depositors, policy-holders, or persons to whom a financial institution, cross-border financial service supplier, or financial service supplier owes a fiduciary duty;

(b) the maintenance of the safety, soundness, integrity, or financial responsibility of a financial institution, cross-border financial service supplier, or financial service supplier; or

(c) ensuring the integrity and stability of a Contracting Party's financial system.

2. Without prejudice to other means of prudential regulation of cross-border trade in financial services, a Contracting Party may require the registration of cross-border financial service suppliers of another Contracting Party and of financial instruments.

Article 9: Effective and Transparent Regulation

1. Each Contracting Party shall ensure that all measures of general application are administered in a reasonable, objective, and impartial manner.

2. Each Contracting Party shall ensure that its laws, regulations, procedures, and administrative rulings of general application with respect to any matter are promptly published or made available in such a manner as to enable interested persons and other Contracting Parties to become acquainted with them. To the extent possible, each Contracting Party shall:

(a) publish in advance any such measures that it proposes to adopt;

(b) provide interested persons and other Contracting Parties a reasonable opportunity to comment on these proposed measures; and

(c) allow reasonable time between the final publication of the measures and the date they become effective.

3. Each Contracting Party shall maintain or establish appropriate mechanisms to respond within a reasonable period of time to an inquiry from any interested person regarding measures of general application.

4. A regulatory authority of a Contracting Party shall make an administrative decision on a completed application of any investor in a financial institution, any cross-border financial service supplier, or any financial institution of other Contracting Parties relating to the supply of a financial service within a reasonable period of time that is justified by the complexity of the application and the normal period of time established for the processing of the application.

Article 10: Payment and Clearing Systems

Under the terms and conditions that accord national treatment, each Contracting

Party shall grant financial service suppliers of other Contracting Parties established in its territory access to payment and clearing systems operated by the Contracting Party, or by an entity exercising governmental authority delegated to it by the Contracting Party, and access to official funding and refinancing facilities available in the normal course of ordinary business. This Article does not confer access to a Contracting Party's lender of last resort facilities.

Article 11: Financial Services Committee

1. The Contracting Parties will hereby establish a Committee on Financial Services (Committee). The principal representative of each Contracting Party shall be an official responsible for financial services.

2. The Committee shall:
   (a) supervise the implementation of this Chapter and its further elaboration;
   (b) consider issues regarding financial services that are referred to it by the Contracting Parties; and
   (c) participate in the dispute settlement procedures

3. The Committee shall meet annually, or as it decides otherwise, to assess the implementation of this Agreement as it applies to financial services.

Article 12: New Financial Services

1. Each Contracting Party shall permit any financial institution of other Contracting Parties to supply any new financial services that it permits its own financial institutions, in like situations, to supply under its laws, on request or notification to the relevant regulator, if required.

2. A Contracting Party may determine the institutional and juridical form through which a new financial service may be supplied and may require authorisation for the supply of the service. If authorisation is required, a decision shall be made within a reasonable period of time and the authorisation may only be refused for prudential reasons.

3. This Article does not prevent a financial institution of a Contracting Party from applying to another Contracting Party for authorising the supply of a financial service that is not supplied within either Contracting Party's territory. The application is subject to the law of the Contracting Party receiving it and is not subject to the obligations of this Article.

Article 13: Expedited Availability of Insurance Services

The Contracting Parties shall recognize the importance of maintaining and developing regulatory procedures to expedite the offering of insurance services by licensed suppliers. These procedures may include: allowing the introduction of products unless the products are disapproved within a reasonable period of time; not requiring product approval or authorisation of insurance lines for insurance other than insurance sold to individuals or compulsory insurances; or not imposing limitations on the number or frequency of product introductions. Where a Contracting Party maintains regulatory product approval procedures, it shall endeavour to maintain or improve those procedures.

Article 14: Performance Requirement

1. The Contracting Parties shall recognize that the performance of a financial institution in its territory by the head office or an affiliate of the financial institution, or by an unrelated service supplier, either inside or outside its territory, is important to the effective management and efficient operation of that financial institution. While a Contracting Party may require financial institutions to ensure compliance with any domestic requirements, it shall recognize the importance of avoiding imposition of any arbitrary requirements on the performance of the financial institutions.

2. For greater certainty, nothing in paragraph 1 prevents a Contracting Party from requiring financial institutions in its territory to retain certain functions.

Article 15: Self-regulatory Organizations

Where a Contracting Party requires financial institutions or cross-border financial service suppliers of other Contracting Parties to be parties of, participate in, or have access to, a self-regulatory organization to supply financial services in or into the territory of that Contracting Party, or grants a privilege or advantage when supplying a financial service through a self-regulatory organization, it shall ensure that the self-regulatory organization observes the obligations under this Agreement.

Article 16: Recognition

1. A Contracting Party may recognize prudential measures of another Contracting Party or a non-Contracting Party in the application of measures covered by this Chapter. The recognition may be:
   (a) accorded autonomously;
   (b) achieved through harmonization or other means; or
   (c) based upon an agreement or arrangement with another Contracting Party or a non-Contracting Party.

2. A Contracting Party that accords recognition of prudential measures under paragraph 1 shall provide adequate opportunities to the other Contracting Parties to demonstrate that circumstances exist in which there are or would be equivalent regulations, oversight, implementation of regulations and, if appropriate, procedures concerning the sharing of information between the relevant Contracting Parties.

3. Where a Contracting Party accords recognition of prudential measures under

paragraph 1(c) and the circumstances set out in paragraph 2 exist, it shall provide adequate opportunity to the other Contracting Parties to negotiate accession to the agreement or arrangement, or to negotiate a comparable agreement or arrangement.

Article 17: Specific Exceptions

1. These provisions will not apply to measures taken by a public entity in pursuit of monetary or exchange rate policies.

2. These provisions do not require any Contracting Party to furnish or allow access to information relating to the affairs and accounts of individual consumers, cross-border financial service suppliers, financial institutions, or to any confidential information which, if disclosed, would interfere with specific regulatory, supervisory, or law enforcement matters, or would otherwise be contrary to the public interest or prejudice legitimate commercial interests of particular enterprises.

3. No Contracting Party shall be prevented from adopting or maintaining measures for prudential reasons including for the protection of investors, depositors, policy holders, or persons to whom a fiduciary duty is owed by a financial institution or cross-border financial service supplier, or to ensure the integrity and stability of the financial system. Where these measures do not conform to the provisions of this Agreement to which this exception applies, they shall not be used as a means of avoiding a Contracting Party's commitments or obligations under those provisions.

4. Nothing herewith shall apply to non-discriminatory measures of general application taken by any public entity in pursuit of monetary and related credit policies or exchange rate policies.

5. A Contracting Party may prevent or limit transfers by a financial institution or cross-border financial service supplier to, or for the benefit of, an affiliate of or person related to such institution or supplier, through the equitable, non-discriminatory and good faith application of measures relating to maintenance of safety, soundness, integrity, or financial responsibility of financial institutions or cross-border financial service suppliers. This paragraph does not prejudice any other provisions of this Agreement that permit a Contracting Party to restrict such transfers.

6. For greater certainty, nothing herein shall be construed to prevent a Contracting Party from adopting or enforcing measures necessary to secure compliance with the laws and regulations that are not inconsistent with this Chapter, including those relating to the prevention of deceptive and fraudulent practices or to deal with the effects of a default on financial services contracts, subject to the requirement that such measures are not applied in a manner which would constitute a means of arbitrary or unjustifiable discrimination between the Contracting Parties or between a Contracting Party and a non-Contracting Party where like conditions prevail, or a disguised restriction on investments in the financial sector or cross-border trade in financial services.

CHAPTER - 11
INFRASTRUCTURE

Article 1: General Provisions

1. It is desirable to establish a favourable legal framework to promote and facilitate the implementation of public and/or privately financed infrastructure projects of Belt and Road by enhancing transparency, fairness and long-term sustainability and removing undesirable restrictions on public and/or private sector participation in infrastructure development and operation.

2. It is desirable to further develop the general principles of transparency, economy and fairness in the award of contracts by public authorities through the establishment of specific procedures for the award of infrastructure projects;

Article 2: Definitions

For the purposes of this Chapter:

"Bidder" or **"bidders"** means persons, including groups thereof, that participate in selection proceedings concerning an infrastructure project;

"Contracting authority" means the public authority that has the power to enter into a Infrastructure Project Contract for the implementation of an infrastructure project;

"Infrastructure Contract" means the mutually binding agreement or agreements between the contracting authority and the Infrastructure Contractor that set forth the terms and conditions for the implementation of an infrastructure project;

"Infrastructure facility" means physical (maybe add "including non-physical" infrastructure facility) facilities and systems that directly or indirectly provide services to the general public;

"Infrastructure project" means the design, Project, development and operation of new infrastructure facilities or the rehabilitation, modernization, expansion or operation of existing infrastructure facilities; (f) "Bidder" or "bidders" means persons, including groups thereof, that participate in selection proceedings concerning an infrastructure project;

"**Infrastructure Project Contractor**" means the person that carries out an infrastructure project under an Infrastructure Project Contract entered into with a contracting authority;

"**Regulatory agency**" means a public authority that is entrusted with the power to issue and enforce rules and regulations governing the infrastructure facility or the provision of the relevant services; and

"**Unsolicited proposal**" means any proposal relating to the implementation of an infrastructure project that is not submitted in response to a request or solicitation issued by the contracting authority within the context of a selection procedure.

Article 3: Authority to enter into Infrastructure Project Contracts

The public authority of the host government/s is considered to have the power to enter into Infrastructure Project Contracts for the implementation of infrastructure projects falling within their respective spheres of competence.

Article 4: Eligible Infrastructure Sectors

Infrastructure Project Contracts may be entered into by the relevant authorities in the sectors as agreed between relevant government/s.

Article 5: Selection of the Infrastructure Project Contractor

1. The selection of the Infrastructure Project Contractor shall be conducted in accordance with rules hereunder.

2. The contracting authority shall engage in pre-selection proceedings with a view to identifying bidders that are suitably qualified to implement the envisaged infrastructure project.

3. The invitation to participate in the pre-selection proceedings shall be widely published.

4. The invitation to participate in the pre-selection proceedings shall include at least the following:

    (a) A description of the infrastructure facility;

    (b) An indication of other essential elements of the project, such as the services to be delivered by the Infrastructure Project Contractor, the financial arrangements envisaged by the contracting authority (for example, whether the project will be entirely financed by user fees or tariffs or whether public or privately funds such as direct payments, loans or guarantees may be provided to the Infrastructure Project Contractor);

    (c) Where already known, a summary of the main required terms of the Infrastructure Project Contract to be entered into;

    (d) The manner and place for the submission of applications for pre- selection and the deadline for the submission, expressed as a specific date and time, allowing sufficient time for bidders to prepare and submit their applications; and

(e) The manner and place for solicitation of the pre-selection documents.

5. The pre-selection documents shall include at least the following information:

(a) The pre-selection criteria in accordance with provisions in Article 6 below;

(b) Whether the contracting authority intends to waive the limitations on the participation of consortia set forth in Article 7;

(c) Whether the contracting authority intends to request only a limited number of pre-selected bidders to submit proposals upon completion of the pre-selection proceedings in accordance with Article 7 and, if applicable, the manner in which this selection will be carried out;

(d) Whether the contracting authority intends to require the successful bidder to establish an independent legal entity established and incorporated under the laws of the host State/s in accordance with Article 25 (related to-Organisation of the Infrastructure Project Contractor).

Article 6: Pre-selection Criteria

1. In order to qualify for the selection proceedings, interested bidders must meet objectively justifiable criteria that the contracting authority considers appropriate in the particular proceedings, as stated in the pre-selection documents. These criteria shall include at least the following:

(a) Adequate professional and technical qualifications, human resources, equipment and other physical facilities as necessary to carry out all the phases of the project, including design, Project, operation and maintenance;

(b) Sufficient ability to manage the financial aspects of the project and capability to sustain its financing requirements; and

(c) Appropriate managerial and organisational capability, reliability and experience, including previous experience in operating similar infrastructure facilities.

Article 7: Participation of consortia

1. The contracting authority, when first inviting the participation of bidders in the selection proceedings, shall allow them to form bidding consortia. The information required from Contracting Parties of bidding consortia to demonstrate their qualifications in accordance with Article 6 shall relate to the consortium as a whole as well as to its individual participants.

2. Unless otherwise stated in the pre-selection documents, each Contracting Party of a consortium may participate, either directly or indirectly, in only one consortium at

the same time. A violation of this rule shall cause the disqualification of the consortium and of the individual Contracting Parties.

3. When considering the qualifications of bidding consortia, the contracting authority shall consider the capabilities of each of the consortium Contracting Parties and assess whether the combined qualifications of the consortium Contracting Parties are adequate to meet the needs of all phases of the project.

Article 8: Decision on Pre-selection

1. The contracting authority shall make a decision with respect to the qualifications of each bidder that has submitted an application for pre-selection. In reaching that decision, the contracting authority shall apply only the criteria that are set forth in the pre-selection documents. All pre-selected bidders shall thereafter be invited by the contracting authority to submit proposals in accordance with Articles 11-17.

2. Notwithstanding Article 10, the contracting authority may, provided that it has made an appropriate statement in the pre-selection documents to that effect, reserve the right to request proposals upon completion of the pre-selection proceedings only from a limited number of bidders that best meet the pre-selection criteria. For this purpose, the contracting authority shall rate the bidders that meet the pre-selection criteria on the basis of the criteria applied to assess their qualifications and draw up the list of bidders that will be invited to submit proposals upon completion of the pre-selection proceedings. In drawing up the list, the contracting authority shall apply only the manner of rating that is set forth in the pre-selection documents.

Article 9: Procedures for Requesting Proposals: Single-Stage and Two-Stage Procedures for Requesting Proposals

1. The contracting authority shall provide a set of the request for proposals and related documents issued in accordance with Article 10 (Related to Content of the request for proposals) to each pre-selected bidder that pays the price, if any, charged for those documents.

2. Notwithstanding the above, the contracting authority may use a two- stage procedure to request proposals from pre-selected bidders when the contracting authority does not deem it to be feasible to describe in the request for proposals the characteristics of the project such as project specifications, performance indicators, financial arrangements or contractual terms in a manner sufficiently detailed and precise to permit final proposals to be formulated.

3. Where a two-stage procedure is used, the following provisions apply:

    (a) The initial request for proposals shall call upon the bidders to submit, in the first stage of the procedure, initial proposals relating to project specifications, performance indicators, financing requirements or other characteristics of the project as well as to the main contractual terms proposed by the contracting authority;

(b) The contracting authority may convene meetings and hold discussions with any of the bidders to clarify questions concerning the initial request for proposals or the initial proposals and accompanying documents submitted by the bidders. The contracting authority shall prepare minutes of any such meeting or discussion containing the questions raised and the clarifications provided by the contracting authority;

(c) Following examination of the proposals received, the contracting authority may review and, as appropriate, revise the initial request for proposals by deleting or modifying any aspect of the initial project specifications, performance indicators, financing requirements or other characteristics of the project, including the main contractual terms, and any criterion for evaluating and comparing proposals and for ascertaining the successful bidder, as set forth in the initial request for proposals, as well as by adding characteristics or criteria to it. The contracting authority shall indicate in the record of the selection proceedings to be kept pursuant to Article 21 (Record of selection and award proceedings) the justification for any revision to the request for proposals. Any such deletion, modification or addition shall be communicated in the invitation to submit final proposals;

(d) In the second stage of the proceedings, the contracting authority shall invite the bidders to submit final proposals with respect to a single set of project specifications, performance indicators or contractual terms in accordance with Articles 10-16 (Article 10-Content of the request for proposals, Article 11-Bid securities, Article 12-Clarifications and modifications, Article 13-Evaluation criteria, Article 14- Comparison and evaluation of proposals, Article 15- Further demonstration of fulfilment of qualification criteria, Article 16- Final negotiations).

Article 10: Content Of The Request For Proposals

1. The request for proposals shall include at least the following information:

(a) General information as may be required by the bidders in order to prepare and submit their proposals;

(b) Project specifications and performance indicators, as appropriate, including the contracting authority's requirements regarding safety and security standards and environmental protection;

(c) The contractual terms proposed by the contracting authority, including an indication of which terms are deemed to be non-negotiable;

(d) The criteria for evaluating proposals and the thresholds, if any, set by the contracting authority for identifying non-responsive proposals; the relative weight to be accorded to each evaluation criterion; and the manner in which the criteria and thresholds are to be applied in the evaluation and rejection of proposals.

Article 11. Bid Securities

1. The request for proposals shall set forth the requirements with respect to the issuer and the nature, form, amount and other principal terms and conditions of the required bid security.

2. A bidder shall not forfeit any bid security that it may have been required to provide, other than in cases of:

(a) Withdrawal or modification of a proposal after the deadline for sub- mission of proposals and, if so stipulated in the request for proposals, before that deadline;

(b) Failure to enter into final negotiations with the contracting authority pursuant to Article 16, paragraph 1 (Final Negotiations);

(c) Failure to submit its best and final offer within the time limit prescribed by the contracting authority pursuant to Articles 16, paragraph 2 (Final Negotiations);

(d) Failure to sign the Infrastructure Project Contract, if required by the contracting authority to do so, after the proposal has been accepted;

(e) Failure to provide required security for the fulfilment of the Infrastructure Project Contract after the proposal has been accepted or to comply with any other condition prior to signing the Infrastructure Project Contract specified in the request for proposals.

Article 12: Clarifications and Modifications

The contracting authority may, whether on its own initiative or as a result of a request for clarification by a bidder, review and, as appropriate, revise any element of the request for proposals as set forth in Article 10 (Content of the request for proposals). The contracting authority shall indicate in the record of the selection proceedings to be kept pursuant to Article 21 (Record of selection and award proceedings) the justification for any revision to the request for proposals. Any such deletion, modification or addition shall be communicated to the bidders in the same manner as the request for proposals at a reasonable time prior to the deadline for submission of proposals.

Article 13: Evaluation Criteria

1. The criteria for the evaluation and comparison of the technical proposals shall include at least the following:

(a) Technical soundness;

(b) Compliance with environmental standards;

(c) Operational feasibility;

(d) Quality of services and measures to ensure their continuity.

2. The criteria for the evaluation and comparison of the financial and commercial proposals shall include, as appropriate:

(a) The present value of the proposed tolls, unit prices and other charges over the concession period;

(b) The present value of the proposed direct payments by the contracting authority, if any;

(c) The costs for design and Project activities, annual operation and maintenance costs, present value of capital costs and operating and maintenance costs;

(d) The extent of financial support, if any, expected from a public authority of the host State;

(e) The soundness of the proposed financial arrangements;

(f) The extent of acceptance of the negotiable contractual terms proposed by the contracting authority in the request for proposals;

(g) The social and economic development potential offered by the proposals.

Article 14: Comparison and Evaluation of Proposals

1. The contracting authority shall compare and evaluate each proposal in accordance with the evaluation criteria, the relative weight accorded to each such criterion and the evaluation process set forth in the request for proposals.

2. For the purposes of paragraph 1, the contracting authority may establish thresholds with respect to quality, technical, financial and commercial aspects. Proposals that fail to achieve the thresholds shall be regarded as non- responsive and rejected from the selection procedure.

Article 15: Further Demonstration of Fulfilment of Qualification Criteria

The contracting authority may require any bidder that has been pre- selected to demonstrate again its qualifications in accordance with the same criteria used for pre-selection. The contracting authority shall disqualify any bidder that fails to demonstrate again its qualifications if requested to do so.

Article 16: Final Negotiations

1. The contracting authority shall rank all responsive proposals on the basis of the evaluation criteria and invite for final negotiation of the Infrastructure Project Contract the bidder that has attained the best rating. Final negotiations shall not concern those contractual terms, if any, that were stated as non-negotiable in the final request for proposals.

2. If it becomes apparent to the contracting authority that the negotiations with the bidder invited will not result in an Infrastructure Project Contract, the contracting authority shall inform the bidder of its intention to terminate the negotiations and give the bidder reasonable time to formulate its best and final offer. If the contracting authority does not find that proposal acceptable, it shall terminate the negotiations with the bidder concerned. The contracting authority shall then invite for negotiations the other bidders in the order of their ranking until it arrives at an Infrastructure Project Contract or rejects all remaining proposals. The contracting authority shall not resume negotiations with a bidder with which negotiations have been terminated pursuant to this paragraph.

Article 17: Negotiation of Infrastructure Project Contracts without Competitive Procedures

1.Circumstances authorizing award without competitive procedures

Subject to approval by the host State/s the contracting authority is authorized to negotiate a Infrastructure Project Contract without using the procedure set forth in Articles 6 to 16 in the following cases:

(a) When there is an urgent need for ensuring continuity in the provision of the service and engaging in the procedures set forth in Articles 6 to 16 would be impractical, provided that the circumstances giving rise to the urgency were neither foreseeable by the contracting authority nor the result of dilatory conduct on its part;

(b) Where the project is of short duration and the anticipated initial investment value does not exceed the amount set forth by the host State as threshold below which a public and/or privately financed infrastructure may be awarded without competitive procedures.

(c) Where the project involves national defence or national security;

(d) Where there is only one source capable of providing the required service, such as when the provision of the service requires the use of intellectual property, trade secrets or other exclusive rights owned or possessed by a certain person or persons;

(e) When an invitation to the pre-selection proceedings or a request for proposals has been issued but no applications or proposals were submitted or all proposals failed to meet the evaluation criteria set forth in the request for proposals and if, in the judgement of the contracting authority, issuing a new invitation to the pre-selection proceedings and a new request for proposals would be unlikely to result in a project award within a required time frame;

(f) In other cases where the host State/s authorizes such an exception for compelling reasons of public interest.

Article 18: Procedures for Negotiation of an Infrastructure Project Contract

1. Where a Infrastructure Project Contract is negotiated without using the procedures set forth in Articles 6-16 the contracting authority shall:

    (a) Except for Infrastructure Project Contracts negotiated pursuant to Article 17, subparagraph (c) (Circumstances authorizing award without competitive procedures), cause a notice of its intention to commence negotiations in respect of an Infrastructure Project Contract to be published in accordance with the relevant law relating to publication procurement notices.

    (b) Engage in negotiations with as many persons as the contracting authority judges capable of carrying out the project as circumstances permit;

    (c) Establish evaluation criteria against which proposals shall be evaluated and ranked.

Article 19: Confidentiality

The contracting authority shall treat proposals in such a manner as to avoid the disclosure of their content to competing bidders. Any discussions, communications and negotiations between the contracting authority and a bidder, shall be confidential. Unless required by law or by a court order or permitted by the request for proposals, no party to the negotiations shall disclose to any other person any technical, price or other information in relation to discussions, communications and negotiations pursuant to the afore- mentioned provisions without the consent of the other party.

Article 20: Notice of Contract Award

Except for Infrastructure Project Contracts awarded pursuant to Article 17, subparagraph (c) (Circumstances authorizing award without competitive procedures), the contracting authority shall cause a notice of the contract award to be published. The notice shall identify the Infrastructure Project Contractor and include a summary of the essential terms of the Infrastructure Project Contract.

Article 21: Record of Selection and Award Proceedings

The contracting authority shall keep an appropriate record of information pertaining to the selection and award proceedings in accordance with the provisions of laws applicable on public procurement that govern record of procurement proceedings

Article 22: Review Procedures

A bidder that claims to have suffered, or that may suffer, loss or injury due to a breach of a duty imposed on the contracting authority by the law may seek review of the contracting authority's acts or failures to act in accordance with the provisions of its laws governing the review of decisions made in applicable procurement proceedings.

Article 23: Contents and Implementation of the Infrastructure Project Contract

The Infrastructure Project Contract shall provide for such matters as the parties deem appropriate, such as matters included in Annex-A of this Chapter.

Article 24: Governing Law

The Infrastructure Project Contract is governed by the law of the host State/s unless otherwise provided in the Infrastructure Project Contract. If an Infrastructure Project runs across more than one country then the law of the Host State will be applicable only on the part of the Project which falls within the Host State territorial jurisdiction.

Article 25: Organisation of the Infrastructure Project Contractor

The contracting authority may require that the successful bidder establish a legal entity incorporated under the laws of the Host State/s, provided that a statement to that effect was made in the pre-selection documents or in the request for proposals, as appropriate. Any requirement relating to the minimum capital of such a legal entity and the procedures for obtaining the approval of the contracting authority to its statute and bylaws and significant changes therein shall be set forth in the Infrastructure Project Contract consistent with the terms of the request for proposals.

Article 26: Ownership of Assets

1. The Infrastructure Project Contract shall specify, as appropriate, which assets are or shall be public property and which assets are or shall be the private property of the Infrastructure Project Contractor. The Infrastructure Project Contract shall in particular identify which assets belong to the following categories:

   (a) Assets, if any, that the Infrastructure Project Contractor is required to return or transfer to the contracting authority or to another entity indicated by the contracting authority in accordance with the terms of the Infrastructure Project Contract;

   (b) Assets, if any, that the contracting authority, at its option, may purchase from the Infrastructure Project Contractor; and

   (c) Assets, if any, that the Infrastructure Project Contractor may retain or dispose of upon expiry or termination of the Infrastructure Project Contract.

Article 27: Acquisition of Rights Related to the Project Site

1. The contracting authority or other public authority under the terms of the law and the Infrastructure Project Contract shall make available to the Infrastructure Project Contractor or, as appropriate, shall assist the Infrastructure Project Contractor in obtaining such rights related to the project site, including title thereto, as may be

necessary for the implementation of the project.

2. Any compulsory acquisition of land that may be required for the implementation of the project shall be carried out in accordance with the provisions of laws that govern compulsory acquisition of private property by public authorities of Host State/s for reasons of public interest.

Article 28: Easements

1. The Infrastructure Project Contractor shall have the right to enter upon, transit through or do work or fix installations upon property of third parties, as appropriate and required for the implementation of the project in accordance with State/s laws that govern easements and other similar rights enjoyed by public utility companies and infrastructure operators under its laws.

2. Any easements that may be required for the implementation of the project shall be created in accordance with the provisions of State/s laws that govern the creation of easements for reasons of public interest.

Article 29: Financial Arrangements

1. The Infrastructure Project Contractor shall have the right to charge, receive or collect tariffs or fees for the use of the facility or its services in accordance with the Infrastructure Project Contract, which shall provide for methods and formulas for the establishment and adjustment of those tariffs or fees in accordance with the rules established by the competent regulatory agency of State/s.

2. The contracting authority shall have the power to agree to make direct payments to the Infrastructure Project Contractor as a substitute for, or in addition to, tariffs or fees for the use of the facility or its services.

Article 30: Security Interests

1. Subject to any restriction that may be contained in the Infrastructure Project Contract, the Infrastructure Project Contractor has the right to create security interests over any of its assets, rights or interests, including those relating to the infrastructure project, as required to secure any financing needed for the project, including, in particular, the following:

 (a) Security over movable or immovable property owned by the Infrastructure Project Contractor or its interests in project assets;

 (b) A pledge of the proceeds of, and receivables owed to the Infrastructure Project Contractor for, the use of the facility or the services it provides.

2. The shareholders of the Infrastructure Project Contractor shall have the right to pledge or create any other security interest in their shares in the Infrastructure Project Contractor.

3. No security under paragraph 1 may be created over public property or other property, assets or rights needed for the provision of a public service, where the creation of such security is prohibited by the law of the host State/s.

Article 31: Assignment of the Infrastructure Project Contract

Except as otherwise provided in Article 30 (Security interests), the rights and obligations of the Infrastructure Project Contractor under the Infrastructure Project Contract may not be assigned to third parties without the consent of the contracting authority. The Infrastructure Project Contract shall set forth the conditions under which the contracting authority shall give its consent to an assignment of the rights and obligations of the Infrastructure Project Contractor under the Infrastructure Project Contract, including the acceptance by the new Infrastructure Project Contractor of all obligations thereunder and evidence of the new Infrastructure Project Contractor's technical and financial capability as necessary for providing the service.

Article 32: Transfer of Controlling Interest in the Infrastructure Project Contractor

Except as otherwise provided in the Infrastructure Project Contract, a controlling interest in the Infrastructure Project Contractor may not be transferred to third parties without the consent of the contracting authority. The Infrastructure Project Contract shall set forth the conditions under which consent of the contracting authority shall be given.

Article 33: Operation of infrastructure

1. The Infrastructure Project Contract shall set forth, as appropriate, the extent of the Infrastructure Project Contractor's obligations to ensure:
   (a) The modification of the service so as to meet the demand for the service;
   (b) The continuity of the service:
   (c) The provision of the service under essentially the same conditions for all users;
   (d) The non-discriminatory access, as appropriate, of other service pro- any public infrastructure network operated by the Infrastructure Project Contractor.

2. The Infrastructure Project Contractor shall have the right to issue and enforce rules governing the use of the facility, subject to the approval of the contracting authority or a regulatory body.

Article 34: Compensation for Specific Changes in Legislation

The Infrastructure Project Contract shall set forth the extent to which the

Infrastructure Project Contractor is entitled to compensation in the event that the cost of the Infrastructure Project Contractor's performance of the Infrastructure Project Contract has substantially increased or that the value that the Infrastructure Project Contractor receives for such performance has substantially diminished, as compared with the costs and the value of performance originally foreseen, as a result of changes in legislation or regulations specifically applicable to the infrastructure facility or the services it provides.

Article 35: Revision of the Infrastructure Project Contract

1. Without prejudice to Article 34 (compensation for specific changes in legislation), the Infrastructure Project Contract shall further set forth the extent to which the Infrastructure Project Contractor is entitled to a revision of the Infrastructure Project Contract with a view to providing compensation in the event that the cost of the Infrastructure Project Contractor's performance of the Infrastructure Project Contract has substantially increased or that the value that the Infrastructure Project Contractor receives for such performance has substantially diminished, as compared with the costs and the value of performance originally foreseen, as a result of:

(a) Changes in economic or financial conditions; or

(b) Changes in legislation or regulations not specifically applicable to the infrastructure facility or the services it provides;

provided that the economic, financial, legislative or regulatory changes:

(a) occur after the conclusion of the contract;

(b) are beyond the control of the Infrastructure Project Contractor; and

(c) are of such a nature that the Infrastructure Project Contractor could not reasonably be expected to have taken them into account at the time the Infrastructure Project Contract was negotiated or to have avoided or overcome their consequences.

2. The Infrastructure Project Contract shall establish procedures for revising the terms of the Infrastructure Project Contract following the occurrence of any such changes.

Article 36: Takeover of an infrastructure Project by the Contracting Authority

Under the circumstances set forth in the Infrastructure Project Contract, the contracting authority has the right to temporarily take over the operation of the facility for the purpose of ensuring the effective and uninterrupted delivery of the service in the event of serious failure by the Infrastructure Project Contractor to perform its obligations and to rectify the breach within a reasonable period of time after having been given notice by the contracting authority to do so.

Article 37: Substitution of the Infrastructure Project Contractor

The contracting authority may agree with the entities extending financing for an infrastructure project and the Infrastructure Project Contractor to provide for the substitution of the Infrastructure Project Contractor by a new entity or person appointed to perform under the existing Infrastructure Project Contract upon serious breach by the Infrastructure Project Contractor or other events that could otherwise justify the termination of the Infrastructure Project Contract or other similar circumstances.

Article 38: Duration, and Extension of the Infrastructure Project Contract

1. The duration of the concession shall be set forth in the concession contract. The contracting authority may not agree to extend its duration except as a result of the following circumstances:
   (a) Delay in completion or interruption of operation due to circumstances beyond the reasonable control of either party;
   (b) Project suspension brought about by acts of the contracting authority or other public authorities;
   (c) Increase in costs arising from requirements of the contracting authority not originally foreseen in the Infrastructure Project Contract, if the Infrastructure Project Contractor would not be able to recover such costs without such extension; or
   (d) Other circumstances, as specified by the Host State/s.

Article 39: Termination of the Infrastructure Project Contract by the Contracting Authority

1. The contracting authority may terminate the Infrastructure Project Contract:
   (a) In the event that it can no longer be reasonably expected that the Infrastructure Project Contractor will be able or willing to perform its obligations, owing to insolvency, serious breach or otherwise;
   (b) For compelling reasons of public interest, subject to payment of compensation to the Infrastructure Project Contractor, the terms of the compensation to be as agreed in the Infrastructure Project Contract;
   (c) Other circumstances that the Host State/s may consider necessary.

Article 40: Termination of the Infrastructure Project Contract by the Infrastructure Project Contractor

1. The Infrastructure Project Contractor may not terminate the Infrastructure Project Contract except under the following circumstances:
   (a) In the event of serious breach by the contracting authority or other public authority of its obligations in connection with the Infrastructure Project

Contract;

(b) If the conditions for a revision of the Infrastructure Project Contract under Paragraph 1 of Article 35 (Revision of the Infrastructure Project Contract) are met, but the parties have failed to agree on a revision of the Infrastructure Project Contract; or

(c) If the cost of the Infrastructure Project Contractor's performance of the Infrastructure Project Contract has substantially increased or the value that the Infrastructure Project Contractor receives for such performance has substantially diminished as a result of acts or omissions of the contracting authority or other public authorities, for instance, pursuant to Article 23 Annex-A, subparagraphs (h)   and (i)   (Contents and implementation of the Infrastructure Project Contract), and the parties have failed to agree on a revision of the Infrastructure Project Contract.

Article 41: Termination of the Infrastructure Project Contract by Either Party

Either party shall have the right to terminate the Infrastructure Project Contract in the event that the performance of its obligations is rendered impossible by circumstances beyond either party's reasonable control. The parties shall also have the right to terminate the Infrastructure Project Contract by mutual consent.

Article 42: Compensation upon Termination of the Infrastructure Project Contract

The Infrastructure Project Contract shall stipulate how compensation due to either party is calculated in the event of termination of the Infrastructure Project Contract, providing, where appropriate, for compensation for the fair value of works performed under the Infrastructure Project Contract, costs incurred or losses sustained by either party, including, as appropriate, lost profits.

Article 43: Wind-up and Transfer Measure upon Expiration or Termination of the Infrastructure Contract

1. The Infrastructure Project Contract shall provide, as appropriate, for:
   (a) Mechanisms and procedures for the transfer of assets to the contracting authority;
   (b) The compensation to which the Infrastructure Project Contractor may be entitled in respect of assets transferred to the contracting authority or to a new Infrastructure Project Contractor or purchased by the contracting authority;
   (c) The transfer of technology required for the operation of the facility;

(d) The training of the contracting authority's personnel or of a successor Infrastructure Project Contractor in the operation and maintenance of the facility;

(e) The provision, by the Infrastructure Project Contractor, of continuing support services and resources, including the supply of spare parts, if required, for a reasonable period after the transfer of the facility to the contracting authority or to a successor Infrastructure Project Contractor.

Article 44: Settlement of Disputes

Disputes between the contracting authority and the Infrastructure Project Contractor, Disputes involving customers or users of the infrastructure facility, other disputes

1. Any disputes arising out of or related to the Belt and Road Infrastructure project shall be settled through the dispute settlement mechanisms of the International Centre of Dispute Prevention and Settlement Organisation (ICDPSAO).

2. Where the Infrastructure Project Contractor provides services to the public or operates infrastructure facilities accessible to the public, the contracting authority may require the Infrastructure Project Contractor to establish simplified and efficient mechanisms for handling claims submitted by its customers or users of the infrastructure facility.

Annex A

The Infrastructure Project Contract shall provide for such matters as the parties deem appropriate, such as:

(a) The nature and scope of works to be performed and services to be provided by the Infrastructure Project Contractor;

(b) The conditions for provision of those services and the extent of exclusivity, if any, of the Infrastructure Project Contractor's rights under the Infrastructure Project Contract;

(c) The assistance that the contracting authority may provide to the Infrastructure Project Contractor in obtaining licences and permits to the extent necessary for the implementation of the infrastructure project;

(d) Any requirements relating to the establishment and minimum capital of a legal entity incorporated in accordance with Article 25 (Organisation of the Infrastructure Project Contractor);

(e) The ownership of assets related to the project and the obligations of the parties, as appropriate, concerning the acquisition of the project site and any necessary easements, in accordance with Articles 26 to 28 (Article 26- Ownership of assets, Article 27- Acquisition of rights related to the project site, Article 28- Easements);

(f) The remuneration of the Infrastructure Project Contractor, whether consisting of tariffs or fees for the use of the facility or the provision of services; the methods and formulas for the establishment or adjustment of any such tariffs or fees; and payments, if any, that may be made by the contracting authority or other public authority;

(g) Procedures for the review and approval of engineering designs, Project plans and specifications by the contracting authority, and the procedures for testing and final inspection, approval and acceptance of the infrastructure facility;

(h) The extent of the Infrastructure Project Contractor's obligations to ensure, as appropriate, the modification of the service so as to meet the actual demand for the service, its continuity and its provision under essentially the same conditions for all users;

(i) The contracting authority's or other public authority's right to monitor the works to be performed and services to be provided by the Infrastructure Project Contractor and the conditions and extent to which the contracting authority or a regulatory agency may order variations in respect of the works and conditions of service or take such other reasonable actions as they may find appropriate to ensure that the infrastructure facility is properly operated and the services are provided in accordance with the applicable legal and contractual requirements;

(j) The extent of the Infrastructure Project Contractor's obligation to provide the contracting authority or a regulatory agency, as appropriate, with reports and other information on its operations;

(k) Mechanisms to deal with additional costs and other consequences that might result from any order issued by the contracting authority or another public authority in connection with subparagraphs (h) and (i) above, including any compensation to which the Infrastructure Project Contractor might be entitled;

(l) Any rights of the contracting authority to review and approve major contracts to be entered into by the Infrastructure Project Contractor, in particular with the Infrastructure Project Contractor's own shareholders or other affiliated persons;

(m) Guarantees of performance to be provided and insurance policies to be maintained by the Infrastructure Project Contractor in connection with the implementation of the infrastructure project;

(n) Remedies available in the event of default of either party;

(o) The extent to which either party may be exempt from liability for failure or delay in complying with any obligation under the Infrastructure Project Contract owing to circumstances beyond its reasonable control;

(p) The duration of the Infrastructure Project Contract and the rights and obligations of the parties upon its expiry or termination;

(q) The manner for calculating compensation pursuant to Article 42 (Compensation upon termination of the Infrastructure Project Contract);

(r) The governing law and the mechanisms for the settlement of disputes that may arise between the contracting authority and the Infrastructure Project Contractor; and

(s) The rights and obligations of the parties with respect to confidential information.

CHAPTER - 12

COMPETITION

Article 1: Definitions

For the purposes of this Chapter:

"Anti-competitive business practices" mean business conduct or transactions that adversely affect competition in the territory of a Contracting Party, such as:

(a) agreements between enterprises, decisions by associations of enterprises and concerted practices, which have as their object or effect the prevention, restriction or distortion of competition in the territory of either Contracting Party as a whole or in a substantial part thereof;

(b) any abuse by one or more enterprises of a dominant position in the territory of either Contracting Party as a whole or in a substantial part thereof;

(c) private monopolization by one or more enterprises in the territory of either Contracting Party as a whole or in a substantial part thereof; or

(d) unfair trade practices; or

(e) concentrations between enterprises, which significantly impede effective competition, in particular as a result of the creation or strengthening of a dominant position or monopoly power in the territory of either Contracting Party as a whole or in a substantial part thereof;

"Undertakings" means natural persons, legal persons and any other organizations that are in engagement of commodities production, operation or service provision.

"State-owned enterprise" means an enterprise that is principally engaged in commercial activities in which a Contracting Party:

(a) directly owns more than 50 per cent of the share capital;

(b) controls, through ownership interests, the exercise of more than 50 per cent of the voting rights; or

(c) holds the power to control the enterprise through any other ownership interest, including indirect or minority ownership;[40] or

(d) holds the power to appoint a majority of members of the board of directors or any other equivalent management body.

Article 2: Objectives

Each Contracting Party understands that proscribing anti-competitive business practices of enterprises including State-owned enterprises (SOEs), implementing competition policies and cooperating on competition issues contribute to preventing the benefits of trade, services and investment liberalization from being undermined and to promoting economic efficiency and consumer welfare and enhances good business practices and ethics.

Article 3: Competition Laws and Authorities

1. Each Contracting Party shall endeavour to maintain or adopt competition laws that promote and protect the competitive process in its market by proscribing anti-competitive business practices.

2. Each Contracting Party shall endeavour to maintain an authority or authorities responsible for the enforcement of its national competition laws.

3. Each Contracting Party shall also endeavour to take appropriate actions, according to each Contracting Party's relevant laws and regulations with respect to anti-competitive business practices, which will prevent the benefits of trade, services and investment liberalization from being undermined.

Article 4: Application of Competition Laws

1. Each Contracting Party shall maintain its competition law that applies to all enterprises in all sectors of the economy and which addresses anti-competitive business practices in an effective manner.

2. Each Contracting Party shall apply its competition law to all enterprises, private or public, engaged in economic activities. This shall not prevent a Contracting Party from providing for exemptions from its competition law, provided that such exemptions are transparent and are limited to those necessary for securing public interest. Such exemptions shall not go beyond what is strictly necessary to achieve the public interest objectives that have been defined by that Contracting Party.

---

40 For the purposes of this subparagraph, a Contracting Party holds the power to control the enterprise if, through an ownership interest, it can determine or direct important matters affecting the enterprise, excluding minority shareholder protections. In determining whether a Contracting Party has this power, all relevant legal and factual elements shall be taken into account on a case-by-case basis. Those elements may include the power to determine or direct commercial operations, including major expenditures or investments; issuances of equity or significant debt offerings; or the restructuring, merger, or dissolution of the enterprise.

Article 5: Principles in Law Enforcement

1. Each Contracting Party shall be consistent with the principles of transparency, non-discrimination, rule of law and procedural fairness in the competition law enforcement.

Article 6: Transparency

1. Each Contracting Party is encouraged to make public, including on the Internet, its laws and regulations concerning competition policy, including procedural rules for an investigation.

2. Each Contracting Party is encouraged to ensure that all final administrative decisions finding a violation of its competition laws are in written form and set out any relevant findings of fact and the reasoning, including legal and, if applicable, economic analysis, on which the decision is based.

3. Each Contracting Party is encouraged to make public the decisions and any orders implementing them in a manner that enables interested persons and other Parties to become acquainted with them. The version of the decisions or orders that the Contracting Party makes available to the public shall not contain business confidential information or other information that is protected by its law from public disclosure.

4. On request of another Contracting Party, a Contracting Party shall strive to make available to the requesting Contracting Party public information concerning:

   (a) its competition law enforcement policies and practices; and

   (b) exemptions and immunities to its national competition laws, provided that the request specifies the particular good or service and market of concern and includes information explaining how the exemption or immunity may hinder trade or investment between the Parties.

Article 7: Non-discrimination

When applying its competition law, each Contracting Party shall respect the principle of non-discrimination for all enterprises, irrespective of the nationality and type of ownership of the enterprises.

Article 8: Procedural Fairness

1. When applying its competition law, each Contracting Party shall respect the principle of procedural fairness for all enterprises, irrespective of the nationality and type of ownership of the enterprises.

2. Each Contracting Party shall ensure that before it imposes a sanction or remedy against a person for violating its national competition laws, it affords that person:

   (a) information about the national competition authority's competition concerns;

   (b) a reasonable opportunity to be represented by counsel; and

(c) a reasonable opportunity to be heard and present evidence in its defence, except that a Contracting Party may provide for the person to be heard and present evidence within a reasonable time after it imposes an interim sanction or remedy.

In particular, each Contracting Party shall afford that person a reasonable opportunity to present evidence or testimony in its defence, including: if applicable, to offer the analysis of a properly qualified expert, to cross-examine any testifying witness; and to review and rebut the evidence introduced in the enforcement proceeding.[41]

3. Each Contracting Party shall adopt or maintain written procedures pursuant to which its national competition law investigations are conducted. If these investigations are not subject to definitive deadlines, each Contracting Party's national competition authorities shall endeavour to conduct their investigations within a reasonable time frame.

4. Each Contracting Party shall adopt or maintain rules of procedure and evidence that apply to enforcement proceedings concerning alleged violations of its national competition laws and the determination of sanctions and remedies thereunder. These rules shall include procedures for introducing evidence, including expert evidence if applicable, and shall apply equally to all parties to a proceeding.

5. Each Contracting Party shall provide a person that is subject to the imposition of a sanction or remedy for violation of its national competition laws with the opportunity to seek review of the sanction or remedy, including review of alleged substantive or procedural errors, in a court or other independent tribunal established under that Contracting Party's laws.

6. If a Contracting Party's national competition authority issues a public notice that reveals the existence of a pending or ongoing investigation, that authority shall avoid implying in that notice that the person referred to in that notice has engaged in the alleged conduct or violated the Contracting Party's national competition laws.

7. If a Contracting Party's national competition authority alleges a violation of its national competition laws, that authority shall be responsible for establishing the legal and factual basis for the alleged violation in an enforcement proceeding.[42]

8. Each Contracting Party shall provide for the protection of business confidential information, and other information treated as confidential under its law, obtained by its national competition authorities during the investigative process. If a Contracting Party's national competition authority uses or intends to use that information in an

---

41 For the purposes of this Article, "enforcement proceedings" means judicial or administrative proceedings following an investigation into the alleged violation of the competition laws.

42 Nothing in this paragraph shall prevent a Contracting Party from requiring that a person against whom such an allegation is made be responsible for establishing certain elements in defence of the allegation.

enforcement proceeding, the Contracting Party shall, if it is permissible under its law and as appropriate, provide a procedure to allow the person under investigation timely access to information that is necessary to prepare an adequate defence to the national competition authority's allegations.

9. Each Contracting Party shall ensure that its national competition authorities afford a person under investigation for possible violation of the national competition laws of that Contracting Party reasonable opportunity to consult with those competition authorities with respect to significant legal, factual or procedural issues that arise during the investigation.

Article 9: Cooperation in Law Enforcement

1. The Contracting Parties recognise the importance of cooperation and coordination in competition field, to promote effective competition law enforcement. Accordingly, each Contracting Party is encouraged to:

(a) cooperate in the area of competition policy by exchanging information on the development of competition policy; and

(b) cooperate, as appropriate, on issues of competition law enforcement, including through notification, consultation and the exchange of information.

2. A Contracting Party's national competition authorities may consider entering into a cooperation arrangement or agreement with the competition authorities of another Contracting Party that sets out mutually agreed terms of cooperation.

3. The Parties agree to cooperate in a manner compatible with their respective laws, regulations and important interests, and within their reasonably available resources.

Article 10: Notification

In a cooperation arrangement or agreement in the meaning of Article 9.2, Contracting Parties' national competition authorities may agree terms of notification, including the following provisions:

(a) Each Contracting Party, through its competition authority or authorities, is encouraged to notify the other Contracting Party of an enforcement activity if it considers that such enforcement activity may substantially affect the other Contracting Party's important interests.

(b) Provided that it is not contrary to the Contracting Parties' competition laws and does not affect any investigation being carried out, the Contracting Parties shall endeavour to notify at an early stage and in a detailed manner which is enough to permit an evaluation in the light of the interests of the other Contracting Party.

(c) The Contracting Parties undertake to exert their best efforts to ensure that notifications are made in the circumstances set out above, taking into account the administrative resources available to them.

Article 11: Exchange of Information

In a cooperation arrangement or agreement in the meaning of Article 9.2, the Contracting Parties' national competition authorities may agree terms of the exchange of Information, including the following provisions:

(a) Each Contracting Party shall endeavour to, upon request of the other Contracting Party, provide information to facilitate effective enforcement of their respective competition laws, provided that it does not affect any ongoing investigation and is compatible with the laws and regulations governing the agencies possessing the information.

(b) Each Contracting Party shall maintain the confidentiality of any information provided as confidential by the competition authority of the other Contracting Party and shall not disclose such information to any entity that is not authorized by the Contracting Party providing information.

Article 12: Technical Cooperation

Recognising that the Contracting Parties can benefit by sharing their diverse experience in developing, applying and enforcing competition law and in developing and implementing competition policies, the Contracting Parties shall consider undertaking mutually agreed technical cooperation activities, subject to available resources, including:

(a) providing advice or training on relevant issues, including through the exchange of officials;

(b) exchanging information and experiences on competition advocacy, including ways to promote a culture of competition; and

(c) assisting a Contracting Party as it implements a new national competition law.

Article 13: Consumer Protection

1. The Contracting Parties recognise the importance of consumer protection policy and enforcement to creating efficient and competitive markets and enhancing consumer welfare in the free trade area.

2. For the purposes of this Article, fraudulent and deceptive commercial activities refer to those fraudulent and deceptive commercial practices that cause actual harm to consumers, or that pose an imminent threat of such harm if not prevented, for example:

(a) a practice of making misrepresentations of material fact, including implied factual misrepresentations, that cause significant detriment to the economic interests of misled consumers;

(b) a practice of failing to deliver products or provide services to consumers after the consumers are charged; or

(c) a practice of charging or debiting consumers' financial, telephone or other accounts without authorisation.

3. Each Contracting Party is encouraged to adopt or maintain consumer protection laws or other laws or regulations that proscribe fraudulent and deceptive commercial activities.[43]

4. The Contracting Parties recognise that fraudulent and deceptive commercial activities increasingly transcend national borders and that cooperation and coordination between the Parties is desirable to effectively address these activities.

5. Accordingly, the Contracting Parties shall promote, as appropriate, cooperation and coordination on matters of mutual interest related to fraudulent and deceptive commercial activities, including in the enforcement of their consumer protection laws.

6. The Contracting Parties shall endeavour to cooperate and coordinate on the matters set out in this Article through the relevant national public bodies or officials responsible for consumer protection policy, laws or enforcement, as determined by each Contracting Party and compatible with their respective laws, regulations and important interests and within their reasonably available resources.

Article 14: Consultation

1. To foster understanding between the Contracting Parties, or to address specific matters that arise under this Chapter, each Contracting Party shall, on request of the other Contracting Party, enter into consultations regarding representations made by the other Contracting Party. In its request, the Contracting Party shall indicate, if relevant, how the matter affects trade or investment between the Parties.

2. Specific matters which can be subject to consultation in the meaning of the preceding paragraph include those regarding enforcement activity by the Contracting Party to which a request for consultations has been addressed, which may substantially affect the requesting Contracting Party's important interests, such as:

(a) enforcement activity against enterprises of the requesting Contracting Party;

(b) enforcement activity resulting in extraterritorial remedies conducted in the requesting Contracting Party; and

(c) lack of enforcement activity resulting in toleration of alleged anticompetitive business practices which may affect the interests of enterprises or consumers of the requesting Contracting Party.

3. The Contracting Party to which a request for consultations has been addressed,

---

43 For greater certainty, the laws or regulations a Party adopts or maintains to proscribe these activities can be civil or criminal in nature.

shall accord full and sympathetic consideration to the concerns raised by the other Contracting Party.

4. To facilitate discussion of the matter that is the subject of the consultations, each Contracting Party shall endeavour to provide relevant non-confidential information to the other Contracting Party, such as:

(a) any relevant findings of fact and the reasoning, including legal and, if applicable, economic analysis, on which the decision is based;

(b) any relevant findings of fact and the reasoning, including legal and, if applicable, economic analysis, which can justify extraterritorial remedies; and

(c) any relevant findings of fact and the reasoning, including legal and, if applicable, economic analysis, which can justify toleration of alleged anticompetitive business practices.

Article 15: Dispute Settlement

If a Contracting Party considers that a given practice continues to affect trade or investment in the sense of this Chapter, it may request consultation to the other Contracting Party in the Joint Commission with a view to facilitating a resolution of the matter.

CHAPTER - 13
ENVIRONMENT

Article 1: Objectives

1. The Contracting Parties recognize that economic development, social development and environmental protection are interdependent and mutually supportive components of sustainable development. They underline the benefit of cooperation on environmental issues as part of a global approach to sustainable development.

2. The Contracting Parties reaffirm their commitments to promoting economic development, resulting from the BRI projects, in such a way as to contribute to the objective of sustainable development and to ensuring that this objective is integrated and reflected in their trade relationship.

3. The Contracting Parties recognise that it is inappropriate to encourage trade or investment by weakening or reducing the protection afforded in their respective environmental laws. Accordingly, a Contracting Party shall not waive or otherwise derogate from, or offer to waive or otherwise derogate from, its environmental laws in a manner that weakens or reduces the protection afforded in those laws in order to encourage trade or investment between the Contracting Parties.

4. The Contracting Parties agree that environmental standards should not be used for protectionist purposes.

Article 2: Scope

Except as otherwise provided in this Chapter, this Chapter applies to the measures including laws and regulations adopted or maintained by the Contracting Parties for addressing environmental issues in relation to BRI.

Article 3: Levels of Protection

1. The Parties reaffirm each Contracting Party's sovereign right to establish its own levels of environmental protection and its own environmental development priorities, and to adopt or modify its environmental laws and policies.

2. Each Contracting Party shall seek to ensure that those laws and policies provide

for and encourage high levels of environmental protection, and shall strive to continue to improve its respective levels of environmental protection.

Article 4: Multilateral Environmental Agreements and Environmental Principles

1. The Contracting Parties recognize that multilateral environmental agreements (hereinafter referred to as "MEAs") play an important role globally and domestically in protecting the environment. The Contracting Parties further recognize that this Chapter can contribute to realizing the goals of such agreements.

2. The Contracting Parties commit to consulting and cooperating as appropriate with respect to negotiations in the MEAs to which Contracting Parties are party on trade-related environmental issues of mutual interest.

3. The Contracting Parties reaffirm their commitments to the effective implementation in their laws and practices of the MEAs to which Contracting Parties are party.

4. The Contracting Parties reaffirm their commitment to the effective implementation in their laws and practices of multilateral environmental agreements to which they are a party, as well as of the environmental principles and obligations reflected namely in the international instruments referred to in Article 1 of this Chapter. They shall strive to further improve the level of environmental protection by all means, including by effective implementation of their environmental laws and regulations.

5. The Contracting Parties recognise that it is inappropriate to encourage trade or investment or any BRI projects by weakening or reducing the protections afforded in domestic environmental laws, regulations, policies and practices. The Contracting Parties agree that environmental standards shall not be used for protectionist trade purposes.

6. The Contracting Parties recognise the importance, when preparing and implementing measures related to the environment, of taking account of scientific, technical and other information, and relevant international guidelines.

Article 5: Promotion of the Dissemination of Goods and Services Favouring the Environment

1. The Contracting Parties shall strive to facilitate and promote investment and dissemination of goods, services, and technologies beneficial to the environment in carrying out the BRI projects.

2. For the purpose of paragraph 1, the Contracting Parties agree to exchange views and will consider cooperation in this area.

3. The Contracting Parties shall encourage cooperation between enterprises in relation to goods, services and technologies that are beneficial to the environment in

carrying out the BRI projects.

Article 6: Enforcement of Environmental Measures Including Laws and Regulations

1. A Contracting Party shall not fail to effectively enforce its environmental measures including laws and regulations, through a sustained or recurring course of action or inaction, in a manner affecting trade or investment between the Contracting Parties.

2. The Contracting Parties recognize that it is inappropriate to encourage trade, services or investment by weakening or reducing the protections afforded in its environmental laws, regulations, policies and practices. Accordingly, neither Contracting Party shall waive or otherwise derogate from such laws, regulations, policies and practices in a manner that weakens or reduces the protections afforded in those laws, regulations, policies and practices.

3. Nothing in this Chapter shall be construed to empower a Contracting Party's authorities to undertake environmental law enforcement activities in the territory of the other Contracting Party.

Article 7: Environmental Impact

1. The Contracting Parties commit to reviewing the impact of the implementation of this Agreement and the BRI projects on environment, at appropriate time after adopting this Agreement, through their respective participative processes and institutions.

2. The Contracting Parties, as appropriate, share information with the other Contracting Party on techniques and methods in reviewing the environmental impacts of this Agreement and the BRI projects.

Article 8: Cooperation

1. Recognizing the importance of cooperation in the field of environment in achieving the goals of sustainable development, the Contracting Parties commit to building on the existing bilateral agreements or arrangements and to further strengthening cooperative activities in areas of common interest.

2. In order to promote the achievement of the objectives of this Chapter and to assist in the fulfillment of their obligations pursuant to it, the Contracting Parties have established the following indicative list of areas of cooperation:

   (a) promotion of the dissemination of environmental goods including environmentally-friendly products and environmental services;
   (b) cooperation on development of environmental technology and promotion of environmental industry;
   (c) exchange of information on policies, activities and measures for

environmental protection;

(d) establishment of environmental think-tanks cooperation mechanisms including exchange of environmental experts;

(e) capacity building which includes workshops, seminars, fairs and exhibition in the field of the environment;

(f) build-up of environmental industry base in respective countries as a pilot area or around the BRI projects; and

(g) other forms of environmental cooperation as the Contracting Parties may deem appropriate.

3. The Contracting Parties shall exert their best efforts to ensure that the applications and benefits of cooperative activities between them are as broad as possible.

Article 9: Institutional Arrangement

1. Each Contracting Party shall designate an office within its administration which shall serve as a contact point with the other Contracting Party for the purpose of implementing this Chapter and the BRI projects.

2. A Contracting Party may through the contact points request consultations regarding any matter arising under this Chapter.

3. The Contracting Parties hereby establish a Committee on Environment and Trade (hereinafter in this Chapter referred to as the "Committee"). The Committee shall comprise senior officials from within the administrations of the Parties.

4. The Committee shall meet when deemed necessary to oversee the implementation of this Chapter.

Article 10: Implementation and Consultations

1. A Contracting Party may through the contact points request consultations within the Committee regarding any matter arising under this Chapter. The Parties shall make every attempt to arrive at a mutually satisfactory resolution of the matter.

2. If a Contracting Party considers that a measure of the other Contracting Party does not comply with the provisions of this Chapter, it may have recourse exclusively to bilateral consultations and dialogue in the Committee or use the International Centre for Dispute Prevention and Settlement Organisations (ICDPASO) Dispute Resolution process.

CHAPTER - 14
LABOUR STANDARDS

Article 1: Definitions

"Forced or Compulsory Labour" shall mean all work or service which is exacted from any person under the menace of any penalty and for which the said person has not offered himself voluntarily.

Nevertheless, for the purposes of this Agreement, the term forced or compulsory labour shall not include –

    (i) any work or service exacted in virtue of compulsory military service laws for work of a purely military character;

    (ii) any work or service which forms part of the normal civic obligations of the citizens of a fully self-governing country;

    (iii)any work or service exacted from any person as a consequence of a conviction in a court of law, provided that the said work or service is carried out under the supervision and control of a public authority and that the said person is not hired to or placed at the disposal of private individuals, companies or associations;

    (iv)any work or service exacted in cases of emergency, that is to say, in the event of war or of a calamity or threatened calamity, such as fire, flood, famine, earthquake, violent epidemic or epizootic diseases, invasion by animal, insect or vegetable pests, and in general any circumstance that would endanger the existence or the well-being of the whole or part of the population;

    (v) minor communal services of a kind which, being performed by the members of the community in the direct interest of the said community, can therefore be considered as normal civic obligations incumbent upon the members of the community, provided that the members of the community or their direct representatives shall have the right to be consulted in regard to the need for such services.

"Central authority" means the highest central authority or authorities designated by a Party and notified to another Contracting Party.

"**Competent Authority**" shall mean either an authority of the metropolitan country or the highest central authority in the territory concerned.

"**Child**" shall apply to all persons under the age of 18.

"**Discrimination**" means

    (a) The term discrimination includes:

        (i) any distinction, exclusion or preference made on the basis of race, colour, sex, religion, political opinion, national extraction or social origin, which has the effect of nullifying or impairing equality of opportunity or treatment in employment or occupation;

        (ii) such other distinction, exclusion or preference which has the effect of nullifying or impairing equality of opportunity or treatment in employment or occupation as may be determined by the Member concerned after consultation with representative employers' and workers' organisations, where such exist, and with other appropriate bodies.

    (b) Any distinction, exclusion or preference in respect of a particular job based on the inherent requirements thereof shall not be deemed to be discrimination.

"**Employment and Occupation**" include access to vocational training, access to employment and to particular occupations, and terms and conditions of employment.

"**Equal remuneration for men and women workers for work of equal value**" refers to rates of remuneration established without discrimination based on sex.

"**ILO**" means the International Labour Organization.

"**ILO Declaration**" means the ILO Declaration on Fundamental Principles and Rights at Work and its Follow-up.

"**Remuneration**" includes the ordinary, basic or minimum wage or salary and any additional emoluments whatsoever payable directly or indirectly, whether in cash or in kind, by the employer to the worker and arising out of the worker's employment;

"**Representative organisations**" means the most representative organisations of employers and workers enjoying the right of freedom of association.

Article 2: General Principles

The Contracting Parties confirm the fundamental principles on which the Belt and Road Labour standard is based are that:

    (a) labour is not a commodity;

    (b) freedom of expression and of association are essential to sustained progress;

    (c) poverty anywhere constitutes a danger to prosperity everywhere;

    (d) the war against want requires to be carried on with unrelenting vigour within each nation, and by continuous and concerted international effort in which the representatives of workers and employers, enjoying equal status with those of governments, join with them in free discussion and democratic decision with a view to the promotion of the common welfare.

(e) all human beings, irrespective of race, creed or sex, have the right to pursue both their material well-being and their spiritual development in conditions of freedom and dignity, of economic security and equal opportunity;

(f) the attainment of the conditions in which this shall be possible must constitute the central aim of national and international policy;

(g) all national and international policies and measures, in particular those of an economic and financial character, should be judged in this light and accepted only in so far as they may be held to promote and not to hinder the achievement of this fundamental objective;

Article 3: Obligations

The Contracting Parties recognise the following shared obligations:

(a) full employment and the raising of standards of living;

(b) the employment of workers in the occupations in which they can have the satisfaction of giving the fullest measure of their skill and attainments and make their greatest contribution to the common well-being;

(c) the provision, as a means to the attainment of this end and under adequate guarantees for all concerned, of facilities for training and the transfer of labour, including migration for employment and settlement;

(d) policies in regard to wages and earnings, hours and other conditions of work calculated to ensure a just share of the fruits of progress to all, and a minimum living wage to all employed and in need of such protection;

(e) the effective recognition of the right of collective bargaining, the cooperation of management and labour in the continuous improvement of productive efficiency, and the collaboration of workers and employers in the preparation and application of social and economic measures;

(f) the extension of social security measures to provide a basic income to all in need of such protection and comprehensive medical care;

(g) adequate protection for the life and health of workers in all occupations;

(h) provision for child welfare and maternity protection;

(i) the provision of adequate nutrition, housing and facilities for recreation and culture;

(j) the assurance of equality of educational and vocational opportunity.

Article 4: Freedom of Association

Each contracting Parties undertake to give effect to the following provisions.

(a) Workers and employers, without distinction whatsoever, shall have the right to establish and, subject only to the rules of concerned, to join organizations of their own choosing without previous authorization.

(b) Workers' and employers' organisations shall have the right to draw up their constitutions and rules, to elect their representatives in full freedom, to organise their administration and activities and to formulate their programs.

(c) The public authorities shall refrain from any interference which would restrict this right or impede the lawful exercise thereof.

(d) Workers' and employers' organisations shall not be liable to be dissolved or suspended by administrative authority.

(e) Workers' and employers' organisations shall have the right to establish and join federations and confederations and any such organization, federation or confederation shall have the right to affiliate with international organisations of workers and employers.

(f) In exercising the rights provided for in this Agreement, workers and employers and their respective organisations, like other persons or organised collectivities, shall respect the law of the land.

Article 5: Right to Organize

1. Each Contracting Party undertakes to take all necessary and appropriate measures to ensure that workers and employers may exercise freely the right to organise.

2. Workers shall enjoy adequate protection against acts of anti-union discrimination in respect of their employment.

3. Such protection shall apply more particularly in respect of acts calculated to—

(a) make the employment of a worker subject to the condition that he shall not join a union or shall relinquish trade union membership;

(b) cause the dismissal of or otherwise prejudice a worker by reason of union membership or because of participation in union activities outside working hours or, with the consent of the employer, within working hours.

4. Workers' and employers' organisations shall enjoy adequate protection against any acts of interference by each other or each other's agents or members in their establishment, functioning or administration.

5. In particular, acts which are designed to promote the establishment of workers' organisations under the domination of employers or employers' organisations, or to support workers' organisations by financial or other means, with the object of placing such organisations under the control of employers or employers' organisations, shall be deemed to constitute acts of interference within the meaning of this Article.

6. Machinery appropriate to national conditions shall be established, where

necessary, for the purpose of ensuring respect for the right to organise as defined in the preceding Articles.

7. Measures appropriate to national conditions shall be taken, where necessary, to encourage and promote the full development and utilisation of machinery for voluntary negotiation between employers or employers' organisations and workers' organisations, with a view to the regulation of terms and conditions of employment by means of collective agreements.

Article 6: Suppression of Forced Labour

1. Each Contracting Party undertakes to suppress the use of forced or compulsory labour in all its forms within the shortest possible period.

2. With a view to this complete suppression, recourse to forced or compulsory labour may be had, during the transitional period, for public purposes only and as an exceptional measure, subject to the conditions and guarantees hereinafter provided.

3. The competent authority shall not impose or permit the imposition of forced or compulsory labour for the benefit of private individuals, companies or associations.

4. No infrastructure projects granted to private individuals, companies or associations shall involve any form of forced or compulsory labour for the production or the collection of products which such private individuals, companies or associations utilise or in which they trade.

5. Where infrastructure projects exist containing provisions involving such forced or compulsory labour, such provisions shall be rescinded as soon as possible.

Article 7: Abolition of Child Labour

1. Each Contracting Party undertakes to pursue a national policy designed to ensure the effective abolition of child labour and to raise progressively the minimum age for admission to employment or work to a level consistent with the fullest physical and mental development of young persons.

2. Each Contracting Party shall specify a minimum age for admission to employment or work within its territory and on means of transport registered in its territory and no one under that age shall be admitted to employment or work in any occupation.

3. The minimum age specified in pursuance of paragraph 1 of this Article shall not be less than the age of completion of compulsory schooling and, in any case, shall not be less than 15 years.

4. Notwithstanding the provisions of paragraph 3 of this Article, a Party whose economy and educational facilities are insufficiently developed may, after consultation with the organisations of employers and workers concerned, where such exist, initially specify a minimum age of 14 years.

5. Each Contracting Member which has specified a minimum age of 14 years in pursuance of the provisions of the preceding paragraph shall include in its reports on the application of this Agreement submitted to all Contracting Parties a statement:

    (a) that its reason for doing so subsists; or

    (b) that it renounces its right to avail itself of the provisions in question as from a stated date.

Article 8: Equal Remuneration

1. Each Contracting Party shall, by means appropriate to the methods in operation for determining rates of remuneration, promote and, in so far as is consistent with such methods, ensure the application to all workers of the principle of equal remuneration for men and women workers for work of equal value.

2. This principle may be applied by means of:

    (a) national laws or regulations

    (b) legally established or recognised machinery for wage determination;

    (c) collective agreements between employers and workers; or

    (d) a combination of these various means.

3. Where such action will assist in giving effect to the provisions of this Chapter measures shall be taken to promote objective appraisal of jobs on the basis of the work to be performed.

4. The methods to be followed in this appraisal may be decided upon by the authorities responsible for the determination of rates of remuneration, or, where such rates are determined by collective agreements, by the parties thereto.

5. Differential rates between workers which correspond, without regard to sex, to differences, as determined by such objective appraisal, in the work to be performed shall not be considered as being contrary to the principle of equal remuneration for men and women workers for work of equal value.

6. Each Contracting Party shall co-operate as appropriate with the employers' and workers' organisations concerned for the purpose of giving effect to the provisions of this Convention.

Article 9: Equality of Opportunity and Treatment

1. Each Contracting Party undertakes to declare and pursue a national policy designed to promote, by methods appropriate to national conditions and practice, equality of opportunity and treatment in respect of employment and occupation, with a view to eliminating any discrimination in respect thereof.

2. Each Contracting Party undertakes, by methods appropriate to national conditions and practice:

    (a) to seek the co-operation of employers' and workers' organisations and other appropriate bodies in promoting the acceptance and observance of this policy;

(b) to enact such legislation and to promote such educational programs as may be calculated to secure the acceptance and observance of the policy;

(c) to repeal any statutory provisions and modify any administrative instructions or practices which are inconsistent with the policy;

(d) to pursue the policy in respect of employment under the direct control of a competent authority;

(e) to ensure observance of the policy in the activities of vocational guidance, vocational training and placement services under the direction of a competent authority;

(f) to indicate in its annual reports on the application of this Agreement, the action taken in pursuance of the policy and the results secured by such action.

Article 10: Labour Inspection

1. Each Contracting Party shall maintain a system of labour inspection in industrial, commercial, infrastructure and agricultural workplaces.

2. The system of labour inspection shall apply to all workplaces in respect of which legal provisions relating to conditions of work and the protection of workers while engaged in their work are enforceable by labour inspectors.

3. National laws or regulations may exempt mining and transport undertakings or parts of such undertakings from the application of this Agreement.

4. The functions of the system of labour inspection shall be:

(a) to secure the enforcement of the legal provisions relating to conditions of work and the protection of workers while engaged in their work, such as provisions relating to hours, wages, safety, health and welfare, the employment of children and young persons, and other connected matters, in so far as such provisions are enforceable by labour inspectors;

(b) to supply technical information and advice to employers and workers concerning the most effective means of complying with the legal provisions;

(c) to bring to the notice of the competent authority defects or abuses not specifically covered by existing legal provisions.

5. Any further duties which may be entrusted to labour inspectors shall not be such as to interfere with the effective discharge of their primary duties or to prejudice in any way the authority and impartiality which are necessary to inspectors in their relations with employers and workers.

6. So far as is compatible with the administrative practice of the Contracting Parties, labour inspection shall be placed under the supervision and control of a central

authority.

 7. The competent authority shall make appropriate arrangements to promote:

  (a) effective co-operation between the inspection services and other Government services and public or private institutions engaged in similar activities; and

  (b) Collaboration between officials of the labour inspectorate and employers and workers or their organisations.

 8. Each Contracting Party shall take the necessary measures to ensure that duly qualified technical experts and specialists, including specialists in medicine, engineering, electricity and chemistry, are associated in the work of inspection, in such manner as may be deemed most appropriate under national conditions, for the purpose of securing the enforcement of the legal provisions relating to the protection of the health and safety of workers while engaged in their work and of investigating the effects of processes, materials and methods of work on the health and safety of workers.

Article 11: Employment Policy

 1. With a view to stimulating economic growth and development, raising levels of living, meeting manpower requirements and overcoming unemployment and underemployment, each Contracting Party shall declare and pursue, as a major goal, an active policy designed to promote full, productive and freely chosen employment.

 2. The said policy shall aim at ensuring that

  (a) there is work for all who are available for and seeking work;

  (b) such work is as productive as possible;

  (c) there is freedom of choice of employment and the fullest possible opportunity for each worker to qualify for, and to use personal skills and endowments in, a well-suited job, irrespective of race, colour, sex, religion, political opinion, national extraction or social origin.

 3. The said policy shall take due account of the stage and level of economic development and the mutual relationships between employment objectives and other economic and social objectives, and shall be pursued by methods that are appropriate to national conditions and practices.

 4. Each Contracting Party shall, by such methods and to such extent as may be appropriate under national conditions:

  (a) decide on and keep under review, within the framework of a co-ordinated economic and social policy, the measures to be adopted for attaining the objectives specified in Clause 1;

  (b) take such steps as may be needed, including when appropriate the establishment of programs, for the application of these measures.

Article 12: Tripartite Consultation

1. Each Contracting Party undertakes to operate procedures which ensure effective consultations, with respect to the matters concerning the activities of the Belt and Road Labour Committee between representatives of the government, of employers and of workers.

2. The nature and form of the procedures provided for in paragraph 1 of this Article shall be determined in each Contracting Party in accordance with national practice, after consultation with the representative organisations, where such organisations exist and such procedures have not yet been established.

3. The representatives of employers and workers for the purposes of the procedures provided for in this Agreement shall be freely chosen by their representative organisations, where such organisations exist.

4. Employers and workers shall be represented on an equal footing on any bodies through which consultations are undertaken.

Article 13: Public Awareness and Procedural Guarantees

1. Each Contracting Party shall promote public awareness of its labour laws, including by ensuring that information related to its labour laws and enforcement and compliance procedures is publicly available.

2. Each Contracting Party shall ensure that persons with a recognised interest under its law in a particular matter have appropriate access to impartial and independent tribunals for the enforcement of the Party's labour laws. These tribunals may include administrative tribunals, quasi-judicial tribunals, judicial tribunals or labour tribunals, as provided for in each Party's law.

3. Each Contracting Party shall ensure that proceedings before these tribunals for the enforcement of its labour laws: are fair, equitable and transparent; comply with due process of law; and do not entail unreasonable fees or time limits or unwarranted delays. Any hearings in these proceedings shall be open to the public, except when the administration of justice otherwise requires, and in accordance with its applicable laws.

4. Each Contracting Party shall ensure that:
   (a) the parties to these proceedings are entitled to support or defend their respective positions, including by presenting information or evidence; and
   (b) final decisions on the merits of the case:
      (i) are based on information or evidence in respect of which the parties were offered the opportunity to be heard;
      (ii) state the reasons on which they are based; and
      (iii)are available in writing without undue delay to the parties to the proceedings and, consistent with its law, to the public.

5. Each Contracting Party shall provide that parties to these proceedings have the

right to seek review or appeal, as appropriate under its law.

6. Each Contracting Party shall ensure that the parties to these proceedings have access to remedies under its law for the effective enforcement of their rights under the Contracting Party's labour laws and that these remedies are executed in a timely manner.

7. Each Contracting Party shall provide procedures to effectively enforce the final decisions of its tribunals in these proceedings.

8. For greater certainty, and without prejudice to whether a tribunal's decision is inconsistent with a Contracting Party's obligations under this Chapter, nothing in this Chapter shall be construed to require a tribunal of a Contracting Party to reopen a decision that it has made in a particular matter.

Article 14: Cooperation

1. The Contracting Parties recognise the importance of cooperation as a mechanism for effective implementation of this Chapter, to enhance opportunities to improve labour standards and to further advance common commitments regarding labour matters, including workers' wellbeing and quality of life and the principles and rights stated in the ILO Declaration.

2. In undertaking cooperative activities, the Contracting Parties shall be guided by the following principles:

(a) consideration of each Contracting Party's priorities, level of development and available resources;

(b) broad involvement of, and mutual benefit to, the Contracting Parties;

(c) relevance of capacity and capability-building activities, including technical assistance between the Contracting Parties to address labour protection issues and activities to promote innovative workplace practices;

(d) generation of measurable, positive and meaningful labour outcomes;

(e) resource efficiency, including through the use of technology, as appropriate, to optimise resources used in cooperative activities;

(f) complementarity with existing regional and multilateral initiatives to address labour issues; and

(g) transparency and public participation.

3. Each Contracting Party may invite the views and, as appropriate, participation of its stakeholders, including worker and employer representatives, in identifying potential areas for cooperation and undertaking cooperative activities. Subject to the agreement of the Parties involved, cooperative activities may occur through bilateral or plurilateral engagement and may involve relevant regional or international organisations, such as the ILO, and non-Contracting Parties.

4. The funding of cooperative activities undertaken within the framework of this

Chapter shall be decided by the Contracting Parties involved on a case-by-case basis.

5. In addition to the cooperative activities outlined in this Article, the Contracting Parties shall, as appropriate, caucus and leverage their respective membership in regional and multilateral fora to further their common interests in addressing labour issues.

6. Areas of cooperation may include:

(a) job creation and the promotion of productive, quality employment, including policies to generate job-rich growth and promote sustainable enterprises and entrepreneurship;

(b) creation of productive, quality employment linked to sustainable growth and skills development for jobs in emerging industries, including environmental industries;

(c) innovative workplace practices to enhance workers' well-being and business and economic competitiveness;

(d) human capital development and the enhancement of employability, including through lifelong learning, continuous education, training and the development and upgrading of skills;

(e) work-life balance;

(f) promotion of improvements in business and labour productivity, particularly in respect of SMEs;

(g) remuneration systems;

(h) promotion of the awareness of and respect for the principles and rights as stated in the ILO Declaration and for the concept of Decent Work as defined by the ILO;

(i) labour laws and practices, including the effective implementation of the principles and rights as stated in the ILO Declaration;

(j) occupational safety and health;

(k) labour administration and adjudication, for example, strengthening capacity, efficiency and effectiveness;

(l) collection and use of labour statistics;

(m) labour inspection, for example, improving compliance and enforcement mechanisms;

(n) addressing the challenges and opportunities of a diverse, multigenerational workforce, including:

(i) promotion of equality and elimination of discrimination in respect of employment and occupation for migrant workers, or in the areas of age, disability and other characteristics not related to merit or the requirements of employment;

(ii) promotion of equality of, elimination of discrimination against, and the employment interests of women; and

(iii) protection of vulnerable workers, including migrant workers, and low-waged, casual or contingent workers;

(o) addressing the labour and employment challenges of economic crises, such as through areas of common interest in the ILO *Global Jobs Pact*;

(p) social protection issues, including workers' compensation in case of occupational injury or illness, pension systems and employment assistance schemes;

(q) best practice for labour relations, for example, improved labour relations, including promotion of best practice in alternative dispute resolution;

(r) social dialogue, including tripartite consultation and partnership;

(s) with respect to labour relations in multi-national enterprises, promoting information sharing and dialogue related to conditions of employment by enterprises operating in two or more Contracting Parties with representative worker organisations in each Contracting Party;

(t) corporate social responsibility; and

(u) other areas as the Parties may decide.

7. The Contracting Parties may undertake activities in the areas of cooperation in paragraph 6 through:

(a) workshops, seminars, dialogues and other fora to share knowledge, experiences and best practices, including online fora and other knowledge-sharing platforms;

(b) study trips, visits and research studies to document and study policies and practices;

(c) collaborative research and development related to best practices in subjects of mutual interest;

(d) specific exchanges of technical expertise and assistance, as appropriate; and

(e) other forms as the Parties may decide.

Article 15: Labour Committee

1. The Contracting Parties hereby establish a Labour Committee composed of senior governmental representatives at the ministerial or other level, as designated by each Contracting Party.

2. The Labour Committee shall meet every two years, unless the Parties decide otherwise.

3. The Labour Committee shall:

(a) consider matters related to this Chapter;

(b) establish and review priorities to guide decisions by the Contracting Parties about labour cooperation and capacity building activities undertaken pursuant to this Chapter, taking into account the principles in Article 14 (Cooperation);

(c) agree on a general work programme in accordance with the priorities established under subparagraph (b);

(d) oversee and evaluate the general work programme;

(e) discuss matters of mutual interest;

(f) facilitate public participation and awareness of the implementation of this Chapter; and

(g) perform any other functions as the Contracting Parties may decide.

4. Every five years, or as otherwise decided by the Contracting Parties, the Labour Committee shall review the implementation of this Chapter with a view to ensuring its effective operation and report the findings and any recommendations to all the Contracting Parties.

5. The Labour Committee may undertake subsequent reviews as agreed by the Contracting Parties.

6. The Labour Committee shall be chaired by each Contracting Party on a rotational basis.

7. All decisions and reports of the Labour Committee shall be made by consensus and be made publicly available, unless the Labour Committee decides otherwise.

8. The Labour Committee shall agree on a joint summary report on its work at the end of each Labour Committee meeting.

9. The Contracting Parties shall, as appropriate, liaise with relevant regional and international organisations, such as the ILO, on matters related to this Chapter. The Council may seek to develop joint proposals or collaborate with those organisations or with non-Parties.

CHAPTER - 15

DISPUTE SETTLEMENT

Article 1: Cooperation

The Contracting Parties shall at all times endeavour to agree on the interpretation and application of this Agreement, and shall make every attempt through cooperation and consultations to arrive at a mutually satisfactory resolution of any matter that might affect its operation or application.

Article 2: Scope

1. Unless otherwise provided in this Agreement, the dispute settlement provisions of this Chapter shall apply:

   (a) with respect to the avoidance or settlement of all disputes between the Contracting Parties regarding the interpretation or application of this Agreement;

   (b) when a Contracting Party considers that an actual or proposed measure of another Contracting Party is or would be inconsistent with an obligation of this Agreement or that another Party has otherwise failed to carry out an obligation under this Agreement; or

   (c) when a Contracting Party considers that a benefit it could reasonably have expected to accrue

is being nullified or impaired as a result of the application of a measure of another Party that is not inconsistent with this Agreement.

Article 3: Choice of Forum

1. If a dispute regarding any matter arises under this Agreement and under another international trade agreement to which the disputing Parties are party, including the WTO Agreement or any bi-lateral or multi-lateral trade agreements, the complaining Party may select the forum in which to settle the dispute.

2. Once a complaining Party has initiated dispute settlement mechanism under this Agreement the forum selected shall be used to the exclusion of other fora.

Article 4: Dispute Settlement Process

The Contracting Parties agree to incorporate the Dispute Settlement Mechanism of International Centre for Dispute Prevention and Settlement Organisation (ICDPASO) in this Chapter, to resolve disputes arising out of this Agreement.

For the purpose of certainty, according to Dispute Settlement Mechanism of ICDPASO), the Contracting Parties agree to:

First use Procedure for Grievance/Good Offices Mechanism of the ICDPASO Dispute Settlement Mechanism to resolve their dispute;

If that dispute and any part of dispute is not resolved through Good Offices, then the Contracting Parties will use Mediation to resolve their disputes either under auspices of ICDPASO or through any other Mediation Organizations;

If that dispute or part of that dispute is not resolved through Mediation, then the Contracting Parties agree to resolve the dispute through Arbitration following rules of Arbitration of the ICDPASO; and

The Contracting Parties, if so desire, appeal the decision of Arbitration Tribunal to the Permanent Appeal Tribunal of the ICDPASO in accordance with the Rules of the Appeal Tribunal of the ICDPASO.

For greater certainty, the Contracting Parties, agree that Appeal process shall not apply on disputes between private parties, disputes between private party/parties against State party or State entity which do not arise a treaty obligation.

Article 5: Code of Conduct for Members of the Tribunal, The Appeal Tribunal and Mediators

The Contracting Parties agree to incorporate "Code of Conduct for Members of the Tribunal, The Appeal Tribunal and Mediators" of the ICDPASO in this Chapter.

Article 6: Transparency Rules

The Contracting Parties agree to incorporate "Transparency Rules" of the ICDPASO in this Chapter.

For greater certainty, the Contracting Party agree that the Rule on Transparency shall apply on investor-state arbitration, State-to-State dispute including appeal process.

For greater certainty, Contracting Parties agree that exception to the Rules on Transparency is equally applicable to mediation mutatis mutandis.

Article 7: Schedule of Fees

Contracting Parties agree to incorporate "Schedule of Fees" of the ICDPASO in this Chapter.

「一帶一路」

合作與夥伴關係協議範本

第一章　總則和定義

第一部分　總則

第一條　總體範圍與框架

各締約方認識到，「一帶一路」倡議以明確的目標、指導原則和優先發展領域為加強經濟合作與發展提供了良好框架。此為構建「一帶一路」倡議參與國的共同體意識邁出了重要的一步。

根據 2015 年發佈的《推動共建絲綢之路經濟帶和 21 世紀海上絲綢之路的願景與行動》，「一帶一路」倡議的一般關鍵性特徵包括通過增進相互理解、信任與交流，推動共同發展繁榮，促進和平友誼。

第二條　主權

「一帶一路」倡議以所有締約方主權平等原則為基礎。

第三條　誠實信用和有約必守

本協議對各締約方均有約束力。所有締約各方應秉承誠實信用的原則行事和履行在本協定下的義務，以享受「一帶一路」倡議的建設成果。

第四條　可持續發展

各締約方承諾將包括聯合國可持續發展目標在內的可持續發展原則納入

「一帶一路」倡議的各個項目。

　　各締約方確保本協定下「一帶一路」項目足夠全面以提高效率和效果，並通過減少貧困和提高社會包容性促進可持續發展。

第五條　法治

　　各締約方致力於依法實施「一帶一路」項目，包括基礎設施建設、金融、投資、知識產權及其他與「一帶一路」項目相關的領域。

第六條　非歧視

　　各締約方應基於市場原則，以非歧視、非任意的方式實施與「一帶一路」項目相關的規則與程序。

第七條　待遇

　　各締約方應公正、客觀地對待其他締約方，包括其投資、企業和國民，並給予其最惠國待遇、國民待遇與公平公正待遇。

　　各締約方應在其領土內保護勞工權利，並為實施「一帶一路」項目的勞工提供安全保障。

第八條　透明度和反腐敗

　　各締約方同意普遍遵循透明度原則。

　　各締約方應持續地、及時地，以無償或收取合理費用的方式向各利益相關方提供所有與「一帶一路」項目有關的政策、法律、法規、行政裁定、許可、認證、資質和註冊要求、技術法規、標準、指南、程序和慣例及其他相關事項的信息。

　　各締約方確認，決心消除「一帶一路」項目中的賄賂和腐敗。

　　各締約方認識到，在公共部門和私人部門都需加強廉潔建設，且各部門就此方面有互助義務。

第九條　正當程序

　　各締約方應尊重當事人所享有的一切合法權利，並應根據締約方各自應當適用的法律為當事人提供正當程序，包括進入上訴程序的權利。

第十條　相互尊重和信任

各締約方同意，在理解「一帶一路」參與國處於不同發展階段、具有不同視角、不同實力和不同優先事項的基礎上，秉承相互尊重、相互信任的精神，推進「一帶一路」倡議。

第十一條　互利

各締約方同意，「一帶一路」倡議須促成一個符合各參與國利益和需求的平衡方案，所有參與國須獲得類似且實質性的利益。

各締約方同意，「一帶一路」項目須重成果而非形式，重成就而非政策。

第十二條　區域團結

各締約方認識到，保持「一帶一路」倡議參與國間密切和持續發展的關係對所有參與國均至關重要。因此，參與國間須維持友好關係和加強地區團結。

第十三條　政府和利益相關方的合作

各締約方同意，「一帶一路」項目的逐步啟動、設計和實施須通過政府機構、企業和利益相關方之間的密切合作來推進。

第十四條　商業慣例和道德規範的標準化

各締約方確保「一帶一路」項目在國際最佳實踐的基礎上實施。任何有關商業慣例和道德規範方面的差異應通過標準化的方式予以解決。

第十五條　溝通、合作和磋商

各締約方應努力推動建立與商貿界及投資者之間有效的交流機制，包括在制定、實施和審議有關「一帶一路」項目的規則和程序時，為各方提供磋商的機會。

各締約方應努力讓工商界及社區組織更有效地參與其中，包括使其更為便捷地獲得項目實施的官方信息，以及使其及時獲得其所提議的政策或措施的反饋意見，特別是當此類措施旨在促進項目時。

　　各締約方須在制定、實施和審議與「一帶一路」項目有關的規則和程序時，讓包括民間團體、非政府組織、工商界、公共部門和學術界在內的所有主體參與其中。

第十六條　規則的簡化和效率

　　各締約方應努力通過推進回應性監管措施，簡化與「一帶一路」項目相關的規則和程序，以減少繁瑣、限制性或不必要的措施。

第十七條　規則的一致性和可預見性

　　各締約方應努力以一致、可預見和統一的方式適用與「一帶一路」項目相關的規則和程序，最大程度地減少不確定性。規則和程序應以非歧視的方式適用，並通過標準政策和操作流程向有關當局提供清晰、準確的程序指引。

第十八條　規則的協調和互認

　　在維護監管權或制定規則權以追求正當目標時，如保護健康、安全或公共道德以及保護可用盡自然資源等，各締約方同意與「一帶一路」項目相關的法規、規則和程序應以國際標準為基礎與國內法規相協調，並在適當的情況下通過互認予以便利。

第十九條　現代化和新技術的使用

　　各締約方應在必要時審議和更新與「一帶一路」項目相關的規則和程序，包括新信息和新商業慣例，並在適當情況下基於所採用的現代技術和新科技進行審議和更新。

　　各締約方致力於促進數字貿易、網絡安全和尊重知識產權。

第二十條　友好與和平解決爭議

　　各締約方應以友好、和平的方式解決與「一帶一路」項目相關的一切爭議，以確保「一帶一路」國家或地區的和平、安全和正義不受危及。

第二部分　一般定義

第二十一條　一般定義

就本協定而言，除非本協定另有規定：

「**一帶一路**」**項目**是指與「一帶一路」倡議相關或為實施「一帶一路」倡議而啓動和開發的項目；

「**GATS**」是指《世界貿易組織協定》附件 1B 包含的《服務貿易總協定》；

「**IMF**」是指國際貨幣基金組織；

「**《國際貨幣基金組織協定》**」是指 1944 年 7 月 22 日在布雷頓森林通過的《國際貨幣基金組織協定》；

「**個人信息**」是指用於識別或可用於識別自然人的任何信息；

「**WCO**」應指 1952 年成立的世界海關組織；

「**TRIPS 協定**」是指《世界貿易組織協定》附件 1C 包含的《與貿易有關的知識產權協定》；

「**UNCITRAL**」是指聯合國貿易法委員會；

「**WTO 協定**」是指於 1994 年 4 月 15 日簽訂的《馬拉喀什建立世界貿易組織協定》。

第二章　發展權

第一條　定義

1. 本協定項下的**「發展權」**是指每一締約方及其國民有權參與、促進和享有經濟、社會、文化的發展，以使所有的經濟權利和自由貿易充分實現。

2. 本協定項下的**「發展權」**亦指本協定以及各締約方批准的其他國際協定和宣言下權利之充分實現。

第二條　國家作為本國人民發展權的義務承擔者

1. 各締約方及其國民是發展的核心主體，且應為發展權的積極參與者和受益者。

2. 各締約方及其國民或單獨或集體對發展負有義務，應考慮對其在共同體中權利及義務的充分尊重，此可單獨確保本協定目標的自由和完全實現，且他們應為發展而促進和保護適當的政治、社會和經濟秩序。

3. 各締約方應制定適當的國家發展政策，以促進和實施發展權，並公平分配由此產生之效益。

第三條　國家在全球和區域層面上作為發展權的集體義務承擔者

1. 各締約方應制定有利於實現發展權的各項規定。

2. 與發展權相關的規定需完全尊重《聯合國憲章》中有關國家間友好關係及合作的國際法原則。

3. 各締約方應相互合作，以確保發展並消除發展障礙。各締約方應以促進發展權並使之成為以主權平等、相互依存、互利合作為基礎的國際經濟新秩序的方式來實現自己的權利和履行自己的義務。

第四條　國家作為他人享有發展權的義務承擔者

應採取必要措施促進發展中國家締約方之發展。各締約方應相互合作，為發展中國家和最不發達國家締約方提供適當方法和設施以促進其全面發展。

第五條　遵守貿易規則

各締約方應堅決消除大規模公然違反貿易規則之行為。

第六條　無歧視的發展權

1. 締約各方應進行合作，旨在促進、鼓勵和加強對所有人的無歧視性發展權的尊重和遵守。

2. 發展權不可分割且相互依存。為實現本協定之目標，應對發展權的實施、促進和保護給予同等關注和迫切考慮。

3. 各締約方應採取措施，消除因不遵守公民政治權、經濟、社會和文化權而造成的發展障礙。

第七條　消除社會不公

各締約方應確保採取有效措施進行適當的經濟和社會改革，以消除一切社會不公。

第八條　公眾和利益相關方的參與

各締約方應鼓勵公眾在所有領域的全面參與，以此作為促進發展和全面實現發展權的一個重要因素。

第九條　逐步增進發展權

各締約方應採取必要步驟確保充分行使和逐步增進發展權，包括在國家和國際層面制定、通過和實施政策、立法及其他措施。

第十條　民心相通

各締約方應鼓勵民心相通，以促進保護發展權的對話、研究和政策。

第十一條　與其他條款的關係

本章所述發展權的所有方面都是不可分割和相互依存的，且每一方面均應置於整體背景之下加以考慮。

第三章　可持續發展

第一條　目標

1. 根據本協定的總則，各締約方承諾將包括聯合國可持續發展目標在內的可持續發展原則納入「一帶一路」倡議的各個項目。

2. 各締約方確保「一帶一路」項目足夠全面以提高效率和效益，並通過減少貧困和提高社會包容性促進可持續發展。

第二條　可持續基礎設施建設

1. 各締約方同意，通過實施「一帶一路」項目，發展優質、可靠、可持續和具適應力的基礎設施，包括區域和跨境基礎設施，以支持經濟發展和人類福祉。重點是通過提供更多的資金、科技與技術支持，使得「一帶一路」沿線國家能夠負擔且公平地獲得基礎設施服務。

2. 各締約方同意以「一帶一路」項目的形式協助現有基礎設施迭代和產業轉型，為此所有「一帶一路」國家和地區應根據其能力採取行動，且通過提高資源利用率以及加大採用清潔與環境友好型技術與工藝，使之具有可持續性。

3. 各締約方同意，根據「一帶一路」沿線國家和地區的國情，促進包容、可持續的工業化，並顯著提高工業在就業和國內生產總值中的比重。

第三條　債務可持續性

各締約方承諾，為「一帶一路」國家多渠道籌集更多資金用於「一帶一路」項目，通過協調政策，酌情促進債務融資、債務減免和債務重組，協助「一帶一路」國家實現債務的長期可持續性。

第四條　可持續投資

1. 各締約方的投資政策應設立公開、非歧視、透明和可預期的投資條件。各締約方的投資政策應為投資者和有形與無形的投資提供法律確定性和強有力的保護，包括訴諸有效的爭端預防和解決機制以及執行程序。每一締約方的爭端解決程序應公平、公開和透明，並應有適當的保障措施以防止被濫用。

2. 每一締約方與投資有關的法規應以透明的方式制定，使所有利益相關方均有機會參與，並將其納入以法治為基礎的制度框架內。

3. 每一締約方的投資政策及影響投資的其他政策，應在國家、區域和國際層面保持一致，旨在促進投資且符合「一帶一路」國家和地區可持續發展與包容性增長的目標。

4. 每一締約方的投資促進政策應以吸引和留住投資為目的，有效和高效地將經濟效益最大化，並輔之以提高透明度和有利於投資者設立、開展和擴大其業務的便利化措施。

5. 每一締約方的投資政策應促進和便利投資者遵循區域性、國際性的最佳實踐，以及可適用的負責任商業行為和公司治理法規。

第五條　可持續生產與消費

各締約方同意為「一帶一路」項目實行「事半功倍」的可持續消費和生產原則，以便通過在全生命周期內減少資源消耗、退化和污染，來增加「一帶一路」項目福利淨收益、促進各項經濟活動、提高「一帶一路」國家和地區人民的生活質量。

第六條　清潔能源

1. 各締約方同意盡可能以「一帶一路」項目的形式，為所有「一帶一路」國家和地區建設、擴建基礎設施和更新技術，以提供現代和可持續性的能源服務。

2. 各締約方同意加強合作，促進獲取清潔能源研究和技術，包括可再生能源、能源利用率、先進和更清潔化石燃料技術，並盡可能通過「一帶一路」項目促進對能源基礎設施和清潔能源技術的投資。

第七條　可持續工作和經濟增長

1. 各締約方同意在「一帶一路」項目中創造條件，為「一帶一路」國家和地區的所有就業人員提供優質的工作機會和體面的工作條件。

2. 各締約方同意立即採取有效措施，在「一帶一路」項目中消除強迫勞動，終止現代奴隸制和人口販賣，並確保禁用一切形式的童工。

3. 各締約方同意保護勞工權利，為在「一帶一路」項目中的所有工人，包括移民工人，特別是女性移民工人以及那些不穩定就業人員，創造安全可靠的工作環境。

第八條　可持續城市和社區

1. 各締約方同意，在實施「一帶一路」項目的同時，推進「一帶一路」國家包容、可持續的城鎮化建設，加強參與性、綜合性、可持續的人類住區規劃和管理能力建設。

2. 關於互聯互通的「一帶一路」項目，各締約方同意向所有人提供安全、可負擔、可獲得、可持續的交通運輸系統，改善道路安全。特別是擴大公共交通、關注弱勢群體如婦女、兒童、殘疾人和老年人的需求。

第九條　氣候變化

各締約方同意，將應對氣候變化的措施納入國家政策、戰略和規劃，以增強「一帶一路」項目對「一帶一路」國家、地區氣候災害和自然災害的抵禦能力和適應能力。

第十條　保護水下生命

1. 對於涉及海洋、河流和水資源的「一帶一路」項目，各締約方同意以可持續方式管理和保護海洋和沿海生態系統，以免產生重大負面影響，包括加強其適應力，採取行動幫助其恢復原狀，以保持海洋健康及富饒。

2. 關於「一帶一路」的陸地項目，各締約方同意預防和顯著減少各類海洋污染，特別是陸上活動所造成的污染，包括海洋廢棄物污染和營養鹽污染。

第十一條　保護陸地生命

1. 各締約方同意在實施「一帶一路」項目時，根據國際協定規定的義務，保護、恢復和可持續利用陸地和內陸的淡水生態系統及其服務，特別是森林、濕地、山麓和旱地。

2. 各締約方同意，在實施「一帶一路」項目的同時，促進對各類森林的可持續管理，停止毀林，恢復退化的森林，並大幅增加「一帶一路」國家和地區的植樹造林和森林再造工作。

3. 各締約方同意，在實施「一帶一路」項目的同時防治荒漠化，恢復退化的土地和土壤，包括受荒漠化、乾旱和洪澇影響的土地，並努力實現「一帶一路」國家和地區土地零退化。

4. 各締約方同意在「一帶一路」項目實施過程中，保護山地生態系統，包括其生物多樣性，以便加強山地生態系統的能力，使其為可持續發展提供必要的益處。

5. 各締約方同意，將生態系統和生物多樣性價值觀納入「一帶一路」項目規劃和發展進程中。

6. 各締約方同意，在實施「一帶一路」項目的同時，從各種渠道動員並大幅增加財政資源，以保護和可持續利用生物多樣性和生態系統。

第十二條　和平、正義與強大機構

1. 各締約方認可並同意，在國際商事爭端預防與解決組織的主持下，以友好、和平的方式解決與「一帶一路」項目相關的一切爭端，確保「一帶一路」國家或地區的和平、安全和正義不受危害。

2. 各締約方亦同意，通過實施「一帶一路」項目及相關活動，達成如下合意：
   (a) 在實施「一帶一路」項目的同時，在國內和國際層面上促進法治，確保所有人都能平等地獲得司法公正；
   (b) 杜絕與「一帶一路」項目實施相關的各種形式的腐敗與賄賂；
   (c) 確保「一帶一路」項目實施中各級決策反應靈敏，且具有包容性、參與性與代表性；
   (d) 通過開展國際合作等方式加強各層級相關國家機構，特別是處於「一帶一路」沿線發展中國家和最不發達國家和地區的國家機構的能力建設，以預防暴力、打擊恐怖主義和犯罪；

(e) 為可持續發展，促進和執行非歧視性法律和政策。

第四章　透明度和反腐敗

第一條　定義

就本章而言：

「**外國公職人員**」指在一外國擔任立法、行政、行政管理或司法職務的任何人，無論經任命或經選舉；以及為一外國，包括公共機構或公共企業，履行一項公共職能的任何人。

「**公共國際組織官員**」指國際職員或經一公共國際組織授權而代表其行事的任何人；

「**公職人員**」指：

(i)　擔任一締約方中立法、行政、行政管理或司法職務的任何人，無論經任命還是經選舉、長期還是臨時、有報酬還是無報酬，且與該人的資歷無關；

(ii)　根據一締約方法律下所定義的並在該締約方法律的相關領域所適用的，為該締約方履行一項公共職能，包括公共機構或公共企業，或提供一項公共服務的任何其他人；或

(iii)　根據一締約方法律定義為公職人員的任何其他人。

「**中小企業**」指任何小型、中型企業，包括微型企業，並可在適用時，根據各締約方國內法律法規或國家政策予以進一步界定。

第二條　適用範圍

本章範圍僅限於促進透明度、以及消除與本協定所涵蓋的任何事項相關的賄賂和腐敗的措施。

第三條　透明度

1. 每一締約方應確保與本協定所涵蓋任何事項有關的政策、法律、法規、行政決定、行政許可、認證、資質和註冊要求、技術法規、標準、指南、程序和慣例，以及對其政策、法律、法規、行政決定、行政許可、認證、資質和註冊要求、技術法規、標準、指南、程序和慣例的任何變更或修訂，最好通過在全國發行的官方公報和/或官方網站上以公開發佈的方式，向所有締約方和利害關係人提供。每一締約方應持續、及時地將該等全國發行的官方公報和/官方網站通知其他締約方。

2. 每一締約方應按照其法律制度，公佈政策建議、討論文件、法規概要或其他文件。該等文件應包含足夠詳細的信息，以告知其他締約方其貿易或投資利益是否及如何受到影響。

第四條　擬議或實際措施的通知

每一締約方應採取與其法律制度相符的必要措施，將可能對本協定的執行產生實質影響或對另一締約方在本協定項下的利益產生實質影響的任何擬議或實際措施，通知其他締約方

第五條　加強制度以提高透明度

每一締約方應依據其國內法的基本原則，努力採取、維持和加強提高透明度的制度，包括技術性貿易措施的透明度，並防止利益衝突。

第六條　維持反腐敗政策和評估

1. 每一締約方應制定和實施或維持與其國內法原則相符的，體現法治、透明度和問責原則，並促進公職人員廉正之有效和協調的反腐敗政策。

2. 每一締約方應努力定期評估相關法律文件和行政措施，以確定其預防和打擊腐敗的充分性。

第七條　刑事定罪

1. 每一締約方應依據其基本法律原則，採取或維持必要的立法或其他措施，將故意實施的下列行為規定為刑事犯罪：

(a) 直接或間接地允諾給予、提議給予或實際給予公職人員或其他人或實體不正當好處，以使該公職人員在履行其法定職責時行為或不行為；

(b) 公職人員為其本人或其他人或實體直接或間接索取或收受不正當好處，以使該公職人員在履行其法定職責時作為或不作為；

(c) 直接或間接地向一外國公職人員或一公共國際組織的官員允諾給予、提議給予或實際給予該公職人員或其他人或實體不正當好處，使該公職人員在履行其法定職責時行為或不行為，以便獲得或保留與進行國際商業活動相關的商業或其他不正當好處；

(d) 幫助、教唆或共謀實施第（a）項至第（c）項所述的任何罪行。

2. 每一締約方應使實施第（a）項至第（d）項所述罪行的人受到與其所犯罪行嚴重性相當的制裁。

第八條　法人責任

每一締約方應根據其國內法原則，採取必要措施，就第七條確定的罪行規定法人責任。

第九條　賠償

每一締約方應採取符合其國內法原則的必要措施，確保因腐敗行為而受到損害的實體或個人有權對該損害的責任者提起法律訴訟以獲得賠償。

第十條　資產非法增加

每一締約方應依照其國內法及其基本原則採取必要的立法和其他措施，將故意實施的資產非法增加規定為犯罪行為，即公職人員的資產顯著增加且不能以其履職期間的合法收入作出合理解釋。

第十一條　反腐敗法律的執行

每一締約方應依據其法律制度的基本原則，有效執行為遵守本章規定而採取或維持的法律或其他措施。

第十二條　有效防止洗錢

每一締約方應依照其國內法律制度確保反洗錢法的存在與有效執行，以對腐敗和犯罪所得的洗錢行為規以實體刑罰。

第十三條　雙邊司法協助

1. 每一締約方應按照其法律和相關條約及安排，最大可能地向另一締約方提供迅速和有效的司法協助，以便一締約方就本協定範圍內的犯罪提起刑事調查和訴訟，以及對一法人提起本協定範圍內的非刑事訴訟。被請求的締約方應毫不遲延地就支持司法協助所需的任何額外資料或文件告知請求方，並依請求通告司法協助的進展和結果。

2. 當一締約方將存在雙重犯罪作為提供司法協助的前提條件時，若被請求司法協助的犯罪行為屬於本協定範圍內的犯罪行為，則認定存在雙重犯罪。

3. 一締約方不應以銀行保密為由，拒絕就本協定範圍內的刑事案件提供司法協助。

第十四條　能力建設和培訓計劃

1. 各締約方應在能力建設方面加強合作，以有效預防和發現腐敗行為，包括與腐敗相關的洗錢行為；以及為官員制定各領域反腐專業培訓計劃，例如對日常業務活動和監視腐敗行為提供技術援助培訓等。

2. 各締約方應努力為企業董事和經理制定反腐培訓計劃，並努力提高私營部門利益相關者的反腐意識。

第十五條　廉潔公共服務

每一締約方應建立公開、公平、高效及促進聘任最佳、最廉潔人員的政府公職人員聘任制度，並建立透明的聘任和晉升機制，以避免任人唯親、濫用裙帶關係和偏袒。

第十六條　獨立和自主

每一締約方應確保負責預防、偵查、起訴和審判腐敗犯罪的人員享有與其職責相適應的獨立自主權，且免受不當影響，並具有收集證據、保護協助偵查機構反腐與保守調查秘密人員的有效手段。

第十七條　有效的紀律措施

每一締約方應確保有關公職人員權責之規則會考慮反腐敗的要求，並規定適當和有效的紀律措施以通過適當的方式，例如行為守則，來進一步規範公職人員應有的行為。

第十八條　公共信息

每一締約方應確保公眾和媒體有依據其國內法律和以不損害行政機關運作效率或以任何其他損害政府機關和個人利益的方式接收和傳播公共信息的自由，特別是關於腐敗問題的信息。

第十九條　私營部門和民間團體的參與

1. 每一締約方，應在其力所能及的範圍內，依照其法律制度的基本原則，採取適當措施，以促進公共部門之外的個人和團體，例如企業、民間團體、非政府組織和社團組織積極參與在影響國際貿易或投資事項中防止和打擊的腐敗，並提高公眾對腐敗的存在、起因、嚴重性以及所生威脅的認識。為此，一締約方可以：

(a) 開展助力於腐敗零容忍的公開信息活動和公眾教育計劃；

(b) 如合適，採取或維持措施以鼓勵專業協會和其他非政府組織全力支持和幫助企業，特別是中小企業，制定內部控制、道德和合規計劃，或採取或維持措施以防止和查明國際貿易和投資中的賄賂和腐敗行為；

(c) 採取或維持措施以鼓勵公司管理層在其公司年度報告中作出聲明，或公開披露其內部控制、道德和合規計劃或措施，包括有助於防止和查明國際貿易和投資中的賄賂和腐敗行為的計劃或措施；以及

(d) 採取或維持措施以尊重、促進和保護尋求、接收、公佈和傳播有關腐敗信息的自由。

2. 每一締約方應努力鼓勵私營企業結合自身結構和規模開展下列活動：

(a) 制定和採取充分的內部審計控制，以幫助預防和查明影響國際貿易

或投資事項中的腐敗行為；以及

（b）確保其賬目和必要的財務報表符合適當的審計和認證程序。

3. 每一締約方應採取適當措施以保證其相關反腐敗機構為公眾所知，且在適當的情況下，提供訪問這些機構的途徑，以就任何可能被認為構成第七條中所述犯罪行為的任何事件進行舉報，包括匿名舉報。

第二十條　與其他協定的關係

除非與本章的目的和宗旨相違背，否則本章中的任何規定不影響各締約方在如下其他公約中的權利和義務：2003 年 10 月 31 日訂於紐約的《聯合國反腐敗公約》、2000 年 11 月 15 日訂於紐約的《聯合國跨國組織犯罪公約》、1997 年 11 月 21 日訂於巴黎的《關於打擊國際商業交易中行賄外國公職人員行為的公約》及其附件、1996 年 3 月 29 日訂於加拉加斯的《美洲反腐敗公約》，或 2003 年 7 月 11 日訂於馬普托的《非洲聯盟預防和打擊腐敗公約》。

第五章　貨物、服務和服務提供者便利化

第一部分

　　各締約方同意減少或消除現有的行政繁文縟節，以促進實施「一帶一路」項目所需的（包括在運輸中的）貨物、服務和服務提供商自由無縫的跨境流動。就此而言，各締約方同意簡化文書工作，實現程序現代化，並協調海關要求，以加快（包括運輸中的）貨物、服務和服務提供者的流動、放行和清關。

第一條　信息共享和可獲得性

1. 信息共享

1.1 各締約方應及時以非歧視和易於獲取的方式公佈和分享以下信息，以便政府、貿易商和其他利益相關方知曉該等信息：

(a) 進口、出口和過境程序（包括港口、機場和其他入境點的手續）以及所需的表格和單證；

(b) 對進口、出口徵收的或與其有關的任何種類的關稅和國內稅適用稅率；

(c) 行政機構對進口、出口或過境收取的或與其有關的規費和費用；

(d) 供海關使用的產品分類或估價規定；

(e) 與原產地規則相關的普遍適用的法律、法規和行政裁定；

(f) 進口、出口或過境的限制或禁止；

(g) 對違反進口、出口或過境程序行為的處罰規定；

(h) 申訴程序；

(i) 與任何一個或多個國家簽署與進口、出口或過境有關的協定或其部分內容；以及

(j) 有關關稅配額管理的程序。

1.2 本條款不應解釋為要求以英文以外的語言發佈或提供信息。

2. 通過互聯網提供的信息

2.1 每一締約方應通過互聯網在可行的範圍內酌情提供和更新以下信息：

(a) 對其進口、出口和過境程序的說明，包括申訴或審查程序，從而使政府、貿易商及其他利害相關方獲悉進口、出口和過境所需的實際步驟；

(b) 對該締約方進口、自該締約方出口或經該締約方過境所需的表格和單證；

(c) 其諮詢點的聯繫信息。

2.2 在可行情況下，第 2.1（a）項所提及之說明亦應提供英文版本。

3. 諮詢點

3.1 每一締約方應在其所能提供的資源範圍內，設立或維持一個或多個諮詢點，以答覆政府、貿易商和其他利害相關方對第 1.1 款所涵蓋事項的合理問詢，並提供第 1.1（a）項要求的表格和單證。

3.2 一關稅同盟的締約方或參與區域一體化（「一帶一路」轄區除外）的締約方可在區域一級設立或維持共同諮詢點，以滿足第 3.1 款關於共同程序的要求。

3.3 鼓勵各締約方不對答覆諮詢及提供所要求的表格和單證收取費用。如收費，各締約方應將其規費和費用的數額限制在所提供服務的近似成本範圍內。

3.4 諮詢點應在各締約方規定的合理時間範圍內答覆諮詢並提供表格和單證。該時限可根據請求的性質或複雜程度而不同。

3.5 鼓勵各締約方通過互聯網提供進一步與貿易有關的信息，包括與貿易

有關的立法和第 1 款提及的其他項目。

4. 通知

各締約方應通知根據第二十三條第 1.1 款設立的「一帶一路」便利化委員會（在本章中稱之為「委員會」）：

（a）公佈第 1.1（a）至（j）項所載項目的官方地點；

（b）第 2.1 款所指的網站鏈接地址；以及

（c）第 3.1 款所指的諮詢點聯繫信息。

第二條　評論機會、生效前信息及磋商

1. 評論機會和生效前信息

1.1 每一締約方應在切實可行的範圍內，以符合其國內法律和法律制度的方式，為貿易商和其他利害相關方提供機會和適當時限，就擬引入或修訂與貨物（包括過境貨物）的流動、放行和清關相關的一般適用的法律法規發表意見。

1.2 每一締約方應在切實可行的範圍內，以符合其國內法律和法律制度的方式，確保與貨物（包括過境貨物）的流動、放行和清關相關的新立或修正的一般適用的法律法規在生效前盡早公佈，或使其相關信息可公開獲得，以便貿易商和其他利害相關方能夠知曉。

1.3 關稅稅率的變更、具有免除效力的措施、因遵守第 1.1 款或第 1.2 款影響其效力的措施、緊急情況下適用的措施或對國內法律和法律制度的微小變更均不包括在第 1.1 款和第 1.2 款之中。

2. 磋商

每一締約方應在適當的情況下規定其邊境機構與其領土內的貿易商或其他利害相關方進行定期磋商。

第三條　預先裁定

1. 每一締約方應以合理的方式並在規定的時間內對已提交包含所有必要信息書面請求的申請人作出預裁定。如一締約方拒絕作出預先裁定，則應及時書

面通知申請人，並說明相關事實和作出決定的依據。

2.當申請中提出的問題出現下列情形時，一締約方可拒絕對申請人作出預先裁定：

　　(a)　所提問題已包含在申請人提請任何政府部門、上訴庭或法院審理的案件中；或

　　(b)　所提問題已由任何上訴庭或法院作出裁決。

3.預先裁定在作出後應在一合理期間內有效，除非作出該裁定所依據的法律、事實或情形已發生變化。

4.一締約方撤銷、變更或廢止該預先裁定，應當書面通知申請人，並列出相關事實和作出決定的依據。一締約方只有在預先裁定的作出是基於不完整、不正確、虛假或誤導性信息的情況下才可撤銷、變更或廢止具有追溯力的該裁定。

5.一締約方作出的預先裁定對請求做出該裁定的申請人的締約方有拘束力。該締約方可規定，預先裁定對申請人具有拘束力。

6.每一締約方應至少公佈：

　　(a)　申請預先裁定的要求，包括需要提供的信息及格式；

　　(b)　作出預先裁定的時限；以及

　　(c)　預先裁定的有效期。

7.每一締約方應根據申請人的書面請求，對預先裁定或對撤銷、變更或廢止預先裁定的決定進行複審。

8.每一締約方在考慮保護商業機密信息需要的同時，應努力公佈其認為對其他利害關係方具有重大利益的預先裁定的任何信息。

9.定義和範圍：

　　(a)　「預先裁定」是在申請中所涵蓋的貨物進口前，一締約方向申請人作出的書面決定，其中規定該締約方在貨物進口時，在如下方面應當給予該貨物的待遇：

　　　　(i)　貨物的稅則分類；以及

　　　　(ii)　貨物的原產地。

　　(b)　除（a）項所規定的預先裁定外，鼓勵各締約方就下列事項作出預先裁定：

(i) 根據特定事實用於確定完稅價格的適當方法、標準及其應用；

(ii) 一締約方申請海關關稅減免要求的適用性；

(iii) 一締約方關於包括關稅配額在內的配額要求的適用情況；以及

(iv) 一締約方認為適宜作出預先裁定的任何其他事項。

(c) 申請人指出口商、進口商或有正當理由的人或其代理人。

(d) 一締約方可要求申請人在其領土內有法人代表或進行註冊。在可行的限度內，該等要求應盡量不限制可申請預先裁定的人員類別，並特別考慮中小企業的具體需要。該等要求應明確透明，且不構成任意的或不正當的歧視。

第四條　申訴或審查程序

1. 每一締約方應規定，海關作出行政決定所針對的任何人在該締約方領土內有權：

(a) 向級別高於或獨立於作出行政決定的官員或機構提出行政申訴或複查或由此類官員或機構進行申訴或複查；及／或

(b) 對該決定進行司法上訴或複審。

2. 一締約方的立法可要求，在提起司法申訴或複查前，先提起行政申訴或複查。

3. 每一締約方應確保，其申訴或複查程序以非歧視的方式進行。

4. 每一締約方應確保，第 1 款（a）項規定的申訴或複審決定：

(a) 未在其法律或法規規定的期限內做出；或

(b) 未能避免不適當拖延，則申訴人有權向行政機關或司法機關提出進一步上訴或要求進一步複審，或向司法機關尋求任何其他救濟。各締約方亦可依誠實信用原則進行磋商或訴諸本協定第十四章（爭端解決）所規定的爭端解決機制。

5. 每一締約方應確保向第 1 款所指人員提供作出行政決定的理由，使其能夠在必要時訴諸上訴或複查程序。

6. 鼓勵每一締約方將本條規定適用於海關以外的相關邊境機構所作出的行政決定。

第五條 增強公正性、非歧視性和透明度的其他措施

1. 增強監管或檢查的通知

如一締約方採用或維持對其相關主管機構發佈通知或指南的系統，旨在增強對通知或指南所涵蓋食品、飲料或飼料的邊境監管或檢查水平以保護其領土內人類、動物或植物的生命或健康，則此種通知或指南的發佈、終止或中止應適用以下紀律：

(a) 該締約方可在適當情況下根據風險發佈通知或指南；

(b) 該締約方可發佈通知或指南，以使其僅統一適用於據以作出通知或指南的衛生和植物檢疫條件適用的入境地點；

(c) 若據以作出通知或指南的情形不復存在或變化後的情形可以具有較低貿易限制的方式處理，則該成員應迅速終止或中止該通知或指南；

(d) 如該締約方決定終止或中止通知或指南，則應適當地以非歧視和易於獲取的方式立即公佈終止或中止聲明，或通知出口締約方或進口商。

2. 扣留

如申報進口貨物因海關或任何其他主管機構檢查而予以扣留，則該締約方應迅速通知承運商或進口商。

3. 檢驗程序

3.1 如申報進口的貨物抵達時所抽取樣品的第一次檢驗結果顯示不利，一締約方可根據請求可給予第二次檢驗機會。

3.2 一締約方應以非歧視和易於獲得的方式公佈可以實施檢驗的實驗室的名稱和地址，或在其提供第 3.1 款所規定的機會的情況下，將該等信息提供給進口商。

3.3 一締約方在貨物放行和清關時應考慮根據第 3.1 款進行的第二次檢驗的結果，並可在適當的情況下接受此次檢驗的結果。

第六條 徵收進口、出口或與進口、出口相關的費用和收費的紀律及處罰

1. 徵收進口、出口或與進口、出口相關的費用和收費的一般紀律

1.1 第 1 款的規定應適用於除進出口關稅和《1994 年關稅與貿易總協定》第三條範圍內的國內稅外的、各締約方對進口、出口貨物徵收或與其相關的所有費用和收費。

1.2 費用和收費信息應按照第一條的規定予以公佈。該等信息應包括將適用的費用和收費、徵收該等費用和收費的原因、主管機構以及支付時間和方式。

1.3 應在新增或修訂的費用和收費的公佈與生效之間留出足夠的時間，但緊急情況除外。此類費用和收費在有關信息公佈之前不得適用。

1.4 各締約方應定期審查其費用和收費，以便在可行的情況下減少費用和收費的數量與種類。

2. 對進口、出口貨物徵收的或與其相關的海關業務辦理費用和收費的特殊紀律

辦理海關業務的費用和收費：

    (a) 應限定在對所涉特定進口、出口操作提供服務或與之相關服務的近似成本內；以及

    (b) 如費用為針對與辦理貨物海關業務密切相關的服務而收取，則無需與特定進口或出口業務相關聯。

3. 處罰紀律

3.1 為第 3 款之目的，「處罰」是指一締約方的海關針對違反其海關法律、法規或程序要求而實施的處罰。

3.2 每一締約方應確保對違反海關法律、法規或程序要求行為的處罰，僅針對其法律所規定的違法行為責任人實施。

3.3 實施的處罰應依照案件的事實和情節而定，且應與違反程度及嚴重性相符。

3.4 每一締約方應確保採取措施以避免:

　　(a) 在罰款和關稅的認定與收取方面存在利益衝突;以及

　　(b) 為不符合第 3.3 款的罰款的評定或徵收提供獎勵。

3.5 每一締約方應確保在對違反海關法律、法規或程序要求的行為進行處罰時,向被處罰者作出書面說明,具體說明該違法行為的性質以及對違法行為處罰的數額或範圍所適用的法律、法規或程序。

3.6 如一當事人在一締約方海關行政部門發現其違法行為之前,主動向海關行政部門披露其違反海關法律、法規或程序要求的行為,則應鼓勵該締約方在確定對其的處罰時,酌情將該等事實作為一個減輕處罰的潛在因素。

3.7 本款的規定適用於對第十一條所提及的過境運輸的處罰。

第七條　貨物放行與清關

1. 抵達前業務處理

1.1 每一締約方應採取或維持允許提交包括艙單在內的進口單證和其他必需信息的程序,以便在貨物抵運前開始辦理業務,以期在貨物抵達後加快放行。

1.2 每一締約方應酌情規定以電子形式預先提交單證,以便在貨物抵達前處理此類單證。

2. 電子支付

每一締約方應在可行的範圍內採取或維持有關程序,允許選擇以電子方式支付海關對進口、出口收取的關稅、國內稅、規費及費用。

3. 將貨物放行與關稅、國內稅、規費及費用的最終確定相分離

3.1 每一締約方應採取或維持程序,規定如關稅、國內稅,規費及費用的最終確定不在貨物抵達前或抵達時作出或不在貨物抵達後盡可能快地作出,則可在最終確定作出前放行貨物,條件是其他所有管理要求均已符合。

3.2 作為此種放行之條件,一締約方可要求:

　　(a) 支付在貨物抵達前或抵達時確定的關稅、國內稅,規費及費用,

對尚未確定的任何數額以保證金、押金或其法律法規規定的其他適當形式提供擔保；或

（b）以保證金、押金或其法律法規規定的其他適當形式提供擔保。

3.3 此類擔保不得超過該締約方所要求的擔保所涵蓋貨物最終應支付的關稅、國內稅、規費及費用的金額。

3.4 如應當處以罰款或罰金的違法行為被發現，則可要求對可能實施的罰款和罰金提供擔保。

3.5 第 3.2 款和第 3.4 款所指擔保應在不再需要時予以退還。

3.6 本條規定不得影響一締約方檢查、扣押、查封、沒收或以任何與其 WTO 以及包括「一帶一路」項目中有效法律文件在內的其他國際條約中的權利、義務相衝突的方式處理貨物的權利。

4. 風險管理

4.1 每一締約方應盡可能為海關監管建立或維持一風險管理制度。

4.2 每一締約方在設計和實施風險管理時，應以避免任意或不合理的歧視，或形成對國際貿易造成變相限制的方式進行。

4.3 每一締約方應將海關監管以及盡可能將其他相關邊境監管集中於高風險貨物，並加速放行低風險貨物。一締約方亦可隨機選擇貨物實施此類監管，作為其風險管理的一部分。

4.4 每一締約方應將通過選擇性標準進行的風險評估作為風險管理的依據。此類選擇性標準可特別包括世界海關組織協調制度代碼、貨物性質和描述、原產國、貨物裝運國、貨物價值、貿易商合規紀錄以及運輸工具類型等。

5. 後續稽查

5.1 為了加快貨物的放行，每一締約方應採取或維持後續稽查，以確保海關和其他相關法律法規得以被遵循。

5.2 每一締約方應以風險為基礎選擇一當事人或貨物進行後續稽查，可包括適當的選擇性標準。每一締約方應以透明的方式進行後續稽查。如該當事人參與後續稽查且結論性結果已得出，則該締約方應立即將稽查結果、被稽查人的權利和義務、以及稽查結果的理由通知被稽查人。

5.3 後續稽查所獲取的信息可用於進一步的行政或司法程序。

5.4 在可行的情況下，各締約方應在實施風險管理時使用後續稽查結果。

6. 平均放行時間的確定和公佈

6.1 鼓勵各締約方根據其需求和能力特別是使用《世界海關組織放行時間研究》等工具，定期並以一致的方式測算和公佈其貨物的平均放行時間。

6.2 鼓勵各締約方與委員會分享其測算平均放行時間的經驗，包括所使用的方法、發現的瓶頸以及由此對效率產生的影響。

7. 對經認證的經營者的貿易便利化措施

7.1 每一締約方應根據第 7.3 款向符合特定標準的經營者，下稱經認證的經營者，提供與進口、出口或過境手續和程序有關的額外的貿易便利化措施。或者，一締約方可通過普遍適用於所有經營者的海關程序，提供該等貿易便利化措施，而無需作出單獨規定。

7.2 成為經認證的經營者的特定標準應與遵守一締約方的法律、法規或程序中規定的要求或不遵守該等要求的風險有關。

 （a）此類標準應予以公佈，可包括：

  （i）遵守海關及其他相關法律法規的適當紀錄；

  （ii）允許進行必要內部控制的紀錄管理系統；

  （iii）財務償債能力，包括在適當情況下提供足夠的擔保或保證；以及

  （iv）供應鏈安全。

 （b）該標準不得：

  （i）設計或實施從而在相同條件的經營者之間給予或造成任意或不合理的歧視；且

  （ii）在可能的限度內，限制中小企業的參與。

7.3 根據第 7.1 款規定的貿易便利化措施應至少包括以下措施中的三項措施：

 （a）酌情降低單證和數據要求；

 （b）酌情降低實際檢查和審查比例；

 （c）酌情加快放行時間；

(d) 關稅、國內稅、規費和費用的延遲支付；

(e) 使用總擔保或減少擔保；

(f) 在一定期限內就全部進口、出口貨物進行一次性海關申報；以及

(g) 在經認證的經營者的場所或海關認可的其他地點辦理貨物清關。

7.4 鼓勵各締約方在國際標準（若存在）的基礎上制定經認證的經營者計劃，除非此類國際標準對實現所追求的合法目標不適宜或無效果。

7.5 為了加強向經營者提供貿易便利化措施，各締約方應向其他締約方提供協商互認經認證的經營者計劃的可能性。

7.6 各締約方應在委員會內交換現行有效的經認證的經營者計劃的相關信息。

8. 快運貨物

8.1 每一締約方應採取或維持程序在保持海關監管的同時，至少允許對做出申請的申請人快速放行通過航空貨運設施入境的貨物。如一締約方使用限制申請人的標準，則該締約方可在公佈的標準中作為申請適用第 8.2 款所述快運貨物待遇的條件，要求申請人應：

(a) 在申請人滿足該締約方關於此類處理在一特定設施中進行的要求的情況下，提供有關處理快運貨物相關的基礎設施，並支付海關費用；

(b) 在快運貨物抵運之前，提交放行所需的信息；

(c) 所確定的費用限於為提供第 8.2 款所述待遇所提供服務的近似成本；

(d) 通過使用內部安保、物流和自提取到送達的追蹤技術，對快運貨物保持高度控制；

(e) 提供從提取到送達的快速運輸；

(f) 承擔向海關繳納貨物一切關稅、國內稅、規費及費用的責任；

(g) 在遵守海關及其他相關法律法規方面有良好的紀錄；

(h) 遵守與有效執行各締約方法律法規和程序要求直接相關的，特別是與第 8.2 款所述待遇有關的其他條件。

8.2 在符合第 8.1 款和第 8.3 款的前提下，各締約方應：

(a) 最大限度減少依據第十條第 1 款放行快運貨物所需的單證，並在可能的情況下，規定對某些貨物可基於一次性提交的信息予以放行；

(b) 規定在正常的情況下，當快運貨物抵運後盡快放行，但條件是放行所需的信息已提交；

(c) 努力將（a）項和（b）項中所述的待遇適用於任何重量或價值的貨物；

(d) 認可一締約方可要求額外入境手續，包括申報單、證明單證及繳納關稅和國內稅，並可根據貨物類型限制這種待遇，前提是這種待遇不限於單據等低價值貨物；以及

(e) 在可能的情況下，除某些規定貨物外，規定免於徵收關稅和國內稅的微量貨值或應徵稅額。符合《1994 年關稅與貿易總協定》第三條的、適用於進口貨物的國內稅，如增值稅和消費稅，不受本條款的約束。

8.3 第 8.1 款和第 8.2 款的任何規定均不影響一締約方檢驗、扣留、扣押、沒收或拒絕貨物入境，或進行後續稽查的權利，包括與使用風險管理系統有關的權利。此外，第 8.1 款和第 8.2 款的任何規定均不妨礙一締約方將要求提交額外信息和完成非自動進口許可要求作為放行的條件。

9. 易腐貨物 [1]

9.1 為了防止易腐貨物可避免的損失或變質，並在符合所有監管要求的情況下，每一締約方應規定易腐貨物：

(a) 在正常情況下，應在盡可能短的時間內予以放行；以及

(b) 在適當的特殊情況下，在海關和其他相關主管機構的工作時間以外進行放行。

9.2 每一締約方應在安排任何可能需要的檢驗時，適當優先考慮易腐貨物。

9.3 每一締約方應安排或允許進口商在易腐貨物放行前對其作適當的儲藏。各締約方可要求進口商安排的任何儲存設施必須經其有關主管機構的批准

---

1 就本條款而言，易腐貨物指由於其自然特性，特別是在缺乏適當儲存條件的情況下，迅速腐爛的貨物。

或指定。將貨物移至儲存設施，包括經認證的經營者移運貨物，如要求，須經有關主管機構批准。在可行並符合國內法的情況下，應進口商請求，該締約方應規定在這些儲存設施中予以放行所需的任何必要程序。

9.4 若易腐貨物的放行出現重大延誤，經書面請求，進口締約方應盡可能就延誤的原因進行通報。

第八條　邊境機構合作

1. 每一締約方應確保，其負責邊境管制以及貨物進口、出口和過境程序的機構與部門相互合作，並協調行動，以便利貿易。

2. 每一締約方應在可能和可行的範圍內，與擁有共同邊界的其他締約方根據共同議定的條款進行合作，以期協調跨境程序，從而便利跨境貿易。此種合作和協調可包括：

　　(a)　工作日和工作時間的協調；

　　(b)　程序和手續的協調；

　　(c)　共用設施的建設與共享；

　　(d)　聯合監管；

　　(e)　一站式邊境監管站的設立。

第九條　與進口、出口和過境相關的手續

1. 手續和單證要求

1.1 為最大限度地減少進口、出口和過境手續的頻率和複雜性，減少和簡化進口、出口和過境單證要求，同時考慮到合法政策目標和其他如情勢變更、相關新信息和商業慣例、方法和技術的可獲得性、國際最佳實踐及利害關係方的投入，每一締約方應對該等手續和單證要求進行審查，並根據審查的結果，酌情確保該等手續和單證要求符合下列要求：

　　(a)　為迅速放行和結關貨物（特別是易腐貨物）而採取和 / 或實施；

　　(b)　以減少交易商和經營者守法的時間和成本的方式而採取和 / 或實施；

　　(c)　在可合理選擇兩項或以上措施以實現政策目標或有關目標的情況

下，選擇對貿易限制最小的措施；以及

（d） 如果不再需要，則不再作出該等要求，包括其中部分要求。

1.2「一帶一路」委員會應酌情制定程序，以便各締約方共享相關信息和最佳做法。

2. 副本的接受

2.1 在適當的情況下，每一締約方應努力接受辦理進口、出口或過境手續所需證明單證的紙質或電子副本。

2.2 如一締約方政府機構已持有此單證的原件，則該締約方的任何其他政府機構應在合適時接受來自持有單證正本的政府機構的紙質或電子副本，以替代正本。

2.3 一締約方不得要求將提交給出口締約方海關的出口報關單正本或副本作為進口的一項要求。

3. 國際標準的使用

3.1 除本協定另有規定外，鼓勵各締約方使用有關國際標準或其部分作為辦理進口、出口或過境手續和程序的依據。

3.2 鼓勵各締約方在力所能及的範圍內參加適當的國際組織對相關國際標準的制定和定期審議。

3.3 委員會應酌情制定程序，使各締約方能夠共享實施國際標準的有關信息和最佳做法。

3.4 委員會亦可邀請有關國際組織討論其關於國際標準方面的工作。在合適的情況下，委員會亦可確定對各締約方具有特別價值的特定標準。

4. 單一窗口

4.1 各締約方應努力建立或維持單一窗口，使貿易商能夠通過單一接入點向參與的主管機構或部門提交貨物進口、出口或過境的單證和／或數據要求。主管機構或部門審查單證和／或數據後，應當將審查結果及時通過單一窗口告知申請人。

4.2 如果文件和／或數據要求已通過單一窗口被接收，參與的主管機構或部門不得提出提交相同文件和／或數據的要求，但在緊急情況和其他已公佈的有限例外情況除外。

4.3 各締約方應將單一窗口的運行細節通知委員會。

4.4 各締約方應在可能和可行的限度內使用信息技術支持單一窗口。

5. 裝運前檢驗

5.1 各締約方不得要求使用與稅則歸類和海關估價有關的裝運前檢驗。

5.2 在不影響各締約方使用第 5.1 款未涵蓋的其他種類的裝運前檢驗的權利的情況下，鼓勵各締約方不對該種使用規定或適用新的要求。

6. 報關代理的使用

6.1 在不影響目前維持報關員特殊地位的部分締約方的重要政策關注的情況下，自本協定生效之日起，各締約方不得強制要求使用報關代理。

6.2 每一締約方應通知委員會，並公佈其使用報關代理的措施。任何後續修改均應及時通知和公佈。

6.3 關於報關代理的許可程序，各締約方應適用透明、客觀的規則。

7. 共同邊境手續和統一單證要求

7.1 每一締約方應在符合第 7.2 款的前提下，在其全部領土內對貨物放行和清關適用共同的海關程序和統一的單證要求。

7.2 本條的任何內容不得妨礙一締約方：

　（a）　根據貨物的性質和類型或其運輸方式，區分其程序和單證要求；

　（b）　在風險管理的基礎上，區分貨物的程序和單證要求；

　（c）　區分其程序和單證要求，以全部或部分免除進口關稅或國內稅；

　（d）　採用電子方式提交或辦理業務；或

　（e）　以與世界貿易組織《衛生和植物檢疫措施實施協定》相一致的方式，區別其程序和單證要求。

8. 拒收入境貨物

8.1 在進口貨物因不符合規定的衛生和植物檢疫法規或技術法規而被一締約

方主管機構拒絕入境的情況下，該締約方應在遵守並符合其法律法規的前提下，允許進口商將被拒收的貨物重新發運或退回給出口商或出口商指定的其他人。

8.2 當給予第 8.1 款規定的選擇權而進口商未在合理期限內行使該權利時，主管機構可採取不同的行動來處理此種違規貨物。

9. 貨物暫准進口及進出境加工

9.1 貨物暫准進口

如貨物為特定目的進入其關稅區、計劃在一定期限內轉出口，且除因使用而引起的正常折舊和損耗外沒有發生任何變化，則每一締約方應按其法律法規規定，允許該貨物運入其關稅區，並有條件地免除全部或部分進口關稅和國內稅。

9.2 進境和出境加工

(a) 每一締約方應按照其法律和法規的規定，允許貨物的進出境加工。對允許出境加工的貨物，根據該締約方的法律和法規，在再進口時可以免徵全部或部分進口關稅和國內稅。

(b) 就本條而言，「進境加工」指貨物運入一締約方關境後，基於該貨物用於製造、加工或修理並隨後出口，有條件的免除全部或部分進口關稅和國內稅或有資格獲得退稅的海關程序。

(c) 就本條而言，「出境加工」指在一締約方關稅區內自由流通的貨物可暫時出口至他國外用於製造、加工或修理並後續再進口的海關程序。

第十條　過境自由

1. 一締約方實施的與過境運輸相關的任何法規或手續：

(a) 若導致其被採用的情形或目標已不復存在，或情形或目標變更後，能夠以更少貿易限制性的合理方式處理時，則不得維持；

(b) 不得以對過境運輸構成變相限制的方式適用。

2. 不得以收取任何有關過境規費或費用影響過境運輸，但運輸費用或相當於過境所產生的行政費用或提供服務的成本費用除外。

3. 各締約方不得尋求、採取或維持對過境運輸的任何自願限制或任何其他類似措施。本要求不影響與管理過境相關的且與 WTO 規則相一致的現行和未來的國內法規、雙邊或多邊安排。

4. 每一締約方應給予經由任何其他締約方領土過境貨物的待遇不低於該等貨物未經其他締約方領土過境而從原產地運至目的地所享受的待遇。

5. 鼓勵各締約方在可行的情況下，為過境運輸提供單獨的基礎設施，如車道、泊位及類似設施。

6. 為實現以下目的且與過境運輸有關的手續、單證要求和海關監管的複雜程度不得超過必要限度：

（a） 貨物識別；以及

（b） 保證滿足過境要求。

7. 貨物一入過境程序並獲准從一締約方領土內的始發地啓運，在其到達締約方領土內的目的地結束過境程序之前，將不必支付任何海關費用或受到不必要的延誤或限制。

8. 各締約方不得對過境貨物實施世界貿易組織《技術性貿易壁壘協定》範圍內的技術法規和合格評價程序。

9. 各締約方應允許並規定在貨物抵達前對過境單證和數據進行提前提交和處理。

10. 過境運輸一經抵達一締約方領土內出境點海關，如符合過境要求，則該海關應立即結束過境操作。

11. 在一締約方要求對過境運輸提供保證金、押金或其他適當貨幣或非貨幣形式的擔保的情況下，該等擔保應僅限於保證該等過境運輸所產生的要求得以滿足。

12. 該締約方一經確定其過境要求已得滿足，則應立即解除擔保。

13. 每一締約方應在符合其法律和法規的情況下，允許包括為同一經營者的多筆交易提供的總擔保或不解除擔保而對後續貨物提供的擔保展期。

14. 每一締約方應公佈其用於設定擔保的相關信息，包括單筆交易擔保，以及在可行情況下的多筆交易擔保。

15. 每一締約方只有在高風險或使用保證無法確保遵守海關法律法規的情況下，方可要求在過境運輸中使用海關押運或海關護送。有關海關押運或海關護送的一般規定，應按照本協定第一條的規定予以公佈。

16. 各締約方應努力相互合作和協調，以促進過境自由。該等合作與協調可包括但不限於在以下方面達成的諒解：

　　(a) 費用；

　　(b) 手續和法律要求；以及

　　(c) 過境制度的實際運行。

　　17. 每一締約方應努力指定一國家過境協調機構，以便接收其他締約方就有關過境業務良好運行所提出來的所有諮詢和建議。

第十一條　海關合作

1. 促進守法和合作的措施

　　1.1 各締約方一致同意，確保貿易商瞭解其守法義務、鼓勵自願守法以允許進口商在適當情況下自我糾錯而不受處罰以及對違法貿易商適用守法措施以實施更為嚴厲的措施。

　　1.2 鼓勵各締約方通過委員會等方式分享海關規定得以遵守方面的最佳實踐。鼓勵各締約方以管理守法措施並提高其有效性為目的，在技術指導或援助和支持能力建設方面開展合作。

2. 交換信息

　　2.1 各締約方應依請求並在遵循本條規定的前提下，在有合理理由懷疑進口或出口申報的真實性和準確性時，交換第 6.1(b) 項和／或 (c) 項所列信息，以便核實該項進口或出口申報。

　　2.2 每一締約方應將其用於交換信息的聯絡點的詳情通知委員會。

3. 核實

　　一締約方只有在對一進出口申報實施適當核實程序並檢查可獲得的有關單證後，方可提出索取信息的請求。

4. 請求

　　4.1 提出請求的締約方應以紙質或電子方式向被請求締約方提供英文書面請求。該請求包括：

(a) 所涉事項，在適當和可獲得的情況下，包括與所涉進口申報相對應的出口申報的序列號；

(b) 請求締約方尋求信息或單證的目的，並在知悉情況下包括該請求所涉人員的姓名和聯繫方式；

(c) 應被請求締約方的要求，在適當的情況下提供對核實的確認；

(d) 請求提供的具體信息或單證；

(e) 提出請求機關的身份認證；

(f) 請求締約方所援引的管轄收集、保護、使用、披露、保留和處置保密信息和個人信息的國內法律和法律制度的規定。

4.2 如請求締約方不能遵守第 4.1 款的任何一項規定，則應在請求中予以說明。

5. 保護和保密

5.1 在符合第 5.2 款的前提下，請求締約方應：

(a) 對被請求締約方提供的所有信息或單證嚴格保密，並至少給予與被請求締約方按第 6.1 款（b）項或（c）項所描述的其國內法律和法律制度規定的同等水平的保護和保密；

(b) 僅向處理所涉事項的海關提供信息或單證，並僅為請求中列明的目的使用該等信息或單證，除非被請求締約方另行書面同意用於其他目的；

(c) 未經被請求締約方的特別書面許可，不得披露信息或單證；

(d) 在任何特定情況下，不得將未經被請求締約方核實的任何信息或單證用作消除疑慮的決定性因素；

(e) 尊重被請求締約方就具體案件提出的關於保留和處置保密信息或單證及個人數據的任何條件；以及

(f) 應請求，將根據所提供的信息或單證就相關事項作出的任何決定和採取的行動通知被請求締約方。

5.2 如提出請求的締約方依照其國內法律和法律制度可能無法遵守第 5.1 款下的任何規定時，則該締約方應在其請求中予以說明。

5.3 被請求締約方對根據第 4 款收到的任何請求和信息核實，應提供與其給予其自身類似信息至少相同水平的保護和保密。

6. 提供信息

6.1 在遵守本條規定的前提下，被請求締約方應迅速：

(a) 以書面形式通過紙質或電子方式作出回覆；

(b) 提供進口或出口申報中列明的具體信息，或在可獲得的情況下，提供申報本身並附要求請求締約方提供保護和保密水平的説明；

(c) 經請求，提供下列用於證明進口或出口申報的單證中所列明的具體信息，或在可獲得的情況下提供單證本身：商業發票、裝箱單、原產地證書和提單，以單證提交的形式提供，無論是紙質的還是電子的，並附要求請求締約方提供保護和保密水平的説明；

(d) 確認所提供的單證為真實副本；

(e) 在可能的情況下，自請求之日起 90 日內，提供信息或對請求作出答覆。

6.2 被請求締約方可根據其國內法律和法律制度，在提供信息前要求得到以下保證，即未經被請求締約方書面許可的情況下，具體信息不得在刑事調查、司法訴訟或非海關訴訟中作為證據使用。如提出請求的締約方不能遵守該等要求，則應向被請求締約方予以説明。

7. 對請求的遲覆或拒絕

7.1 在下列情況下，被請求締約方可對提供信息的請求予以遲覆或部分或全部拒絕，並應將該等行為的理由通知提出請求的締約方：

(a) 與被請求締約方國內法律和法律制度所體現的公共利益相抵觸；

(b) 其國內法律和法律制度禁止發佈該信息。在此種情況下，應向提出請求的締約方提供相關具體引文的副本；

(c) 提供信息將妨礙執法或干擾正在進行的行政或司法調查、起訴或訴訟；

(d) 管轄收集、保護、使用、披露、保留和處置保密信息或個人信息的國內法律和法律制度要求獲得進口商或出口商的同意，而該等同意尚未獲得；或

（e）提供信息的請求在被請求締約方關於要求保留單證的法律規定失效後才收到。

7.2 在第 4.2 款、第 5.2 款或第 6.2 款的情況下，是否執行該等請求應由被請求締約方自行決定。

8. 互惠

如果提出請求的締約方認為，若被請求締約方提出類似請求，其將無法執行，或其尚未適用本條規定，則應在請求中對該等事實予以説明。是否執行該等請求應由被請求締約方自行決定。

9. 行政負擔

9.1 提出請求的締約方應考慮答覆信息請求對被請求締約方資源和成本的影響。該請求締約方應考慮尋求請求獲得答覆的財務利益與被請求締約方為提供信息所做努力之間的相稱性。

9.2 如果被請求締約方從一個或多個提出請求的締約方處收到數量多到或範圍寬到難以處理，且在合理期限內難以滿足的信息請求，可要求一個或多個提出請求的締約方按照重要性對其請求進行排序，以便在其資源範圍內就實際處理限額達成一致。在雙方未達成共識的情況下，則被請求締約方可根據自身排序結果自行決定執行該等請求。

10. 限制

不得要求被請求締約方：

（a）修改其進口、出口申報的格式或程序；

（b）索取除第 6.1（c）項提及的在進口或出口申報中提交的單證以外的其他單證；

（c）發起諮詢，以獲得信息；

（d）修改保留此類信息的期限；

（e）在已採用電子格式的單證的情況下，還要求提供紙質單證；

（f）翻譯信息；

（g）核實信息的準確性；或

（h） 提供可能損害公私企業合法商業利益的信息。

11. 未經授權的使用或披露

11.1 如若違反本條項下關於交換信息的使用或披露，則已接收到信息的請求締約方應立即將該等未經授權的使用或披露之詳情告知提供信息的被請求締約方，並且：

（a） 採取必要措施對違反行為予以補救；

（b） 採取必要措施防止將來的任何違反行為；以及

（c） 將根據第（a）項和第（b）項採取的措施通知被請求締約方。

11.2 被請求締約方可中止其根據本條對請求締約方所負的義務直至第 11.1 款規定的措施得以實施。

12. 雙邊和區域協議

12.1 本條任何規定不得妨礙一締約方締結或維持一項共享或交換海關信息和數據，包括在安全和快速基礎上如自動或在貨物抵達前共享或交換海關信息和數據的雙邊、多邊或區域協議。

12.2 本條任何規定不得解釋為改變或影響一締約方在該等雙邊、多邊或區域協議項下的權利和義務，或為管理各締約方在該等其他協議項下的海關信息和數據的交換。

第二部分　機構安排和最後條款

第十二條　機構安排

1.「一帶一路」便利化委員會

1.1 特此設立便利化委員會。

1.2 委員會應對所有締約方開放，並選舉產生委員會主席。委員會應根據本協定有關規定的需要和設想舉行會議，每年至少一次，以便為締約方提供機會就有關本協定的實施或促進本協定目標實現的任何事項進行磋商。委員會應履行本協定或各締約方賦予其的各項職責，並應制定自己的議事規則。

1.3 委員會可按要求設立附屬機構。所有該等機構應向委員會報告。

1.4 委員會應制定可使各締約方在適當的情況下分享有關信息和最佳實踐的程序。

1.5 委員會應與貿易便利化領域的國際組織，如世界海關組織，保持密切聯繫，以期獲得有關本協定實施和管理的最佳建議，並確保避免不必要的重複工作。為此，委員會可邀請該等組織或其附屬機構的代表：

　　（a）出席委員會會議；以及

　　（b）討論有關實施本協定的具體事宜。

1.6 委員會應在本協定生效後四年內且在生效後定期對本協定的運作和實施情況進行審查。

1.7 鼓勵各締約方向委員會提出有關本協定實施和適用的問題。

1.8 委員會應鼓勵和便利各締約方就本協定項下的具體問題進行專門討論，以期迅速達成令各方滿意的解決辦法。

2. 國家便利化委員會

每一締約方應設立和 / 或維持國家貿易便利化委員會或指定一個現有機制，以便利本協定條款的國內協調和實施。

第十三條　最後條款

1. 就本協定而言,「締約方」一詞被視為包括該締約方的主管機構。

2. 本協定所有條款對所有締約方具有約束力。

第六章　數字經濟

第一部分　定義

第一條　定義

就本章而言：

「計算設施」指用於商業用途的信息處理或存儲的計算機服務器和存儲設備；

「涵蓋的人」指：

    (a)　第七章「投資」第一條「定義」中所定義的「涵蓋投資」；或

    (b)　按《服務貿易總協定》第二十八條（g）項中所定義的一締約方的服務提供者，但不包括按本協定「金融」一章「定義」的「涵蓋的人」；

「數字產品」指電腦程序、文本、視頻、圖像、聲音紀錄，或其他經數字化編碼、生產用於商業銷售或分銷、可通過電子方式傳輸的產品；[2,3]

「電子認證」指驗證電子通信的締約方或交易締約方的身份並保證電子通信完整性的過程或行為；

2　為進一步明確，數字產品不包括以數字化表現的金融工具，例如貨幣。

3　數字產品的定義不得被理解為反映一締約方對通過電子傳輸的數字產品貿易應被歸入服務貿易或貨物貿易的觀點。

「**電子發票**」指供應商和購買者之間使用結構化數字格式自動創建、交換和處理支付請求；

「**電子支付**」指付款人通過電子方式將可接受的貨幣債權轉移給收款人；

「**電子簽名**」指電子文件或信息中所含有、附加、與之有邏輯聯繫的電子形式的數據，該等數據可被用於識別與電子文件或信息有關的簽名人身份，並表明簽名人對電子文件或信息中所含信息之認可；

「**電子傳輸或通過電子方式傳輸**」指任何使用電磁形式進行的傳輸，包括光子形式；

「**政府信息**」指由中央政府掌握的非專有信息，包括數據；

「**個人信息**」指關於一已確認或可確認的自然人的任何信息，包括數據；

「**貿易管理文件**」指由一締約方簽發或控制的、必須由或為進口商或出口商填寫的與貨物進口或出口有關的表格。

「**非應邀商業電子信息**」指出於商業或營銷目的，未經接收人同意，或儘管接收人已明確拒絕，但是通過互聯網接入服務提供者或在每一締約方法律法規所規定的限度內通過其他電信服務，仍向其電子地址發送的電子信息。

第二部分 範圍與一般規定

第二條 範圍與一般規定 [4]

1. 各締約方認識到數字貿易帶來的經濟增長和機遇，及認識到構建促進消費者對數字貿易的信心，避免對數字貿易的使用和發展設置不必要障礙的框架的重要性。

2. 本章的目標還包括：

(a) 促進各締約方間的數字貿易，以及全球範圍內數字貿易的更廣泛應用；

4　本章與其他各章內容不一致之處，以其他各章內容為準。

（b）致力於為數字貿易的使用創造一個信任和有信心的環境；以及

（c）加強各締約方在數字貿易發展方面的合作。

3.本章應適用於一締約方採取或維持的影響電子方式貿易的措施。

4.本章不得適用於：

（a）政府採購；或

（b）締約方或以其名義持有或處理的信息，或與此類信息相關的措施，包括與信息收集相關的措施。

第三部分　數字產品

第三條　海關關稅

1. 任何締約方不得對一締約方的人員與另一締約方的人員之間的電子傳輸，包括以電子方式傳輸的內容徵收關稅。

2. 為明確起見，第 1 款不得阻止締約方對以電子方式傳輸的內容徵收國內稅、費用或其他收費，只要此類國內稅、費用或收費以符合本協定的方式徵收。

第四條　關於數字產品的非歧視待遇

1. 任何締約方對在另一締約方領土內創造、製作、發佈、簽約、委託或首次以商業條款提供的數字產品的待遇，或給予作者、表演者、生產者、開發者或所有者為另一締約方人員的數字產品的待遇，不得低於其給予其他同類數字產品的待遇。[5]

2. 第 1 款不適用於與第八章（知識產權）項下的權利和義務出現任何不一致的情況。

5　為進一步明確，如一非締約方的數字產品屬於「同類數字產品」，則就本款而言，這一產品將被視為「其他同類數字產品」。

3. 各締約方理解，本條不適用於一締約方提供的補貼或撥款，包括政府支持的貸款、擔保和保險。

4. 本條不得適用於廣播。

第四部分　電子商務

第五條　國內電子交易框架

1. 每一締約方應維持與聯合國貿易法委員會《1996 年電子商務示範法》或 2005 年 11 月 23 日於紐約通過的《聯合國國際合同使用電子通信公約》的原則相一致的管轄電子交易的法律框架。

2. 每一締約方應努力：

　(a)　避免對電子交易施加任何不必要的監管負擔；及

　(b)　在制定電子交易的法律框架過程中便利利害關係人提出建議。

　(c)　通過《貿易法委員會電子可轉讓紀錄示範法》（2017）。

第六條　電子認證和電子簽名

1. 除非其法律項下另有規定，否則一締約方不得僅根據一簽名是電子方式而否認該簽名的法律效力。

2. 任何締約方不得對電子認證採取或維持下列措施：

　(a)　禁止電子交易一當事方就該交易共同確定適當的認證方法；或

　(b)　阻止一電子交易當事方獲得向司法或行政機構證明其交易符合有關認證的任何法律要求的機會。

3. 儘管有第 2 款，但一締約方可針對一特定交易類型，要求認證方法符合特定性能標準，或經一依照法律認可的授權機構認證。

4. 各締約方應鼓勵使用可交互操作的電子認證。

第七條　電子發票

1. 締約方認識到電子發票的重要性，電子發票可以提高商業交易的效率、準確性和可靠性。締約方還認識到，保證各自領土內用於電子發票的系統與其他締約方領土內用於電子發票的系統可交互操作的益處。

2. 締約方應努力保證在其領土內實施與電子發票相關的措施旨在支持各締約方電子發票框架之間的跨境交互操作性。為此，每一締約方應根據國際框架制定與電子發票相關的措施。

3. 締約方認識到促進全球採用交互電子發票系統的經濟重要性。為此，締約方應就促進採用交互電子發票系統分享最佳實踐和開展合作。

4. 締約方應就促進、鼓勵、支持或便利企業採用電子發票的倡議開展合作。為此，締約方應努力：

    (a) 促進支持電子發票的政策、基礎設施、程序的建設；及

    (b) 培養使用電子發票的意識和增強能力建設。

第八條　電子支付

1. 為促進電子支付的快速發展，特別是由非銀行、非金融機構和金融科技企業提供的電子支付，締約方認識到為跨境電子支付發展一個高效、安全和可靠環境的重要性，包括通過：

    (a) 促進採用和使用國際公認的電子支付標準；

    (b) 促進電子支付基礎設施的交互性和相互聯繫；以及

    (c) 鼓勵電子支付服務的創新和競爭。

2. 為此目的，締約方應：

    (a) 公開各自關於電子支付的法規，包括有關監管批准、許可要求、程序和技術標準；

    (b) 努力及時完成關於監管或許可批准的決定；

    (c) 在獲得電子支付系統運作所需的服務和基礎設施方面，不得任意或無理地歧視金融機構和非金融機構；

    (d) 對於相關的電子支付系統，採用電子支付信息的國際標準，以便在金融機構和服務提供商之間進行電子數據交換，使電子支付系統之間具有更大的互操作性；

(e) 促進開放平台和架構的使用，如通過應用程序編程接口（API）提供的工具和協議，並鼓勵支付服務提供商在可能的情況下安全地將其產品和服務的 API 提供給第三方，以促進電子支付領域更大的可交互性、創新和競爭；及

(f) 促進創新和競爭，及時推出新的金融和電子支付產品和服務，例如通過採用監管和行業沙盒。

3. 鑒於第 1 款的規定，締約方認識到通過法規維護電子支付系統的安全、效率、信任和保障的重要性，並認識到法規和政策的通過和執行應與支付服務提供者承擔的風險相稱。

第九條　無紙化貿易

1. 每一締約方應努力：

(a) 以電子方式向公眾提供貿易管理文件；及

(b) 接受以電子方式提交的貿易管理文件作為與此種文件紙質版具有同等法律效力的文件。

(c) 在可行的情況下，各締約方應以英文提供（a）項所述的貿易管理文件。

2. 注意到 WTO《貿易便利化協定》中的義務，每一締約方應努力建立或設立單一窗口，使個人能夠通過一單一接入點向參與的主管機關或機構提交貨物進口、出口或過境的貿易管理單證和數據要求。

3. 各締約方應與另一締約方的單一窗口建立或保持無縫、可信和安全的互連，以促進與貿易管理文件有關的數據交換，這些可包括：

(a) 原產地證書；

(b) 非操縱性證明；以及

(c) 締約方共同確定的任何其他文件。

4. 各締約方應努力開發數據交換系統，以支持各締約方主管當局之間交換與第 3 款所述貿易管理文件有關的數據。

5. 各締約方應：

(a) 對第 3 款和第 4 款中提到的所有交換數據嚴格保密，並至少給予與披露方的國內法律和法律制度所規定的相同水平的保護和保密；

（b）只向負責的海關當局提供第 3 款和第 4 款中提到的交換數據，並只為締約各方共同確定的目的使用這些數據；以及

（c）未經披露方的具體書面許可，不得披露第 3 款和第 4 款中提及的交換數據。

6. 各締約方承認在其境內的企業之間交換商業貿易活動中使用的電子紀錄的重要性。為此，各締約方應酌情促進其各自領土之間的企業在商業跨境貿易活動中使用和交換電子紀錄，包括支持開發數據交換系統。

7. 各締約方認識到，第 4 款和第 6 款中提到的數據交換系統應盡可能地相互兼容和互通。為此，各締約方應努力在數據交換系統的開發和管理方面制定和採用國際公認的標準。

8. 各締約方應就促進、鼓勵、支持和 / 或推動本條所述數據交換系統的使用和採用的舉措進行合作和協作，包括但不限於通過以下方式：

（a）分享信息和經驗，包括交流數據交換系統開發和管理方面的最佳做法；以及

（b）在數據交換系統的開發和管理方面開展試點項目合作。

9. 各締約方應在雙邊和國際論壇上進行合作，以促進接受貿易管理文件的電子版和企業間商業貿易活動中使用的電子紀錄。

10. 在制定規定無紙化貿易使用的倡議時，各締約方應努力考慮國際組織議定的方法。

第十條　快運貨物

1. 締約方認識到電子商務在促進貿易方面發揮着重要作用。為便利航空快運，各締約方應保證以可預見、一致和透明的方式實施各自的海關程序。

2. 各締約方應對航空快運採用或設立快速海關程序，同時保持適當海關監管和選擇。這些程序應：

（a）規定在快運貨物抵達前提交和處理放行貨物所需的信息；

（b）允許一次性提交涵蓋一票快運貨物中所有貨物的信息，例如貨單，如可能，應允許通過電子方式提交；[6]

（c）在可能的限度內，規定放行某些貨物的最少單證數；

6　為進一步明確，可要求提供額外單證作為放行條件。

(d) 在正常情況下，只要貨物已抵達，規定在提交必要海關單證後 4 小時內放行快運貨物；以及

(e) 對任何重量或價值的裝運貨物適用，認識到一締約方可能根據貨物重量或價值要求辦理正式入境手續（包括申報和證明文件、支付關稅）作為放行條件。

3. 如一締約方未向所有裝運貨物提供 2（a）項至 2（e）項規定的待遇，則該締約方應規定可向航空快運貨物提供此種待遇的單獨和快速的海關程序。

4. 在可能的情況下，各締約方應：

(a) 在其法律中規定一個最低價值，低於該價值的貨物不徵收關稅或稅款；

(b) 對低於其設定值的貨物不徵收關稅或稅款；以及

(c) 酌情審查其設定值，同時考慮相關因素，如通貨膨脹率、對貿易便利化的影響、對風險管理的影響、與稅額相比的徵稅行政成本、跨境貿易交易成本、對中小企業的影響或與徵收關稅相關的其他因素。

5. 第 4 款不應適用於限制性或控制性貨物的運輸，如須遵守進口許可證或類似要求的貨物。

第十一條　接入和使用互聯網開展數字貿易的原則

在遵守適用政策、法律和法規的前提下，各締約方認識到其領土內的消費者有能力受益於下述行為：

(a) 在遵守合理網絡管理的前提下，按消費者選擇接入和使用互聯網上可獲得的服務和應用；[7]

(b) 將消費者選擇的終端用戶設備接入互聯網，只要該設備不損害網絡；以及

(c) 獲取消費者的互聯網接入服務提供者的網絡管理實踐的信息。

---

[7] 各締約方認識到一互聯網接入服務提供者對其用戶獨家提供特定內容屬不違背這一原則的行為。

第十二條　互聯互通費用分攤

各締約方認識到尋求國際互聯網連接的一提供者應能夠與另一締約方的提供者在商業基礎上進行談判。這些談判可包括就補償相關提供者建立、運營和維護設施開展的談判。

第十三條　非應邀商業電子信息 [8]

1. 每一締約方應就非應邀商業電子信息採取或維持下列措施：
   （a）要求非應邀商業電子信息提供者促進接收人阻止繼續接收此種信息的能力；
   （b）要求按每一締約方法律法規的規定，獲得接收人就接收商業電子信息的同意；或
   （c）通過其他方式規定將非應邀商業電子信息減至最低程度。

2. 每一締約方應規定向未遵守根據第 1 款採取或維持的措施的非應邀商業電子信息提供者的追償權。

3. 各締約方應努力就共同關注的適當案件中的非應邀商業電子信息監管進行合作。

第十四條　源代碼

1. 任何締約方不得將要求轉移或獲得另一締約方的人所擁有的軟件源代碼作為在其領土內進口、分銷、銷售或使用該軟件或含有該軟件產品的條件。

2. 就本條而言，第 1 款項下的軟件限於大眾市場軟件或含有該軟件的產品，不包括用於關鍵基礎設施的軟件。

3. 本條中任何內容不得阻止：
   （a）在商業談判合同中包含或實施與提供源代碼相關的條款和條件；或
   （b）一締約方要求對軟件源代碼作出使該軟件符合與本協定不相抵觸的法律或法規所必需的修改。

4. 本條不排除一締約方的政府機構、執法機構、監管機構或司法機關（「相關機構」）要求另一締約方的人保存或提供軟件的源代碼或該源代碼中表

8　一締約方在實施其關於非應邀商業電子信息的法律框架之日前不適用本條。

達的算法給相關機構，以便進行調查、檢查、審查、執法行動或司法或行政程序，[9] 但需根據該締約方的法律和法規採取保障措施，防止未經授權的披露。

5. 本條不得理解為影響與專利申請或已授予專利相關的要求，包括司法機構對專利爭端發佈的任何命令，但需防範未經一締約方法律或實踐授權的披露行為。

第十五條　在線消費者保護

1. 各締約方認識到採取和維持透明和有效的措施以保護消費者在進行數字貿易時免受詐騙和商業欺詐活動侵害的重要性。為此，各締約方應在適當的情況下就具有共同利益的有關詐騙和商業欺詐活動的事項上加強合作與協調，包括執行各自的消費者保護法。[10]

2. 在本條中，欺詐性和欺騙性商業活動是指那些具有欺詐性或欺騙性並對消費者造成實際傷害，或者如果不加以防止，會造成這種傷害的潛在威脅的商業行為。例如：

　　(a) 對重要事實進行虛假陳述，包括隱含的事實虛假陳述，可能對被誤導的消費者的經濟利益造成重大損害；

　　(b) 在向消費者收費後未向其交付產品或提供服務；或

　　(c) 未經授權對消費者的金融、數字或其他賬戶進行收費或扣款。

3. 每一締約方應採取或維持消費者保護法，以禁止對從事在線商業活動消費者造成損害或潛在損害的詐騙和商業欺詐活動。

4. 締約各方認識到各自國家消費者保護機構或其他相關機構在跨境數字貿易相關活動中開展合作用以提高消費者福利的重要性。為此，締約雙方確認開展線上商業活動的合作。

5. 為此目的，對於線上商業活動，締約方應酌情並在遵守每一締約方法律法規的情況下，促進就對消費者造成實際傷害或如果不加以阻止，會有這種傷

9　如果商業秘密所有者聲稱該軟件源代碼具有商業秘密的地位，則這種披露不應解釋為對這種地位產生負面影響。

10　各締約方應努力通過其指定的負責消費者保護政策、立法及執法事務的國內公共機構或官員，就本條所載事項，以與各自法律、法規和重要利益相符的方式，在各自合理可獲得的資源範圍內，開展合作與協調。

害的緊迫威脅的欺詐和欺騙商業行為相關的共同利益事項進行合作，包括消費者保護法執法方面，就線上商業活動進行合作。

6. 締約方承認機制的益處，包括替代性爭端解決方案，以便利解決與電子商務交易相關的索賠要求。

第五部分　個人信息和數據保護

第十六條　個人信息保護[11]

1. 各締約方認識到保護數字貿易用戶個人信息的經濟和社會效益，及其對增強消費者對數字貿易信心的貢獻。

2. 為此目的，每一締約方應採用或維持規定數字貿易用戶個人信息保護的法律框架。各締約方在制定其個人信息保護的法律框架時，應考慮相關國際機構的原則和指南。[12]

3. 每一締約方在保護數字貿易用戶免受其管轄範圍內發生的個人信息保護侵害方面應努力採取非歧視的作法。

4. 每一締約方應公佈其為數字貿易用戶提供的有關個人信息保護的信息，包括：

　　(a) 個人如何尋求救濟；以及

　　(b) 企業如何遵守與個人信息保護有關的任何法律要求。

5. 鑒於各締約方可採取不同的法律途徑保護個人信息，各締約方應鼓勵建立促進不同制度間兼容性和交互性的機制。這類機制可包括對監管結果的承認，無論是自主給予還是通過共同安排，或通過更廣泛的國際框架。為此，締約方應努力就在其管轄範圍內適用的任何此類機制交換信息，並探討如何擴大

11　不要求一締約方在其實施保護數字貿易用戶個人數據的法律框架之日前適用本條。

12　為進一步明確，一締約方可通過採取或維持措施以符合本款中的義務，例如全面保護隱私、個人信息或個人數據的法律、涵蓋隱私的特定部門法律或規定執行由企業作出與隱私相關的自願承諾的法律。

此類機制或其他適當安排，以促進各機制間的兼容性和交互性。

6.締約各方應努力共同促進採用共同的跨境信息傳輸機制。

第十七條　接入與使用公共電信服務

1.每一締約方應保證，任何締約方的企業可將公共電信服務用於在其領土內或跨境傳輸信息，包括公司內部通信以及訪問任何締約方領土內數據庫所包含的，或以機器可讀形式存儲的信息。

2.一締約方可採取必要措施，以保證信息的安全性和機密性，並保護公共電信網絡或服務的終端使用者的個人數據隱私，只要上述措施不以對服務貿易構成任意的或不合理的歧視或構成變相限制的方式實施。

3.每一締約方應保證，如因互聯互通安排獲得公共電信服務供應商和終端使用者的、或與之有關的敏感商業信息，其領土內的公共電信服務供應商採取合理措施保護該信息的機密性，並保證這些服務商僅為提供上述服務而使用此類信息。

第十八條　開放政府數據

1.各締約方認識到便利公共訪問和使用政府信息可以促進經濟和社會發展，和創新；

2.各締約方應當努力合作識別各締約方能擴大訪問和使用開放政府數據的方式，以便增進與產生商業機會；

3.本條項下的合作可包括如下述活動：

(a) 鼓勵在開放政府數據集的基礎上開發新產品和服務；及

(b) 促進使用和開發開放政府數據許可模式，以標準化的公共許可形式在線提供，使開放政府數據能夠為締約方各自法律法規所允許的任何目的，由任何人自由獲取、使用和共享，且依賴於開放政府數據格式。

第六部分　跨境信息流動

第十九條　通過電子方式跨境傳輸信息

1. 各締約方認識到每一締約方可對通過電子方式傳輸信息設置各自的監管要求。

2. 當此活動是以第 3 款下涵蓋的人進行的商業行為時，每一締約方應允許通過電子方式跨境傳輸信息，包括個人信息。

3. 本條中任何內容不得阻止一締約方為實現合法公共政策目標而採取或維持與第 2 款不符的措施，只要該措施：

(a)　不以構成任意或不合理歧視或對貿易構成變相限制的方式適用；及

(b)　不對信息傳輸施以超出實現目標所需限度的限制。

第二十條　計算設施的位置

1. 各締約方認識到每一締約方可就計算設施的使用設有各自的監管要求，包括尋求保證通信安全性和機密性的要求。

2. 任何締約方不得要求一涵蓋的人在該締約方領土內將使用或設置計算設施作為在其領土內開展業務的條件。

3. 本條中任何內容不得阻止一締約方為實現合法公共政策目標而採取或維持與第 2 款不一致的措施，只要該措施：

(a)　不以構成任意或不合理歧視或對貿易構成變相限制的方式適用；及

(b)　不對計算設施的使用或位置施以超出實現目標所需限度的限制。

第二十一條　合作

1. 認識到數字貿易的全球性，各締約方應努力：

    (a)　就有關數字貿易的法規、政策、執行和合規交流信息與分享經驗，包括：

        (i)　個人信息保護，特別是就加強現有執行隱私保護法律的國際合作機制；

        (ii)　電子通信安全；

        (iii)　電子認證；

        (iv)　政府利用數字工具和技術提高政府績效；以及

        (v)　使用密碼學的信息和通信技術產品

    (b)　就促進和發展進一步全球隱私制度交互性的機制合作和保持對話；

    (c)　積極參與區域和多邊論壇，以促進數字貿易的發展；

    (d)　鼓勵私營部門制定自律方法以促進數字貿易繁榮，包括行為準則、示範合同、指南和執行機制；

    (e)　促進殘疾人獲得信息和通信技術；

    (f)　促進數字包容以確保所有人與商業機構獲得其所需以參與、貢獻於與獲益於數字經濟；以及

2. 締約雙方應考慮建立論壇，解決上述任何問題，或與本章實施相關的其他問題。

第二十二條　中小企業和初創企業

1. 各締約方認識到中小企業在維持數字經濟動力與增進數字經濟競爭力的重要地位；

2. 各締約方認識到私營部門在根據本章實施的中小企業和初創企業合作中不可或缺的作用；

3. 為促進各締約方間開展更強有力的合作以增強中小企業和初創企業在數

字經濟中的貿易與投資機會，各締約方應當：

(a) 繼續與其他締約方合作，就利用數字工具與技術幫助中小企業和初創企業獲得資金與信貸、中小企業和初創企業參與政府採購機會以及有助於中小企業和初創企業適應數字經濟的其他領域交流信息與最佳實踐；及

(b) 鼓勵各締約方中小企業和初創企業參與有助於其與國際供應商、買家與其他潛在商業夥伴聯繫的平台；

4. 各締約方應努力增進中小企業和初創企業的數字對話。對話可包括來自各締約方的私營部門、非政府組織、學術界與其他利益相關方。

第二十三條　數據創新

1. 各締約方認識到，數字化和數字經濟中的數據使用可促進經濟增長。為支持以電子方式進行的信息跨境傳輸，促進數字經濟中的數據驅動型創新，各締約方進一步認識到，有必要創造一個能夠和支持並有利於實驗和創新的環境，包括在適用情況下使用監管沙盒。

2. 各締約方應努力通過以下方式支持數據創新：

(a) 合作開展數據共享項目，包括涉及研究人員、學術界和產業界的項目，根據需要使用監管沙盒，以證明通過電子手段跨境傳輸信息的好處；

(b) 合作制定數據可移植性的政策和標準；以及

(c) 分享與數據創新有關的研究和行業實踐。

第二十四條　數字經濟中的競爭

1. 認識到締約方可受益於分享其在競爭法執法及競爭政策制定實施以應對數字經濟所帶來挑戰方面的經驗，締約各方應努力做到：

(a) 就競爭政策和有效的競爭法執行活動交流信息並分享最佳做法，以促進和保護數字市場的競爭環境；

(b) 確保締約方的數字市場是開放的、可競爭的和有效的；以及

(c) 通過提供諮詢或培訓，包括通過官員交流，加強締約方之間的合作，以識別和減少數字市場中的反競爭行為。

2. 締約方應酌情就數字市場中競爭法執法問題進行合作，包括通過磋商和交流信息。

第二十五條　數字經濟的標準、技術法規和合格評定程序

1. 締約方承認標準、技術法規和合格評定程序對促進運作良好的數字經濟和通過提高兼容性、交互性和可靠性減少貿易壁壘的重要性和貢獻。

2. 締約方應努力參與各方共同感興趣的區域、多邊或國際論壇並開展合作，按照以下原則和程序，促進與數字經濟有關的標準的制定和採用：

 (a)　有關標準制定的信息和程序應易於獲取，並通過既定機制通知和傳達給標準化機構的成員；

 (b)　標準制定過程應在可行的範圍內允許公開和非歧視性的參與；

 (c)　標準制定過程應確保通過的標準是公正和一致的，並促進其應用和傳播；以及

 (d)　標準化機構應繼續努力和合作，以保持標準的有效性和與目標和情況的相關性。

3. 締約方認識到，促進跨境承認合格評定結果的機制可以支持數字經濟。這種機制包括：

 (a)　相關合格評定機構之間的自願安排；以及

 (b)　使用締約各方都是締約方的區域或國際承認協定或安排。

4. 為此，締約方應努力做到：

 (a)　交流信息，分享經驗和意見，包括在技術援助／能力建設方面的合作，以及按照各方確定的條款和條件，就與數字經濟有關的標準、技術法規和合格評定程序的制定和應用進行對話；

 (b)　積極參加各締約方參加的區域、多邊和國際論壇，以制定與數字經濟有關的標準，並在共同關心的領域促進其採用；

 (c)　確定、制定和促進與數字經濟有關的標準領域的聯合倡議；

 (d)　應另一締約方的要求，積極考慮就與數字經濟有關的標準、技術法規和合格評定程序等共同關心的問題提出合作建議；以及

 (e)　促進締約方政府和非政府機構在共同關心的問題上的合作，包括跨境研究或試驗項目，以便在締約方和行業之間對標準、技術法規和

合格評估程序有更多的瞭解。

5. 締約方承認在制定、通過和應用有關數字經濟的標準、技術法規和合格評定程序方面，信息交流和透明度的重要性。每一締約方應努力做到：

(a) 根據要求，在締約方商定的合理期限內，如有可能，在 60 天內，以印刷品或電子方式提供與本國數字經濟有關的標準、技術法規和合格評估程序的信息；以及

(b) 如有要求，且已具有，提供英文全文或摘要版。

第八部分　網絡安全

第二十六條　網絡安全合作

1. 各締約方認識到，對網絡安全的威脅將破壞對數字貿易的信心。因此，各締約方應努力：

(a) 增強負責網絡安全事件應對的國家實體的能力；以及

(b) 加強現有合作機制，在識別和減少影響電子網絡的惡意入侵或惡意代碼傳播、利用此種機制迅速應對網絡安全事件，以及共享信息以提高意識和最佳實踐方面開展合作。

2. 鑒於網絡安全威脅的不斷發展變化，各締約方認識，在應對此類威脅方面，基於風險的方法可能比規範性法規更有效。因此，各締約方應努力採用並鼓勵其管轄範圍內的企業採用基於風險的方法。該類方法依賴於基於共識的標準和風險管理最佳實踐，以識別和防範網絡安全風險，並監測、應對網絡安全事件並從網絡安全事件中恢復。

3. 在符合共同利益的情況下，締約方應在網絡問題領域開展合作，分享最佳做法，並通過合作性的實際行動，在適用現有國際法和負責任的國家行為規範及網絡建立信任措施的基礎上，促進和保護一個開放、自由、穩定、和平和安全的網絡空間。

第二十七條　網絡安全和保障

1. 締約方認識到，安全可靠的網絡環境對數字經濟起到支撐作用。

2. 締約方認識到採取多方利益攸關的方式解決網絡安全和保障問題的重要性。

3. 締約方應努力合作，以推動形成影響網絡安全和保障的全球問題的合作解決方案。

第九部分　透明度

第二十八條　透明度

1. 每一締約方應盡快公佈有關或影響本章實施的一般適用的所有有關措施，或如上述情況不可行，以其他方式使公眾獲悉，包括在可行的情況下在互聯網上公佈。

2. 每一締約方應盡快答覆另一締約方關於特定信息的相關請求，該信息是關於該締約方與本章實施相關或影響本章實施的一般適用的任何措施。

第七章　投資

第一部分

第一條　定義

就本章而言：

「**中央政府**」指：

對於【國家】，【】；以及

對於【國家】，【】；

「**中心**」指根據《關於解決國家與他國國民之間的投資爭端的公約》設立的國際投資爭端解決中心。

「**申請人**」指與另一締約方產生投資爭端的一締約方的投資者。

「**涵蓋投資**」指對於一締約方，指截至本章生效之日在一締約方領土內存在的另一締約方投資者的投資，或在此後設立、獲得或擴大的投資。

「**爭端雙方**」指申請人和被申請人。

「**爭端一方**」指申請人或被申請人。

「**企業**」指根據適用法律組成或組織的任何實體，無論是否以營利為目的，無論是私人還是政府所有或控制，包括公司、信託、合夥、獨資企業、合資企業、協會或類似組織；以及企業的分支機構。

「**一締約方的企業**」指根據一締約方的法律組成或組織的企業，或位於一締約方領土內並在該領土內開展經營活動的分支機構。

「**現有**」指在本章生效之日時生效。

「**可自由使用貨幣**」指國際貨幣基金組織根據《國際貨幣基金組織協定》確定的「可自由使用貨幣」。

「**政府採購**」指政府為公共目的而獲得或使用貨物、服務或其任何組合的過程。該過程不以商業銷售或轉售為目的，也不以商業銷售或轉售而用於生產或提供貨物或服務為目的。

「**《ICSID 附加便利規則》**」指《國際投資爭端解決中心秘書處關於程序管理的附加便利規則》。

「**《ICSID 公約》**」指 1965 年 3 月 18 日於華盛頓通過的《關於解決國家與他國國民之間的投資爭端的公約》。

「**投資**」指一投資者直接或間接，擁有或控制的，具有投資特徵的各種資產，此類特徵包括承諾資本或其他資源的投入、收益或利潤的期待或風險的承擔等。投資可採取的形式包括：

    (a)   一家企業；

    (b)   一家企業中的股份、股票和其他形式的參股；

    (c)   債券、無擔保債券、其他債務工具和貸款；

    (d)   期貨、期權和其他衍生品；

    (e)   總承包、建設、管理、生產、特許權、收入分成及其他類似合同；

    (f)   知識產權；

    (g)   根據國內法律授予的批准、授權、許可和其他類似權利；[13] 以及

    (h)   其他有形或無形財產、動產或不動產及相關財產權利，例如租賃、抵押、留置和質押。

「**投資協議**」指一締約方國家機構[14] 與一涵蓋投資或另一締約方的投資者之間的一書面協議[15]，涵蓋投資或投資者根據該協議設立或獲得不同於該書面協議

13　為進一步明確，「投資」不包括在司法或行政訴訟中的指令或判決。

14　為本定義之目的，「國家機構」指 (a) 就【國家】而言，【】；以及 (b) 就【國家】而言，【】。

15　書面協議指當事人雙方簽署的書面形式的協議，無論是單個文件還是多個文件，創設權利和義務的交換，並根據第三十三條第 2 款（準據法）對雙方當事人均具有約束力。為進一步明確，(a) 行政或司法機關的單方行為，例如由一締約方在其監管職權內辦法的許可、執照或授權，或法令、命令、或判決本身；以及 (b) 行政或司法法令或命令不得被視為書面協議。

本身的一涵蓋投資，且該協議授予該涵蓋投資或投資者下列權利：

    (a) 關於一國家權力控制的自然資源，如勘探、開採、冶煉、運輸、分銷或銷售；

    (b) 代表該締約方向公眾提供服務，包括發電或配電、水處理或配送、或電信；或

    (c) 承擔基礎設施項目，例如公路、橋樑、運河、堤壩或管道的建設，但是條件是基礎設施並非專門或主要供政府使用及為政府的利益。

「投資授權」[16] 指一締約方外國投資管理機構給予另一締約方的一涵蓋投資或投資者的授權。

「非締約方投資者」 對於一締約方而言，指試圖、正在或已經在該締約方領土內進行投資的投資者，但其不屬於任一締約方的投資者；

「締約方投資者」 指試圖、正在或已經在另一締約方領土內投資的一締約方或其國有企業，或締約方的國民或企業；但前提條件是具有雙重國籍的自然人應被視為僅具有其主要有效國籍的國家的國民。

「措施」 指任何法律、法規、程序、要求或慣例。

「國民」 指：

    (a) 就【國家】而言，【】；以及

    (b) 就【國家】，【】。

「《紐約公約》」 指 1958 年 6 月 10 日於紐約通過的聯合國《承認和執行外國仲裁裁決的公約》。

「爭端締約方」 指不屬一投資爭端當事方的任一締約方。

「人」 指一自然人或一企業。

「一締約方的人」 指一締約方的國民或企業。

「受保護信息」 指機密商業信息，或根據一締約方法律享有保密特權或受保護不應洩露的信息。

「地方政府」 指：

    (a) 就【國家】而言，【】；以及

    (b) 就【國家】而言，【】。

---

16 為進一步明確，一締約方為執行具有普遍適用性的法律（例如競爭法）而採取的行動不屬於本定義範圍。

「**被申請人**」指作為一項投資爭端當事方的一締約方。

「**秘書長**」指國際投資爭端解決中心的秘書長。

「**國有企業**」指一締約方擁有或通過所有者權益控制的企業。

「**領土**」指：

(a) 就【國家】而言，【】；

(b) 就【國家】，【】。

(c) 就每一締約方而言，該締約方的領海和領海以外的任何區域，根據《聯合國海洋法公約》所反映的習慣國際法，締約方可在該區域內行使主權或管轄權。

「**TRIPS 協定**」是指《WTO 協定》附件 1C 所載的《與貿易有關的知識產權協定》。[17]

「**《UNICITRAL 仲裁規則》**」指聯合國國際貿易法委員會的仲裁規則。

「**世貿組織協定**」是指 1994 年 4 月 15 日簽署的《馬拉喀什建立世界貿易組織協定》。

第二條　範圍

1. 本章適用於一締約方採取或維持的與下列內容相關的措施：

(a) 另一締約方的投資者；

(b) 涵蓋投資；以及

(c) 就第十條（業績要求）、第十四條（投資與環境）以及第十五條（投資與勞工）而言，該締約方領土內的所有投資。

2. 一締約方在第一部分下的義務應適用於：

(a) 由該締約方[18]授權行使任何監管、行政或其他政府權力的國有企業或其他人；以及

(b) 該締約方的行政分支。

3. 為進一步明確，對於本協定生效之日前發生的一行為或事實或曾經存在

17　為了更加明確，「TRIPS 協議」包括締約國之間對 WTO 成員根據 WTO 協議給予的 TRIPS 協議任何條款的任何有效豁免。

18　為進一步明確，被授權的政府權力包括立法授權、向國有企業或其他人授予政府權力、或授權國有企業或其他人行使政府權力的政府命令、指示或其他行動。

但已終止的情況，本章對該締約方不得具有約束力。

第三條　與其他協定的關係

1. 認識到各締約方希望本協定與其現有國際協定共存的意圖，每一締約方確認：

    (a) 對於包括《世界貿易組織協定》在內的所有締約方均為締約方的現行國際協定而言，其對其他締約方有關的現有權利和義務；以及

    (b) 對於有關該締約方和至少一其他締約方均為締約方的現行國際協定而言，其對該另一個締約方或多個締約方的現有權利和義務，視具體情況而定。

2. 如一締約方認為，本協定的條款與該締約方和至少一其他締約方為當事方的另一協定的一條款不一致，則應請求該另一協定的相關締約方應進行磋商，以期達成令雙方滿意的解決辦法。本款不影響一締約方在第二部分項下的權利和義務。[19]

第四條　國民待遇

1. 在設立、獲得、擴大、管理、經營、運營和出售或以其他方式處置在其領土內的投資方面，每一締約方應給予另一締約方投資者的待遇不低於在相似情況下該締約方給予本國投資者的待遇。

2. 在設立、獲得、擴大、管理、經營、運營和出售或以其他方式處置投資方面，每一締約方應給予涵蓋投資的待遇不低於在相似情況下該締約方給予本國投資者在其領土內投資的待遇。

3. 對於一地區政府而言，一締約方根據第 1 款和第 2 款所給予的待遇，指不低於該地區政府在相似情況下給予其作為一部分的在該締約方地區內居住的自然人和根據該締約方地區政府的法律組成的企業的待遇。

第五條　最惠國待遇

1. 在設立、獲得、擴大、管理、經營、運營和出售或以其他方式處置在其

19　就本協定的適用而言，各締約方同意，一協定對貨物、服務、投資或人提供的待遇優於本協議項下所給予待遇的事實，並不意味着存在第 2 款規定的不一致。

領土內投資方面，每一締約方應給予另一締約方投資者的待遇不低於在相似情況下該締約方給予任何非締約方投資者的待遇。

2. 在設立、獲得、擴大、管理、經營、運營和出售或以其他方式處置投資方面，每一締約方應給予涵蓋投資的待遇不低於在相似情況下該締約方給予任何非締約方投資者在其領土內投資的待遇。

3. 為進一步明確，本條中所指的待遇不包括國際爭端解決程序或機制，例如本章第二部分（投資者 - 國家間爭端解決）所包括的程序或機制。

第六條　最低標準待遇 [20]

1. 每一締約方應依照習慣國際法給予涵蓋投資包括公平公正待遇及充分保護和安全在內的待遇。

2. 為進一步明確，第 1 款規定將習慣國際法中給予外國人的最低標準待遇作為給予涵蓋投資的最低標準待遇。「公平公正待遇」和「充分保護和安全」的概念不要求締約方給予額外的或超出該標準所要求的待遇，且不創設額外的實體權利。第 1 款中的義務要求：

(a)「公平公正待遇」包括依照世界主要法律制度中所包含的正當程序原則，在刑事、民事或行政裁決程序中不拒絕司法的義務；以及

(b)「充分保護和安全」要求每一締約方提供習慣國際法所要求的治安保護水平。

3. 關於存在違反本協定另一條款或另一單獨國際協定的決定並不能證明違反本條的情況存在。

4. 儘管有第十四條第 5 款（b）項（補貼和贈款）的規定，就與其領土內的武裝衝突或內亂而使投資所遭受損失所採取或維持的措施而言，每一締約方應給予另一締約方的投資者以及涵蓋投資非歧視待遇。

5. 儘管有第 4 款的規定，如一締約方的投資者在另一締約方的領土內，在第 4 款所述情況下，由於下列原因而遭受損失：

(a) 涵蓋投資全部或部分為後一締約方的軍隊或政府徵用；或

(b) 涵蓋投資全部或部分被後一締約方的軍隊或政府在非情勢所必需的情況下破壞，則後一締約方針對該損失向投資者要求恢復原狀或進

20　第六條（最低標準待遇）應依照附件一加以解釋。

行賠償，或酌情同時恢復原狀和進行賠償。任何賠償應及時、充分和有效並依照第八條（徵收和補償）第 2 款至第 4 款適用。

6. 第 4 款不適用於與第四條（國民待遇）不一致但符合第十六條（不符措施）第 5 款（b）（補貼和贈款）的補貼相關的現行措施。

第七條　武裝衝突或內亂情況下的待遇

1. 儘管有第十六條（不符措施），每一締約方應就採取或維持與其領土內的武裝衝突或內亂而使投資所遭受損失相關的措施方面，應給予另一締約方的投資者和涵蓋投資非歧視待遇。

2. 儘管有第 1 款，但是如一締約方的投資者在第 1 款所指的情況下因下列原因在另一締約方領土內遭受損失：

(a) 涵蓋投資全部或部分為後一締約方的軍隊或政府徵用；或

(b) 涵蓋投資全部或部分被後一締約方的軍隊或政府在非情勢所必需的
情況下破壞，

則後一締約方針對該損失向投資者恢復原狀或進行賠償，或酌情同時恢復原狀和進行賠償。

3. 第 1 款不得適用於與第四條（國民待遇）不一致的現行補貼或贈款措施，但適用於第十六條（不符措施）。

第八條　徵收和補償 [21]

1. 任何締約方對一涵蓋投資不得直接徵收或實行國有化，或通過等同於徵收和實行國有化（「徵收」）的措施間接徵收或實行國有化，除非符合下列條件：

(a) 為公共目的；

(b) 以非歧視的方式進行；

(c) 支付及時、充分和有效的補償；以及

(d) 根據正當法律程序和第六條（最低標準待遇）第 1 款至第 3 款進行。

2. 第 1（c）款所指的補償應：

(a) 無遲延支付；

21　第八條（徵收和補償）應依照附件一和附件二進行解釋。

(b) 等同於緊接徵收發生前（「徵收之日」）被徵收投資的公平市場價值；

(c) 不反映因徵收意圖提前公開而發生的任何價值變化；以及

(d) 可全部實現並可自由轉移。

3. 如公平市場價值以可自由使用貨幣計價，則第 1 款（c）項所提的補償不得低於徵收之日的公平市場價值，另加以該貨幣合理商業利率計算的徵收之日至付款之日產生的利息。

4. 如公平市場價值以不可自由使用貨幣計價，則第 1 款（c）項所提的以付款之日市場匯率轉換為支付貨幣的補償不得低於：

(a) 根據當日市場匯率轉換為可自由使用貨幣之徵收之日的公平市場價值；另加

(b) 以該可自由使用貨幣的合理商業利率計算的徵收之日至付款之日產生的利息。

5. 本條不適用於依照《TRIPS 協定》對一知識產權強制許可的頒發，也不適用於知識產權的撤銷、限制或創設，只要此類頒發、撤銷、限制和創造符合《與貿易相關的知識產權協定》。

6. 為進一步明確，一締約方就不發放、繼續發放或維持一補貼或贈款的決定，或就修改或減少一補貼或贈款的決定：

(a) 在法律或合同項下無就發放、繼續發放或維持該補貼或贈款的任何具體承諾；或

(b) 依照該補貼或贈款的發放、繼續發放、修改、減少和維持所附任何條款或條件做出，

則單獨該決定本身不構成徵收。

第九條　轉移

1. 每一締約方應允許與涵蓋投資相關的所有轉移可自由進出其領土且無遲延。此類轉移包括：

(a) 資本出資；

(b) 利潤、股息、資本收益、以及全部或部分出售涵蓋投資所得，或全部或部分清算涵蓋投資所得；

(c) 利息、特許權使用費、管理費、技術指導費和其他費用；

(d) 根據一合同所付款項，包括貸款協議；

(e) 根據第六條第 4 款和第 5 款以及第八條所付款項；以及

(f) 一爭端產生的款項。

2. 每一締約方應允許與一涵蓋投資相關的轉移以按轉移之時市場匯率換算的可自由使用貨幣進行。

3. 每一締約方應允許按一締約方與一涵蓋投資或與另一締約方投資者的書面協議中所授權或載明的與一涵蓋投資相關的實物回報。

4. 儘管有第 1 款至第 3 款，一締約方可對下列情況通過公正、非歧視和善意適用其法律以阻止轉移：

(a) 破產、無力償還債務或保護債權人的權利；

(b) 發行、買賣或交易證券、期貨、期權或衍生品；

(c) 刑事或刑事犯罪；

(d) 為協助執法或金融監管部門提供必要的財務報告或紀錄；或

(e) 保證司法或行政程序的命令或判決得以遵守。

第十條　業績要求

1. 對於一締約方或一非締約方的投資者在其領土內的投資的設立、獲得、擴大、管理、經營、運營、出售或其他處置方面，任何締約方不得施加或強制執行任何要求，或強制要求作出任何承諾或保證：[22]

(a) 出口達到一指定水平或比例的貨物或服務；

(b) 當地含量達到一指定水平或比例；

(c) 購買、使用其領土內生產的貨物，或給予此類貨物優惠，或要求自其領土內的人購買貨物；

(d) 以任何方式將進口量或進口額與出口量或出口額或與該投資有關的外匯流入金額相關聯；

(e) 通過以任何方式將該投資生產或提供的貨物或服務與其出口量或出口額或外匯收入相關聯，限制此類貨物或服務在其領土內的銷售；

22　為進一步明確，第 2 款中所指的獲得或繼續獲得一優惠的條件不構成第 1 款而言的「承諾或保證」。

(f)　要求向其領土內的人轉讓一特定技術、一生產工序或其他專有知識；

(g)　要求僅可自該締約方領土向一特定地區市場或向世界市場供應該投資所生產的貨物或提供的服務。

(h)　(i)　在其領土內購買、使用該締約方或該締約方的人的技術，或給予此種技術優惠；[23] 或

　　　(ii)　要求在其領土內阻止購買或使用一特定技術，或阻止給予該特定技術優惠，

以便基於國籍對該締約方的投資者、投資或技術或該締約方的人提供保護。

2. 對於一締約方或一非締約方的投資者在其領土內投資的設立、獲取、擴大、管理、經營、運營、出售或其他處置，任何締約方不得將遵守下列任何要求作為獲得或繼續獲得一優惠的條件：

(a)　當地含量達到一指定水平或比例；

(b)　購買、使用其領土內生產的貨物，或給予此類貨物優惠，或向其領土內的人購買貨物；

(c)　以任何方式將進口量或進口額與出口量或出口額或與該投資有關的外匯流入金額相關聯；或

(d)　通過以任何方式將該投資生產或提供的貨物或服務與其出口量或出口額或外匯收入相關聯，限制此類貨物或服務在其領土內的銷售。

3. (a)　第 2 款中任何內容不得解釋為阻止一締約方將遵守在其領土內確定生產地點、提供服務、培訓或僱傭員工、建設或擴大特定設施、開展研發的要求作為一締約方或一非締約方的投資者在該締約方領土內的投資獲得或繼續獲得一優惠的條件。

(b)　第 1 款第 (f) 和 (h) 項不得適用於：

　　(i)　如一締約方依照《TRIPS 協定》第三十一條授權使用一知識產權，或對於要求披露屬於《TRIPS 協定》第三十九條範圍內的專有信息且符合該條的措施；或

23　就本條而言，「該締約方或該締約方的人的技術」一詞包括由該締約方或該締約方的人所擁有的技術，及該締約方或該締約方的人擁有獨佔許可的技術。

(ii) 當該要求由法院、行政法庭或競爭機構實施，或承諾或保護由法院、行政法庭或競爭機構強制執行，以糾正一項根據該締約方競爭法經司法或行政程序確定為反競爭行為的作法。[24]

(c) 只要此類措施不以任意或不合理的方式實施，或不構成對國際貿易或投資的變相限制，則第 1 款 (b)、(c)、(f) 項和第 2 款 (a)、(b) 項不得解釋為阻止一締約方採取或維持下列措施，包括環境措施：

(i) 保證遵守不與本章相抵觸的法律法規所必需的措施；

(ii) 保護人類、動物或植物的生命或健康所必需的措施；或

(iii) 與保護生物或非生物的可用盡自然資源相關的措施。

(d) 第 1 款 (a)、(b)、(c) 項和第 2 款 (a)、(b) 項不得適用於與出口促進和對外援助計劃相關的貨物或服務的資格要求。

(e) 第 1 款 (b)、(c)、(f)、(g) 項和第 2 款 (a) 和 (b) 項不得適用於政府採購。

(f) 第 2 款 (a) 和 (b) 項不得適用於由一進口締約方對獲得優惠關稅或優惠配額資格所必需的貨物成分施加的要求。

(g) 第 1 款 (h) 和 (i) 項不得解釋為阻止一締約方採取或維持保護合法公共福利目標的措施，只要此類措施不以任意或不合理的方式適用，或不構成對國際貿易或投資的變相限制。

4. 為進一步明確，第 1 款和第 2 款不得適用於該兩款中所列之外的其他承諾、保證或要求。

5. 本條在一締約方未施加或要求該承諾、保證或要求的情況下，不能阻止私人當事方之間實施任何承諾、保證或要求。

6. 每一締約方的投資者和在其領土內經營的企業，應努力將國際承認的公司社會責任標準自願納入其實踐和內部政策，如各締約方認可或支持的原則聲明。這些原則可涉及如勞工、環境、人權、社區關係和反腐敗問題。

第十一條　高級管理人員和董事會

1. 一締約方不得要求屬一涵蓋投資的該締約方的一企業任命一具有特定國籍的自然人擔任一高級管理職務。

24　各締約方認識到專利並不必然授予市場支配力。

2. 一締約方可要求屬一涵蓋投資的該締約方的一企業的董事會或董事會的任何委員會的半數以上成員具有一特定國籍或在該締約方領土內居住，只要該要求不實質損害該投資者控制其投資的能力。

第十二條　與投資有關的法律和決定的公佈

1. 每一締約方應確保其：

(a) 普遍適用的法律、法規、程序和行政裁決；以及

(b) 有關於本章涵蓋的任何事項相關的裁決應立即公佈或以其他方式使公眾獲悉。

2. 為本條之目的，「普遍適用的行政裁決」指適用於其一般管轄範圍內的所有人和事實情況，並確立為行為規範的行政裁決或解釋，但不包括：

(a) 在行政或準司法程序中作出的裁定或裁決，適用於特定案件中締約另一方的特定投資或投資者；或

(b) 對某一特定行為或做法作出裁定的裁決。

第十三條　透明度和反腐敗

1. 根據本協定第四章（透明度和反腐敗），各締約方同意就改進本條、第十二條和第三十二條載明的透明度實踐的方式進行定期磋商。

2. 公佈

在可能的範圍內，每一締約方應：

(a) 提前公佈其擬採取的第十二條第 1 款（a）項所指的任何措施；以及

(b) 為利害關係人和其他締約方提供合理機會，對這些擬議的措施進行評論。

3. 對於根據第 2 款（a）項公佈的、與本章涵蓋的任何事項相關的、普遍適用的中央政府的擬議法規，每一締約方：

(a) 應在全國發行的一份正式刊物上公佈擬議的法規，並應鼓勵通過額外的渠道散發此種法規；

(b) 在多數情況下，應該在公眾意見徵集截止日前 60 日將擬議法規予以公佈；

(c) 應在該等公佈中包括對擬議法規目的和原理的解釋；以及

(d) 在通過最終法規時，應處理在徵集意見期內收到的重要實質性意見，並在其官方刊物或政府互聯網站的顯著位置，解釋其對擬議法規所做的實質性修改。

4. 對於其中央級政府通過的、與本章涵蓋的任何事項有關的、普遍適用的法規，每一締約方：

(a) 應在全國發行的一份正式刊物上公佈法規，並應鼓勵通過其他渠道發行法規；以及

(b) 應在公佈中包含對法規目的和原理的解釋。

5. 信息的提供

(a) 若提出請求的締約方認為任何實際或擬議的措施可能對本章的實施產生重大影響，或在其他方面對其在本章項下的利益產生重大影響，則一締約方應根據另一締約方的請求，及時提供信息並就有關的問題作出答覆。

(b) 本款項下的任何請求或信息應通過相關聯絡點提供給其他締約方。

(c) 根據本款提供的任何信息不得影響所涉措施是否符合本章規定。

6. 行政程序

為了以一致、公正和合理的方式實施第十二條第 1 款 (a) 項所指的各項措施，對於涉及另一締約方的特定涵蓋投資或投資者的具體案件，每一締約方應保證在其行政程序中遵守下列規定：

(a) 受程序直接影響的其他締約方的涵蓋投資或投資者在啓動程序時，應盡可能根據國內程序向其發出合理的通知，包括對程序性質的說明、據以啓動程序的權限說明、以及對所涉及任何問題的總體說明；

(b) 在作出任何最終行政行為之前，在時間、程序的性質和公共利益允許的情況下，給予此類人提供事實和論據以支持他們立場的合理機會；以及

(c) 其程序符合國內法。

7. 覆議和申訴

(a) 每一締約方應設立或維持司法、準司法、行政法庭或程序，以便及

時審查並在必要時糾正有關本章節所涉事項的最終行政行為。此類法庭應公正且獨立於受委託負責行政執行的部門或管理機構，且不應與該等事項的結果有任何實質性利害關係。

(b) 每一締約方應保證在任何此類法庭或程序中，使得各當事方均有權：

(i) 支持各自立場或為各自立場辯護的合理機會；以及

(ii) 根據證據和提交的紀錄作出的決定，或依據國內法的要求，根據行政機構編纂的紀錄作出決定。

(c) 每一締約方應確保，在可按國內法規定進行上訴或進一步審議的情況下，該決定應由與所涉行政行為有關的部門或管理機構實施，並應規範該等部門或管理機構的實踐。

8. 標準設定

(a) 每一締約方應允許其他締約方的人參與制定其中央政府機構的標準和技術法規。[25] 每一締約方該等標準和中央政府合格評定程序的制定，應允許其他締約方的人以不低於給予本國人的條件參與。

(b) 每一締約方應建議其領土內的非政府標準化機構允許其他締約方的人參與此種機構的標準制定。各締約方應建議其領土內的非政府標準化機構允許其他締約方的人參與制定此種標準及此種機構對合格評定程序的制定，其條件不應低於其給予該締約方的人的待遇。

(c) 第 8 款 (a) 項和 (b) 項不適用於：

(i) 《世界貿易組織關於衛生和植物檢疫措施適用規則》附件一中規定的衛生和植物檢疫措施；或

(ii) 政府機構為其生產或消費要求制定的採購規格。

(d) 為第 8 款 (a) 項和 (b) 項之目的，「中央政府機構」、「標準」、「技術法規」和「合格評定程序」應具有《世界貿易組織貿易技術壁壘協定》附件一中賦予這些術語的含義。與附件一相符，後三個術語不包括提供服務的標準、技術法規或合格評定程序。

9. 反腐敗措施

25　一締約方可通過如下方式履行此項義務，例如，為利害關係人提供對其擬制定的措施提出意見的合理機會，並在制定措施時考慮這些意見。

以本協定第四章（透明度和反腐敗）為準：

(a) 每一締約方應採取或維持必要的立法及其他措施，將其管轄範圍內的任何人在影響國際貿易或投資的事項中故意實施的下列行為，確定為其法律項下的刑事犯罪：

   (i) 直接或間接地允諾給予、提議給予或實際給予公職人員或其他人或實體不正當利益，以使該公職人員在履行或執行他或她的公務方面作為或不作為；

   (ii) 公職人員為其或其他人或實體直接或間接索取或收受一項不正當利益，以使該公職人員在履行或執行他或她的公務方面作為或不作為；

   (iii) 直接或間接地允諾給予、提議給予或實際給予外國公職人員或一公共國際組織官員不正當利益，以使該公職人員在履行公務或執行他或她的公務方面作為或不作為，以便在開展國際商業務方面獲得或保留商業或其他不當利益；以及

   (iv) 幫助、教唆或共謀實施第 (i) 至 (iii) 項所述之任何違法行為。

(b) 每一締約方應按照第 1 款或第 5 款所述違法行為的嚴重性對其進行懲罰。

(c) 每一締約方採取或維持與其法律原則相一致的必要措施，確定法人對第 1 款或第 5 款中所述違法行為應承擔的責任。特別是，各締約方尤其應確保對第 1 款或第 5 款中所述違法行為承擔責任的法人，應受到有效、適當且具勸戒作用的刑事或非刑事制裁，包括金錢制裁。

(d) 任何締約方不得允許受其管轄的人從稅款中扣除因第 1 款所述違法行為而產生的相關費用。

(e) 為防止腐敗，各締約方應依照其法律法規，採取或維持關於賬簿和紀錄保存、財務報表披露以及會計和審計準則的必要措施，以禁止為實施第 1 款所述之任何違法行為而作出的下列行為：

   (i) 設立賬外賬目；

   (ii) 進行賬外交易或性質不明的交易活動；

   (iii) 將不存在的支出入賬；

（iv）錄入未正確識別的負債對象

（v）使用虛假文件；以及

（vi）在法律規定的時限屆滿前故意提前銷毀記賬憑證。

（f）每一締約方應考慮採取或維持措施，以保護秉持善意並有合理依據向主管機構舉報有關第 1 款或第 5 款所述違法行為事實的人免受任何不公正待遇。

第十四條　投資與環境

以本協定第三章（可持續發展）和第十三章（環境）為準：

1. 各締約方認識到，其各自的環境法律和政策及其參與的多邊環境協定在保護環境方面發揮的重要作用。

2. 各締約方認識到，通過削弱或減少國內環境法律提供的保護來鼓勵投資是不適當的。因此，每一締約方不得為鼓勵在其領土內設立、獲得、擴大、或保留投資，而放棄或以其他方式減損、或提議放棄或以其他方式減損其環境法律 26 提供的保護，或將通過持續或反覆的作為或不作為而使該等環境法律無法有效執行。

3. 各締約方認識到，每一締約方保留在監管、合規、調查和檢察等事項方面行使自由裁量的權利，並保留在被確定為優先事項的其他環境事項方面分配執法資源的權利。據此，各締約方理解，在一締約方的作為或不作為反映出合理使用資源分配的自由裁量權，或做出關於資源分配的善意決定，則締約國遵守了第 2 款。

4. 為本條之目的，「環境法律」指每一締約方的法律、法規或其規定，其主要目的是通過下列方式保護環境，或防止對人類、動物或植物的生命或健康造成危險：

（a）防止、減少或控制污染物或環境污染物的釋放或排放；

（b）對環境有害或有毒的化學品、物質、材料和廢棄物的控制，以及相關信息的發佈；或

（c）保護或養護野生動植物群，包括瀕危物種、其棲息地和特別自然保護區，

26　如果一締約方依照放棄或減損之規定，放棄或減損環境法律，則第 2 款不適用。

在締約方領土範圍內，但不包括與勞工安全或健康直接相關的任何法規或條例或其規定。

5. 本章的任何內容不得解釋為阻止一締約方採取、維持或執行其認為適當的、符合本章規定的任何措施，以確保在其領土內的投資活動是以對環境問題敏感的方式進行。

6. 一締約方可就本條項下產生的任何問題，通過書面方式要求與其他締約方進行磋商。其他締約方應在收到磋商請求之日起三十日內對磋商請求作出答覆。嗣後，各締約方應進行磋商，努力達成各方滿意的解決方案。

7. 各締約方確認，每一締約方可在適當的情況下就本條項下產生的任何問題，為公眾參與提供機會。

第十五條　投資與勞工

根據本協定第十四章（勞工標準）：

1. 各締約方重申各自作為國際勞工組織成員的義務及在國際勞工組織《國際勞工組織關於工作中基本原則和權利宣言及其後續措施》中所承擔的義務。

2. 各締約方認識到，通過削弱或減少國內勞工法律提供的保護來鼓勵投資是不適當的。因此，當與第 3 款第（a）至（e）項所指的勞工權利相抵觸時，每一締約方不得為鼓勵在其領土內設立、獲得、擴大、或保留投資，而放棄或以其他方式減損、或提議放棄或以其他方式減損其勞工法律提供的保護，或通過持續或反覆的作為或不作為而使該等勞工法律無法有效執行。

3. 為本條之目的，「勞工法」指與下列直接相關的每一締約方的成文法、法規或其規定：

　　（a）結社自由；

　　（b）對集體談判權的有效承認；

　　（c）消除一切形式的強迫或強制勞動；

　　（d）有效廢除童工並禁止最惡劣形式的童工；

　　（e）消除就業和職業方面的歧視；以及

　　（f）與最低工資、工作時間、職業安全和健康相關的、可接受的工作條件。

4. 一締約方可就本條項下產生的任何問題，通過書面方式要求與其他締約方進行磋商。其他締約方應在收到磋商請求之日起三十日內對磋商請求作出答覆。嗣後，各締約方應進行磋商，努力達成各方滿意的解決方案。

5. 各締約方確認，每一締約方可在適當的情況下就本條項下產生的任何事項，為公眾參與提供機會。

6. 自然人因商務需要入境及短暫居住

(a) 本款適用於各締約方根據（d）項以設立為目的之商務訪客和企業內部調動人員入境和在其領土內短暫居住的措施。

(b) 本款不得適用於影響尋求進入一締約方就業市場的自然人的措施，也不得適用於永久性的與公民身份、居留或就業相關的措施。

(c) 本章的任何內容不得阻止一締約方採取管理自然人入境或在其領土內短暫居住的措施，包括為保護其邊境完整和保證自然人有序跨境流動所需的措施，只要實施該等措施不會減損或喪失任何締約方在本款具體承諾條件項下所獲得的利益。[27]

(d) 為本款之目的：

(i) 「商務訪客」指在設立的企業中擔任高級職務的自然人。除設立需要外，不提供服務或從事其他經濟活動，且不從東道國締約方境內取得報酬。

(ii) 「企業內部調動人員」指在其他締約方境內受僱於法人、法人分支機構或作為其合夥人滿一年，並臨時轉入該等法人的子公司、分公司或總公司的自然人[28] 該等自然人屬於以下兩類：

(iii) 「經理人員」指在法人中擔任高級職務，主要領導企業的經營管理，主要接受董事會或企業股東或其他同等職位人員的監督或指導，至少包括：領導企業或其部門或分支機構；及監督和控制其他監督人員、專業人員或管理人員的工作；擁有招聘和辭退、或建議招聘和辭退、或其他與人事有關的行為的權力。

(iv) 「專業人員」指在法人中工作的、具有對企業的生產、研究設備、技術、程序或者管理所必需的專門知識的人員。在評估該

---

27 僅要求某些國家的自然人辦理簽證而不要求其他國家的自然人辦理簽證，不應單獨被視為喪失或減損某項具體承諾的利益。

28 為進一步明確，可要求經理人員和專業人員證明其具有轉入企業所需的專業資格和經驗。

等知識時，不僅要考慮與企業相關的特定知識，還要考慮該等人員是否具有需要專門技術知識的特定工種或行業所需要的資歷，包括是否為公認的專業人員。

(e) 為設立目的而進行的商務訪問，在任何 12 個月的停留期，最長不得超過 90 天；經理人員和專業人員的停留期，最長不得超過三年。

(f) 以一締約方對企業訪客和企業內部調動人員的相關當地保留為準（如有）：

(i) 一締約方應允許企業內部調動人員和設立的商務訪客入境和短暫居住。

(ii) 一締約方不應在部分或全部領土範圍內，以數量配額或經濟需求測試的形式，對特定行業為設立公司而允許商務訪客入境的自然人，或無論是在其部分或全部領土上，對特定行業的投資者可僱傭的企業內部調動人員的自然人的總數，進行限制。

(iii) 每一締約方應就其領土內的、其他締約方的企業內部調動人員和設立的商務訪客的暫時居留給予國民待遇。為本款之目的，應比照適用《服務貿易總協定》第十七條之國民待遇。[29]

(g) 為進一步明確，根據本款（自然人為商業目的的入境和臨時停留）准予的臨時入境，並不取代根據授予締約方領土內現行有效的法律和法規對從事某一職業或開展某一活動所需的資格要求，但這些要求不得與本章下的義務相抵觸。

第十六條　不符措施

1. 第四條、第五條、第十條（業績要求）和第十一條不得適用於：

(a) 一締約方在下列政府層級維持的任何現行不符措施：

(i) 中央一級政府，為該締約方在其附件一或附件三減讓表中所列；

(ii) 區域一級政府，為該締約方在其附件一或附件三減讓表中所列，或

(iii) 地方一級政府。

29　為進一步明確，各締約方同意，該承諾適用於本章承諾範圍涵蓋的所有行業的經濟活動。

(b) （a）項中所指的任何不符措施之延續或及時更新；或

(c) 就（a）項中所指的任何不符措施的修正，只要與該措施緊接修正前的情況相比，該修正未降低該措施與第四條（國民待遇）、第五條（最惠國待遇）、第十條（業績要求）或第十一條（高級管理人員和董事會）的相符程度。

2. 第四條（國民待遇）、第五條（最惠國待遇）、第十條（業績要求）或第十一條（高級管理人員和董事會）不適用於一締約方對於其在附件二減讓表中所列部門、分部門或活動採取或維持的任何措施。

3. 任何締約方不得根據在本協定對其生效之日採取的、其附件二減讓表所涵蓋的任何措施，要求另一締約方的投資者以其國籍為由出售或以其他方式處置在該措施生效時已存在的投資。

4.（a）第四條不得適用於屬對下列條款所施義務之例外或減損範圍內的任何措施：

(i) 第四條（國民待遇）；或

(ii) 《TRIPS 協定》的第三條。

(b) 第五條不得適用於屬於《TRIPS 協定》第五條範圍內的任何措施，或作為下列條款所施義務之例外或減損：

(i) 第四條（國民待遇）；或

(ii) 《TRIPS 協定》第四條。

5. 第四條（國民待遇）、第五條（最惠國待遇）和第十一條（高級管理人員和董事會）不得適用於：

(a) 政府採購；或

(b) 一締約方給予的補貼或贈款，包括政府支持的貸款、擔保和保險。

第十七條　代位

如一締約方或該締約方指定的任何機關、機構、法定團體或公司根據其所簽訂的與一涵蓋投資有關的擔保、保險合同或其他形式的補償協議向該締約方的一投資者進行支付的，則該涵蓋投資所在領土所屬其他締約方應承認任何權利的代位或轉讓，而該權利為該投資者對於涵蓋投資在本章下如非代位則本應享有的權利，且該投資者不得在代位的限度內尋求這些權利。

第十八條　特殊手續和信息要求

1. 第四條（國民待遇）不得解釋為阻止一締約方採取或維持一措施，以規定與一涵蓋投資有關的特殊手續，例如投資註冊的居住要求，或要求一涵蓋投資應根據該締約方的法律或法規合法設立，只要這些手續不實質損害該締約方根據本章對另一締約方的投資者和涵蓋投資所提供的保護。

2. 儘管有第四條（國民待遇）和第五條（最惠國待遇），但是一締約方可僅基於信息或統計目的，要求另一締約方的投資者或其涵蓋投資提供與該投資有關的信息。該締約方應保護屬機密性質的商業信息不被披露而導致損害投資者或涵蓋投資的競爭地位。本款中任何內容不得解釋為阻止一締約方以其他方式獲得或披露與公正和善意適用其法律有關的信息。

第十九條　不減損

為使一締約方的投資者或涵蓋投資有權享受比本章給予的更優惠待遇，本章不應減損下列任何一項：

1. 一締約方的法律或法規、行政實踐或程序、行政或裁決決定；

2. 一締約方的國際法律義務；或

3. 一締約方承擔的義務，包括投資授權或投資協定包含的義務。

第二十條　拒絕給予利益

1. 一締約方可拒絕將本章的利益給予屬其他締約方企業的該其他締約方的一投資者和投資者的投資，如該企業為一非締約方的人或拒絕給予利益的締約方所擁有或控制：

(a) 與該非締約方無保持外交關係；或

(b) 針對該非締約方或非締約方的人採取或維持措施以禁止與該企業進行交易，或如本章的利益被授予該企業或其投資，則會違反或規避此類措施。

2. 一締約方可拒絕將本章之利益給予為另一締約方一投資者之企業以及該投資者的投資，如該企業在另一締約方領土內無實質經營活動且一非締約方或拒絕給予利益締約方的人擁有或控制該企業。

第二十一條　基本安全

各締約方同意善意適用「基本安全」措施，並接受以「基本安全」的名義採取的任何措施應為可受法院裁判。

本章的任何內容不得解釋為：

1. 要求一締約方提供或允許獲得其認為披露後會違背其基本安全利益的任何信息；或

2. 阻止一締約方採取其認為對履行有關維持或恢復國際和平與安全，或保護自身基本安全利益的義務所必須的措施。

第二十二條　信息披露

本章的任何內容不得解釋為要求一締約方提供或允許訪問機密信息，如果披露該機密信息會妨礙執法或違反公共利益，或損害特定的公共或私人企業的合法商業利益。

第二十三條　金融服務

以本協定第十章（金融服務）為準：

1. 儘管根據本章的其他規定，不應阻止一締約方出於審慎原因而採取或維持有關金融服務的措施，包括出於保護投資者、存款人、投保人，或出於保護金融服務提供者對其負有信義義務的人，或出於確保金融系統的完整與穩定而採取或維持的此類措施。[30] 在此類措施與本章規定不符的情況下，不得用以規避本章項下該締約方的承諾或義務。

2.（a）本章的任何內容不適用於任何公共實體為執行貨幣及相關信貸政策或匯率政策而採取的普遍適用的非歧視措施。本款不應影響締約方在第九條（轉移）或第十條（業績要求）項下的義務。[31]

（b）為本款之目的，「公共實體」指一締約方的中央銀行或金融機構。

3. 在申請人根據本章第二部分提出仲裁申請的情況下，而被申請人援引第

30　各締約方理解，「審慎原因」包括維護單個金融機構的安全性、健全性、完整性或金融責任，以及維護支付和清算系統的安全性、財務和運營完整性。

31　為進一步明確，為追求貨幣及相關信貸政策或匯率政策而採取的普遍適用的措施不包括明確宣佈失效或修改與計價貨幣或匯率有關的合同條款的措施。

1 款或第 2 款作為抗辯，則下列規定適用於：

(a) 被申請人應在根據第二部分將仲裁請求提交仲裁之日起 120 天內，以書面形式向各締約方的主管金融機構[32] 提交請求，要求共同決定第 1 款或第 2 款是否以及在多大程度上構成對仲裁請求的有效抗辯。如果仲裁庭已經組成，被申請人應迅速向仲裁庭提交該請求的副本。仲裁可就僅依據 (d) 項的請求進行。

(b) 各締約方的金融機構應隨時準備相互磋商，並應嘗試以善意作出 (a) 項所述的決定。任何此類決定應立即送交爭端雙方，且還應送交仲裁庭（如仲裁庭組成）。此類決定對仲裁庭具有約束力。

(c) 如各締約方的主管金融機構在收到 (a) 項下被申請人要求共同決定的書面請求之日起 120 天內未作出該項所述的決定，仲裁庭應對該主管金融機構未解決的問題作出決定。應適用第二部分的規定，除非根據本項作出修改。

(i) 在任何尚未被任命的所有仲裁員時，爭端各締約方應採取適當措施，以確保仲裁庭具有金融服務法律或實務方面的專門知識或經驗。應在任命首席仲裁員時考慮特定候選人有關爭端產生的特定金融服務部門的專門知識。

(ii) 在被申請人按照 (a) 項提出共同決定的請求之前，如已根據第二十七條第 3 款任命首席仲裁員的，則應根據爭端任一締約方的要求予以替換該仲裁員，且仲裁庭應根據第 (c) (i) 項重新組成。如在仲裁程序根據第 (d) 項重新開始之日起 30 天內，爭端各締約方未就任命新的首席仲裁員達成一致意見的，則秘書長應根據第 (c) (i) 項的要求任命首席仲裁員。

(iii) 仲裁庭不得因主管金融機構未作出第 (a) 項所述的決定而推斷適用第 1 款或第 2 款。

(iv) 非爭端締約方可就第 1 款或第 2 款是否以及在多大程度上構成對仲裁請求的有效抗辯，向仲裁庭提出口頭和書面陳述。為仲裁之目的，應推定非爭端締約方就第 1 款或第 2 款所持的立場與被申請人不一致，除非其作出該等陳述。

---

32 為本條之目的，「主管金融機構」，就【國家】而言，指【】；就【國家】而言，指【】。

(d) 第 (a) 項所指的仲裁可在下列情況下處理仲裁請求：

(i) 爭端締約方和仲裁庭（如組成）均收到主管金融機構的共同決定之日後之 10 日後；或

(ii) 第 (c) 項規定主管金融機構的 120 天期限屆滿後之 10 日後。

(e) 應被申請人在第 (c) 項所指的共同決定的 120 天期限屆滿後 30 日內提出請求，或者，如果在 120 日期限屆滿時仲裁庭尚未組成，則在仲裁庭組成後 30 日內提出請求，仲裁庭應在決定被申請人援引第 1 款或第 2 款作為抗辯之主張的實體之前，對第 (c) 項所指的主管金融機構尚未解決的一項或多項問題處理並作出決定。被申請人未能提出此種請求無損被申請人在仲裁的任何適當階段援引第 1 款或第 2 款作為抗辯的權利。

4. 在發生本章第三部分項下的爭端且一締約方主管金融機構向其他締約方主管金融機構作出爭端涉及金融服務的書面通知時，除根據本款和第 5 款另有修改外，適用第三部分。

(a) 各締約方的主管金融機構應負責就該等爭端相互進行磋商，且在收到該等通知之日起 180 日內，將磋商報告送交各締約方。一締約方只能在 180 日期限屆滿後根據第三部分將爭端提交仲裁。

(b) 任一締約方均可將此類報告送交根據第三部分組成的、裁決所指爭端或相似爭端的仲裁庭，或送交根據本章第二部分組成的、裁決由引起該第三部分項下爭端之相同事件或情形的主張之仲裁庭。

5. 在一締約方根據第 4 款將涉及金融服務的爭端提交本章第三部分仲裁的情況下，並在爭端提交仲裁之日起 30 日內，應任何締約方的要求，每一締約方在任命所有尚未任命的仲裁員時，應採取適當措施確保仲裁庭具有金融服務法律或實踐的專門知識或經驗。應在任命首席仲裁員時考慮特定候選人有關金融服務的專門知識。

6. 儘管有第十三條第 2 至 4 款，每一締約方在可行的限度內，

(a) 應提前公佈其擬採取的、與金融服務相關的、任何具有普遍適用性的法規及其目的；

(b) 應向利害關係人和其他締約方提供對該擬議法規進行評論的合理機會；以及

（c）　應在通過最終法規時，以書面形式說明從利害關係人處收到的、與擬議法規相關的重要實質性評論。

7.「金融服務」一詞應與《服務貿易總協定》金融服務附件第 5（a）項具有相同含義。

8.為進一步明確，不得將本章的任何內容解釋為阻止一締約方採取或實施與其他締約方在金融機構的投資者或涵蓋投資有關的措施，這些措施是為確保遵守與本章不相抵觸的法律法規相抵觸所必需的措施，包括與防止和欺詐行為有關的措施，或處理違約對金融服務合同的影響的措施，但這些措施的適用方式不得在情形類似的國家間構成任意或不合理的歧視手段，或構成對金融機構投資的變相限制。

第二十四條　稅收

1.除本條規定外，第一部分的任何內容不得施加與稅收措施相關的義務。

2.第八條（徵收和補償）應適用於所有的稅收措施，除非申請人主張一項稅收措施涉及徵收。只有在下列情況下，該等申請人方可根據第二部分將主張提交仲裁：

（a）　申請人以就該等稅收措施是否涉及徵收問題，書面向各締約方主管稅務機構[33]提出；

（b）　自該提交之日起 180 日內，各締約方的主管稅務機構未能就該等徵收措施不是徵收達成一致。

3.在第 4 款的前提下，第十條（業績要求）第 2 至 4 款應適用於所有稅收措施。

4.本章的任何內容不得影響任何締約方在任何稅收協定項下的權利和義務。如本章與任何此類協定相抵觸，則在相抵觸的範圍內適用該等協定。如各締約方之間有稅收協定，該協定項下的主管機構應自行負責確定本章與該等協定之間是否相抵觸。

33　為本條之目的，「主管稅務機關」：(a) 對【國家】而言，指【】。(b) 對【國家】而言，指【】。

第二十五條　生效、期限和終止 [34]

1. 本章應自各締約方交換批准書之日起 30 日後生效。本協定有效期為 10 年，且除非依據第 2 款予以終止，本協定在有效期後繼續有效。

2. 一締約方可在本章第一個 10 年期限屆滿時或此後的任何時間終止本章，但應提前一年書面通知其他締約方。

3. 終止之日起的 10 年內，除延伸至設立或獲得涵蓋投資的條款範圍外，所有其他條款應繼續適用於終止之日前設立或獲得的涵蓋投資。

第二部分　爭端解決

第二十六條　磋商和談判

1. 當發生投資爭端時，申請人和被申請人應首先通過磋商和談判尋求解決爭端。磋商和談判可包括使用不具有拘束力的第三方程序，如斡旋、調解或調停。

2. 申請人應向被申請人提交對所涉事項的事實做簡要說明的磋商書面請求。

3. 為進一步明確，不得將啓動磋商和談判解釋為承認仲裁庭的管轄權。

第二十七條　提交仲裁請求

1. 如爭端締約方認為投資爭端不能通過磋商和談判解決：

　（a）　申請人可自行將請求提交本部分項下仲裁：

　　（i）　被申請人已經違反

　　　（A）第三條至第十條項下的義務，

　　　（B）投資授權，或

　　　（C）投資協議；

　　　以及

34　本條僅能在一締約方因其自身的獨特原因，無法就本章作為本協定的一部分作出一攬子承諾的情況下適用。

（ii）申請人已因此類違約產生損失或損害；以及

（b）申請人可代表被申請人企業，而該企業為申請人直接或間接擁有或控制的法人，將請求提交本部分項下仲裁：

（i）被申請人已違反

（A）第三條至第十條項下的義務，

（B）投資授權，或

（C）投資協議；

以及

（ii）該企業已因此類違約產生損失或損害，前提條件是申請人只有在請求的標的和被請求的損害賠償依據相關投資協議與涵蓋投資的設立或獲得、或尋求設立或獲得直接相關時，方可依據第（a）（i）（C）項或第（b）（i）（C）項提出違反一投資協議的主張。

2. 在提交任何本部分項下仲裁請求至少 90 日前，申請人應向被申請人送達其提交仲裁請求意向的書面通知（「意向通知」）。該通知應載明：

（a）申請人的姓名和地址；如代表企業提出仲裁請求的，則該企業的名稱、地址和註冊地；

（b）就每一請求，被指稱已違反之本章規定、投資授權或投資協議以及任何其他相關條款；

（c）每一請求的法律和事實依據；以及

（d）尋求的救濟和主張的損害賠償之大概數額。

3. 如引起仲裁請求的事件發生時間已超過六個月，申請人可將第 1 款所指的請求提交如下機構：

（a）《關於解決國家與他國國民之間的投資爭端的公約》和《國際投資爭端解決中心仲裁規則》項下，前提是被申訴方和非爭端締約方均為《關於解決國家與他國國民之間的投資爭端的公約》的締約方；

（b）《國際投資爭端解決中心附加便利規則》項下，前提是被申訴方或非爭端締約方均為《關於解決國家與他國國民之間的投資爭端的公約》的締約方；

（c）《聯合國國際貿易法委員會仲裁規則》項下；或

(d) 國際商事爭端預防與解決組織爭端解決機制的數套規則項下；[35]

4. 當申請人發出如下仲裁通知或仲裁請求（「仲裁通知」）時，應將一請求視為提交本部分項下仲裁：

(a) 秘書長接收的《關於解決國家與他國國民之間的投資爭端的公約》所指的仲裁通知；

(b) 秘書長接收的《國際投資爭端解決中心附加便利規則》附件三第二條所指的仲裁通知；

(c) 被申請人接收的《聯合國國際貿易法委員會仲裁規則》第三條所指的仲裁通知和《聯合國國際貿易法委員會仲裁規則》第二十條所指的仲裁申請書；或

(d) 被申請人接收的根據第 3 款（d）項選擇的國際商事爭端預防與解決組織的規則所指的仲裁通知。

應將申請人在提交仲裁通知後首次提出的請求在可適用仲裁規則項下其接收之日視為提交本部分項下仲裁。

5. 除本章另有規定，第 3 款項下可適用的且在本部分項下提交一項或多項仲裁請求之日有效的仲裁規則應適用於該仲裁。

6. 申請人應在仲裁通知中提供：

(a) 申請人指定的仲裁員姓名；或

(b) 申請人書面同意秘書長任命該等仲裁員。

第二十八條　各締約方之同意仲裁

1. 每一締約方同意依據本章將請求提交本部分項下仲裁。

2. 第 1 款項下的同意和本部分項下提交仲裁請求應滿足下列要求：

(a) 爭端當事方的書面同意符合《關於解決國家與他國國民之間的投資爭端的公約》第二章（中心的管轄權）和《國際投資爭端解決中心附加便利規則》；【以及】

(b) 就「書面協議」，符合《紐約公約》第二條。

35　為進一步明確，如一方選擇適用國際商事爭端預防與解決組織的規則，則爭端解決程序應適用該等規則，而不受本章爭端解決規則的約束。為進一步明確，本章應視為已經包含了國際商事爭端預防與解決組織爭端解決機制的規則。

第二十九條　各締約方同意的條件和限制

1. 如自申請人第一次知道或應當知道第二十七條第 1 款項下違約之日起，以及知道或應當知道申請人〔就第二十七條第 1 款（a）項提出的請求而言〕或企業〔就第二十七條第 1 款（b）項提出的請求而言〕已受損失或損害之日起，超過三年的，不得將任何請求提交本部分項下仲裁。

2. 不得將任何請求提交本部分項下仲裁，除非：

(a) 申請人以書面形式同意依據本章列明的程序進行仲裁；以及

(b) 仲裁通知附有，

(i) 對於根據第二十七條第 1 款（a）項提交仲裁的請求，申請人的書面聲明放棄，以及

(ii) 對於根據第二十七條第 1 款（b）項提交仲裁的請求，申請人和企業的書面聲明

放棄根據任一締約方法律在任何行政法庭或法院、或其他爭端解決程序的，對任何被指控構成第二十七條所列一違反行為的任何措施啟動或繼續任何程序的任何權利。

2. 儘管有第 2 款（b）項的規定，申請人〔就第二十七條第 1 款（a）項下提出的請求〕和申請人或企業〔就第二十七條第 1 款（b）項提出的請求〕可提起或繼續尋求臨時禁令救濟且不涉及向被申請人的司法或行政法庭支付金錢賠償的訴訟，只要提起該訴訟完全是為了在仲裁程序進行期間維護申請人或企業的權益。

第三十條　仲裁員的選擇

1. 除非爭端方另有約定，否則仲裁庭應由三名仲裁員組成。每一爭端方指定一名仲裁員，第三名仲裁員應經爭端方共同指定並擔任首席仲裁員。

2. 秘書長應作為根據本節所提交仲裁的指定機構。

3. 在遵守第二十七條第 4 款的前提下，如仲裁庭在根據本節提交仲裁請求之日後 75 日內仍未組成的，則應爭端一方請求，秘書長應行使他或她的自由裁量權，指定尚未指定的一名或多名仲裁員。

4. 就《關於解決國家與他國國民之間的投資爭端的公約》第三十九條和《國際投資爭端解決中心附加便利規則》附件 C 第七條而言，並在不損害以國

籍之外的理由對一仲裁員提出異議的情況下：

(a) 被申請人同意根據《關於解決國家與他國國民之間的投資爭端的公約》和《國際投資爭端解決中心附加便利規則》設立的仲裁庭的每一名成員的指定；

(b) 第二十七條第 1 款（a）項所指的申請人，只有在該申請人以書面形式同意仲裁庭每一人員指定的條件下，方可根據本節提交根據《關於解決國家與他國國民之間的投資爭端的公約》或《國際投資爭端解決中心附加便利規則》進行仲裁的請求或繼續一請求；以及

(c) 第二十七條第 1 款（b）項中所指的申請人，只有在該申請人和企業書面同意仲裁庭每一人員指定的條件下，方可根據本節提交根據《關於解決國家與他國國民之間的投資爭端的公約》或《國際投資爭端解決中心附加便利規則》進行仲裁的請求或繼續一請求。

第三十一條　仲裁程序的進行

1. 各爭端方可根據第二十七條第 3 款適用的仲裁規則議定任何仲裁地。如爭端方無法達成一致，則仲裁庭應根據適用的仲裁規則確定仲裁地點，條件是該地點應位於一屬《紐約公約》締約方的領土內。

2. 非爭端締約方可就本章的解釋向仲裁庭提交口頭和書面陳述。

3. 仲裁庭應有權力接受和考慮非爭端方的人或實體提交的法庭之友陳述。

4. 在不損害仲裁庭作為先決問題處理其他異議的職權的前提下，仲裁庭應作為先決問題處理被申請人提出的異議並作出裁決，作為一法律事項，所提交的一請求並非一可根據第三十七條作出有利於申請人裁決的請求。

(a) 此種異議應在仲裁庭組成後盡快提交仲裁庭，且在任何情況下均不得遲於仲裁庭選定的被申請人提交答辯狀的日期（或，在對仲裁通知進行修改的情況下，則為仲裁庭選定的被申請人提交對修改作出答覆的日期）。

(b) 在收到本款項下的異議後，仲裁庭應中止針對實體問題的任何程序，設定考慮該異議的時間表，該時間表與已設定的考慮其他先決問題的時間表相一致，對異議作出決定或裁決並闡述有關理由。

(c) 在對本款項下的異議作出決定時，仲裁庭應假定申請人用於支持仲

裁通知（或其任何修改）中任何請求的事實指控是真實的，且在根據《聯合國國際貿易法委員會仲裁規則》提交的一爭端中，《聯合國國際貿易法委員會仲裁規則》第二十條所指的仲裁請求也是真實的。仲裁庭還可考慮無爭議的任何其他相關事實。

(d) 被申請人不會僅因根據本款提出或未提出任何異議，或使用第 5 款列明的快速程序而放棄對權限提出異議或放棄關於實體問題的論據。

5. 如被申請人在仲裁庭組成後 45 日內提出請求，則仲裁庭應快速裁決第 4 款下的異議，以及該爭端不屬於仲裁庭管轄權範圍的異議。仲裁庭應中止關於實體問題的任何程序，並不遲於該請求提出之日後 150 日內發佈關於異議的決定或裁決並陳述相關理由。但是，如爭端一方請求舉行聽證會，仲裁庭可再用 30 日時間發佈決定或裁決。無論是否請求舉行聽證會，仲裁庭可在表明存在特別原因的情況下短暫推遲發佈其決定或裁決，時間不得超過 30 日。

6. 如仲裁庭就被申請人根據第 4 款或第 5 款提出的異議作出決定，如確有必要，則仲裁庭可裁決勝訴方承擔在提出或抗辯異議過程中產生的合理費用和律師費。在確定此種裁決是必要時，仲裁庭應考慮申請人的請求或被申請人的異議是否是輕率的，並應向爭端方提供合理的評論機會。

7. 被申請人不得將申請人依據一保險合同或擔保合同已獲得或將獲得對其聲稱的全部或部分損失的賠償或其他補償，作出其所聲稱的抗辯、反訴或抵消權的理由或任何其他理由。

8. 仲裁庭可下令採取臨時保全措施以維護一爭端方的權利，或以保證仲裁庭的管轄權充分有效，包括作出保全由一爭端方擁有或控制的證據的命令或保護仲裁庭的管轄權的命令。仲裁庭不得下令扣押或下令禁止適用被指控構成第二十七條所指違反情況的一措施。就本款而言，命令包括建議。

9. (a) 在根據本節進行的任何仲裁中，應爭端一方請求，仲裁庭在發佈一項有關責任的決定或裁決之前，應將其擬議的決定或裁決傳送各爭端方和非爭端締約方。在仲裁庭傳送其擬議的決定或裁決後 60 日內，各爭端方可就其擬議的決定或裁決的任何方面向仲裁庭提交書面評論。仲裁庭應對任何評論予以考慮，並不遲於 60 日的評論期期滿後 45 日發佈其決定或裁決。

(b) (a) 項不適用於根據本部分進行並根據第 10 款可作出上訴的任何

仲裁。

10. 如將來在其他機制性安排下設立審查投資者與國家間爭端解決仲裁庭裁決的上訴機制，則各締約方應考慮根據第三十七條作出的裁決是否適用該等上訴機制。各締約方應努力確保其考慮採用的任何此類上訴機制關於程序透明度的規定與第三十二條所確立的透明度條款相類似。

第三十二條　仲裁程序的透明度

1. 在第 2 款和第 4 款的前提下，被申請人應在收到下列文書後，迅速將文書傳送給非爭端締約方，並使公眾可獲得該等文件：

  (a) 意向通知；

  (b) 仲裁通知；

  (c) 爭端一方向仲裁庭提交的訴狀、備忘錄和摘要，以及依據第三十一條第 2 款（非爭端締約方的書面陳述）、第 3 款（法庭之友陳述）和第三十六條（合併審理）提交的任何書面陳述；

  (d) 仲裁庭的庭審紀要或筆錄（如可獲得）；以及

  (e) 仲裁庭的命令、裁決和決定。

2. 仲裁庭應舉行向公眾開放的聽證會，並應經與爭端方磋商後確定適當的行政安排。然而，任一爭端方意圖在聽證會中使用指定為受保護的信息，則應當據此通知仲裁庭。仲裁庭應作出適當安排以保護該信息不被披露。

3. 本節中任何內容，不要求被申請人披露受保護的信息，或者提供或允許獲取被申請人依據第二十一條（基本安全）或第二十二條（信息披露）可拒絕披露的信息。

4. 向仲裁庭提交的任何受保護的信息應依照下列程序以防止被披露：

  (a) 在遵守（d）項的前提下，如提供信息的爭端一方依據（b）項明確將其指定為受保護的信息，則各爭端方和仲裁庭均不得將該信息向非爭端締約方或公眾披露；

  (b) 聲稱某些信息構成受保護信息的任何爭端方，應在向仲裁庭提交該等信息時明確指定該信息屬保護信息；

  (c) 爭端一方在提交聲明包含受保護信息的文件時，應同時提交一份不包含受保護信息的該文件的編輯版本。只有該編輯版本應提供給非

爭端締約方，並依據第 1 款予以公佈；以及

(d) 仲裁庭應對聲稱信息包含受保護信息的指定所提任何異議作出決定。如果仲裁庭確定對該信息所作指定不適當，則提交信息的爭端一方可（i）全部或部分撤回包含該信息的陳述，或（ii）同意依據仲裁庭的確定和（c）項，重新提交完整的和經編輯的文件並作出正確指定。在以上任一情況下，另一爭端方均應在必要時重新提交完整的和經編輯的文件，或去除由首次提交該信息的爭端一方根據（i）項撤回的信息，或對該信息重新作出指定以符合首次提交該信息的爭端一方根據（ii）項所作指定。

5. 本節中任何內容不限制被申請人向公眾提供其根據法律要求予以披露的信息。

第三十三條　準據法

1. 在遵守第 3 款的前提下，若根據第二十七條第 1 款（a）（i）（A）項或第 1 款（b）（i）（A）項提出仲裁申請時，則仲裁庭應根據本章和適用的國際法規則對爭議問題作出決定。

2. 在遵守第 3 款和本節的其他規定前提下，如一請求根據第二十七條第 1 款（a）（i）（B）或（C）項或第二十七條第 1 款（b）（i）（B）或（C）項提交仲裁，則仲裁庭應適用：

(a) 在相關投資授權或投資協議中載明的法律規則、或各爭端方可能另有議定的法律規則；或

(b) 如果法律規則未予載明或無另外約定：

　　(i)　被申請人的法律，包括其衝突法；[36] 以及

　　(ii) 可適用的國際法規則。

3. 各締約方通過為本條之目的而指定的代表作出的、聲明對本章規定進行解釋的聯合決定，對仲裁庭具有拘束力，且仲裁庭作出的任何決定或裁決必須與該等聯合決定相一致。

---

36 「被申請人的法律」指具有適當管轄權的國內法院或法庭在同一案件中適用的法律。

第三十四條　對附件的解釋

1. 如被申請人以被指控違反的措施屬於附件一、附件二或附件三中載明的條目範圍為由進行抗辯，則應被申請人的請求，仲裁庭應請求各締約方就此問題作出解釋。各締約方應在該請求送達之日起 90 日內，以書面形式將表明其解釋的聯合決定提交仲裁庭。

2. 各締約方通過其為本條之目的指定的代表根據第 1 款作出的聯合決定，對仲裁庭具有拘束力，且仲裁庭作出的任何決定或裁決必須與該聯合決定相一致。如各締約方未能在 90 日內作出該等決定，則仲裁庭應對該問題作出決定。

第三十五條　專家報告

在不影響經適用的仲裁規則授權指定其他類型專家的情況下，仲裁庭可應爭端一方的請求，除非各爭端方不同意，自行指定一名或多名專家，就爭端一方在程序中提出的有關環境、健康、安全或其他科學事項的任何事實問題提交書面報告，但需遵守各爭端方可能議定的條款和條件。

第三十六條　合併審理

1. 如兩個或多個請求根據第二十七條第 1 款分別提交仲裁，而該請求包含共同的法律或事實問題且產生自相同事件或情況，則任一爭端方可依照尋求為合併審理命令所涵蓋的所有爭端方達成的一致意見，或依據第 2 款至第 10 款的條款尋求合併審理的命令。

2. 根據本條尋求合併審理命令的爭端一方，應以書面形式向秘書長和尋求為該命令所涵蓋的爭端方送達請求，並在請求中說明：

    (a) 尋求為該命令所涵蓋的所有爭端方的名稱和地址；

    (b) 所尋求命令的性質；以及

    (c) 尋求該命令的理由。

3. 除非秘書長在收到根據第 2 款所提請求之後 30 日內發現該請求明顯無依據，否則應根據本條設立仲裁庭。

4. 除非尋求為該命令所涵蓋的所有爭端方另有議定，否則根據本條設立的仲裁庭應由三名仲裁員組成：

    (a) 經各申請人一致同意指定的一名仲裁員；

(b) 由被申請人指定的一名仲裁員；以及

(c) 由秘書長指定的首席仲裁員，但前提是首席仲裁員不得為任一締約方的國民。

5. 如在秘書長收到根據第 2 款所提請求之日後 60 日內，被申請人或申請人未能依據第 4 款指定一名仲裁員，則應尋求為該命令所涵蓋的任一爭端方之請求，秘書長應指定一名或數名尚未指定的仲裁員。如被申請人未能指定仲裁員的，則秘書長應指定一名爭端締約方的國民；以及如申請人未能指定仲裁員的，秘書長應指定一名非爭端締約方的國民。

6. 如根據本條設立的仲裁庭確信，根據第二十七條第 1 款提交仲裁的兩個或多個請求包含一共同法律或事實問題，且產生自相同事件或情況，則為公正有效解決該請求，仲裁庭可在聽取各爭端方的意見後通過命令：

(a) 對全部或部分請求一併行使管轄權、進行聽審和作出確定；

(b) 對一項或數項請求行使管轄權、進行聽審和作出確定，仲裁庭認為該確定有助於其他請求的解決；或

(c) 指示一此前根據第三十條設立的仲裁庭對全部或部分請求一併行使管轄權、進行審理並作出確定，條件是：

(i) 應先前不屬該仲裁庭的爭端一方的一申請人的請求，該仲裁庭應由其原有成員重新組成，但申請人的仲裁庭應依據第 4 款 (a) 項和第 5 款指定；以及

(ii) 仲裁庭應決定任何此前的審理是否需要重複。

7. 如已根據本條設立仲裁庭，則根據第二十七條第 1 款已經提交請求且未根據第 2 款提交的請求中未被提名的一申請人，可以向仲裁庭提出關於將其包括在根據第 6 款作出的任何命令中的書面請求，並應在請求中載明：

(a) 申請人的名稱和地址；

(b) 所尋求的命令的性質；以及

(c) 尋求命令的理由。

申請人應將其請求的副本遞送秘書長。

8. 根據本條設立的仲裁庭應依據《聯合國國際貿易法委員會仲裁規則》進行其仲裁，但需按經本節修改後的規則。

9. 根據第三十條設立的仲裁庭不得對根據本條設立或受到指示的仲裁庭已

行使管轄權的一項請求或一請求的一部分行使決定權。

10. 應爭端一方申請，根據本條設立的仲裁庭在作出第 6 款下的決定前，可命令根據第三十條（仲裁員的選擇）設立的仲裁庭的程序予以暫停，除非後一仲裁庭已經停止仲裁程序。

第三十七條　裁決

1. 如仲裁庭對被申請人作出最終裁決，則仲裁庭只能單獨或一併就下列各項作出裁決：

(a) 金錢賠償及任何適用利息；以及

(b) 財產返還，在此情況下裁決應規定被申請人可支付金錢賠償及適用利息以替代返還。

仲裁庭還可依據本章和適用的仲裁規則對費用和律師費作出裁決。

2. 在遵守第 1 款的前提下，如一請求根據第二十七條第 1 款（b）項提交仲裁，則：

(a) 返還財產的裁決應規定返還對象為該企業；

(b) 金錢賠償及任何適用利息的裁決應規定有關款項的支付對象為該企業；以及

(c) 裁決應規定該裁決的作出不損害任何人在適用的國內法規定的救濟中可能享有的任何權利。

3. 仲裁庭不得作出懲罰性損害賠償的裁決。

4. 仲裁庭作出的裁決除對各爭端方和特定案件以外不具有拘束力。

5. 在遵守第 6 款和臨時裁決適用的審議程序的前提下，爭端一方應立即遵守和履行一裁決。

6. 爭端一方不得尋求執行一最終裁決，直至：

(a) 對於根據《關於解決國家與他國國民間投資爭端公約》作出的最終裁決，

(i) 自作出裁決之日起已滿 120 日且無爭端方要求修改或撤銷該裁決；或

(ii) 修改或撤銷程序已完成；以及

(b) 對於根據《國際投資爭端解決中心附加便利規則》、《聯合國國際

貿易法委員會仲裁規則》或根據第二十七條第 3 款（d）項所選擇的規則作出的最終裁決，

(i) 自作出裁決之日起已滿 90 日，且無爭端方啟動修改、取消或撤銷該裁決的程序；或

(ii) 法院已駁回或准許修改、取消或撤銷裁決的申請，且無進一步上訴。

7. 每一締約方應就在其領土內執行裁決作出規定。

8. 如被申請人未能遵守或履行最終裁決，則應在非爭端締約方遞交請求後，根據第四十一條（國家間爭端解決）設立一仲裁庭。在不損害適用的國際法規則項下其他救濟的情況下，該請求締約方可在該等程序中尋求：

(a) 就未能遵守或履行最終裁決的行為與本章的義務不一致作出確定；以及

(b) 對被申請人遵守或履行最終裁決提出建議。

9. 無論是否已根據第 8 款進行有關程序，爭端一方可根據《關於解決國家與他國國民間投資爭端公約》或《紐約公約》（或《美洲國家間公約》）尋求執行一仲裁裁決。

10. 根據本節提交仲裁的請求應被視為產生自就《紐約公約》第一條（和《美洲國家間公約》第一條）而言的一商業關係或交易。

第三十八條　一般例外

1.《1994 年關稅與貿易總協定》第二十條及其解釋性説明併入本協定，成為本協定之一部分，並比照適用。

2. 各締約方理解，《1994 年關稅與貿易總協定》第二十條（b）項所指的措施包括為保護人類、動物或植物生命或健康所必需的環境措施，且《1994 年關稅與服務貿易總協定》第二十條（g）項適用於與保護可用盡的生物和非生物自然資源有關的措施。

3.《服務貿易總協定》第十四條（a）、（b）和（c）項併入本協定，成為本協定的一部分，並比照適用。各締約方理解，《服務貿易總協定》第十四條（b）項所指的措施包括為保護人類、動物或植物的聲明或健康所必須的環境措施。

4. 本協定的任何內容不得解釋為阻止一締約方採取經世界貿易組織爭端解決機構授權或根據採取行動的締約方和被採取行動的締約方均為締約方的自由貿易協定項下爭端解決小組的裁決而採取的行動，包括維持或增加關稅。

第三十九條　附件和腳註

附件和腳註應為本章的組成部分。

第四十條　文書送達

對一締約方的通知和其他文書應送達至附件三為該締約方指定的地點。

第四十一條　國家間爭端解決

1. 在遵守第 5 款的前提下，各締約方之間涉及本章解釋或適用的爭議，如不能通過磋商或其他外交途徑解決的，應根據任一締約方之請求，提交仲裁。由仲裁庭依據可適用的國際法規則作出具有約束力的決定或裁決。各締約方之間如無相反的約定，適用《聯合國國際貿易法委員會仲裁規則》，除非各締約方或本章另有修改。

2. 除非各締約方另有協議，仲裁庭應由三名仲裁員組成，每一締約方各指定一名仲裁員，第三名仲裁員為各當事締約方同意指定的首席仲裁員。如根據本節提交仲裁請求後 75 日內仲裁庭尚未組成的，則應任一當事締約方請求，秘書長應行使他或她的自由裁量權，指定尚未指定的一名或數名仲裁員。

3. 仲裁員的費用和仲裁程序的其他費用由各締約方平均負擔。但仲裁庭可以自行決定指定一締約方負擔較高比例的費用。

4. 第三十一條第 3 款（法庭之友提交）、第三十二條（仲裁程序的透明度）、第三十三條（準據法）第 1 款和第 3 款以及第三十四條（對附件的解釋）

應比照適用於本條項下的仲裁。

5. 第 1 款至第 4 款不適用於第十二條或第十三條項下產生的事項。

第四十二條　外國投資委員會

1. 各締約方特此設立外國投資委員會（以下簡稱「委員會」），由各締約方的內閣級代表或其指定人員組成。

2. 委員會應：

(a) 監督本章的實施；

(b) 監督其進一步闡述；

(c) 解決因解釋或適用產生的爭議；

(d) 採納對本章的規定具有拘束力的解釋；

(e) 採納根據國際商事爭端預防與解決組織相關規則在調解程序中達成的、各締約方均同意的解決方案；

(f) 監督根據本章設立的所有委員會和工作組的工作；

(g) 考慮可能影響本章實施的任何其他事項。

3. 委員會有權：

(a) 設立臨時或常設委員會、工作組或專家小組，並向其委派職責；

(b) 向非政府人士或團體徵求意見；以及

(c) 在執行其職責時採取各締約方同意的其他行動。

4. 委員會應建立其規則和程序。除委員會另行同意外，委員會的所有決定應經各締約方一致同意後作出。

5. 委員會應每年至少召開一次例會。委員會定期會議應由各締約方輪流主持。

附件一　習慣國際法

締約方確認如下共同理解，即一般意義上的「習慣國際法」和在第六條（最低待遇標準）和附件二（徵收）中特別提及的「習慣國際法」源於國家出於法律義務意識而遵循的普遍和一貫的慣例。關於第六條（最低待遇標準），習慣國際法關於外國人待遇的最低標準指保護外國人經濟權利和利益的所有習慣國際法原則。

附件二 徵收

締約方確認對下列事項的共同理解：

1. 第八條（徵收與補償）第 1 款旨在反應有關各締約方與徵收相關義務的習慣國際法。

2. 一締約方的一項或一系列行動不構成徵收，除非對一項投資的有形或無形財產權或財產權益造成影響。

3. 第八條（徵收與補償）第 1 款處理兩類情形。第一類為直接徵收，即一投資被國有化或通過正式轉讓所有權或完全沒收而被直接沒收。

4. 第八條（徵收與補償）第 1 款處理的第二類情形為間接徵收，即一締約方的一項或一系列行動具有與直接徵收同等效果，而無需正式轉移所有權或完全沒收。

(a) 就一締約方的一項或一系列行動在特定事實情況下是否構成間接徵收所作確定，需逐案根據事實進行調查，並考慮包括下列其他因素：

(i) 儘管一締約方的一項或一系列行動已對一投資的經濟價值有不利影響，但是單獨政府行為的經濟影響本身並不能證明已發生間接徵收；

(ii) 政府行為對基於投資的明顯合理預期的影響程度；以及

(iii) 政府行為的性質。

(b) 除非在極少數情況下，一締約方為保護如公共健康、安全和環境的合法公共福祉目標而採取的非歧視性管制行動不構成間接徵收。

附件三　向一締約方送達文件

【國家】

通知和其他文件應送達【國家】至：【填寫送達通知和其他文件的地點【國家】】

【國家】

通知和其他文件應送達【國家】至：【填寫送達通知和其他文件的地點【國家】】

第八章　知識產權

第一條　定義

就本章而言，除非出現相反意思：

「**地理標識**」指識別某一貨物來源於一締約方領土的標誌，或來源於該領土內某一地區或某一地方的標誌，而該貨物的質量、聲譽或其他特性主要是由於其地理來源而產生的；

「**知識產權**」指《TRIPS 協定》中定義和描述的版權及相關權利、商標權、地理標識、工業外觀設計、集成電路的專利和布圖設計（拓撲圖）、植物品種權、以及對未披露信息的權利；

「**一締約方國民**」，就相關權利而言，包括該締約方符合《TRIPS 協定》第一條第 3 款所列協定中保護資格標準的實體；

「**《巴黎公約》**」指 1967 年 7 月 14 日在斯德哥爾摩修訂的《保護工業產權巴黎公約》。

「**表演**」指固定在錄音製品上的表演，除非另有說明；

「**《TRIPS 協定》**」指《世界知識產權協定》附件一 C 所載的《與貿易有關的知識產權協定》；以及

「**WIPO**」指世界知識產權組織。

第二條　目標

1. 知識產權的保護和實施應有助於促進技術創新，有助於技術轉讓與傳播，有助於技術知識的生產者和使用者相互受益，並有助於社會和經濟福祉，以及平衡權利人、使用者的合法利益和公共利益。

2. 本章旨在通過有效和充分的知識產權創造、利用、保護和執法，促進更深層次的經濟一體化與合作，以實施「一帶一路」項目，減少對貿易和投資的扭曲和阻礙，同時認識到：

    （a）各締約方不同的經濟發展水平、經濟實力和國內法律制度的差異；

    （b）促進創新和創造的需要；

    （c）需要在知識產權權利人的權利、使用者的合法權益以及包括公共健康在內的社會公共利益之間保持適當的平衡；

    （d）促進信息、知識、內容、文化和藝術傳播的重要性；以及

    （e）建立和維護透明的知識產權制度，推動和維護充分有效的知識產權保護和執法，為權利人和使用者提供信心以幫助「一帶一路」項目的實施。

3. 知識產權的保護和實施應有助於技術創新和技術轉讓與傳播，有助於技術知識的生產者和使用者間相互受益，並有助於社會和經濟福祉，以及權利和義務的平衡。

第三條　原則

各締約方認識到：

    （a）知識產權保護促進經濟社會發展，減少對國際貿易的扭曲和阻礙；

    （b）知識產權制度本身不應成為合法貿易的障礙；

    （c）只要符合《TRIPS 協定》[37] 及本章的規定，為防止知識產權持有人濫用知識產權，或採取不合理地限制貿易、反競爭或對國際技術轉讓造成不利影響的做法，可能需要採取適當措施。

第四條　國際協定

每一締約方申明其對《TRIPS 協定》及其他任何締約方均為締約方的多邊協定的承諾。鼓勵各締約方遵守與知識產權有關的國際義務。對《TRIPS 協定》或各締約方為締約方的其他與知識產權有關的多邊協定的任何違反，不必然構成對本協定的違反；反之亦然，對本協定的違反不必然構成對《TRIPS 協定》及其他與知識產權有關的多邊協定的違反。

37　為進一步明確，「TRIPS 協定」包括任何經修訂並生效的議定書，以及世界貿易組織締約方之間根據《世界貿易組織協定》授予的對《TRIPS 協定》任何規定的任何棄權。

為進一步明確，各締約方同意將《TRIPS 協定》第一部分（總則和基本原則）、第二部分（知識產權的可用性、範圍和使用的標準）、第三部分（知識產權的執法）、第四部分（知識產權的獲取和維護及各締約方之間的相關程序）的規定納入本協定。無論一締約方是否為世界貿易組織的成員，均應遵守該納入部分。

第五條　國民待遇

1. 對本章涵蓋的所有類型知識產權，每一締約方在知識產權保護方面給予其他締約方國民的待遇，不得低於其給予本國國民的待遇，但應遵守《TRIPS 協定》和在世界知識產權組織主持下締結的多邊協定規定的例外情況。

2. 就本條而言，「保護」包括影響知識產權的可用性、獲取、範圍、維護和執行的事項，以及影響本章涵蓋的知識產權使用的事項。

3. 一締約方可就其司法和行政程序而減損第 1 款，包括要求其他締約方國民在其領土內指定送達訴訟文書的地址或在其領土內指定代理人，只要此類減損是：

(a) 為確保遵守與本章不相抵觸的法律法規；以及

(b) 沒有以構成對貿易的變相限制的方式實施。

4. 第 1 款不適用於在世界知識產權組織主持下締結的、與知識產權的獲取或維護有關的多邊協定所規定的程序。

第六條　透明度

1. 每一締約方應努力使其與知識產權保護和執行有關的普遍適用的法律、法規、程序和行政裁決可在網上獲取，以協助其知識產權體系運作的透明度。

2. 每一締約方在遵守其法律的前提下，應努力使其所公佈的、與申請商標、地理標誌、外觀設立、專利和植物品種權有關的信息可在網上獲取。

3. 每一締約方在遵守其法律的前提下，使其已公佈的註冊或授予的商標、地理標誌、外觀設計、專利和植物品種權的信息在互聯網上可獲得，以使公眾能夠知曉該等註冊或授予的權利。

第七條　知識產權與公共衛生

各締約方承認世界貿易組織部長級會議於 2001 年 11 月 14 日通過的《關於 TRIPS 協定與公共衛生的多哈宣言》所確定的原則，並確認本章規定不影響該宣言。特別是，各締約方就本章達成以下諒解：

(a) 各締約方確認有權充分使用《關於 TRIPS 協定與公共衛生的多哈宣言》中所確認的靈活性；

(b) 各締約方同意，本章不阻止、也不應阻止一締約方採取保護公共衛生的措施；以及

(c) 各締約方確認，本章的解釋和實施能夠且應該支持各締約方保護公共衛生，特別是促進人人獲得藥品的權利。

為承認各締約方獲得藥品和公共衛生的承諾，本章不得、亦不應阻止《TRIPS 協定》第三十一條之二及其附件和附錄的有效適用。

各締約方認識到，關於實施《TRIPS 協定》第三十一條之二及其附錄的國際努力的貢獻之重要性。

各締約方同意，在發生大流行病如新冠肺炎的情況下，可暫停本章的實施，以便「一帶一路」司法轄區或地區的廣大公眾能夠獲得疫苗、藥品或相關設備。當大流行病得到控制，或者有足夠的疫苗、藥品或相關設備的時候，本章將恢復實施。各締約方在本章暫停實施期間所採取的任何措施，不應解釋為對本章的違反。

第八條　知識產權用盡

本章的任何內容不得阻止各締約方在其法律制度內確定是否適用及在何種條件下適用知識產權的權利用盡。

第九條　獲取和維護的程序

各締約方應：

(a) 持續完善審核和註冊制度，包括通過完善審核程序和質量體系等措施；

(b) 向申請人提供書面通信說明拒絕授予或註冊知識產權的理由；

(c) 為利害關係方提供反對知識產權授予或註冊的機會，或者就現有知

識產權尋求撤銷、註銷或無效的機會；

(d) 要求書面說明異議、撤銷、註冊或無效決定的理由；以及

(e) 就本條而言，「書面」和「書面通訊」包括電子形式的書面信息和通訊。

第十條　著作權和相關權利的保護

1. 在不影響各締約方均為締約方的國際協定所規定的義務的情況下，每一締約方應按照其法律、法規和本章，對作品的作者、表演者、錄音製品的製作者以及對其作品、表演、錄音製品和廣播的廣播組織分別給予和確保充分和有效的保護。[38]

2. 每一締約方應規定，作者、表演者、錄音製品製作者和廣播組織有權允許或禁止以任何方式或形式複製其作品、表演、錄音製品和廣播。

3. 每一締約方應規定，無論廣播是通過有線或空中，包括通過有線或衛星傳輸，其保護期不得少於廣播發生後 50 年。

第十一條　向公眾廣播和傳播

1. 將以商業目的出版的錄音製品直接或間接用於向公眾進行廣播或任何傳播的，表演者和錄音製品製作者應享有獲得報酬的權利。

2. 每一締約方應給予廣播組織排他性的權利，以授權或禁止：

(a) 其廣播的重播；

(b) 固定其廣播節目；以及

(c) 未經其同意，複製其廣播節目的錄製品。

第十二條　限制和例外

每一締約方應將對排他性權利的限制或例外限定於某些特定情況，不得與作品、表演、錄音製品或廣播的正常利用相衝突，而不得不合理損害權利人的合法權益。

38　為進一步明確，作品包括電影攝影作品、攝影作品和計算機程序。

第十三條　作為商標的標誌類型

各締約方同意，就作為商標的標誌（包括視覺標誌和聲音標誌）的保護方式進行合作。此外，每一締約方應盡最大努力註冊氣味商標。一締約方可要求對商標進行簡要和精確的描述或圖形表示，或如適用，則兩者均包括。

第十四條　商標保護

1. 每一締約方應給予商品和服務的商標權利人充分和有效的保護。

2. 任何締約方不得作為註冊條件而要求標記可被視覺感知，也不得僅以該標記由聲音組成為由而拒絕註冊一商標。

3. 每一締約方應規定，註冊商標的所有人應享有專有權，以阻止第三方未經該所有人同意而在貿易過程中對與所有權人已註冊商標的貨物或服務相同或類似的貨物或服務使用相同或類似的標記，如該種使用可能導致出現混淆的可能性。在對相同商品或服務使用相同標記的情況下，應推定存在混淆的可能性。上述權利不得影響任何現有的在先權利，也不得影響各締約方在使用的基礎上提供權利可用性的可能性。

4. 每一締約方應規定，具有欺騙性的標誌不得作為商標使用，也不得作為商標註冊。

第十五條　馳名商標

各締約方應至少按照《TRIPS 協定》第十六條第 2 款和第十六條第 3 款，以及 1883 年 3 月 20 日在巴黎簽署的《保護工業產權巴黎公約》第六條之二，為馳名商標提供保護。

第十六條　商標權的例外

各締約方可對商標所授予的權利規定有限的例外，如對描述性詞語的合理使用，前提是這些例外考慮到商標所有人和第三方的合法利益。

第十七條　地理標誌

1. 各締約方認識到地理標誌可通過商標或專門制度或其他法律手段予以保護。

2. 在不損害《TRIPS 協定》第二十二條和第二十三條的情況下，各締約方應根據本章，採取一切必要措施，確保對用於指稱原產於各締約方領土內的商品的地理標誌給予相互保護。

第十八條　專利保護

1. 在遵守第 2 款和第 3 款的前提下，所有技術領域中的任何發明，無論是產品還是方法，均可獲得專利，只要該發明具有新穎性、包含創造性步驟且可供工業應用。

2. 每一締約方可拒絕對某些發明授予專利權，如在其領土內防止此類發明的商業利用是維護公共秩序或道德，包括保護人類、動物或植物的生命或健康或避免對環境造成嚴重破壞所必需的，只要此類拒絕授予並非僅因該等利用為其法律所禁止。

3. 每一締約方還可拒絕對下列內容授予專利權：

(a)　用於人或動物治療的診斷、治療和外科手術方法；以及

(b)　植物和除微生物以外的動物，以及除非生物或微生物學方法外的生產植物或動物的主要生物方法。

4. 每一締約方可對專利所授予的專有權規定有限例外，只要此類例外不會與專利的正常利用發生不合理的抵觸，也不會不合理地損害專利所有人的合法利益，同時考慮到第三方的合法利益。

5. 各締約方可根據國內法律和法規，對申請人的專利申請提供加速審查。各締約方同意就該等事項加強合作。

第十九條　植物育種者的權利

各締約方應通過其主管機構合作，鼓勵和促進植物育種者權利的保護和發展，以期：

(a)　更好地協調各締約方植物育種者權利管理制度，包括加強對有共同利益物種的保護和信息交流；

(b)　減少各締約方之間植物育種者權利審查系統的不必要重複程序；以及

(c)　促進國際植物育種者權利法律、標準和實踐的改革和進一步發展，

包括在「一帶一路」區域內。

第二十條　對未披露信息的保護

1. 在確保有效防止不正當競爭的過程中，每一締約方應依據第 2 款保護未披露的信息。

2. 自然人和法人應有能力防止在未經其同意的情況下，以違反誠實商業慣例的方式向他人披露、獲取或使用其合法控制的信息，[39] 只要此類信息：

   (a) 是秘密的。此類信息作為一個整體或作為其部件的精確結構和組成，並不為通常處理這類信息的圈子內的人所普遍知曉，並不為其容易獲得；

   (b) 因其秘密性而具有商業價值；以及

   (c) 已由合法控制此類信息的人採取合理的保密措施。

第二十一條　遺傳資源和傳統知識領域的合作

1. 各締約方認識到，知識產權制度和遺傳資源相關傳統知識與兩者之間的相關性，在該傳統知識與知識產權制度相關聯的情況下。

2. 各締約方應努力通過各自負責知識產權的機關或其他有關機構合作，以提高對與遺傳資源有關的傳統知識問題和遺傳資源的理解。

3. 各締約方應努力開展高質量專利審查，審查的內容可包括：

   (a) 在確定現有技術時，可考慮遺傳資源相關傳統知識的可公開獲得的相關文獻信息；

   (b) 給予第三方機會以書面形式向主管審查機構引用可能影響專利性的現有技術披露，包括與遺傳資源相關傳統知識有關的現有技術披露；

   (c) 如適用且適當，使用包含遺傳資源相關傳統知識的數據庫或數字圖書館；以及

   (d) 在培訓審查涉及遺傳資源相關傳統知識的專利申請專利審查員方面進行合作。

39　就本規定而言，「違反誠實商業慣例」至少指諸如違約、洩密和誘使違約等行為，並包括第三方在知悉或存在重大過失而未知悉獲取涉及此類慣例的情況下獲取未披露的信息。

第二十二條　執行

1. 每一締約方承諾實施有效的知識產權執法制度，以消除侵犯知識產權的商品和服務貿易。

2. 每一締約方應根據《TRIPS 協定》規定可適用的刑事訴訟程序和罰則，至少以防商業規模的故意假冒商標或盜版行為。可用的救濟措施應包括足以提供威懾的監禁和/或罰款，並與適用於相應嚴重性犯罪的處罰水平相一致。

3. 各締約方同意，為了通過替代方式（即為「替代性爭議解決」）解決爭議，特別是仲裁和調解，任何直接或附帶涉及知識產權的爭議均應被視為能夠通過仲裁和調解解決，且不得違反各締約方的公共政策。知識產權爭議包括：

(a) 關於知識產權的可執行性、侵權、存續、有效性、所有權、範圍、期限或任何其他方面的爭議；

(b) 關於知識產權交易的爭議；以及

(c) 關於知識產權的任何應付賠償的爭議。

第二十三條　邊境措施

1. 每一締約方應確保，對權利人啓動程序以暫停放行涉嫌假冒商標或盜版商品的要求不得不合理地阻止其訴諸此類程序。

2. 如果其主管機構已確定商品為假冒商標或盜版商品（或已扣押該等涉嫌商品），則每一締約方應規定其主管機構有權限至少將發貨人和收貨人的名稱和地址，以及相關商品的數量通知權利人。

3. 每一締約方應規定，其海關部門可依據職權啓動有關進出口貨物涉嫌假冒商標或盜版商品的邊境措施。

4. 每一締約方應確保其法律、法規或政策允許相關主管機構在收到信息或投訴後，依法採取措施阻止假冒商標或盜版商品的出口。

5. 各締約方可將被視為非商業性的少量貨物的進口或出口排除在本條的適用範圍之外。

第二十四條　合作

1. 各締約方應努力就本章所涵蓋的事項進行合作，例如通過按每一締約方確定的其各自知識產權機構或其他機構之間的適當協調、培訓和信息交流。合作可涵蓋如下領域：

    (a) 國內和國際知識產權政策的發展情況；

    (b) 知識產權管理和註冊制度；

    (c) 與知識產權有關的教育和意識；

    (d) 與下列各項相關的知識產權問題：

        (i)   小型及中型企業；

        (ii) 科學、技術和創新活動；以及

        (iii) 技術的產生、轉讓和傳播；

    (e) 涉及在研究、創新和經濟增長中使用知識產權的政策；

    (f) 多邊知識產權協定的實施，例如在世界知識產權組織主持下締結或管理的協定；以及

    (g) 對發展中國家的技術援助。

2. 各締約方將考慮根據既定安排在有共同利益的領域持續合作的機會，以改善各自法轄區內知識產權制度（包括行政程序）的運作。此種合作包括但不限於：

    (a) 專利審查中的成果分享；

    (b) 知識產權的執法；

    (c) 加強在如下領域的合作關係：

        (i)   應其他締約方的要求，在打擊跨境知識產權犯罪時，就證據收集、技術援助和信息共享方面提供必要的合作；

        (ii) 在線版權執法的交流與合作；

        (iii) 節能和綠色技術的技術轉讓；

        (iv) 各締約方達成共識的其他領域。

    (d) 提高公眾對知識產權問題的意識；

    (e) 提高專利審查質量和效率；以及

    (f) 降低獲得專利授權的複雜性和成本。

3. 每一締約方將依據本章第六條考慮其他締約方在公共衛生危機中提出的援助請求。

第二十五條　諮詢機制：知識產權委員會

1. 為有效實施和操作本章，各締約方特此設立一知識產權委員會（「委員會」）。

2. 委員會的職能應為：

　　(a)　審查和監督本章的實施和操作；

　　(b)　討論與本章涵蓋的知識產權相關的任何問題；以及

　　(c)　向「一帶一路」聯合委員會報告其調查結果。

3. 委員會應由每一締約方的代表組成。

4. 委員會應在各締約方議定的地點、時間和方式舉行會議。

第九章　公共衛生

第一條　適用的目標與範圍

1. 各締約方擁護《世界衛生組織組織法》序言，該序言提出，享有最高且能獲得的健康標準是每個個人的基本權利之一，不因種族、宗教、政治信仰、經濟或社會條件的不同而不同。不同國家在促進健康和控制疾病上的發展不一，特別是在傳染病控制方面的差異，實為一種共同的危害。

2. 各締約方重申《國際衛生條例》中確立的原則，承諾在公平、團結和誠信的基礎上，包括通過「一帶一路」等項目，發展和保持大流行病的防範和應對能力。

3. 各締約方承認世貿組織部長級會議於 2001 年 11 月 14 日通過的《關於 TRIPS 協定與公共衛生的多哈宣言》所確立的原則，並確認本章的規定不影響該宣言。

4. 特別是，各締約方已就本章達成以下諒解：

    (a) 各締約方確認有權充分利用《關於〈與貿易有關的知識產權協定〉與公共健康問題的多哈宣言》中被正式承認的靈活性；

    (b) 各締約方同意，本章不會也不應妨礙一締約方採取措施以保護公眾健康；以及

    (c) 各締約方確認，本章能夠而且應當以支持每一締約方有權保護公眾健康，特別是促進人人獲得藥品的方式加以解釋和實施。

5. 認識到各締約方對獲得藥品和公共健康的承諾，本章不會也不應妨礙對《與貿易有關的知識產權協定》第三十一條之二以及《與貿易有關的知識產權協定》附件和附錄的有效利用。

6. 締約方認識到促進國際努力以實施《與貿易有關的知識產權協定》第

三十一條之二以及《與貿易有關的知識產權協定》附件和附錄的重要性。

7. 各締約方同意大流行病在性質上屬於一種特殊情況，並同意在發生國際關注的突發公共衛生事件（例如 COVID-19）時，本協定第八章（知識產權）的實施可被暫停，以便疫苗、氧氣供應、個人防護裝備、藥品或相關設備，能最大限度地在「一帶一路」轄區或區域內向公眾提供。一旦大流行病得到控制或有足夠的疫苗、藥物或相關設備提供，則本協定第八章（知識產權）的實施應予以恢復。各締約方在本協議第八章（知識產權）暫停實施期間採取的任何措施不得解釋為對本章規定的違反。

第二條　預防、防範和應對方面的區域團結

各締約方同意，在可能的情況下，通過「一帶一路」項目支持和加強區域規劃、預防、防範和應對疾病傳播，包括通過衛生系統的準備與抵禦。特別要考慮低收入或中低收入締約國的需求，秉着友好和區域團結的精神，共同承諾不讓任何一方掉隊。

第三條　信息共享與協調

各締約方認識到並理解及時獲取信息和有效風險交流的重要性，因此，各締約方同意通過在「一帶一路」國家和地區開展研發合作、技術和信息共享等方式加強區域能力建設，以識別健康威脅。

每一締約國應根據其本國法律，努力制止在媒體、社交網絡上或以其他方式傳播有關公共衛生事件、預防和反流行病措施及行為的虛假或誤導性信息，從而增強公眾信心。

各締約方之間為執行本章規定而進行的信息交流應僅限於和平目的，和保護「一帶一路」國家和地區之公眾。

第四條　數據互操作性

1. 各締約方應盡可能努力相互提供技術援助，並通過與社會文化相適應的信息和風險通報管理以及定期更新的早期預警系統傳播信息，以便根據現有最佳信息評估和逐步更新國家、區域或全球風險。

2. 為了加強數據互操作性，各締約方應盡可能，基於開放標準、開放源代

碼及確保減少濫用和偽造風險，以數字或紙質方式發佈健康文件與證書，並確保對此類文件中所含個人數據的保護與安全。

第五條　協作和獲得衛生服務

各締約方認識到，大流行病對一線工作者，尤其是衛生工作者、窮人和弱勢群體，特別是發展中國家的此類人員的影響尤為嚴重。各締約方同意加強區域合作，並盡可能通過「一帶一路」項目促進獲得有效公共衛生應對所需的衛生產品、衛生技術和專門知識。

第六條　可預測的供應鏈和物流網絡

各締約方同意做出合理努力，酌情促進和協調基本衛生保健工作者的流動、確保對國際關注的突發公共衛生事件中的基本醫療產品供應鏈的保護、遣返旅行者，並盡可能避免對區域交通、貿易、生計、人權以及「一帶一路」國家和地區公平獲得衛生產品、衛生保健技術和專門知識形成不必要的干擾。

第七條　加強公共衛生知識普及

各締約方承諾通過「一帶一路」項目增強公眾意識，並基於科學和證據，促進科學、公共衛生和大流行病知識在民眾中的普及。

各締約方應努力促進科研，並就「一帶一路」國家中妨礙對公共衛生和社會措施的遵守、對疫苗的信心和接種、對適當治療方法的採用以及對科學和政府機關的信任的各種因素提供政策參考信息。

第十章　金融

第一條　定義

「締約方」指批准或加入本協定的國家；

「金融服務」指具有金融性質的任何服務，包括保險及保險相關服務、銀行及其他金融服務（保險除外），以及具有金融性質的服務所附帶或附屬的服務。金融服務包括下列活動：

(a) 保險及其相關服務

   (i) 壽險或非壽險的直接保險（包括共同保險）；

   (ii) 再保險和轉分保；

   (iii) 保險中介，例如經紀和代理；

   (iv) 保險附屬服務，例如諮詢、精算、風險評估和理賠服務；以及

(b) 銀行和其他金融服務（保險除外）：

   (i) 接受公眾存款和其他應償還資金；

   (ii) 所有類型的貸款，包括消費信貸、抵押信貸、商業交易的代理和融資；

   (iii) 金融租賃；

   (iv) 所有支付和貨幣轉移服務，包括信用卡、賒賬卡、貸記卡、旅行支票和銀行匯票；

   (v) 擔保和承諾；

   (vi) 交易市場、場外交易市場或其他市場自行交易或代客交易之如下列：

     (A) 貨幣市場票據（包括支票、匯票、存單）；

     (B) 外匯；

(C) 衍生品，包括但不僅限於期貨和期權；

(D) 匯率和利率工具，包括掉期和遠期匯率和利率協定等產品；

(E) 可轉讓證券；或

(F) 其他轉讓票據和金融資產，包括金銀條塊；

(vii) 參與各類證券的發行，包括承銷和募集代理（公開或者私人），並提供與該發行相關的服務；

(viii) 貨幣經紀；

(ix) 資產管理，如現金或投資組合管理、所有形式的集合投資管理、養老基金管理、託管、存款和信託服務；

(x) 金融資產的結算和清算服務，包括證券、衍生品和其他可轉讓票據；

(xi) 提供和轉移金融信息、金融數據處理和相關軟件；或

(xii) 就（i）至（xi）項中所列的所有活動提供諮詢、中介和其他附屬金融服務，包括徵信與分析、投資和投資組合的研究和諮詢、收購諮詢、公司重組和戰略諮詢；

「**金融機構**」指根據一締約方法律在其領土內獲准開展業務並作為金融機構接受監管或監督的任何金融中介或其他企業，包括總部位於另一締約方領土內的金融機構在該締約方領土內設立的分支機構；

「**金融服務提供者**」指在一締約方領土內從事提供金融服務業務與尋求或正在以跨境提供的方式提供金融服務的企業，包括該締約方的公共實體；

「**公共實體**」指：

(a) 一締約方的政府、中央銀行或貨幣管理機構，或一締約方擁有或控制的實體，主要執行政府職能或為政府目的而活動，但不包括主要以商業條件提供金融服務的實體；或

(b) 在履行這些職能時，履行通常由中央銀行或貨幣管理機構履行的職能的私人實體；

「**金融服務貿易**」指提供下列金融服務：

(a) 自一締約方領土向另一締約方領土提供金融服務；

(b) 在一締約方領土內向另一締約方的人提供金融服務；或

(c) 一締約方的國民在另一締約方領土內提供金融服務。

第二條　適用範圍

1. 本章應適用於一締約方採取或維持的與下列內容相關的措施：

(a) 該締約方的金融機構；

(b) 該締約方的投資者，以及這些投資者對該締約方領土內金融機構的投資；以及

(c) 跨境金融服務貿易。

2. 本章不得適用於一締約方採取或維持的與下列內容相關的措施：

(a) 構成公共退休計劃或法定社會保障制度一部分的活動或服務；或

(b) 代表該締約方或由該締約方擔保或使用該締約方的財政資源開展的活動或服務，包括其公共實體，

但本章僅適用於一締約方允許其金融機構從事 (a) 項或 (b) 項中所指任何活動或服務時與公共實體或金融機構競爭的情況。

3. 本章不得適用於金融服務的政府採購。

4. 本章不得適用於有關跨境提供金融服務的補貼或贈款，包括政府支持貸款、擔保和保險。

第三條　國民待遇

1. 每一締約方在設立、獲得、擴大、管理、經營、運營、出售或其他處置在其領土內的金融機構及對金融機構的投資方面，應給予另一締約方投資者不低於其在相似情況下給予本國投資者的待遇。

2. 每一締約方在設立、獲取、擴大、管理、經營、運營、出售或其他處置金融機構和投資方面，應給予另一締約方的金融機構以及另一締約方投資者對金融機構的投資不低於其在相似情況下給予本國金融機構和本國投資者對金融機構投資的待遇。

3. 為進一步明確，一締約方根據第 1 款和第 2 款給予的待遇，對於一地區層級政府而言，指不低於該地區政府在相似情況下給予其作為該締約方一部分的投資者、金融機構和投資者對金融機構投資的最優惠待遇。

4. 就國民待遇義務而言，對於相關服務提供，一締約方給予另一締約方的

跨境金融服務提供者不低於其在相似情況下給予本國金融服務提供者的待遇。

第四條　最惠國待遇

每一締約方應給予：

(a) 另一締約方的投資者不低於其在相似情況下給予任何其他締約方投資者的待遇；

(b) 另一締約方的金融機構不低於其在相似情況下給予任何其他締約方的金融機構的待遇；

(c) 另一締約方的投資者在金融機構的投資不低於其在相似情況下給予任何其他締約方的投資者對金融機構投資的待遇；以及

(d) 另一締約方的跨境金融服務提供者不低於其在相似情況下給予任何其他締約方跨境金融服務提供者的待遇。

第五條　市場准入

任一締約方不得對另一締約方的金融機構或另一締約方的投資者在其全部領土內或在國家、省、地區或地方政府領土內設立金融機構的市場准入採取或維持下列措施：

(a) 對下列各項施加限制：

(i) 無論以數量配額、壟斷、專營服務提供者的形式，還是以經濟需求測試要求的形式，限制金融機構的數量；

(ii) 以數量配額或經濟需求測試要求的形式，限制金融服務交易或資產總值；

(iii) 以配額或經濟需求測試要求的形式，限制金融服務業務總數或以指定數量單位表示的金融服務產出總量；

(iv) 以限制境外投資金融機構的最高股比、限制單個或合計外投資金融機構投資總額的方式，限制外資參與度；或

(v) 以數量配額或經濟需求測試要求的形式，限制特定金融服務部門或金融機構可僱傭的、提供具體金融服務所必需且直接相關的自然人總數；或

(b) 限制或要求金融機構通過特定類型法律實體或合資企業提供服務。

第六條　跨境貿易

1. 每一締約方根據給予國民待遇的條款和條件，應允許另一締約方的跨境金融服務提供者提供金融服務。

2. 每一締約方應允許位於其領土內的人員及其國民（無論位於何處）向位於許可締約方以外的另一締約方領土內的跨境金融提供者購買金融服務。該項義務並不要求締約方允許此類供應商在其領土內從事經營或招攬業務。一締約方可就此義務的目的對「從事經營」和「招攬業務」作出定義，但該定義不得與本章的規定相抵觸。

3. 在不影響對跨境金融服務貿易進行審慎監管的其他手段的前提下，一締約方可要求另一締約方的跨境金融服務提供者和金融工具提供者進行登記或取得授權。

第七條　信息的傳輸和處理

1. 每一締約方應允許另一締約方金融機構或跨境金融服務提供者在其正常業務過程中需要進行數據處理的情況下，以電子或其他形式將信息轉移出境或入境。

2. 每一締約方應維持適當的安全措施以保護隱私，特別是涉及個人信息的傳輸。如傳輸金融信息涉及個人信息，應遵守傳輸來源之締約方境內關於個人信息保護的立法。

第八條　審慎措施

1. 本協定不阻止一締約方出於審慎原因而採取或維持合理的措施，包括：

   (a) 對投資者、存款人、保單持有人或金融機構、跨境金融服務提供者或金融服務提供者對其負有信託義務的人的保護；

   (b) 維護金融機構、跨境金融服務提供者或金融服務提供者的安全、健全、誠信或財務責任；或

   (c) 確保一締約方財政系統的完整和穩定。

2. 在不影響對跨境金融服務貿易實施其他審慎監管方法的前提下，一締約方可要求對另一締約方的跨境金融服務提供者及金融工具進行登記。

第九條　有效和透明的監管

1. 每一締約方應保證所有普遍適用的措施以合理、客觀和公正的方式進行管理。

2. 每一締約方應保證及時公佈或提供與任何事項相關的法律、法規、程序及普遍適用的行政裁決，以便利害關係人和其他締約方對其進行瞭解。每一締約方應盡可能：

(a) 提前公佈其擬採用的任何該等措施；

(b) 給予利害關係人和其他締約方對擬議措施提出意見的合理機會；以及

(c) 允許措施最終公佈之日與生效之日間留有合理時間。

3. 每一締約方應維持或設立適當機制，以在一合理期限內答覆利害關係人對普遍適用措施的問詢。

4. 一締約方監管機構應在合理期間內對另一締約方的任一金融機構的投資者、任一金融機構或任一跨境金融服務提供者提出的與提供金融服務相關的完整申請作出行政決定，該合理期限應與該申請的複雜程度和處理該申請的正常時間相匹配。

第十條　支付和清算系統

根據給予國民待遇的條款和條件，每一締約方應允許在其領土內設立的另一締約方的金融服務提供者接入該締約方或履行該締約方授予政府職能的實體運營的支付清算系統，並訪問正常業務過程中可獲得的官方融資和再融資便利。本條並非旨在授權其獲得該締約方最終貸款人安排。

第十一條　金融服務委員會

1. 各締約方特此設立金融服務委員會（下稱「委員會」）。每一締約方的首席代表應為負責金融服務的一官員。

2. 委員會應：

(a) 監督本章及其進一步詳述內容的執行；

(b) 審議各締約方提交委員會的關於金融服務的議題；以及

(c) 參加爭端解決程序。

3. 委員會應每年召開會議，或在其決定的其他時間召開會議，以評估本協定適用金融服務條款的執行情況。

第十二條　新金融服務

1. 每一締約方應允許另一締約方的金融機構提供該締約方在其法律項下允許其本國金融機構在相似情況下提供的任一新金融服務。如有必要，應請求或通知相關監管機關。

2. 一締約方可確定提供新金融服務可使用的組織和法律形式，並可要求提供該服務獲得授權。如授權為必需，則該締約方應在合理期限內決定是否給予授權且僅可因審慎理由拒絕授權。

3. 本條不妨礙一締約方的金融機構向另一締約方申請授權其提供不在任何締約方領土內提供的金融服務。該申請應受接受該申請的締約方法律管轄，而不受本條義務的限制。

第十三條　快速提供保險服務

各締約方應認識到維持和制定監管程序以加快獲得授權的保險服務提供者提供保險服務的重要性。這些程序可包括：允許推出產品，除非這些產品在一合理期限內不被批准；不要求保險產品獲得批准或授權，但向個人銷售的保險或強制保險除外；或不限制推出產品的數量或頻率。如一締約方維持監管產品批准程序，則該締約方應努力維持或完善此種程序。

第十四條　業績要求

1. 各締約方應認識到，金融機構總部或其分支機構，或與其無關聯的服務提供者在其領土內外的業績，對該金融機構的有效管理和高效運行是重要的。儘管一締約方可要求金融機構確保遵守任何國內要求，但應認識到避免對金融機構的業績強加任何任意要求的重要性。

2. 為進一步明確，第 1 款的規定不阻止一締約方要求其領土內的金融機構保留某些職能。

第十五條　自律組織

如一締約方要求其他締約方的金融機構或跨境金融服務提供者在其領土內提供或向其領土提供金融服務時需成為自律組織成員或參加或接觸自律組織，或通過自律組織提供服務時授予特權或給予優惠，則該締約方應保證該自律組織遵守本協定項下的義務。

第十六條　承認

1. 一締約方可在實施本章所涵蓋措施時承認另一締約方或一非締約方的審慎措施。該承認可：

　(a)　自主給予；

　(b)　通過協調或其他方式實現；或

　(c)　根據與另一締約方或一非締約方的協定或安排。

2. 根據第 1 款對審慎措施給予承認的一締約方應向其他締約方提供充分的機會，以證明已存在或將有等效法規、監督和法規執行以及，如適當，相關締約方之間共享信息程序的情況。

3. 如在一締約方根據第 1 款（c）項對審慎措施給予承認且存在第 2 款所列情形，則該締約方應向其他締約方提供談判加入該協定或安排或談判類似協定或安排的充分機會。

第十七條　特定例外

1. 本章規定不適用於公共實體為推行貨幣或匯率政策而採取的措施。

2. 本章規定不要求任何締約方提供或允許查閱與個人消費者、跨境金融服務提供者、金融機構的事務和賬戶有關的信息，也不要求提供或允許查閱任何一旦披露將會影響特定監管、監督或執法事項，或會違反公共利益或損害特定企業合法商業利益的保密信息。

3. 不得阻止一締約方以審慎為由而採取或維持措施，包括為保護投資者、存款人、投保人或保護金融機構或跨境金融服務提供者對其負有信託責任的人，或為保證金融系統的完整和穩定而採取的措施。若此種措施不符合本例外所適用本協定條款的情況下，此類措施不得作為一締約方逃避其根據這些條款承擔的承諾或義務的手段。

4. 本章中任何內容不得適用於任何公共實體為推行貨幣和相關信貸政策或匯率政策而採取的普遍適用的非歧視措施。

5. 一締約方可通過公平、非歧視和善意適用有關維護金融機構或跨境金融服務提供者的安全、健全、完整性或金融責任措施，阻止或限制一金融機構或跨境金融服務提供者向與該機構或提供者相關的附屬機構或人進行轉移，或為此類附屬機構或人的利益進行轉移。本款不影響本協定中允許一締約方限制轉移的任何其他條款。

6. 為進一步明確，本章中任何內容均不得解釋為阻止一締約方採取或執行必要措施，以確保遵守與本章不相抵觸的法律或法規，包括有關防止欺騙和欺詐行為或處理涉及金融服務合同違約影響的措施，但須符合以下要求，即此類措施不得以在條件相似的締約方之間或在締約方與非締約方之間構成任意或不合理歧視的方式實施，或構成對金融行業的投資或跨境金融服務貿易的變相限制的方式實施。

第十一章　基礎設施

第一條　總則

1. 希望通過提高透明度、公正性和長期可持續性，以及通過消除公共和／或私人部門參與基礎設施開發和運營的不利限制，建立有利於促進和推動實施「一帶一路」公共和／或私人融資基礎設施項目的法律框架。

2. 希望通過建立具體的基礎設施項目招標程序，進一步發展公共機構在合同招標中透明、經濟和公平的總體原則；

第二條　定義

就本章而言：

「投標人」指參與基礎設施項目遴選程序的主體，包括其集團；

「締約機構」指有權為實施基礎設施項目而簽訂基礎設施項目合同的公共機構；

「基礎設施合同」指締約機構和基礎設施承包商之間就實施基礎設施項目條款和條件所達成的具有約束力的協議；

「基礎設施」指直接或間接向公眾提供服務的物理設施和系統（可增加「包括非物理基礎設施」）；

「基礎設施項目」指新基礎設施的設計、項目、開發和運營或現有基礎設施的修復、現代化、擴建或運營；

「基礎設施項目承包商」指根據與締約機構簽訂基礎設施項目合同並實施基礎設施項目的人；

「監管機構」指被授權發佈或執行管理基礎設施或相關服務的提供的條例和法規的公共機構；以及

「非應標建議書」指非為回應締約機構在遴選程序中發出的請求或招標邀請書而提交的與實施基礎設施項目有關的任何建議書。

第三條　簽訂基礎設施項目合同的權限

東道國政府公共機構有權就其職權範圍內實施的基礎設施項目簽訂基礎設施項目合同。

第四條　適格的基礎設施行業

相關機構可在相關政府達成一致的行業簽訂基礎設施項目合同。

第五條　基礎設施項目承包商的選擇

1.應當按照本章以下規定選擇基礎設施項目承包商。

2.締約機構應當進行預選程序，以確認有資質實施擬議基礎設施項目的投標人。

3.應當廣泛向社會公佈參加預選程序的邀請。

4.參加預選程序的邀請應當至少包括以下內容：

　(a)　對基礎設施的描述；

　(b)　注明項目的其他基本要素，如將由基礎設施項目承包商提供的服務、締約機構設想的財務安排（例如，項目資金的來源是否全部來自用戶使用費或收費；或是否可以向基礎設施承包商提供公共或私人資金，如直接付款、貸款或擔保）；

　(c)　在已知的情況下，擬簽訂的基礎設施項目合同主要必備條款的內容摘要；

　(d)　以明確的日期和時間載明提交預選申請的方式和地點及其截止時間，使投標人有充足的時間準備和提交申請；以及

　(e)　索取預選文件的方式及地點。

5.預選文件應當包括至少以下內容：

　(a)　根據下文第六條確定的預選標準；

　(b)　締約機構是否擬放棄第七條對聯合體參與投標的限制；

　(c)　在按照第七條完成預選程序後，締約機構是否僅有意要求有限數量

的預選投標人提交建議書且在適用的情況下實行此種方式作選擇；

(d) 締約機關是否擬要求中標人根據東道國法律以及第二十五條（基礎設施項目承包商的組織）的規定成立和註冊的獨立法人實體。

第六條　預選標準

1. 為有資格參加遴選程序，有意向的投標人必須符合締約機構在預選文件中所述的其認為在特定程序中客觀、合理的標準。此類標準應當至少包括下列內容：

(a) 具備開展項目所有階段（包括設計、項目、運營和維護）所需的足夠的專業技術資格、人力資源、設備和其他物質設施；

(b) 有足夠的能力管理項目的財務事項，並有足夠的能力維持其融資需求；以及

(c) 適當的管理和組織能力、可靠性和經驗，包括此前運營相似基礎設施的經驗。

第七條　聯合體參與投標

1. 締約機構在首次邀請投標人參加遴選程序時，應當允許其形成投標聯合體。投標聯合體的參與方依據第六條規定而提供的資質證明信息，應當涉及整個聯合體及各個參與方。

2. 除預選文件另有說明，聯合體中的每一參與方同時只能直接或間接參加一個聯合體。違反本條規則則將導致聯合體和相關參與方喪失資格。

3. 締約機構在考慮投標聯合體的資質時，應當考慮聯合體各參與方的能力，並評估聯合體各參與方的綜合資質能否滿足項目各階段的需要。

第八條　預選決定

1. 締約機構應當對提交預選申請的每個投標人進行資格審查並作出決定。在作出這一決定時，締約機構應當僅適用預選文件中設定的標準。締約機關應當在作出決定後邀請所有通過預選的投標人按照第十一條至第十七條的規定提交建議書。

2. 儘管有第十條的規定，但可以在預選文件中做出適當說明的情況下，締

約機構可保留在預選程序完成後僅向有限數量的最符合預選標準的投標人徵求建議書的權利。為此，締約機關應當根據用於評估投標人資質的標準對符合預選標準的投標人進行評級，並擬定完成預選程序後被邀請提交建議書的投標人名單。在編製該名單時，締約機構應當僅採用預選文件中規定的評級方式。

第九條　徵求建議書的程序：一階段徵求建議書程序與二階段徵求建議書程序

1. 如預選定的投標人需支付招標文件費用的，則締約機構應當向其每人提供一套依據第十條（與招標邀請書的內容相關）發佈的招標邀請書和有關文件。

2. 儘管有上款規定，但在締約機構認為無法在招標邀請書中以充分詳細和準確的方式描述如工程規格、業績指標、財務安排或合同條款等工程特點以形成最終招標邀請書的情況下，締約機構可採用兩階段程序，從預選定的投標人中徵求建議書。

3. 以下規定適用於採用兩階段程序的情形：

(a) 初階招標邀請書應當要求投標人在程序的第一階段提交與項目規格、業績指標、融資要求或項目其他特性以及由締約機構提出的主要合同條款相關的初期建議書；

(b) 締約機構可與任何投標人召開會議、進行討論，釋明與初階招標邀請書以及投標人提交的初期建議書及其附隨文件有關的問題。締約機構應當為任何該等會議或討論作紀錄，其中應包含提出的問題和締約機構作出的解釋；

(c) 締約機關可以在審閱已收到的投標書後，審查並酌情修改初階招標邀請書，方式包括刪除或修訂其中最初的項目規格、業績指標、融資要求或項目其他特徵，包括主要合同條款；刪除或修訂初階招標邀請書中設定的評審和比較建議書與確定中標人的任何標準，以及增加項目的特性或標準。締約機構應在根據第二十一條保存的遴選程序的紀錄中說明對招標邀請書進行任何修改的理由。任何該等刪除、修改或增加均應當在邀請提交最終建議書時予以告知；

(d) 在程序的第二階段，締約機構應當依據第十條至第十六條的規定，邀請投標人就單套工程規格、業績指標或合同條款提交最終建議書。

第十條　招標邀請書的內容

1. 招標邀請書應當至少包括以下內容：

(a) 投標人為準備和提交建議書而可能需要的一般信息；

(b) 項目規格和業績指標，適當包括締約機構對安全和保障標準及環境保護的要求；

(c) 締約機構提出的合同條款，包括指明不可協商的條款；

(d) 評審建議書的標準以及締約機構為確認非回應性建議書所設定的門檻（如有）；對每項評審標準賦予的相對權重；以及在評審和否決建議書的過程中適用該等標準和門檻的方式。

第十一條　投標擔保

1. 招標邀請書應當載明有關招標人的要求以及投標擔保所需的性質、形式、金額及其他主要條款和條件。

2. 投標人不得喪失其或所需提供的任何投標擔保，但下列情況除外：

(a) 在提交建議書的截止日期後以及（如招標邀請書中另有規定）在該截止日期前撤回或修改建議書；

(b) 未能依據第十六條第 1 款（最終談判）與締約機構進行最終談判；

(c) 未能在締約機構根據第十六條第 2 款（最終談判）規定的期限內提交最佳和最終報價；

(d) 在建議書被接受後，如締約機構要求簽訂基礎設施項目合同，而未能履行這一要求；

(e) 未能在建議書被接受後提供為履行基礎設施項目合同所需的擔保或未能在簽署基礎設施項目合同之前遵守招標邀請書中規定的任何其他條件。

第十二條　釋明和修改

締約機構可主動或根據投標人的釋明請求，就第十條（招標邀請書的內容）規定的招標邀請書中的任何內容進行審查和酌情修改。締約機構應在根據

第二十一條（選擇和授予程序的紀錄）保存的遴選程序的紀錄中說明對招標邀請書作任何修改的理由。任何此類刪除、修改或增加應當在提交建議書截止日期前的合理時間內以與招標邀請書相同的方式通知投標人。

第十三條　評審標準

1. 對技術建議書的評審和比較標準應當至少包括以下內容：
   (a) 技術可靠性；
   (b) 符合環境標準；
   (c) 經營可行性；
   (d) 服務質量和確保其連續性的措施。
2. 對財務和商務建議書的評審和比較標準應當視情況包括：
   (a) 在特許經營期內擬收取的通行費、單價和其他費用的現值；
   (b) 擬由締約機構直接支付的現值（如有）；
   (c) 設計和項目活動成本、年度運營和維護成本、資本成本及運營和維護成本的現值；
   (d) 東道國公共機構預期提供財務支持的程度（如有）；
   (e) 擬議財務安排的穩健性；
   (f) 締約機構在招標邀請書中提出的可談判合同條款的接受程度；
   (g) 建議書體現的社會經濟發展潛力。

第十四條　建議書的比較和評審

1. 締約機構應當根據招標邀請書中的評審標準、每一標準的相對權重及評審程序，對每一建議書進行比較和評審。

2. 就第 1 款而言，締約機構可設定質量、技術、財務和商務方面的門檻。未達到門檻的建議書將被視為非回應性建議書，並在遴選程序中予以否決。

第十五條　滿足資質標準的進一步論證

締約機構可以要求被預選的投標人按照與預選相同的標準重新證明其資質。不能按照要求重新證明其資質的，締約機關應當取消其投標資格。

第十六條　最終談判

1. 締約機構應當依據評審標準對所有回應性建議書進行排名，並邀請得分最高的投標人進行基礎設施項目合同的最終談判。最終談判不應涉及在最終招標邀請書中聲明不可談判的合同條款（如有）。

2. 如果締約機構明確認為無法通過談判與被邀請的投標人達成基礎設施項目合同的，締約機構應當將其終止談判的意向通知投標人，並給予投標人合理時間制定最佳和最終報價。如果締約機構認為無法接受該建議書，則應當終止與相關投標人的談判。然後，締約機關應當按照排名邀請其他投標人進行談判，直至達成基礎設施項目合同或否決所有剩餘建議書。締約機構不得恢復與根據本款規定被終止談判投標人的談判。

第十七條　不適用競爭性程序的基礎設施項目合同談判

1. 不適用競爭性程序授予合同的情形

在下列情況下，經東道國批准，締約機構有權在不適用第六條至第十六條規定程序的情況下就基礎設施項目合同進行談判：

(a) 當出現緊急需要保證提供服務連續性且在適用第六條至第十六條規定程序不切實際的情況，如若引起該緊急狀況的情形是締約機構無法預見且非由締約機構的遲延行為所導致；

(b) 若項目期限較短，且預期初始投資值不超過東道國設定的最低限額，對低於該限額的公共和／或私人資助的基礎設施授予可以不經競爭性程序；

(c) 當項目涉及國防或國家安全的；

(d) 當能夠提供所要求的服務為單一來源，例如提供服務需要使用某人或某些人擁有的知識產權、商業秘密或其他排他性權利；

(e) 當已經發佈預選程序邀請書或招標邀請書，但尚未提交申請或建議書，或所有建議書均未達到招標邀請書列明的評審標準，且締約機構認為重新發佈預選程序邀請書或招標邀請書不可能在規定的時限內實現項目授予；

(f) 東道國為了必要的公共利益授權作出例外規定的其他情況。

第十八條　基礎設施項目合同的談判程序

1. 如基礎設施項目合同的談判未適用第六條至第十六條規定的程序，締約機構應：

    （a）　除根據第十七條（c）項（不適用競爭性程序授予合同的情形）談判的基礎設施項目合同外，根據與公開採購通知有關的相關法律發佈開始基礎設施項目合同談判的意向通知。

    （b）　在條件允許的情況下，與締約機構認為有能力實施項目的、盡可能多的人進行談判；

    （c）　制定評審標準，並對照該標準對建議書進行評審和排名。

第十九條　保密

締約機構應當以避免將其內容披露給競爭投標人的方式處理建議書。締約機構與投標人之間的任何討論、溝通和談判均應當保密。除非法律規定或根據法院命令或招標邀請書允許，未經另一方同意，參加談判的任何一方不得向任何其他人披露根據上述條款進行的與討論、溝通和談判相關的任何技術、價格或其他信息。

第二十條　授予合同通知

除依據第十七條（c）項授予的基礎設施項目合同外，締約機關應當公佈授予合同通知書。該通知書應當標明基礎設施項目的承包商，並包括基礎設施項目合同基本條款的摘要。

第二十一條　選擇和授予同程序的紀錄

締約機構應按照規制與公共採購有關的，紀錄採購程序的法律規定，對與選擇和授予程序有關的信息進行適當紀錄。

第二十二條　審查程序

如果投標人主張其因締約機構違反法定義務而遭受或可能遭受損失或損害，該投標人可根據適用於審查採購程序中作出的決定的法律規定，尋求對締約機構的作為或不作為進行審查。

第二十三條　基礎設施項目合同的內容及實施

基礎設施項目合同應當約定雙方認為合適的事項，例如本章附件一所列事項。

第二十四條　準據法

除非另有規定，基礎設施項目合同由東道國法律管轄。如基礎設施項目跨越多個國家，則東道國法律僅適用於項目位於東道國領土管轄範圍內的部分。

第二十五條　基礎設施項目承包商的組織

締約機構可以要求中標人在東道國法律下成立一個法律實體，前提是在預選文件或招標邀請書中酌情明確該等要求。任何有關該等法人實體最低資本的要求，以及獲得締約機關對其章程和組織性文件及其重大變更批准的程序，均應當在基礎設施項目合同中載明，並與招標邀請書中條款保持一致。

第二十六條　資產所有權

1. 基礎設施項目合同應當酌情說明哪些資產屬於或應屬於公共財產，哪些資產屬於或應屬於基礎設施項目承包商的私有財產。基礎設施項目合同應當特別明確哪些資產屬於下列類別：

(a) 根據基礎設施項目合同的條款，要求基礎設施項目承包商返還或轉讓給締約機構或締約機構指定的其他實體的資產（如有）；

(b) 締約機構可以選擇從基礎設施項目承包商處購買的資產（如有）；以及

(c) 在基礎設施項目合同到期或終止時，基礎設施項目承包商可以保留或處置的資產（如有）。

第二十七條　與項目場地有關權利的取得

1. 根據法律和基礎設施項目合同的規定，締約機構或其他公共機關應當向基礎設施項目承包商提供或在適當情況下協助基礎設施項目承包商獲得與項目場地有關的權利，包括項目場地所有權，以確保項目的實施。

2. 項目實施可能需要的任何土地強制徵用，應當按照東道國公共機構基於公共利益的強制徵用私有財產的法律規定進行。

第二十八條　地役權

1. 基礎設施項目承包商應有權依據締約方有關地役權的法律以及公用事業公司和基礎設施運營商法定享有的其他相似權利，在且為實施項目需要的適當情況下，進入、穿越第三方財產或在其上施工或安裝固定物。

2. 為項目實施所需之地役權設立，應依據締約方管轄為公共利益之需設定地役權的法律辦理。

第二十九條　財務安排

1. 基礎設施項目承包商應有權根據基礎設施項目合同收取、接收使用設施或服務的費用。基礎設施項目合同應依據締約方主管機構制定的規則，提供確定和調整此類費用的方法和公式。

2. 締約機構有權同意向基礎設施項目承包商進行直接支付，以作為代替或額外支付設施使用或服務提供所收取的費用。

第三十條　擔保權益

1. 以基礎設施項目合同中包含的任何限制為準，基礎設施項目承包商有權在其任何資產、權利或利益（包括與基礎設施項目有關的資產、權利或利益）上設定擔保權益，以擔保項目所需的任何融資，特別包括下列內容：

  (a) 在基礎設施項目承包商擁有的動產或不動產或其在項目資產中的權益上設立的擔保；

  (b) 就使用設施或基礎設施項目承包商提供的服務所產生的收益以及就該等使用而對其所欠的應收賬款設定的質押。

2. 基礎設施項目承包商的股東應有權在其持有的基礎設施項目承包商的股份上設定質押或任何其他擔保權益。

3. 不得在締約方法律禁止的情況下就公共財產或提供公共服務所需的其他財產、資產或權利設定第 1 款項下的擔保。

第三十一條　基礎設施項目合同的轉讓

除第三十條（擔保權益）另有規定外，未經締約機構同意，基礎設施項目承包商在基礎設施項目合同項下的權利和義務不得轉讓給第三方。基礎設施項目合同應規定締約機構同意轉讓基礎設施項目承包商在該合同項下的權利和義務的條件，包括新的基礎設施項目承包商接受該合同項下的全部義務，以及新的基礎設施項目承包商具備提供服務所必需的技術和財務能力的證明。

第三十二條　基礎設施項目承包商控股權的轉移

除基礎設施項目合同另有規定外，未經締約機構同意，基礎設施項目承包商的控股權不得轉讓給第三方。基礎設施項目合同中應明確締約機構同意的條件。

第三十三條　基礎設施的運營

1. 基礎設施項目合同應適當規定基礎設施項目承包商有義務確保：
   (a) 改變服務以滿足服務的需求；
   (b) 服務的持續性；
   (c) 服務的提供應以基本上相同的條件適用於所有用戶；
   (d) 在適當情況下，非歧視性地獲得有利於基礎設施項目承包商運營的任何公共基礎設施網絡的其他服務。

2. 基礎設施項目承包商應有權發佈和執行與設施使用有關的規則，但需經締約機構或監管機構的批准。

第三十四條　具體立法變更的補償

基礎設施項目合同應載明，如因特定適用於基礎設施或其提供服務的立法或法規發生變化，而導致較最初預期的基礎設施項目合同履行成本和價值相比，基礎設施項目承包商履行基礎設施項目合同的成本實質性地增加，或其因履行該等合同而使所獲價值實質性地減少時，基礎設施承包商有權獲得何種程度的補償。

第三十五條　基礎設施項目合同的修改

1. 在不影響第三十四條（具體立法變更的補償）的前提下，基礎設施項目合同應進一步規定，基礎設施項目承包商有權對基礎設施項目合同進行變更的限度，以便在與最初預期的履行基礎設施項目合同的成本和價值相比，由於下列事項而導致基礎設施項目承包商履行基礎設施項目合同的成本實質性增加或因履行該等合同而使獲得的價值實質性減少的情況下，向基礎設施項目承包商進行補償：

(a)　經濟或財務狀況的變化；或

(b)　非特定適用於基礎設施或其提供服務的立法或法規發生變化；

但前提為經濟、財務、立法或監管方面發生變更：

(a)　發生在合同簽訂後；

(b)　超出基礎設施項目承包商控制的範圍；以及

(c)　其性質是基礎設施項目承包商在基礎設施項目合同談判時，無法合理預期並作考量，或進行規避或就其後果加以解決。

2. 基礎設施項目合同應規定，在發生任何這些變化後，修改基礎設施項目合同條款的程序。

第三十六條　締約機構對基礎設施項目的接管

在基礎設施項目合同約定的情形下，當基礎設施項目承包商嚴重不能履行其義務且在締約機構通知其在合理期限內糾正違約後未能糾正違約時，締約機構有權臨時接管基礎設施的運營以保證有效和不間斷地提供服務。

第三十七條　替換基礎設施項目承包商

締約機構可與為基礎設施項目提供融資的實體和基礎設施項目承包商達成協議，規定在基礎設施項目承包商嚴重違約或出現其他可能導致終止基礎設施項目合同的情形或其他類似情形下，通過指定新的實體或個人履行現有在基礎設施項目合同以替換基礎設施項目承包商。

第三十八條　基礎設施項目合同的期限和延期

1. 特許經營的期限應在特許經營合同中規定。除因下列情況外，締約機構不可同意延長其期限：

(a) 因超出任何一方合理控制的情形而延遲完工或中斷經營；

(b) 因締約機構或其他公共機構的行為而導致項目停工；

(c) 因締約機構的要求而引起成本增加，而該等增加在基礎設施項目合同中無法事先預見，且不延期則基礎設施項目承包商無法收回該等費用；或

(d) 東道國規定的其他情形。

第三十九條　締約機關終止基礎設施項目合同

1. 在下列情況下，締約機關可終止基礎設施項目合同：

(a) 由於資不抵債、嚴重違約或其他原因，無法合理預期基礎設施項目承包商能夠或願意履行其義務；

(b) 由於公共利益的充分理由，在向基礎設施項目承包商支付賠償金的前提下，賠償條款按基礎設施項目合同中約定；

(c) 東道國認為必要的其他情況。

第四十條　基礎設施項目承包商終止基礎設施項目合同

1. 除下列情形外，基礎設施項目承包商不可終止基礎設施項目合同：

(a) 締約機構或其他公共機構嚴重違反與基礎設施項目合同有關的義務；

(b) 如符合第三十五條第 1 款（基礎設施項目合同的修改）規定的修改基礎設施項目合同的條件，但雙方就基礎設施項目合同的修改不能達成一致；

(c) 如由於締約機構或其他公共機構的作為或不作為〔例如根據第二十三條附件一的第 (h) 項和第 (i) 項〕，而導致基礎設施項目承包商履行基礎設施項目合同的成本大幅增加，或其因該等履行而獲得的價值大幅減少，且雙方未能就基礎設施項目合同的修改達成一致。

第四十一條　任何一方終止基礎設施項目合同

任何一方均應有權在因超出其合理控制情形而無法履行義務的情況下終止

基礎設施項目合同。雙方亦應有權經協商一致終止基礎設施項目合同。

第四十二條　基礎設施項目合同終止時的賠償

基礎設施項目合同應規定在基礎設施項目合同終止的情況下，如何計算向任何一方支付的賠償，且在適當的情況下，對基礎設施項目合同項下已履行工程的公允價值以及任何一方帶來的成本或承擔的損失（酌情包括利潤損失）進行賠償。

第四十三條　基礎設施項目合同期滿或終止時的清盤和移交措施

1. 基礎設施項目合同應酌情規定：
   (a)　向締約機構移交資產的機制和程序；
   (b)　基礎設施項目承包商可能有權就向締約機構或新基礎設施項目承包商轉讓的資產或締約機構購買的資產獲得的賠償；
   (c)　設施運營所需的技術轉讓；
   (d)　對締約機構的人員或基礎設施項目承包商的繼任者進行設施運營和維護的培訓；
   (e)　在設施移交給締約機構或基礎設施項目承包商的繼任者後的合理期限內，基礎設施項目承包商提供持續支持服務和資源，包括備件供應（如需要）。

第四十四條　爭議解決

締約機關與基礎設施項目承包商之間的爭議、基礎設施客戶或使用者之間的爭議，其他爭議

1. 任何因「一帶一路」基礎設施項目產生的或與之有關的爭議，均應通過國際商事爭議預防與解決組織的爭議解決機制解決。

2. 如基礎設施項目承包商向社會公眾提供服務或面向社會公眾運營基礎設施，締約機構可要求基礎設施項目承包商建立簡便、高效的機制，以處理其客戶或基礎設施使用者提出的索賠。

附件一

基礎設施項目合同應對締約方認為適宜的事項作出規定，如：

(a) 基礎設施項目承包商擬履行的工程和提供服務的性質和範圍；

(b) 提供此種服務的條件以及基礎設施項目承包商在基礎設施項目合同項下的權利的排他性（如有）；

(c) 締約主管機關在實施基礎設施項目所需的範圍內，可向基礎設施項目承包商提供協助，以獲得執照和許可協證；

(d) 根據第二十五條（基礎設施項目承包商的組織），與法人實體的成立和最低資本有關的任何要求；

(e) 依據第二十六條至第二十八條（第二十六條資產所有權，第二十七條與項目場地有關權利的取得，第二十八條地役權），與項目有關的資產所有權，以及各方在獲得項目場地和任何必要的地役權方面的義務；

(f) 基礎設施項目承包商的報酬，無論是包括使用設施或提供服務的費用或關稅；設立或調整任何此類關稅或費用的方法和公式；以及締約機關或其他公共機關可能支付的任何款項（如有）；

(g) 締約機關審查和批准工程設計、項目計劃和規格的程序，以及基礎設施的試驗、竣工檢查、驗收和工程接收程序；

(h) 基礎設施項目承包商酌情保證修改服務以滿足對服務的實際需求、服務的連續性和在基本相同的條件下向所有用戶提供服務的義務；

(i) 締約機關或其他公共機構對基礎設施項目承包商擬實施的工程和提供的服務進行監督的權利，以及締約機關或監管機構可以命令改變工程和服務的條件和程度，或採取其認為適當的其他合理行動，以確保依據適用法律和合同的要求正常運營基礎設施和提供服務；

(j) 基礎設施項目承包商酌情向締約機關或監管機構提供與其運營相關的報告和其他信息的義務；

(k) 處理因締約機關或另一公共機構就上述（h）和（i）發佈的任何命

令而產生的額外費用和其他後果的機制，包括基礎設施項目承包商可能有權獲得的任何賠償；

(1) 締約機關審查和批准基礎設施項目承包商簽訂的主要合同的任何權利，特別是與基礎設施項目承包商的股東或其他關聯方簽訂的合同；

(m) 基礎設施項目承包商就基礎設施項目的實施提供的履約保函和保單；

(n) 任何一方違約時可獲得的救濟；

(o) 任何一方因超出其合理控制範圍的情況而未能或延遲履行基礎設施項目合同項下的任何義務時可被免責的程度；

(p) 基礎設施項目合同的期限以及合同期滿或終止時各方的權利和義務；

(q) 根據第四十二條（基礎設施項目合同終止時的賠償），計算賠償的方法；

(r) 締約機關與基礎設施項目承包商之間可能產生的爭議，適用的法律和爭議解決機制；

(s) 各方有關保密信息的權利和義務。

第十二章　競爭

第一條　定義

就本章而言：

「反競爭商業行為」指對一締約方境內市場產生負面影響的商業行為或交易，例如：

    (a) 在締約一方全境或大部分地區，試圖造成或者實際具有排除、限制、扭曲競爭效果的企業協議、聯合決定或協同行為；

    (b) 在一締約方全境或大部分地區，一家或數家具有支配地位企業濫用支配地位的行為；

    (c) 在一締約方全境或大部分地區，一家或數家企業的私人壟斷行為；或

    (d) 不公平貿易行為；或

    (e) 在一締約方全境或大部分地區，顯著妨礙有效競爭，特別是形成或加強市場支配地位或市場壟斷力量的經營者集中；

「經營者」指從事商品生產、經營或提供服務的自然人、法人和任何其他組織。

「國有企業」指主要從事商業活動的企業且一締約方在該企業中：

    (a) 直接擁有 50% 以上股份資本；

    (b) 通過所有權利益控制 50% 以上投票權的行使；或

    (c) 通過任何其他所有者權益（包括間接或少數所有權），擁有對該企

業的控制權；[40] 或者

    (d) 擁有任命董事會或其他同等管理機構過半數成員的權力。

第二條　目標

    締約方認識到，禁止經營者（包括國有企業）的反競爭商業行為，執行競爭政策，針對競爭問題開展合作，有助於防止貿易、服務和投資自由化利益受損，有利於提高經濟效率和消費者福利，並加強良好的商業慣例和道德規範。

第三條　競爭法和主管機關

    1. 締約方應努力維持或實施競爭法，禁止反競爭商業行為，促進和保護市場競爭過程。

    2. 締約方應努力保持設立一個或多個主管機關，負責其本國競爭法執法。

    3. 締約方還應努力依據各自的相關法律法規，對反競爭商業行為採取相應措施，防止貿易、服務和投資自由化受損。

第四條　競爭法的適用

    1. 締約方應維持其國家競爭法，該法應適用於所有經濟領域內的所有企業，並以有效的方式處理反競爭商業行為。

    2. 締約方應將其競爭法適用於所有從事經濟活動的私營或公營企業。該條款不應妨礙締約方規定其競爭法的豁免，但此種豁免必須是透明的，並僅限於為維護公共利益所必需的。此種豁免不應超出實現該締約方所確定的公共利益目標所絕對必要的範圍。

第五條　執法原則

    1. 締約方競爭執法應符合透明、非歧視、法治和程序正義原則。

40　為本項之目的，如果締約方能夠通過所有者權益決定或指導影響企業的重要事項，不包括對少數股東的保護，則該締約方擁有控制企業的權利。在確定締約方是否擁有此項權力時，應逐案考慮所有相關的法律和事實要素。這些要素可包括決定或指導商業運營的權力，其中包括重大支出或投資、發行股票或重大債券、或企業重組、合併或解散等。

第六條　透明度

1. 鼓勵每一締約方通過網絡公開等方式公開其有關競爭政策的法律法規，包括調查的程序規則在內。

2. 鼓勵每一締約方保證，所有認定違反其國家競爭法的最終行政決定均以書面形式作出，並列出事實認定和論證過程，包括作出決定所依據的法律分析，且如適用，包括經濟分析。

3. 鼓勵每一締約方以方便利害關係人和其他締約方知悉的方式，公佈決定及執行該決定的任何命令。該締約方公佈的決定或命令的版本不包含商業秘密或受該締約方法律保護不得公開披露的其他信息。

4. 應另一締約方請求，一締約方應努力向該提出請求的締約方提供有關下列內容的公開信息：

　　(a)　其競爭法的執法政策和實踐；及

　　(b)　對其國家競爭法的免於適用和責任豁免，只要該請求中列明特定貨物或服務和關注的市場並包括說明該免於適用或責任豁免如何妨礙締約方之間的貿易或投資的信息。

第七條　非歧視

締約方應遵照非歧視原則適用其競爭法，不分企業的國籍和所有制性質。

第八條　程序公正

1. 締約方應遵照程序公正原則適用其競爭法，不分企業的國籍和所有制性質。

2. 每一締約方應確保，在對一人因違反其國家競爭法而實施處罰或救濟之前，向其提供：

　　(a)　關於國家競爭主管機關的競爭關注的信息；

　　(b)　由律師代理的合理機會；以及

　　(c)　在答辯中陳述意見和提交證據的合理機會，但一締約方可規定在其實施臨時處罰或救濟後的一段合理時間內允許其陳述意見和提交證據。

特別是，每一締約方應向該人提供提交證據或證詞進行抗辯的合理機會，包括：如適用，提供合格專家的分析意見、對任何證人進行交叉詢問、以及審閱和反駁在執行程序中提交的證據。[41]

3. 每一締約方應採取或設立書面程序，據以開展國家競爭法調查。如未對這些調查規定最終期限，則每一締約方的國家競爭主管機關應努力在合理時間內開展調查。

4. 每一締約方應採取或設立程序和證據規則，適用於對涉嫌違反其國內競爭法行為的執法程序及據此作出的處罰和救濟決定。這些規則應包括證據引入程序，應包括專家證據（如適用），並應平等適用於程序中的所有當事方。

5. 每一締約方應向因違反其國內競爭法而受到處罰或救濟的人提供尋求對處罰或救濟進行審查的機會，包括在法院或根據該締約方法律設立的其他獨立法庭中對所主張的實體或程序錯誤進行審查。

6. 如一締約方的國家競爭主管機關發佈公告，披露一項未決或正在進行的調查，則該主管機關應避免在公告中暗示其中所指之人已經從事涉嫌行為或已經違反該締約方的國家競爭法。

7. 如一締約方的國家競爭主管機關指控存在違反其國家競爭法的行為，則該主管機關應在執法程序中負責就其指控的違法行為確定法律和事實基礎。[42]

8. 每一締約方應規定保護國家競爭主管機關在調查過程中獲得的商業機密信息和根據其法律按機密信息處理的其他信息。如一締約方的國家競爭主管機關在執法程序中使用或有意使用該信息，則在其法律允許且適當的情況下，該締約方應規定一程序，允許被調查人可及時獲得為準備針對該國家競爭主管機關的指控進行充分辯護所需的必要信息。

9. 每一締約方應確保其國家競爭主管機關向因可能違反該締約方國內競爭法而接受調查的人員提供合理的機會，使其就調查過程中出現的重大法律、事實或程序問題諮詢競爭主管機關。

第九條　執法合作

1. 締約方認識到在競爭領域加強合作與協調，對促進競爭法的有效執行的重要性。為此，鼓勵每一締約方：

41　就本條而言，「執法程序」指對涉嫌違反競爭法的行為進行調查後的司法或行政覆議程序。

42　本款中任何內容均不妨礙一締約方要求被指控的人在對指控進行抗辯時負責證明特定要件。

（a） 通過交流關於制定競爭政策的信息在競爭政策領域進行合作；以及

（b） 酌情就競爭法執行問題進行合作，包括通知、磋商和信息交流。

2.一締約方的國家競爭主管機關可考慮與另一締約方的競爭主管機關訂立列明雙方議定的合作條款的合作安排或協議。

3.締約方同意以符合其各自法律、法規和重大利益的方式，並在各自可合理獲得的資源範圍內開展合作。

第十條　通報

就本章第九條第 2 款項下的合作安排或協議而言，締約方的國家競爭主管機關可商定以下內容的通報條件：

（a） 鼓勵締約方通過其競爭主管機關向另一締約方競爭主管機關通報其執法活動，若締約方認為其執法活動可能對另一締約方的重要利益產生實質性影響。

（b） 在不違反締約方的競爭法，且不影響任何正在進行的調查的情況下，締約方應盡量在調查的早期階段向另一方通報。通報應足夠詳細，以使另一締約方能夠進行利益評估。

（c） 締約方承諾，在各自可用的行政資源內，盡最大努力保證按照上述要求進行通報。

第十一條　信息交換

就本章第九條第 2 款項下的合作安排或協議而言，締約方的國家競爭主管機關可商定信息交換的條件，包括以下規定：

（a） 締約方在不影響正在進行的調查，且符合有關法律法規的情況下，應另一締約方請求，應盡力提供相關信息，以便對方進行有效的競爭執法。

（b） 締約方對另一締約方提供的秘密信息應當予以保密，不得將相關信息洩露給任何未經提供信息的締約方認可的機構。

第十二條　技術合作

認識到締約方可從分享其在制定、適用和執行競爭法及制定和實施競爭政策過程中所積累的不同經驗中獲益，締約方應考慮在可獲得的資源範圍內開展相互同意的技術合作活動，包括：

(a) 就相關問題提供建議或培訓，包括通過官員交流；

(b) 交流關於競爭宣傳的信息和經驗，包括促進競爭文化的途徑；以及

(c) 在一締約方實施其新的國家競爭法時提供援助。

第十三條　消費者保護

1. 締約方認識到消費者保護政策和執法對於在本自由貿易區內建設高效率和競爭性市場及提高消費者福利的重要性。

2. 就本條而言，欺詐和欺騙性商業活動指對消費者造成實際損害或如不加制止即會造成此種損害的迫近威脅的欺詐和欺騙性商業做法，例如：

(a) 導致被誤導的消費者的經濟利益明顯受損的對重要事實進行虛假陳述的做法，包括暗示性事實虛假陳述；

(b) 在收取消費者費用後未向消費者交付產品或服務的做法；或

(c) 未經授權而對消費者財務、電話或其他賬戶收費或借記的做法。

3. 鼓勵每一締約方採取或維持消費者保護法或其他法律或法規，以禁止欺詐和欺騙性商業行為。[43]

4. 締約方認識到跨越國境的欺詐和欺騙性商業行為不斷增加，宜通過締約方之間的合作和協調有效應對此類活動。

5. 因此，締約方應酌情推動就涉及欺詐和欺騙性商業行為的具有共同利益的問題開展合作和協調，包括在各自消費者保護法的執行方面。

6. 締約方應努力通過其確定的負責消費者保護政策、法律或執行的相關國家公共機構或官員，在與各自法律、法規和重要利益相一致的前提下，在各自合理可獲得的資源範圍內，就本條所列事項開展合作和協調。

第十四條　磋商

1. 為促進各締約方之間的相互理解，或為處理本章執行過程中出現的特定事項，一締約方應另一締約方要求，應就對方提出的關注與其進行磋商。提

---

[43] 為進一步明確，一締約方採取或維持的禁止此類活動的法律或法規可以屬民事或刑事性質。

出磋商請求的締約方應在請求中指明相關事項如何影響各締約方間的貿易或投資。

　2. 前款所指可進行磋商的具體事項，包括涉及磋商請求的締約方執法活動的事項，這些事項可能對提出請求的締約方的重要利益產生實質性影響，例如：

(a) 針對提出請求締約方企業的執法活動；

(b) 導致在請求締約方進行域外救濟的執法活動；以及

(c) 缺乏執法活動，導致容忍可能影響請求締約方企業或消費者利益的所謂反競爭商業行為。

　3. 締約方對提出磋商請求的另一締約方的關注應當給予充分諒解和考慮。

　4. 為便利就有關事項進行磋商，一締約方應盡量向另一締約方提供相關非保密信息，例如：

(a) 任何相關的事實調查結果和推理，包括決定所依據的法律分析和（如適用）經濟分析；

(b) 任何相關的事實調查結果和推理，包括法律分析和（如適用）經濟分析，可證明域外救濟的正當性；以及

(c) 任何相關的事實調查結果和推理，包括法律分析和（如適用）經濟分析，可證明容忍所謂的反競爭商業行為是合理的。

第十五條　爭端解決

　若一締約方認為某一做法持續影響本章意義上的貿易或投資，可請求在聯合委員會中與另一締約方進行磋商，以促進該事項的解決。

第十三章　環境

第一條　目標

1. 締約方認識到，經濟發展、社會發展和環境保護是可持續發展相互依存、相互支持的組成部分。各方強調在環境議題的合作獲益是實現全球可持續發展的努力的一部分。

2. 締約方重申其承諾，致力於促進「一帶一路」項目的經濟發展，以有助於實現可持續發展目標，並確保這一目標被納入和反映在締約方的貿易關係中。

3. 締約方認識到，不宜通過弱化或減少各自環境法提供的保護以鼓勵貿易或投資。為此，締約方不得以影響締約方之間貿易或投資的方式，豁免或減損，或提議豁免或減損其環境法。

4. 締約方同意，環境標準不得用於貿易保護主義之目的。

第二條　範圍

除非本章另有規定，本章適用於締約方為解決與「一帶一路」倡議相關的環境問題而採取或維持的包括法律和法規在內的各種措施。

第三條　保護水平

1. 締約方重申，各自擁有確定自身環境保護水平及其環境發展優先領域，以及制定或修訂其環境法律和政策的主權權利。

2. 締約方應努力確保這些法律和政策有助於並鼓勵高水平的環境保護，並應努力持續提高各自的環境保護水平。

第四條 多邊環境協定和環境原則

1. 締約方認識到，多邊環境協定在全球和締約方國內層面對保護環境保護發揮着重要作用。締約方進一步認識到，本章有助於實現多邊環境協定的目標。

2. 締約方承諾，在締約方參加的多邊環境協定的談判中，可在適當時就共同感興趣的、與貿易相關的環境問題進行磋商與合作。

3. 締約方重申其承諾，在各自的法律和實踐中，有效實施其參加的多邊環境協定。

4. 締約方重申其承諾，在其法律和實踐中有效實施其參加的多邊環境協定，以及本章第一條所指國際文書中所體現的環境原則和義務。締約方應努力通過各種途徑，包括有效實施環境法律和法規，進一步提高環境保護水平。

5. 締約方認識到，通過弱化或減少國內環境法律、法規、政策和實踐所提供的保護以鼓勵貿易、投資或「一帶一路」項目是不適當的。締約方同意，環境標準不得用於貿易保護主義之目的。

6. 締約方認識到，在制定和實施與環境有關的措施時，考慮科學、技術和其他信息以及有關國際準則的重要性。

第五條 促進有利於環境的貨物和服務推廣

1. 締約方應努力便利和促進有利於環境的貨物、服務和技術的投資和推廣，以開展「一帶一路」項目。

2. 為第 1 款之目的，締約方同意交換意見，並將考慮就此領域開展合作。

3. 締約方應鼓勵企業在實施「一帶一路」項目中就有利於環境的貨物、服務和技術進行合作。

第六條 包括法律、法規在內的環境措施的執行

1. 締約方不得通過持續或不間斷的行為或有意的不作為，而未能有效執行其包括法律法規在內的環境措施，以影響各締約方之間貿易或投資的方式。

2. 締約方認識到，通過削弱或減少其各自環境法律、法規、政策和實踐所賦予的保護來鼓勵貿易、服務或投資是不恰當的。因此，任何締約方不得以削弱或減少這些法律、法規、政策和實踐所賦予的保護的方式而放棄或貶損這些

法律、法規、政策和實踐。

3. 本章的任何內容都不得被解釋為授權一締約方主管機關在另一締約方領土內開展環境執法活動。

第七條　環境影響

1. 締約方承諾，在通過本協定被採納後的適當時間，通過各自的參與性程序和機構，評估本協定和「一帶一路」項目的實施對環境的影響。

2. 締約方在適當時與另一締約方分享關於本協定和「一帶一路」項目環境影響評估的技術和方法的信息。

第八條　合作

1. 締約方認識到，環境領域合作對於實現可持續發展目標的重要性，承諾以現有的雙邊協定或安排為基礎，在有共同利益的領域深化合作。

2. 為推動實現本章目標，並有助於履行本章規定的相關義務，締約方確定在以下領域合作的指示性清單：

　　(a)　推廣包括環境友好產品在內的環境產品和環境服務；

　　(b)　環境技術開發與環境產業促進的合作；

　　(c)　交流關於環境保護的政策、活動和措施的信息；

　　(d)　建立包括環境專家交流的環境智庫合作機制；

　　(e)　能力建設，包括環境領域的專題會、研討會、博覽會和展覽會；

　　(f)　在各締約國建立作為試點地區或圍繞「一帶一路」項目的環境產業示範區基地；以及

　　(g)　締約方認為適當的其他形式的環境合作。

3. 締約方應盡最大努力，確保各方合作活動的應用和成效盡可能廣泛。

第九條　制度安排

1. 為實施本章和「一帶一路」項目之目的，每一締約方應在其行政部門內指定一個辦公室，作為與其他締約方的聯絡點。

2. 一締約方可通過聯絡點，請求另一締約方就本章產生的任何事項進行磋商。

3. 締約方特此設立環境與貿易委員會（以下簡稱「委員會」）。委員會應由締約方行政部門的若干高級官員組成。

4. 委員會應在認為必要時開會，以監督本章的執行。

第十條　實施與磋商

1. 一締約方可通過聯絡點，請求就本章下產生的任何事項在委員會內進行磋商。締約方應盡一切努力就該等事項達成各方滿意的解決方案。

2. 如一締約方認為，另一締約方的措施不符合本章的規定，可訴諸委員會的雙邊磋商與對話（排他性），或使用國際商事爭端預防與解決組織的爭端解決程序。

第十四章　勞工標準

第一條　定義

「強迫或強制勞動」 指以懲罰相威脅，強使任何人從事其本人不曾表示自願從事的所有工作和勞務。

但為本公約目的，「強迫或強制勞動」一詞不包括：

(i)　任何工作或勞務是根據義務兵役法強徵以代替純軍事性工作者；

(ii)　作為一個完全自治國家的正常公民義務一部分的任何勞動或勞務；

(iii)　任何人因法庭判定有罪而被迫從事的任何工作或勞務，但上述工作或勞務必須由政府當局監督和管理，該人員不得由私人、公司或社團僱傭或處置；

(iv)　任何工作或勞務，因緊急情況而強徵者。所謂緊急情況係指戰爭或災害或災難威脅，例如火災、水災、饑荒、地震、猛烈流行病或動物瘟疫、動物、昆蟲或植物害蟲的侵害以及一般來說可能危及全部或部分居民的生存或福利的任何情況；

(v)　由社區成員為該社區直接利益而從事的，故可視為社區成員應履行的正常公民義務的輕微社區勞動，但這些勞務是否需要，社區成員或其直接選出的代表應有被徵詢協商的權利；

「中央部門」 是指由一締約方指定並通知另一締約方的最高中央機構。

「主管部門」 是指一國本土的主管部門或有關地區的最高中央部門。

「兒童」 適用於所有未滿 18 周歲的人。

「歧視」 是指：

(a)　歧視一詞包括：

(i)　基於種族、膚色、性別、宗教、政治見解、民族血統或社會出身的任何區別、排斥或特惠，其效果為取消或損害就業或職業方面的機會平等或待遇平等；

(ii) 相關締約方在同僱主代表組織和工人代表組織——如果這種組織存在——以及其他有關機構磋商後可能確定其效果為取消或損害就業或職業方面的機會平等或待遇平等的其他區別、排斥或特惠。

(b) 基於特殊工作本身的要求的任何區別、排斥或特惠，不應視為歧視。

「**就業**」和「**職業**」指獲得職業上的訓練、獲得就業及獲得特殊職業、以及就業的條件。

「**男女同工同酬**」指報酬率的訂定，不得有性別上的歧視。

「**ILO**」是指「國際勞工組織」。

「**《國際勞工組織宣言》**」是指國際勞工組織《關於工作中基本原則和權利宣言》及其後續措施。

「**報酬**」指普通的、基本的或最低限度的工資或薪金，以及任何其他因工人的工作而由僱主直接或間接地以現金或實物支付給工人的酬金；

「**代表組織**」是指享有結社自由權利的最具有代表性的僱主組織和工人組織。

第二條　總則

締約方確認，「一帶一路」勞工標準所基於的基本原則是：

(a) 勞動不是商品；

(b) 言論自由和結社自由是不斷進步的必要條件；

(c) 任何地方的貧困對一切地方的繁榮構成威脅；

(d) 反對貧困的鬥爭需要各國在國內以堅持不懈的精力進行，還需要國際社會作持續一致的努力。在此努力中，工人和僱主代表享有和政府代表同等的地位，和政府代表一起參加自由討論和民主決議，以增進共同福利；

(e) 全人類不分種族、信仰或性別，均有權在自由、尊嚴、經濟保障和機會均等的條件下，謀求物質福利和精神發展；

(f) 為實現上述目標而創造條件，應成為國家和國際政策的中心目標；

(g) 所有國家和國際政策和措施，特別是經濟與財政政策和措施，均應從這一角度考慮，並應促進這一基本目標的實現；

第三條　義務

締約方承認，有下列共同義務：

(a) 促進充分就業和提高生活水平；

(b) 僱傭工人從事他們可以充分衡量其技能和成就，並為公共福祉做出最大貢獻的職業；

(c) 作為實現上述目標的手段，並在有關各方得到充分保障的情況下，提供培訓和勞動力轉移便利，包括為就業和定居而移徙；

(d) 關於工資和收入、工時和其他工作條件的政策，旨在確保所有人公平分享進步成果，並確保所有就業和需要這種保護的人都能獲得最低生活工資；

(e) 有效地承認集體談判權，管理層和勞工在不斷提高生產效率方面的合作，以及工人和僱主在制定和實施社會和經濟措施方面的合作；

(f) 擴大社會保障措施，向所有需要此種保障和綜合醫療的人提供基本收入；

(g) 充分保護所有職業工人的生命和健康；

(h) 提供兒童福利和生育保護；

(i) 提供充足的營養、住房以及娛樂和文化設施；

(j) 確保教育和職業機會平等。

第四條　結社自由

締約方承諾有效實施下列各項規定：

(a) 凡工人及僱主，無分軒輊，不須經過事前批准手續，均有權建立他們自己願意建立的組織，和在僅僅遵守有關組織的規章的情況下，加入他們自己願意加入的組織。

(b) 工人組織及僱主組織均有權制定他們自己的組織法和規章、充分自由地選舉他們自己的代表、規劃他們自己的行政和活動，並制定他們自己的計劃。

(c) 公共機關不得作出任何足以使此項權利受到限制或其合法行使受到阻礙的干涉。

(d) 行政機關不得解散工人組織及僱主組織或暫停他們的活動。

(e) 工人組織及僱主組織均應有權成立或加入各種協會和聯合會,任何此類組織、協會或聯合會應有權加入國際性工人組織及僱主組織。

(f) 工人、僱主及他們各自的組織在行使本協定規定的權利時,應同其他人及其他有組織的團體一樣,遵守當地法律。

第五條　組織權

1. 締約方承諾,採取一切必要和適當的措施,以確保工人和僱主均可以自由地行使組織權。

2. 工人應享有充分的保護,以防止在就業方面發生任何排斥工會的歧視行為。

3. 這種保護應特別應用於針對含有以下目的的行為:

(a) 將不得加入工會或必須放棄工會會籍作為僱傭工人的條件;

(b) 由於工人加入了工會或者在業餘時間或經僱主許可在工作時間參加了工會活動而將其解僱,或以其他手段予以打擊。

4. 工人組織和僱主組織均應享有充分的保護,以防止在組織的建立、運轉和管理等方面,發生一方直接或通過代理人或會員干涉另一方的任何行為。

5. 特別是其意在促使建立受僱主或僱主組織操縱的工人組織的行為,或通過財政手段或其他方式支持工人組織以期把它們置於僱主或僱主組織控制之下的行為,應被認為構成本條所稱的干涉行為。

6. 為保證以上各條所規定的組織權利受到尊重,必要時應建立符合國情的機構。

7. 必要時應採取符合國情的措施,鼓勵和推動在僱主或僱主組織同工人組織之間,最廣泛地發展與使用集體協議的自願談判程序,以便通過這種方式確定就業條款和條件。

第六條　禁止強迫勞動

1. 每一締約方承諾，在可能範圍內最短期間，制止強迫或強制勞動的一切使用形式。

2. 為了徹底制止強迫或強制勞動，在過渡期間，僅於為公共目的和作為例外措施時，可使用強迫或強制勞動，並須受以下所訂條件和保證的限制。

3. 主管部門不得為私人、公司或社團的利益徵用或准許徵用強迫或強制勞動。

4. 給予私人、公司或社團的基礎設施項目，不得附有徵用任何形式的強迫或強制勞動之權，以從事生產或收集這些私人、公司或社團所利用或買賣的產品。

5. 若基礎設施項目中存在此類強迫或強制勞動的規定，應儘早廢止這些規定。

第七條　廢除童工

1. 每一締約方承諾，執行一項國家政策，以保證有效地廢除童工並將准予就業或工作的最低年齡逐步提高到符合年輕人身心最充分發展的水平。

2. 每一締約方應詳細說明准予在其領土內及在其領土註冊的運輸工具上就業或工作的最低年齡，未滿該年齡者不得允許其受僱於或從事任何職業。

3. 根據本條第 1 款規定的最低年齡應不低於完成義務教育的年齡，並在任何情況下不得低於 15 歲。

4. 儘管有本條第 3 款的規定，若締約方的經濟和教育設施不夠發達，得在與相關的僱主組織和工人組織（如存在此種組織）協商後，初步規定最低年齡為 14 歲。

5. 根據上述規定已定最低年齡為 14 歲的締約方，應在其按照本協定規定提交的報告中，向所有締約方說明：

　　(a)　如此做的理由；或

　　(b)　自規定日期起放棄其援用有關規定的權利。

第八條　同工同酬

1. 每一締約方應以符合現行決定薪酬辦法的適當方法促進並在符合這些辦法的範圍內保證男女同工同酬的原則對一切工人適用。

2. 這一原則可通過以下方式適用：

    (a) 國家法律或法規；

    (b) 依法設立或在法律上得到承認的工資決定機構；

    (c) 僱主與工人間的集體協議；或

    (d) 這三種方法的混合。

3. 在行動有助於實施本章規定的情況下，應採取措施去促進在實際工作的基礎上對各種職位作客觀評價。

4. 評價的方法可由負責決定薪酬率的主管機關決定。如果這種薪酬率係以集體協議決定，則可由協議的有關各方決定。

5. 工人間報酬率的差異，如果是基於這種客觀評價所確定的實際工作的差異，而與性別無關，則不應視為違反男女同工同酬的原則。

6. 每一締約方應酌情與有關的僱主組織和工人組織合作，以實施本協定的各項規定。

第九條　機會和待遇平等

1. 每一締約方承諾，宣佈並執行一種旨在以適合本國條件及習慣的方法，促進就業和職業方面的機會平等和待遇平等的國家政策，以消除就業和職業方面的任何歧視。

2. 每一締約方承諾，以適合本國條件及習慣的方法：

    (a) 尋求僱主組織和工人組織以及其他有關機構的合作，以促進對這一政策的接受和遵行；

    (b) 制定旨在使這一政策得到接受和遵行的法律，並促進旨在使這一政策得到接受和遵行的教育計劃；

    (c) 廢止與這一政策相抵觸的任何法律規定，並修改與這一政策相抵觸的任何行政命令或慣例；

    (d) 在主管部門的直接控制下執行就業政策；

    (e) 保證職業指導、職業培訓和安置服務等活動，均在主管部門的監督下，遵行這一政策；

    (f) 在其關於本協定適用情況的年度報告中，說明為執行這一政策而採取的行動以及這種行動所得的結果。

第十條　勞動監察

1. 締約方應維持在工業、商業、基礎設施和農業工作場所的勞動監察制度。

2. 勞動監察制度應適用於勞動監察員執行有關勞動條件和勞動者保護的法律規定的所有工作場所。

3. 締約方法律或法規可豁免採礦和運輸企業或其中的一部分適用本協定。

4. 勞動監察制度的職能應為：

(a) 在可由勞動監察員實施的情況下，保證執行有關工作條件和保護在崗工人的法律規定，如有關工時、工資、安全、健康和福利、兒童和青少年就業及其他相關事項的規定；

(b) 向僱主和工人提供有關遵守法律規定的最有效手段的技術信息和建議；

(c) 提請主管部門注意現行法律條款中未具體涉及的缺陷或弊端。

5. 任何可能委託給勞動監察員的進一步的職責，不得妨礙其有效履行其主要職責，或以任何方式損害監察員在與僱主和工人的關係中所必需的權威和公正性。

6. 在符合締約方行政慣例的範圍內，勞動監察應置於中央機關的監督和控制之下。

7. 主管部門應作出適當的安排，促進：

(a) 監察部門和其他政府部門與從事類似活動的公共或私營機構的有效合作；以及

(b) 勞動監察官員與僱主、工人或其組織之間的合作。

8. 每一締約方應採取必要措施，確保具有適當資格的技術專家和專業人員，包括醫學、工程、電氣和化學方面的專家，以符合其國情的最適當的方式參與勞動監察工作，以確保執行有關保護工人在工作期間的安全與健康的法律規定，並調查工作過程、材料和工作方法對工人健康與安全的影響。

第十一條　就業政策

1. 為了刺激經濟增長和發展、提高生活水平、應付人力需要和克服失業和就業不足起見，每一締約方，作為主要目標，應宣佈和推行一種旨在促進充分就業、生產性就業和自由選擇職業的積極政策。

    2. 該政策的目的應在於保證：

      (a) 凡能夠工作並尋求工作的人都可以獲得工作；

      (b) 此項工作盡可能是富有成效的；

      (c) 自由選擇職業，使每一工人都有最大可能的機會去取得擔任其適於擔任的工作的資格，並對該項工作使用他的技能和才能，不分種族、膚色、性別、宗教、政治見解、國籍或社會出身。

    3. 該政策應適當地顧到經濟發展的程度和水平，以及就業目標同別的經濟和社會目標間的相互關係，並應通過適合於國家條件和實踐的方法實施。

    4. 每一締約方應通過此種方法並在可能適合國情的範圍內：

      (a) 於一個經濟和社會政策結合的體系內，決定為達成第 1 款所述目標而採取的措施，並對這些措施經常加以檢查；

      (b) 採取為執行這些措施而可能需要的步驟，包括酌情制定各種計劃在內。

第十二條　三方磋商

    1. 每一締約方承諾，運用各種程序保證就與「一帶一路」勞工委員會活動的有關事項，在政府、僱主和工人代表之間進行有效的磋商。

    2. 本條第 1 款規定的程序的性質和形式，由締約方與代表性組織（如有該類組織存在及此種程序尚未建立）磋商後，根據國家慣例決定。

    3. 以本協定所規定的程序為目的的僱主和工人代表應由他們的代表性組織（如果此類組織存在）自由選任。

    4. 僱主和工人應以平等地位參加從事磋商的任何機構。

第十三條　公眾認識與程序保證

    1. 每一締約方應提高公眾對其勞工法的認識，包括通過保證與其勞工法、執行和遵守程序相關的信息可公開獲得。

    2. 每一締約方應保證，根據其法律對一特定事項擁有被認可利益的人可適當使用執行該締約方勞工法的公正和獨立的法庭。按每一締約方的法律中所規定的，這些法庭可包括行政法庭、準司法法庭、司法法庭或勞動法庭。

3. 每一締約方應保證這些法庭執行其勞工法的程序：公平、公正且透明；符合正當法律程序；不收取不合理費用或設置不合理時限，或無理拖延。這些程序中的任何聽證會應依照其適用法律向公眾開放，除非司法機關另有要求。

4. 每一締約方應保證：

(a) 這些程序的當事方有權支持各自立場或為各自立場進行辯護，包括提交信息或證據；以及

(b) 對案件實體問題的最終裁決：

(i) 根據當事方被給予聽證機會的信息或證據作出的；

(ii) 陳述作出裁決的理由；以及

(iii) 以書面形式向這些程序當事方提供，不得有不當遲延，並在符合其法律的情況下向公眾提供。

5. 每一締約方應規定，這些程序的當事方有權酌情依法尋求審查或上訴。

6. 每一締約方應保證，這些程序的當事方可獲得其法律下的救濟，以有效執行其在該締約方勞工法下的權利，且這些救濟及時得到執行。

7. 每一締約方應規定程序以有效執行其法庭在這些程序中作出的最終裁決。

8. 為進一步明確，在不影響法庭的裁決是否與該締約方在本章下義務相一致的情況下，本章中任何內容不得解釋為要求一締約方的法庭重新審理對一特定事項已作出的裁決。

第十四條　合作

1. 締約方認識到，合作作為有效執行本章機制的重要性，以增加提高勞工標準的機會，進一步推進關於勞工問題的共同承諾，包括工人福利、生活質量以及《國際勞工組織宣言》中所述原則和權利。

2. 在開展合作活動時，締約方應遵循下列原則：

(a) 考慮每一締約方的優先領域、發展水平及可獲得的資源；

(b) 締約方的廣泛參與和共同利益；

(c) 能力與能力建設活動的相關性，包括締約方之間為處理勞工保護問題開展的技術援助及為促進創新工作場所實踐進行的活動；

(d) 產生可衡量、積極的和有意義的勞動成果；

(e) 資源效率，包括酌情使用技術以優化合作活動所使用的資源；

(f) 與處理勞工問題的現行區域和多邊倡議互補；以及

(g) 透明度與公眾參與。

3. 在確定潛在合作領域和開展合作活動時，每一締約方可邀請包括工人和僱主代表在內的利益相關方發表意見，並酌情邀請其參加。在遵守所涉締約方議定的前提下，合作活動可通過雙邊或諸邊參與方式進行，並可涉及國際勞工組織等相關區域或國際組織以及非締約方。

4. 在本章範圍內開展合作活動的資金問題應由所涉締約方在個案基礎上決定。

5. 除本條所列的合作活動外，締約方應酌情利用各自在區域和多邊場合的成員身份加強協調，以增進在處理勞工問題方面的共同利益。

6. 合作領域可包括：

(a) 創造就業和促進生產性、高質量就業，包括創造更多就業的增長、促進可持續企業和企業家精神的政策；

(b) 創造與可持續增長相關的生產性和高質量就業以及培養包括環境產業在內的新興產業就業所需技能；

(c) 提升工人福利、商業及經濟競爭力的創新性工作實踐；

(d) 人力資本開發及就業能力提高，包括通過終身學習、繼續教育、培訓以及技能開發和提高；

(e) 工作與生活的平衡；

(f) 促進商業和勞動生產力的改善，特別是對於中小企業；

(g) 薪酬制度；

(h) 促進對《國際勞工組織宣言》中所述原則和權利及國際勞工組織「體面勞動」概念的認識和尊重；

(i) 勞工法和實踐，包括《國際勞工組織宣言》中所述原則和權利的有效執行；

(j) 職業安全衛生；

(k) 勞動行政管理和裁決，例如提高能力、效率和效力；

(l) 勞工統計數據的收集和使用；

(m) 勞動監察，例如改善遵守與執行機制；

(n) 應對多元化、多代際勞動力帶來的機遇和挑戰，包括：

(i) 在外來工人就業和職業方面，或在年齡、殘疾及其他與崗位績効或要求無關的特徵方面，促進平等，消除歧視；

  (ii) 推動婦女平等和就業利益，消除婦女歧視；以及

  (iii) 保護弱勢工人，包括外來工人及低工資、非正式工或臨時工；

(o) 應對經濟危機帶來的勞工和就業挑戰，例如通過國際勞工組織《全球就業協定》中的共同利益領域；

(p) 社會保護問題，包括出現職業傷害或疾病時對工人的賠償、養老金制度以及就業援助計劃；

(q) 勞動關係最佳實踐，例如改善勞動關係，包括促進替代性爭議解決方面的最佳實踐；

(r) 社會對話，包括三方協商和夥伴關係；

(s) 對於跨國企業中的勞動關係，促進在兩個或多個締約方運營的企業與每一締約方的代表性工人組織就就業條件進行信息分享和對話；

(t) 企業社會責任；以及

(u) 締約方可能決定的其他領域。

7. 締約方可通過下列方式開展第 6 款中合作領域的活動：

(a) 講習班、研討會、對話及其他論壇以分享知識、經驗和最佳實踐，包括在線論壇和其他知識分享平台；

(b) 考察、訪問及研究性學習文件以及學習政策和實踐；

(c) 對具有共同利益議題的最佳實踐開展合作研究和開發；

(d) 酌情就技術專長和援助開展具體交流；以及

(e) 締約方可能決定的其他形式。

第十五條 勞工委員會

1. 締約方特此設立勞工委員會，由每一締約方指定的部級或其他級別的高級政府代表組成。

2. 勞工委員會應每兩年召開一次會議，除非締約方另有決定。

3. 勞工委員會應：

(a) 審議與本章相關的事項；

(b) 設定和審議優先事項，以指導締約方作出關於根據本章開展的勞工合作和能力建設活動的決定，同時考慮第十四條（合作）中的原

則；

(c) 根據（b）項設立的優先事項商定總體工作計劃；

(d) 監督和評估總體工作計劃；

(e) 討論具有共同利益的問題；

(f) 促進公眾對本章執行的參與和認知；以及

(g) 履行締約方可能決定的其他職能。

4. 每五年，或按締約方所決定的其他時間，勞工委員會應審議本章實施情況以確保有效實施，並向所有締約方報告審查結果和任何建議。

5. 勞工委員會可按締約方所議定的開展後續審議。

6. 勞工委員會主席應由每一締約方輪流擔任。

7. 勞工委員會所有決定和報告應經協商一致作出並向公眾提供，除非勞工委員會另有決定。

8. 勞工委員會應在每一勞工委員會會議結束時議定一份關於其工作的聯合摘要報告。

9. 締約方應酌情與相關區域和國際組織就與本章相關的事項進行聯絡，例如國際勞工組織。勞工委員會可尋求與這些組織或非締約方制定聯合提案或開展合作。

第十五章　爭端解決

第一條　合作

　　締約方應始終努力對本協定的解釋和適用達成一致，並應盡一切努力通過合作與磋商就可能影響本協定運用或適用的任何事項達成雙方滿意的解決辦法。

第二條　範圍

　　1.除非本協定中另有規定，否則本章的爭端解決條款應適用於：

　　　(a)　在避免或解決締約方之間有關本協定的解釋或適用方面的所有爭端；

　　　(b)　一締約方認為另一締約方的實際措施或擬議措施與本協定的義務不一致或將會出現不一致的情況，或另一締約方在其他方面未能履行本協定項下的義務的情況，或

　　　(c)　一締約方認為由於另一締約方實施與本協定不相抵觸的措施，其可合理預期獲得的利益正在喪失或減損的情況。

第三條　爭端解決場所的選擇

　　1.如一爭端涉及本協定項下和包括《世界貿易組織協定》或任何雙邊或多邊貿易協定在內的爭端方均為參加方的另一國際貿易協定項下產生的任何事項，則起訴方可選擇解決爭端的場所。

　　2.一旦起訴方啟動本協定項下的爭端解決機制，則應使用所選擇的場所而同時排除其他場所。

第四條　爭端解決程序

締約方同意將國際商事爭端預防與解決組織的爭端解決機制納入本章，以解決因本協定引起的爭端。

為明確起見，根據國際商事爭端預防與解決組織的爭端解決機制，締約方同意：

首先使用國際商事爭端預防與解決組織的申訴／斡旋機制程序解決其爭端；

若該爭端或爭端的任何部分未能通過斡旋解決，則締約方將在國際商事爭端預防與解決組織的主持下或通過任何其他調解組織，使用調解解決其爭端；

如果該爭端或其任何部分未能通過調解解決，則締約方同意按照國際商事爭端預防與解決組織的仲裁規則，通過仲裁解決其爭端；以及

若締約方欲對仲裁庭裁決提出上訴，則可根據國際商事爭端預防與解決組織的上訴規則向其常設上訴庭提出上訴。

為進一步明確起見，締約方同意，上訴程序不適用於私人當事方之間、以及私人當事方與締約方或國家實體之間的爭端，這些爭端不產生條約義務。

第五條　仲裁員、上訴庭成員和調解員的行為守則

締約方同意，將國際商事爭端預防與解決組織的《仲裁員、上訴庭成員和調解員的行為守則》納入本章。

第六條　透明度規則

締約方同意，將國際商事爭端預防與解決組織的《透明度規則》納入本章。

為進一步明確，締約方同意，《透明度規則》適用於投資者與東道國之間的仲裁以及各締約國之間的仲裁，包括上訴程序。

為進一步明確，締約方同意，《透明度規則》的例外規定比照適用於調解。

第七條　費用

締約方同意，將國際商事爭端預防與解決組織的《費用》納入本章。

The Belt and Road Cooperation and Partnership Model Agreement

Edited by Guiguo Wang, Rajesh Sharma

Editor Cheung Hin Chung

Designer Amanda Woo

Published by Joint Publishing (H.K.) Co., Ltd.

20/F., North Point Industrial Building, 499 King's Road, North Point, Hong Kong

Distributed by SUP Publishing Logistics (H.K.) Ltd.

16/F., Tsuen Wan Industrial Centre, 220-248 Texaco Road, Tsuen Wan, N.T., Hong Kong

Printed by Elegance Printing & Book Binding Co., Ltd.

Block A, 4/F., 6 Wing Yip Street, Kwun Tong, Kowloon, Hong Kong

First Published in October 2023

ISBN 978-962-04-5350-2 (Softcover)

ISBN 978-962-04-5362-5 (Hardcover)

© 2023 Joint Publishing (H.K.) Co., Ltd.

Published & Printed in Hong Kong, China.

「一帶一路」合作與夥伴關係協議範本

編　　者	王貴國　Rajesh Sharma
責任編輯	張軒誦
書籍設計	吳冠曼
出　　版	三聯書店（香港）有限公司
	香港北角英皇道四九九號北角工業大廈二十樓
香港發行	香港聯合書刊物流有限公司
	香港新界荃灣德士古道二二〇至二四八號十六樓
印　　刷	美雅印刷製本有限公司
	香港九龍觀塘榮業街六號四樓 A 室
版　　次	二〇二三年十月香港第一版第一次印刷
規　　格	十六開（170 mm × 240 mm）四〇〇面
國際書號	ISBN 978-962-04-5350-2（平裝）
	ISBN 978-962-04-5362-5（精裝）

© 2023 三聯書店（香港）有限公司

Published & Printed in Hong Kong, China.